# Plight and Fate of Women During and Following GENOCIDE

# Plight and Fate of Women During and Following GENOCIDE

GENOCIDE:
A CRITICAL BIBLIOGRAPHIC REVIEW
VOLUME 7

## Samuel Totten, editor

**Transaction Publishers**
New Brunswick (U.S.A.) and London (U.K.)

This book is printed on acid-free paper that meets the American National Standard for Permanence of Paper for Printed Library Materials.

Library of Congress Catalog Number: 2008038491
ISBN: 978-1-4128-0827-9
Printed in the United States of America

Library of Congress Cataloging-in-Publication

Totten, Samuel
    Plight and fate of women during and following genocide / Samuel Totten.
        p. cm. -- (Genocide: A critical bibliographic review, v. 7)
    Includes bibliographical references and index.
    ISBN 978-1-4128-0827-9 (alk. paper)
        1. Genocide. 2. Women--Crimes against. 3. Crimes against human-
    ity--History--20th century. 4. Crimes against humantiy--History--21st
    century. I. Title.
HV6322.7.T687 2008
364.15'1082--dc22

2008038491

# Contents

# Introduction

*Samuel Totten*

The plight and fate of female victims during the course of genocide is both similar to and, in some respects, radically and profoundly different from their male counterparts. During the course of genocide, female victims, like males, suffer demonization, ostracism, discrimination, and the deprivation of their basic human rights. Likewise, they are often rounded up, deported, and killed. But, unlike most men, they have also been subjected to rape, gang rape, and mass rape. Likewise, during the course of various genocides, many females have been forced to become "sex slaves." Furthermore, such assaults and degradation can, and often does, result in pregnancies and horrible injuries to their reproductive systems.

The horror and pain suffered by females do not end with the act of rape. There is always the fear, and reality, of being infected with HIV/AIDS. Concomitantly, there is the fear, and reality, of becoming pregnant as a result of having been raped. Then, there is the birth of the babies ("rape babies" as they are referred to in Rwanda today). In many cases, the very sight of the babies and children remind the mothers of the horrific violations they suffered. In certain cases, mothers harbor a deep-seated hatred and/or distain for such babies/children, which results in even more misery. Often times the hatred is so great that the children born of rape leave home early on in order to fend for themselves on the street.

In many societies (including Bosnia-Herzegovina, Rwanda, and Darfur, to name but three) those females who have been raped during a genocide are not only ostracized by their fellow citizens but by their very family members (This is particularly true in more conservative and/or traditional societies.) Some, such as black African females in Darfur, are perceived as "damaged goods," and thus considered unfit for marriage. Many are also forced from their homes, thus having to fend for themselves and their children to the best of their ability.

None of the above even begins to get at the shame the victims experience during the sexual assaults or the shame most, if not all, carry with them for the rest of their lives—*not* as a result of something they did, but as a result of *something horrific that was done to them.*

1

As the number of volumes in the *Genocide: A Critical Bibliographic Review* series increased over the years, it became increasingly evident to me that the plight and fate of women constituted a lacuna of sorts within the series. Granted, the topic has been alluded to in various chapters in various volumes of the series, but only in a limited way. That realization led to the decision to dedicate an entire issue to examining the plight and fate of females in a single volume.

At least since early adolescence I have been sickened and angered by reports of sexual assaults on females. Such disgust and anger only grew over the course of my thirty plus years as a human rights activist and then genocide scholar. Indeed, for years I have agonized over what could and should be done to halt such terrible atrocities against girls and women. That was true despite the fact that only relatively recently was the horror of such attacks on females "personalized" for me. First, in July/August 2004, I served as one of the twenty-four investigators with the U.S. State Department's and the Coalition of International Justice's Darfur Atrocities Documentation Project. The express purpose of the project was to interview black African refugees from the Darfur region of Sudan in order to collect data that could be analyzed by the State Department to ascertain whether genocide had been and/or was continuing to be perpetrated by the government of Sudan and the *Janjaweed* (Arab militia). During the course of my time in a refugee camp in Goz Beida, Chad, I came face to face with many females who had been raped, gang-raped, and impregnated as a result of such rape. Women (we didn't interview anyone under the age of eighteen) and the relatives of women who had been attacked spoke about their (the women) being forced to do "lewd dances," being raped in fields, and gang raped in their homes in front of their family members. I heard, for example, a story about a woman who was gang-raped by so many men so many times that she could not walk and was thus carried from deep within Darfur to Chad by her relatives. I also heard, time and again, that even though they, the women who had been sexually assaulted, had been in the refugee camp for six months and more, none had received a medical check-up.

Then, in July and August 2006, I conducted a series of interviews with survivors of the 1994 Rwandan genocide in order to ascertain the perspective of general citizens vis-à-vis the value and efficacy of *gacaca* (an adapted form of a precolonial process of conflict resolution to try cases of alleged perpetrators of genocide.) During the course of my interviews, I heard numerous stories about young girls and women who had been raped, ganged raped, impregnated, and often killed by their Hutu assailants.

The sorrow one feels when hearing such stories, while looking in the eyes of the victims and/or their parents or siblings, is nearly overwhelming. And the sorrow is not something that evaporates with time. In light of that simple but profound fact, one has to wonder how the victims make it through their daily existence.

Although working on this latest volume has been emotionally taxing, it has been an honor working with such a fine group of scholars/authors, none of whom have previously appeared in this bibliographic series. The authors run the gamut from well-established scholars to newly minted PhDs and PhD candidates. Collectively, they have helped to produce one of the most unique volumes in this series.

In developing the volume, I envisioned authors addressing a host of key issues which, in the end, would provide a solid overview of the historical and contemporary plight and fate of females in the face of genocide and its aftermath. Although I believe that goal has been accomplished, ultimately, it is up to readers to make that judgment.

Numerous chapters focus on the plight and fate of females during specific cases of genocide: the Ottoman Turk genocide of the Armenians, the Holocaust, the 1971 genocide in Bangladesh, the 1975-1979 Khmer Rouge perpetrated genocide, the 1994 Rwandan genocide, genocide perpetrated during the crisis in the former Yugoslavia, and the ongoing genocide in Darfur (2003-today). Initially, I contemplated including chapters on genocides that were perpetrated earlier than the twentieth century (especially one or two on the indigenous peoples in the Americas), but repeated efforts to solicit such chapters came to naught. Ultimately, in an attempt to at least, in part, present the history of the issue of rape and genocide, I solicited a chapter on the evolution of international law and the plight and fate of women during the course of genocide.

In "Women and the Armenian Genocide: The Victim, The Living Martyr," Rubina Permooian, Research Associate in the Department of Near Eastern Languages and Cultures at the University of California, Los Angeles (UCLA), argues that "More vulnerable and less well-equipped physically and emotionally [than the men], especially during the forced deportations from their homes and villages of 1915, [Armenian women and girls] often had to take charge of the remnants of the family and face particularly tragic choices—to throw themselves down cliffs, to surrender to the raging waters of the Euphrates, or to live the life of a concubine in a Turkish or Kurdish harem; indeed, decisions to live or die, none of which offered true salvation, yet all of which demanded heavy compromises or extraordinary courage." In discussing the latter, Permooian examines how the females' experiences affected their entire lives as well as those of their children.

In "Women and the Holocaust," Helene Sinnreich, director of Judaic and Holocaust Studies at Youngstown State University, notes that while male and female victims "shared" and suffered many common experiences during the course of the Holocaust, there were also "a variety of experiences unique to women which gender scholars in recent years have uncovered. These include victimization connected to sexuality, women's role as mothers, as well as societal expectations of women." Continuing, she reports that "Already during World War II itself, the special place of women during the Holocaust was a topic raised by the historian Emmanuel Ringelblum. Remarkably, after the war, there was a lag in interest among professional historians writing about women and the

Holocaust. In fact, until about a decade ago (e.g., the late 1990s), there was very little historical work published on the particulars of women's experience during the Holocaust." She goes on to provide a solid overview of the breadth and depth of scholarly work that addresses a host of issues germane to the plight and fate of females during the Holocaust.

In "The Bangladesh Genocide: The Plight of Women," Angela Debnath, a Ph.D. candidate at University College of London and an adjunct professor of international relations at the American University of Rome, Italy, examines the immediate and long-term impact of the 1971 Bangladesh genocide on Bangladeshi females. Significantly, she notes that the subsequent violence "inflicted upon women by their own state, community leaders, and peers in the aftermath of the conflict" was more social than physical in nature. In that regard, she examines "how the dynamics of violent conflict frequently transfigure women from individuals of worth into a homogeneous terrain of conflict, an extension of the physical battlefield." Ultimately, she explores "what the females' experiences in 1971 and afterwards reveal about Bangladeshi society and the state, the ideology of nationalism and of nation-building, and the crime of genocide."

In "Death, Shattered Families, and Living as Widows in Cambodia," Judy Ledgerwood, associate professor in the Department of Anthropology and Center for Southeast Asian Studies at Northern Illinois University, addresses the plight and fate of Cambodian females during and following the Khmer Rouge-perpetrated genocide in Cambodia (1975-1979). At the outset of her chapter, she states that the specific plight of women during the Cambodian genocide "has not been the focus of research, though there are data available on aspects of social change, women's physical and mental health, sexual violence and women's roles in the revolution." Continuing, she notes that "there is more research on women in the post-revolutionary years, including that which addresses the social effects of large numbers of widows, changing social patterns in the wake of widespread death and displacement, and new economic roles for women — new forms of labor in the 1980s, and migration to work in garment factories and the sex industry in the 1990s."

In "The Crisis in the Former Yugoslavia and Its Impact on the Lives of Women and Girls," Ivana Macek, assistant professor in Genocide Studies at Uppsala University, Sweden, examines the complex array of situations that women found themselves caught up in during the long and drawn out crisis in the former Yugoslavia during the 1990s. In part, she discusses the impact of the war on the daily lives of women, women who worked as anti-war activists and then morphed into nationalists, the mass rape of females, and life in the post-conflict period. Of the mass rapes perpetrated in the former Yugoslavia, she assets that, ultimately, "the women were recognized only in their role as members of a nation and the means for men of the other nation to humiliate and conquer the men of the raped women's nation. That is, the multilayered shame and the bodily harm that the women actually experienced was not truly accounted for."

Samuel Totten's chapter, "The Plight and Fate of Female Victims During and Following the 1994 Rwandan Genocide," is based on historical and field-based research. In the chapter, he provides an overview of a host of critical issues, including but not limited to the following: the ostensible purpose of the mass rape of young girls and women during the course of the genocide; the role of female collaborators and killers; the plight and fate of "rape babies" and their mothers; the impact of the Akayesu trial on international law; and the numerous and painful challenges that female survivors continue to face in the aftermath of the genocide.

In the last chapter that addresses a specific genocide, "Genocide in Darfur: The Mass Rape of Black African Women and Girls," Totten provides insights into the causes of the genocide in Darfur, the sexual attacks on females of all ages and the genocidal aspects of such, and the ramifications of the latter for the individual girls and women as well as the black Africans as an ethnic group.

In a thought-provoking chapter entitled "Rape and Genocide," Dr. Fran Pilch, professor of political science at the United States Air Force Academy, discusses the fact that "the concept of rape as genocide began to emerge in the 1990s, when the systematic use of rape during the conflict in the former Yugoslavia was used as an instrument to attack both individual women and the groups to which they belonged." Continuing she observes that "The combination of the rising importance of non-governmental organizations, enhanced communications through new technology, and the formation of the ad hoc tribunals created to address crimes in the former Yugoslavia and Rwanda also served to generate a deepened concern about the role of rape in the destruction of communities." In the course of her analysis, Pilch examines how the understanding of the role of sexual violence in genocide found legal expression in the groundbreaking Akayesu decision at the International Criminal Tribunal for Rwanda (ICTR).

In her well-written and well-argued chapter, "The Evolution of Gender Crimes in International Law," Nicole Hallett, lecturer at the Yale University School of Law, first discusses how sexual violence was perpetrated in Bosnia and Rwanda as a tool of genocide, and then provides an analysis as to "how the horror of those genocides transformed gender crimes from 'the least condemned war crime[s]' to an emerging area of international criminal law."

Valerie Oosterveld, assistant professor in the Faculty of Law at the University of Western Ontario (Canada), first notes and then argues the following in her chapter entitled "Prosecution of Gender-based Acts of Genocide Under International Law": "'Gender' is not included in the list of targeted groups in the definition of genocide found in the 1948 Convention on the Prevention and Punishment of the Crime of Genocide, and that exclusion is replicated in the 1998 Rome Statute of the International Criminal Court. That does not mean, however, that gender is not a relevant consideration in the prosecution of genocide. Various gender-based acts clearly fall within the prohibited acts included in the genocide definition and gender interacts with the definition's list of targeted groups—national, ethnic, racial or religious—in a myriad of ways. Thus, the prosecution of genocide must take into account the fact that gender deeply informs how genocide is carried out." In her chapter, she provides solid rationales and examples to support the aforementioned points and assertions.

Finally, in "The Post-Genocidal Period and Its Impact on Women," Tazreena Sajjad , a third-year Ph.D student at the School of International Service at American University in Washington D.C., discusses the phenomenon of post-genocidal trauma and examines the ways in which post-genocidal trauma directly impacts women. In doing so, she examines the context of such trauma and the many and complex challenges societies face in responding to such. She goes on to delineate some of the interventions and strategies that have been most effective in addressing this phenomenon.

My hope is that this seventh volume in the *Genocide: A Critical Bibliographic Review* series will provoke debate, discussion, reflection and, ultimately, action—action by concerned individuals, organizations, nations, nongovernmental organizations, and the international community. To ignore the issues presented herein (e.g., the ongoing mass rape of girls and women across the globe during periods of war and genocide, the ostracism of females who have suffered rape, the terrible psychological and physical wounds the victims carry with them each and every day of their lives, the plight of the offspring of those who have been raped, the critical need for medical and psychological services for those who have suffered rape) would be unconscionable—and to address them later rather than sooner would only add insult to injury as many of the issues have been shunted aside for far too long already.

# 1

# Women and the Armenian Genocide: The Victim, the Living Martyr

*Rubina Peroomian*

## Introduction

The events of 1915 mark the beginning of the culmination of a series of calamities that befell the Armenian population of the Ottoman Empire. These events, spanning about a quarter of a century—beginning with the Hamidian massacres of 1894–1896, continuing with the Cilician massacres of 1909, and ending with the Kemalist campaign of 1919–1923—constitute what is known today as the Armenian Genocide. As a result of the calculated and systematic destruction of Armenian life in the Ottoman Empire, an estimated one and a half million Armenians lost their lives and about five hundred thousand survivors fled the country and scattered around the world. Today, aside from a dwindling Armenian community of about 50,000 in Istanbul, it is estimated that about one hundred thousand forcibly Islamized Armenians continue to live throughout Turkey, a modern republic in which the presence of Armenians in their homeland of 3,000 years, as well as the edifices of their culture and heritage, are no more, wiped off the map as they are from the memory of its Turkish citizens.

During this darkest period of Armenian history, Armenian women were victimized by a prolonged agony. More vulnerable and less well-equipped physically and emotionally, especially during the forced deportations from their homes and villages of 1915, they had to take charge of the remnants of the family and face particularly tragic choices, to throw themselves down cliffs, to surrender to the raging waters of the Euphrates, or to live the life of a concubine in a Turkish or Kurdish harem—decisions to live or die, none of which offered true salvation, yet all of which demanded heavy compromises or extraordinary courage. Women who survived lived with the traumatic memory of the past and

7

its impact, never able to lead a normal life. Moreover, willingly or unwillingly, they affected their children's perception of the world and of their identity as a person and as an ethnic Armenian.

This chapter and the annotated bibliography that follows it focus on the plight of Armenian women as victims and survivors of the Genocide, and point to the need for more in-depth research and study in this field. The bibliography leaves out the huge corpus of Genocide literature written in Armenian and thus only includes works that are accessible to the English-speaking audience. Due to the constraints of space, the entries are limited. Further titles can be found in Richard G. Hovannisian (1980, pp. 17-43), Samuel Totten (1991b, pp. 7-43), and Hamo Vassilian (1992).

## Through and Beyond the Darkest Period of Armenian History

### The Impact of Events Preceding 1915

The memory of the cataclysmic events preceding 1915 permeated the Armenian psyche of the late nineteenth and early twentieth centuries. Within the confines of their families, the elders spoke of their traumatic experience as survivors. Eyewitness accounts detailed the plight of Armenian women, mothers witnessing their daughters being raped, their sons and husbands being tortured and killed in front of their eyes; young women being forced into conjugal relationships with their Turkish or Kurdish abductors, bearing their children, and then, in extreme cases, in a moment of rage and revenge, killing the innocent offspring and running away insane. Eyewitness accounts also spoke of women who took up arms and fought shoulder to shoulder with *fedayee*s (freedom fighters) in the incomparably scant defense that Armenians put up against the Turkish army or the incessant Kurdish assaults. During this period, towns and villages were ruined, thousands of lives were lost, but total destruction did not occur (Dadrian, 1995, pp. 141-157, 181-183). The survivors continued their lives in their ravaged homes and ransacked towns and villages. Rebirth was possible, and women played a major role in this revival. Armenians survived and continued to thrive, despite continuing discrimination and persecution.

### The Total Destruction

The premeditated and planned massacres and deportations of Armenians beginning in the spring of 1915 destroyed the fabric of Armenian life in its ancestral homeland. The entire Armenian population was swept away. There was not even a flicker of hope for rebirth and revival.

The annihilation of Armenians was executed in phases (Dadrian, p. 221), and Armenian women were victimized throughout in various ways. The Turkish government proceeded, as Henry Morgenthau, the American ambassador to Turkey (1913–1916), asserts, by first turning Armenians into defenseless masses in order to make their slaughter less difficult (Morgenthau, 1975, p. 302). Contrary to the pre-1908 revolution of the Young Turks, Armenian men were permitted to serve in the army and receive military training, and some even possessed arms. The total annihilation could not begin without first liquidating them. As Turkey entered World War I, able-bodied Armenian men were conscripted into the army, but shortly after being conscripted, they were segregated, disarmed, formed into labor battalions, and murdered (Morgenthau, 1975, pp. 302-303). A minuscule number survived the butchery to recount what was going on in the army. Such butchery was followed by the decree of general disarmament during which all Armenians had to surrender all weapons, even instruments such as kitchen knives or any implements that resembled weapons. The decree was implemented with utmost cruelty. The tortures inflicted on Armenian victims—the *bastinado*, the horse-shoeing, the pulling out of eyebrows, beards, and nails—are horrific to even contemplate. Speaking of such, Morgenthau (1975) wrote:

> The gendarmes treated women with the same cruelty and indecency as the men. There are cases on record in which women accused of concealing weapons were stripped naked and whipped with branches freshly cut from trees, and these beatings were even inflicted on women who were with child. Violations so commonly accompanied these searches that Armenian women and girls, on the approach of the gendarmes, would flee to the woods, the hills, or to mountain caves. (p. 305)

The next phase was the arrest of Armenian men, mostly in leadership positions, in every town and village. On the night of April 23–24, 1915, the Armenian secular and religious leaders and prominent intellectuals in Istanbul and other large cities were arrested and either executed outright or killed on the road to exile. This calculated strategy turned the Armenian population into defenseless and frantic masses of women, children, and elderly men who had escaped death in the previous phases.

The way was now paved for the full-fledged implementation of the annihilation of the Armenian population. The defenseless people of towns and villages were driven out of their homes and deported south to the desert. The manner in which the orders for deportation were carried out differed in each locale. The time granted for preparation varied from no time at all to a few days.

*Difficult Choices*

In almost every household, with the men of the family murdered or imprisoned, it was now up to the women to assume responsibility and make the difficult decisions, first, to accept the loss of the murdered or imprisoned husband or son, and then to prepare for the journey. Preparation entailed anticipating every possibility, what to take along, and whether or not entrust a young child to the care of a volunteering neighbor—with the hope of returning and reclaiming the child. A survivor interviewed by the Miller and Miller (1993) remembers how difficult it was to part from her mother, sisters, and grandmother. Her mother had decided to allow her to be deported with her fiancé's family, because she would not be able to protect and watch over all four of her daughters. As luck would have it, she was the only survivor of the family. Other interviewees recalled the preparations: the mother of one wanted to kill one of their five hundred sheep in order to prepare food to take along, but the Turks had stolen all of them; the mother of another bribed a soldier to get a good pair of shoes for her daughter; other mothers buried their precious possessions, gold and jewelry, in the hope of recovering them when they returned (Miller and Miller, 1993, pp. 68-72). In many places, the government had given assurances that the deportations were a temporary safety measure, simply a matter of relocating Armenians from the war zone.

Many families were given the option to convert to Islam and avoid deportation. It was up to the women to make that difficult decision and face the long-term compunction of having betrayed the Christian faith of their ancestors. But even in these cases, their troubles did not end with their conversion. They had to surrender their children to Turkish orphanages where they were to be brought up as true Muslims. Obviously, the government did not trust the converts of the older generation of Armenians.

Caravans of deportees left each town and village throughout Anatolia, carrying Armenians to their fate. Most deportees went on foot, while others with better means hired carts or pack animals to carry their belongings or a sick or elderly member of their family. Usually one or more gendarmes accompanied the caravans to "protect" the deportees. Instead, the latter alerted the surrounding Muslim villagers and/or bands of chettes—criminals released from jails and given free rein in the countryside to assist with the extermination of the deportees—of the approaching convoy, then stepped aside and allowed them to loot, rape, and kill at will. After a few days, all the deportees were in the same situation, with their belongings stolen, and their carts and horses or donkeys gone.

Unable to bear the hardships of the road and the weeks of walking without food and water, the older and weaker men and women often slowed down and fell behind. In turn, the gendarmes shot them or left them to die by the roadside. Survivors recall their mothers crafting makeshift shoes by wrapping cloth around their children's bare feet, but these ripped easily on the thorns and stones on the road. Mothers kept making these wrappers until they ran out of materials, blankets, and clothing. Many survivors also remember their mothers teaching them the Armenian alphabet, drawing with a stick in the desert sand, in the hope that after their own certain death, their children would keep the memory of their identity alive. Those who still had their Bibles would read to the children to soothe the pain of hunger and thirst (Miller and Miller, 1993).

The deportees would walk all day and stop at night to rest in the open air or under makeshift tents. They would cling to each other for protection and hide the young girls, because the gendarmes or the nearby tribesmen usually attacked the camp at night to prey on young girls.

From April to October 1915, thousands and thousands of wretched women and children filled the roads, prey to continuous assaults, hunger, thirst, epidemic diseases, and the scorching desert sun. The death march passed through circuitous country roads and rugged mountain passes crowded with the rotting corpses, covered with worms, of those left behind from previous caravans. The route that was chosen avoided populated villages so that the deportees could not get food, water, or help of any kind. Even when the route took them by a stream or a well, the gendarmes would prohibit the deportees from approaching the water. The deportees became walking skeletons, skin and bone, barefoot, half-naked, their skin encrusted with dirt and filth and blackened and dehydrated from the blistering sun and literally dying of thirst, they craved water. But those who ran to the water were shot.

Women were separated from their children and husbands from their wives. The men, who had not been arrested before the deportation, along with the older boys, were separated from the caravans and shot or killed with bayonets (Hovannisian, 1986, p. 29).

People were not allowed to stop to bury their dead. Pregnant women were not allowed to stop and give birth. Those who had babies had to bundle their newborn in a piece of their own clothing and move on. These were the lucky ones, who saw their offspring. Others, stabbed with bayonets, had their fetuses taken out and thrown in the air or crushed against a rock. Speaking of such horrors, Morgenthau (1975) wrote:

> There were women who held up their babies to strangers, begging them to take them and save them from their tormentors, and failing this, they would throw them into wells or leave them behind bushes, that at least they might die undisturbed. Behind was left a small army of girls, who had been sold as slaves—frequently for a *medjidie*, or about eighty cents—and who, after serving the brutal purposes of their purchasers, were forced to live lives of prostitution. (p. 317)

A woman survivor from Malgara, who was six years old during the deportations (UCLA Armenian Oral History collection), recounted the following story: The gendarmes separated the children from their parents and led them to a small village nearby. They were to be sold to Bedouin Arabs the next day. It was already dark, she recalled, but the children could see the flames of a big fire in the distance. They could also smell burning flesh. Frightened and distraught, they huddled together and watched the flames finally die down. In the darkness of the night they found a thin stream running nearby. They were so thirsty that they drank the water. It was a little salty and tasted funny. The next morning when they looked at each other they were terrified. Their faces were covered with blood, the blood of their parents and fellow deportees burned alive the night before. The survivor recounted this with tears in her eyes and confessed with pain that she cannot get rid of the image deeply imprinted in her memory.

Reverend F. H. Leslie, an American missionary in Urfa at the time of the genocide, reported about the caravans of women and girls passing the city each day, noting how they were "constantly robbed of their money, bedding, clothing, and beaten, criminally abused and abducted along the way" (quoted in Miller and Miller, 1993, p. 21). American missionaries also reported the most terrible scenes along the banks of the Euphrates. More specifically, they told how gendarmes pushed the Armenian women into the water and shot at them if they tried to swim away, or how women themselves jumped into the river with their children in their arms to put an end to their torturous life and/or to avoid becoming prey to the perpetrator's sexual appetite.

Suicide was not always an option, as human instinct drove the wretched women into the tricky game of survival, a game that could defy moral standards and rob human dignity and normal patterns of behavior of their meaning. There are reports of instances of cannibalism in the desert of Deir-el-Zor, were tens of thousands of Armenians were first pushed and then "herded." After months of dehumanizing, incapacitating suffering, the few remnants of women and children were left in the desert to die. They were faced with the choice of either starving to death or eating the corpses of their own children, who themselves had died of starvation. Thus, the Turkish atrocities did not end with murder and plunder; in certain cases, those Armenians who remained alive, but just barely, were reduced to the status of lowly animals, thus shifting the burden of guilt onto the wretched survivors who had to go on living a tormented life of lingering shame and remorse (Hovannisian, 1986, p.178).

## A Self-Assigned Mission

Despite numerous hardships, some survived to tell the story of Armenian suffering, and many interviewees (UCLA Armenian Oral History collection) attest to that self-assigned mission. These eyewitness accounts and testimonies are valuable insights that, as Samuel Totten (1991a) puts it in his analysis of the importance of first-person accounts, provide "a means to penetrate deeper into the dark depths of genocide" (p. 322).

Pailatsu Kaptanian, for example, wrote her 298-page eyewitness account *Tsavak* (the name of her baby boy who did not survive), for the express purpose of helping the European representatives at the postwar negotiation table to see the truth as to what happened to the Armenian people at the hands of the Ottoman Turks.

Bertha (Berjouhi) Nakshian Ketchian, firmly believed, "We—the survivors—are living eyewitnesses of the Genocide of Armenians by the Turks. What was documented in writing and pictures at the time is now being denied." She was determined to fight against denial, to join the struggle for world recognition of the Armenian Genocide, believing that "recognition of the crime does not bring the victims back, but it eases somewhat the pain of the living" (Ketchian, 1988, pp. ix-x). Other similarly motivated memoirs are listed in the annotated bibliography accompanying this essay.

*A Lifetime of Disillusionment and Nightmares*

It is difficult to live a normal healthy life, as healing and reconciliation become impossible when one's trust in humanity is shattered, when the traumatic ordeal of the past is fueled by the perpetrator's unwavering denialist stance. Historical documentation as well as the testimonies of many survivors speak of the participation of Turkish and Kurdish mobs in the looting and carnage. Turkish neighbors refused to buy the goods that Armenians offered before the 1915 deportations in order to procure funds for the journey ahead. Instead, many rushed to move into Armenian homes even before the inhabitants were evacuated (UCLA Armenian Oral History collection). During the postwar Kemalist campaign in Smyrna (Izmir), the Turkish neighbors of Armenians and Greeks helped the Ottoman army identify Armenian and Greek homes and to set them on fire after looting and killing the inhabitants (Housepian, 1988, pp. 155-167). They also burned the Armenian church with hundreds of refugees inside. And Turkish officers preyed on the Armenian women who were driven out of their homes and gathered on the quay (Smyrna Tragedy). Many survivors speak of the betrayal and complicity of a close and trusted Turkish friend of the family. This was an enigma that continued to weigh heavily among the survivors' painful memories. Disillusionment was coupled with anger when the world praised Kemal Ataturk, the father of modern Turkey, but also the perpetrator of the Smyrna Tragedy.

Almost all of the survivors spoke of nightmares haunting them and affecting their behavior. The horrors they experienced live on in the deep layers of their memory and are propelled to the surface in their sleep, when the willful suppression of these images is not functioning.

The ordeal continued. Women survivors of the Armenian Genocide carried the burden of horrifying memories and transmitted it to their offspring, even if they tried to suppress the memory by not talking about their past. And thus, the memory remained alive in the next generation and the one after that, and such memory, of course, constitutes an important component of the Armenian ethnic identity—and also as an important factor in their outlook on life.

## Critical Challenges Facing the Field

While the study of the Armenian Genocide has made important strides, gender analysis is quite a new field within that domain. It has yet to find acceptance and the recognition of its importance among genocide scholars, such that they come to understand that one need not be a feminist or a woman scholar to focus on the experiences of women victims in genocidal situations. This is particularly true in the case of Armenian Genocide studies.

Another major challenge to this field is the lack of information about the thousands of Armenian women who were "rescued" (most often not with altruistic motivation, but for egotistic reasons) or abducted and forcibly converted to Islam. No gender analysis would be complete without in-depth research on the life experiences of these women. And here, we come late. Most of these women are dead and buried now, and buried with them are their stories that never had a chance to reach receptive ears and fill a small gap in the history of the Armenian Genocide, as well as the history of multiethnic Turkish society believed to be uniform and uninterrupted.

An interesting and newly revealed twist in this area is the hostile attitude among the children of runaway Armenian concubines, those women who eventually took refuge in Armenian communities outside Turkey. This is a double-edged sword, a continuing source of suffering for the mothers—the guilt of their unholy conjugal life with a Turk and the pain of having abandoned their children—and a source of anger and hatred for their offspring, having been told about their Armenian mothers who ran off and left them behind as orphans. Research in this area is essential.

## Avenues to New Possibilities for Progress

The main opening for progress in the study of the plight of the Armenian women victims of the Genocide is the keen interest of third-generation Armenians in the experience of their grandmothers. Evidence of this is the increasing number of publications of their stories in memoirs, and the use of their stories for deeper analysis. Another phenomenon that inspires optimism for progress in this field is the recent change of atmosphere in Turkey. The wall of silence surrounding the Armenian issue has been breached, and many Turkish intellectuals are challenging the official stand and demanding that the Turkish government confront the past. Because of this change, there has been a relaxation, albeit slight, in the rigid Turkish policy of enforced silence about the Armenian Genocide, allowing the emergence of memoirs, biographies, and fiction that entertain the subject of the Armenian Genocide and explore the lives of survivors hitherto assumed to be totally integrated and immersed in Turkish society. It is only recently that we have become aware of the lifelong trauma engulfing these survivors, and how the past has shaped the identity of the generations born to them. Migirdic Margosyan's *Gavur Mahallesi* (The Infidels' Quarter), Fethiye Cetin's *Anneannem* (My Maternal Grandmother), and Kemal Yalcin's *Seninle Guler Yuregim* (You Rejoice My Heart) are pacesetters.

## Conclusion

In-depth analysis of the experiences of Armenian women—victims and survivors—would certainly help to expand our knowledge of the Armenian

Genocide. In this respect, increased momentum in the study of existing sources is crucial. But more important is to bring to light the experience of Islamized Armenian women in Turkey, and that is possible only with the help of Turkish and Turkish-Armenian intellectuals and a favorable atmosphere in Turkey.

The Armenian survivors who have now almost all passed on were denied the satisfaction of seeing the criminal admit the crime—a unique situation in the Armenian case—which could have had a psychological, even a therapeutic effect. They passed with a bitter grievance weighing on their souls. Now, it is the second- and third-generation survivors who live with these unsettled accounts of the past. They deserve belated reconciliation for the sake of a peaceful future and for the sake of humanity, and this reconciliation will be possible only when the official Turkish stance vis-à-vis the Armenian Genocide is reversed.

## References

Boyajian, Levon, and Grigorian, Haigaz (1986). Psychological sequelae of the Armenian Genocide, pp. 177-185. In Richard G. Hovannisian (Ed.). *The Armenian Genocide in Perspective*. New Brunswick, NJ: Transaction Publishers.

Dadrian, Vahakn N. (1995). The *History of the Armenian Genocide: Ethnic Conflict from the Balkans to Anatolia to the Caucasus*. Providence and Oxford: Berghahn Books.

Hovannisian, Richard G. (Ed.) (1980). *The Armenian Holocaust: A Bibliography Relating to the Deportations, Massacres, and Dispersion of the Armenian People*, 1915-1923. Cambridge, MA: National Association for Armenian Studies and Research: Armenian Heritage Press.

Hovannisian, Richard G (1986). The historical dimensions of the Armenian Question, 1878-1923. In Hovannisian, Richard G (Ed.). *The Armenian Genocide in Perspective*. New Brunswick, NJ: Transaction Publishers, pp. 19-41.

Hovannisian, Richard G. (2003). Bitter-sweet memories: The last generation of Ottoman Armenians, pp. 113-124. In Richard G. Hovannisian (Ed.). *Looking Backward, Moving Forward, Confronting the Armenian Genocide*. New Brunswick, NJ: Transaction Publishers.

Housepian Dobkin, Marjorie (1988). *Smyrna 1922: The Destruction of a City*. Kent, OH: Kent State University Press.

Miller, Donald E., and, Touryan-Miller, Lorna (1993). *Survivors: An Oral History of the Armenian Genocide*. Berkeley and Los Angeles: University of California Press.

Morgenthau, Henry (1975). *Ambassador Morgenthau's Story*. Plandome, NY: New Age Publishers.

Totten, Samuel (1991a). First-person accounts of genocide, pp. 321-362. In Israel W. Charny (Ed.) *Genocide: A Critical Bibliographic Review*, Volume 2. London: Mansell Publishers.

Totten, Samuel (1991b). The Ottoman genocide of the Armenians, pp. 7-43. In Samuel Totten (Compiler/Editor) *First-Person Accounts of Genocidal Acts Committed in the Twentieth Century: An Annotated Bibliography*. Westport, CT: Greenwood Press.

Vassilian, Hamo (Ed.) (1992). *The Armenian Genocide: A Comprehensive Bibliography and Library Resource Guide*. Glendale, CA: Armenian Reference Books.

## Annotated Bibliography

*Diaries*

Jacobson, Maria (2001). *Diaries of a Danish Missionary, Harpoot, 1907-1917*. Kristen Vind (Tr.), Ara Sarafian (Ed.). Princeton, NJ and London: Gomidas Institute Books, 266 pp.
Jacobson describes the convoys of deportees, mostly women and children, passing through Harpoot (Kharbert), the missionary orphanage. In doing so, she recounts she and her colleagues were forced to close the orphanage down and as a result had to relocate the orphans. She witnessed Turkish families taking in Armenian children, giving them Turkish names and forcing them to convert.

*Eyewitness Accounts*

Lambert, Rose (1911). *Hadjin and the Armenian Massacres*. New York, Chicago, Toronto, London, and Edinburgh: Fleming H. Revell Company. 106 pp.
    The author, a missionary stationed in Hadjin, recounts the 1909 massacres and the Armenian defense of the city. Similar episodes are recorded by Zapel Esayan in *Averaknerun mej* (Amid the Ruins).

Mugerditchian Esther (circa 1917). *From Turkish Toils: The Narrative of an Armenian Family's Escape*. New York: George H. Doran Company Publishers, 45 pp.
    Esther wrote this long letter in Armenian to her husband, an employee of the British Consular Service in Diarbekir stationed in Egypt. She described in detail the hardship of the family, and how, disguised as Kurds, they escaped the Turkish atrocities. The letter was translated into English in 1919 with a message from the author, "Cherish in your hearts the feeling of vengeance for our hundreds of thousands of martyrs."

Parmelee, Ruth M. (2002). *A Pioneer in the Euphrates Valley*. Princeton, NJ and London: Gomidas Institute, 68 pp.
    Dr. Ruth Parmelee was an American medical missionary in the Ottoman Empire during World War I. This book is a testimony of Turkish atrocities against Armenians in the region.

*Memoirs and Autobiographies*

Bedoukian, Kerop (1978). *The Urchin: An Armenian's Escape*. London: Butler and Tanner Ltd. 186 pp. (Also published as *Some of us Survived*. New York: Farrar Straus Giroux, 242 pp.)
    Bedoukian was nine years old when the deportation of Armenians in Sivaz began. The memoirs are dedicated to his mother and sister who shared his

horrifying ordeal, and who protected him, allowing him to survive and escape to freedom. He remembers her mother's utmost sacrifice for her children and her begging for bread in Turkish houses where Armenian women were taken in as concubines.

Martin, Ramela (1989). *Out of Darkness*. Cambridge, MA: Zoryan Institute Publication, 220 pp.

Born in the Pilibosian family in Malatia, Ramela was a little girl during the years of deportation and massacres. She soon found herself left alone with her mother on the deportation road. She lost her mother, too, and struggled all alone until she found her way into an orphanage, where she witnessed children dying from hunger and illnesses. Reaching Greece, and freedom, was a miracle.

Minassian, John (1986). *Many Hills Yet to Climb: Memoirs of an Armenian Deportee*. Santa Barbara, CA: Jim Cook, Publisher, 255 pp.

John Minassian was born in Sivaz. He was a student at the American Teachers College when the Great War broke out. He survived the genocide to write a detailed account of the Armenian suffering. This story is also the sad story of women of different walks of life subjected to dehumanizing atrocities.

Muggerditchian Shipley, Alice (1983). *We Walked Then Ran*. Phoenix, AZ: A. M. Shipley, 290 pp.

The author was born into a diplomatic family. Her father was in the service of the British government in Egypt when the deportations began. Alice tells the story of her escape from the Turkish atrocities with her mother and siblings.

Naim Bey (1965). *The Memoirs of Naim Bey* (second printing). Compiled by Antonian, Aram. Newtone Square, PA: Armenian Historical Research Association, 84 pp.

In this compilation of Official Turkish Documents on the deportations and massacres of Armenians, Antonian is making heard the voice of a Turkish official who reluctantly carried out his superiors' orders. After the war, Naim Bey handed over the documents he had still kept to Antonian and on behest of Antonian wrote his memoirs in which the harrowing events and the suffering of women are described.

Najarian, Peter (1986). *Daughters of Memory*. Berkeley, CA: City Miner Books, 157 pp.

Women survivors of the Genocide, living in the United States, get together every so often and relate their experiences during the deportations of 1915. Najarian shows how indelible are the imprints of these memories, always present in the lives of these women.

Nakshian Ketchian, Bertha (1988). *In the Shadow of the Fortress: The Genocide Remembered*. Cambridge, MA: Zoryan Institute Publication. 151 pp.

Bertha (Berjuhi) remembers her childhood in Husenig, in the Province of Kharbert. She describes women, children and old men during the Death March, young women being kidnapped, attractive children taken away by Arabs and Kurds, women hurling themselves down the cliffs. She remembers her grandmother trying hard to keep the family together. Bertha ended up in an orphanage in Kharbert after the remnants of her family managed to return from Aleppo.

Soghoian, Florence M. (1997). *Portrait of a Survivor*. Hanover, MA: The Christopher Publishing House, 147 pp.

Soghoian relates the story of her mother, Shnorhig, who was deported from Zeitun at the age of seven. Her father was a soldier in the Turkish army and away from the family at the time. They never heard from him again. Her family members were separated from each other in that chaotic crowd on the road of deportation. She was left alone in the streets of Marash and was taken to the orphanage there. Later, she was reunited with her mother, the only other survivor of their large family.

Surmelian, Levon Z. (1945). *I Ask You Ladies and Gentlemen*. New York: E. P. Dutton & Co., Inc., 316 pp.

This autobiography is one of the first English-language works on the Armenian Genocide. The tragedy of 1915 is described through the eyes of a young boy. It is a documentary with a poetic language, and reflected in it is the philosophy of life of someone who has come face to face with death a few times in his childhood.

Tabibian, Negdar K. (1988). *Destined to Survive: An Autobiography*. Laverne, CA: American-Armenian International College, University of Laverne, 140 pp.

Tabibian tells the story of the defense of Van and the exodus of the people of Van just before the Turkish reoccupation of the region. She took to the road with her grandparents, mother, younger sister, and older sister with her newborn baby. The men of the family had all fallen during the battle to defend the city.

*Biography*

Bagdasarian, Adam (2000). *Forgotten Fire*. New York: DK Publishing, Inc. 273 pp.

Twelve-year-old Vahan's childhood abruptly ended when he watched horror-stricken the execution of his two older brothers by gendarmes in their own garden in Bitlis. The book is based on Bagdasarian's great uncle, Vahan's life story. Female members of the family and fellow deportees are vividly portrayed throughout the story.

Balakian, Peter (1997). *Black Dog of Fate*. New York: Broadway Books, 289 pp.

This is a testimony of Balakian's discovery of the traumatic past that his family and his ancestors had experienced. Against a backdrop of historical facts, Balakian narrates the story of his grandmother, which is the story of many victims and survivors of the Armenian Genocide.

Katchadourian, Stina (1994). *Efronia, an Armenian Love Story*. Boston, MA: Northeastern University Press, 221 pp.

Efronia's memoir of some 500 pages, written in Armenian, was translated into English by her son and then turned into a piece of literary work by her non-Armenian daughter-in-law. Efronia was born into a well-educated family in Aintab. She planned to enter the Marash College for Girls when the Great War broke out. From that moment, her story is the turbulent life of a family in their struggle to survive. Meanwhile, Efronia's love story with a young Persian man was an outrageous occurrence for the time. She always had the chance to turn her back to the family's tradition and Christian faith and escape with her lover to safety and personal happiness, but she chose to suffer with her family. She survived and, much later in life, reluctantly chose a partner in marriage. This story of forbidden love gives a different view of woman's suffering in those tumultuous years.

Kherdian, David (1979). *The Road from Home: The Story of an Armenian Girl*. New York: Greenwillow Books, 238 pp.

Kherdian relates the story of his mother Veron, born in Azizia into a well-to-do family. At the age of sixteen, she was deported with her family and survived unspeakable hardship.

Manoukian, Mariam, and Manoukian, Elize (2005). *On the Other Side of Mount Ararat: A Story of a Vanished City*. Glendale, CA: Abril Publishng, 177 pp.

In the voice of her grandmother, Mariam Manoukian and her daughter Elize depict the life of the Kosparian family and, in general, the life of Armenians in Van in the years between 1913 and 1915. Women of different generations are portrayed in their everyday life: their beliefs, their fears, their bravery, and their suffering through the hardship of the exodus from Van, escaping the encroaching Turkish army. This book is the result of the efforts of third and fourth generation Armenians to recount the memories of a tragic past that have remained imprinted in the minds of generations to come.

Mouradian, Kay (2005). *A Gift in the Sunlight: An Armenian Story*. London and Reading: Taderon Press, 205 pp.

Mouradian wrote her mother's story on her behest. To furnish a historical background for these heartrending stories, reminiscences of the years of massacres she grew up with, she began her research, and the deeper she delved, the more convinced she became that what she was to write was more than her mother's story; "it is also the story of every Armenian who survived that tragic historical event that continues to be glossed over by the modern world."

Tashjian, Alice A. (1995). *Silences: My Mother's Will to Survive*. Princeton, NJ: Blue Pansy Publishing, 98 pp.

This is the story of Iskouhi Parounagian of Sivaz, the author's mother, a story that has come alive through mother-daughter conversations. Still in her teens, Iskouhi lost her mother to the hardships of the Death March. Orphaned and alone, she wandered for days without food until a Turkish woman picked her up and took her home. But sheltering Armenians was dangerous, and Turks who did that, faced jail or even death. Iskouhi was driven out, but the Turkish woman was kind enough to accompany her until she could join a caravan of Armenians, to be followed by further ordeals.

*Fiction*

Aharonian Marcom, Micheline (2001). *Three Apples Fell from Heaven*. New York: Riverhead Books, 270 pp.

This novel is based on Micheline's maternal grandmother's story and includes the horrifying experience of other men and women during the years 1915-1917. The author is a third generation half-Armenian half-American woman who, despite her mother's resolve not to talk about the harrowing stories that she herself had been raised with, set out to discover the past.

Edgarian, Carol (1994). *Rise the Euphrates*. New York: Random House Books, 370 pp.

Edgarian blends the facts of the Armenian Genocide with the traumatic experience of the survivor generation, specifically, that of her grandmother. She highlights the attractions and fun and multiple opportunities that American culture can offer a third-generation Armenian teenager and demonstrates that no matter how deeply assimilated with the culture and lifestyle of the mainstream and aloof from the Armenian past, this American-born generation still carries traces of the wounds of the Genocide.

Hacikyan, Agop J., and Jean-Yves Soucy (2001). *A Summer without Dawn*. Toronto, Ontario: McClelland & Stewart Inc. Publishers, 545 pp.

This novel was first published in French, *Un eté sans aube*. It is a detailed description of Vartan and Maro Balian's ordeal through the years of genocide. Maro struggles to save her only son as she bears the disgrace and humiliation of a concubine in her "rescuer's" harem. She represents the collective persona of all women facing the same predicament, exemplifying the life-long ordeal of women, who had to leave behind their children, fruits of the unholy conjugal life with their abductors, and escape to freedom.

Kricorian, Nancy (1999). *Zabelle*. New York: Avon Books, 241pp.

This is the story of Zabelle Chahasbanian, from her childhood in Hadjin to her immigration to the United States, with frequent flashbacks into the darkest years of her life during the deportations.

Shirinian, Lorne (2002). *Memory's Orphans*. Kingston, Ontario: Blue Heron Press. 101pp.

This is a collection of short stories about individuals in search of their place in the New World. Whether they were born somewhere in Turkey (Western Armenia), survived the Genocide and took refuge in the Diaspora, or were born in the Diaspora but lived with the transmitted memory of the genocide, they are outsiders, marginal people, who are here and there simultaneously. This is clearly the effects of the genocide on the survivors and generations of survivors.

*Secondary Material*

Akcam, Taner (2006). *A Shameful Act: The Armenian Genocide and the Question of Turkish Responsibility*. New York: Metropolitan Books, Henry Holt and Company, 483 pp.

In the light of Turkish nationalism and the goals of the Young Turks, this Turkish historian presents his view of the Armenian massacres. While discussing the massacres and deportations, he also speaks of the fate of women (see, particularly, pp. 174-204).

Balakian, Nona (1958). *The Armenian American Writer*. New York: Armenian General Benevolent Union of America, 32 pp.

This is a short introduction into the works of the first generation Armenian writers who wrote in English. Balakian analyses their work, their motives, and the imprint of the Old Country on their writings.

Balakian, Peter (2003). *The Burning Tigris: The Armenian Genocide and America's Response*. New York: HarperCollins Publishers, 475 pp.

Using archival materials and eyewitness accounts, Balakian presents the history of the Armenian Genocide. He provides valuable information on the lot of Armenian women, their experience during the deportation, their forcible conversions and abduction into harems, and the sexual violence perpetrated against them.

Bedrosian, Margaret (1991). *The Magical Pine Ring: Armenian American Literature*. Detroit, MI: Wayne State University Press, 249 pp.

This is a compilation of essays analyzing the works of various Armenian-American writers in their quest to find their identity and to come to terms with their collective traumatic past. Bedrosian herself is a second generation survivor, and her own past has affected her approach to these writers.

Dicanio, Margaret (2002). *Memory Fragments from the Armenian Genocide: A Mosaic of a Shared Heritage*. New York, Lincoln, Shanghai: Mystery and Suspense Press, 243 pp.

Discanio has recorded the life stories of thirty-one second-generation men and women survivors, all of whom exemplify the philosophy that "doing well is doing good." This is a credo handed down to them by their survivor parents and the memory of their family members who perished during the Genocide. They uphold their culture and heritage and do well in life as if taking revenge on the Turkish campaign to wipe out Armenians.

Hovannisian, Richard G. (1992). "Intervention and Shades of Altruism During the Armenian Genocide," pp. 173-207 (CHECK THIS). In Richard G. Hovannisian (Ed.) *The Armenian Genocide, History, Politics, Ethics*. New York: St. Martin's Press.

Hovannisian, one of the doyens of research on the Armenian Genocide, analyzes oral histories of the Armenian genocide into order too attempt to gain insight into the motivations of those who intervened on the behalf of the Armenians. He shows these interventions to be humanitarian, obviously, not counting the cases of sexual exploitation, forced labor, bribery, etc. This essay is important to the topic under discussion because cases of good Turks saving Armenian women for solely humanitarian reasons have not been addressed in the body of this essay.

Mergerian, Barbara, and Renjilian-Burgy, Joy (Eds.) (2000). *Voices of Armenian Women. Papers Presented at the International Conference on Armenian Women. Paris, France*. Belmont, MA: AIWA Press, Armenian International Women's Association, 333 pp.

The first section of this volume (pp. 1-49) comprises five essays dealing with the impact of the Armenian Genocide on women survivors and their offspring.

Miller, Donald E., and, Touryan Miller, Lorna (1992). "Women and Children of the Armenian Genocide," pp. 152-172. In Richard G. Hovannisian (Ed.) *The Armenian Genocide, History, Politics, Ethics*. New York: St. Martin's Press.

Based on interviews of survivors through the years, the Millers delineate the experience of women, identifying their gender-specific physical and emotional suffering.

Moranian, Suzanne Elizabeth (1992). "Bearing Witness: The Missionary Archives as Evidence of the Armenian Genocide," pp. 103-128. In Richard G. Hovannisian (Ed.) *The Armenian Genocide, History, Politics, Ethics*. New York: St. Martin's Press.

Moranian discusses missionary activities in the Ottoman Empire, especially during the massacres and deportations, and cites their reports. She describes how difficult it was for the missionaries to witness the deportation, knowing that the deportees "faced almost certain death." Anna Birge, for example, remembers women and children jammed into cattle cars going south without food and water: "One woman gave birth to twins in one of the cattle cars, and upon crossing a river, the woman hurled herself and her two infants into the water." Toward the end of the Genocide, the Turkish government exempted the Armenian Catholics and Protestants from deportation, but most of them were already gone.

Peroomian, Rubina (1993). *Literary Responses to Catastrophe: A Comparison of the Armenian and the Jewish Experience*. Atlanta, GA: Scholars Press, 238 pp.

Through the literary responses to the Genocide by the first generation Armenian literati, the author examines the plight of the Armenian people and their differing reactions to the horrors of genocide. The predicament of women in their prolonged agony is also discussed.

Peroomian, Rubina (2003). New Directions in Literary Responses to the Armenian Genocide," pp. 157-180. In Richard G. Hovannisian (Ed.) *Looking Backward, Moving Forward: Confronting the Armenian Genocide*. New Brunswick, NJ: Transaction Publishers.

The author examines the contextualization of the Armenian Genocide by the second- and third-generation writers, stresses the power of artistic literature as an instrument of memory and mission and as an indicator of the metamorphosis of ethnic identity. Through this analysis, the second- and third-generation Armenian women's perception of the past and its impact on the present is discussed.

Peroomian, Rubina (2003)."When Death Is a Blessing and Life a Prolonged Agony: Women Victims of Genocide," pp. 314-332. In Colin Tatz, Peter Arnold, and Sandra Tatz (Eds.), *Genocide, Perspectives II: Essays on Holocaust and Genocide*. Sydney: Brandl & Schlesinger with the Australian Institute for Holocaust & Genocide Studies.

This gender-specific analysis discusses women's plight during the Genocide and the impact of the traumatic past on survivors as reflected in memoirs, eyewitness accounts, and fiction.

Rowe, Victoria (2003). *A History of Armenian Women's Writing: 1880-1922*. London: Cambridge Scholars Press Ltd., 301 pp.

This book contains a comprehensive bibliography of works of Armenian women writers and those focusing on Armenian women. Chapter 6 deals specifically with women's experience of exile and genocide.

Shirinian, George N. (2001). "The Armenian Massacres of 1894-1897: A Bibliography." *Armenian Review*, 47 (1-2), 113-164.

This compilation of material (historical background, documents, memoirs and eyewitness accounts) about the massacres in individual cities and towns and policies of the Great Powers is a valuable contribution to the research and understanding of the massacres of that era—and specifically the plight of the Armenian women caught in that turmoil.

Shirinian, Lorne (1990). *Armenian-North American Literature, a Critical Introduction: Genocide, Diaspora, and Symbols.* Lewiston, Quinston, Lampeter, Canada: The Edwin Mellen Press, 304 pp.

Shirinian explores the ways Armenians in North America relate to the Armenian Genocide and discusses how there is a certain unity in the texts at the level of the collective symbol of the Armenian Genocide.

Shirinian Lorne (1998). "Survivor Memoirs of the Armenian Genocide as Cultural History," pp. 165-174. In Richard G. Hovannisian (Ed.) *Remembrance and Denial: The Case of the Armenian Genocide.* Detroit, MI: Wayne State University Press.

In this essay, the author discusses the difference between written accounts/memoirs and oral history. He maintains that memoirs are part history and "contribute to and form a major component of the collective memory of the Armenian nation." The importance to the subject at hand is the background and analysis it provides for the many memoirs by women survivors listed in this bibliography.

Shirinian, Lorne (2000). *Writing Memory: The Search for Home in Armenian Diaspora Literature as Cultural Practice.* Kingston, Ontario: Blue Heron Press, 189 pp.

Examined are the role of the memory of the Genocide in the Armenian Diaspora communities, and the hardship of living away from home. "Home" here is a substitute for Western Armenia that was swept clean of its indigenous people during the Genocide.

Staub, Ervin (2003). "Healing and Reconciliation, pp. 263-274. In Richard G. Hovannisian (Ed.) *Looking Backward, Moving Forward, Confronting the Armenian Genocide.* New Brunswick, NJ: Transaction Publishers.

The author deals with the post-traumatic stress disorder and its relevance to Armenian survivors, stressing the need to reconcile with the past.

Topalian, S. Shake (1999). "Daughters and Granddaughters of Survivors: From Horror to Finding our own Voices," pp. 224-331. In Mark A. Mamigonian (Ed.) *The Armenians of New England.* MA: National Association for Armenian Studies and Research, Armenian Heritage Press.

The author discusses the impact of the genocidal experience on Armenian women and how they transmit that psychological effect as they raise their daughters and granddaughters.

# 2

# Women and the Holocaust

*Helene J. Sinnreich*

## Introduction

*"The historian of the future who will write about
the events of our days will have to devote a special
page to the Jewish woman and her place in this
war. The Jewish woman has assumed a special
chapter in Jewish history. In the abyss of darkness
she was a pillar of strength and courage."*
— *Emmanuel Ringelblum writing
in the Warsaw Ghetto[1]*

During the Holocaust, women, like their male counterparts, were subjected to a vast array of conditions which differed depending on geographical location, Nazis decrees, legislation, and actions, the progression of the war. In various places and times, women were subjected to humiliating and restrictive legislation, forced into new roles as conditions transformed or separated families, and suffered genocidal conditions, including incarceration in ghettos and concentration camps, being massacred by soldiers or members of mobile killing units which murdered men, women, and children during the initial invasion period, or being sent away to forced labor. Women's experiences during the Holocaust also included attempts to evade German genocidal plans by going into hiding whether through living in a secret hiding space or posing as a non-Jew, or through participation in resistance movements such as smuggling munitions or serving as partisan fighters. In addition to these common experiences shared between male and female victims of the Holocaust, there were a variety of experiences unique to women which gender scholars in recent years have uncovered. These include victimization connected to sexuality, women's role as mothers, as well as societal expectations of women.

Already during World War II itself, the special place of women during the Holocaust was a topic raised by the historian Emmanuel Ringelblum. Remarkably, after the war, there was a lag in interest among professional historians writing about women and the Holocaust. In fact, until about a decade ago (e.g., the late 1990s), there was very little historical work published on the particulars of women's experience during the Holocaust. As Joan Ringelheim, one of the early proponents of applying gender analysis to Holocaust Studies, has pointed out, this is ironic as one of the hallmarks of the genocide is the fact that women and children were targeted.

During the immediate postwar period and through the 1980s, there were some collections of women's testimony, wonderful fodder for analytic research, published but not much in the way of synthetic works. The exception to this was the pioneering work of Joan Ringelheim, whose volume, co-edited with Esther Katz, *Proceedings of the Conference on Women Surviving the Holocaust* appeared in 1983. A year later, in 1984, Renate Bridenthal, Atina Grossmann and Marion Kaplan edited *When Biology Became Destiny: Women in Weimar and Nazi Germany*. Unsurprisingly, much of this early work has since been critiqued by proponents of modern trends in gender studies. For example, in "Gender, Genocide, and Jewish Memory," Sara Horowitz (2000) contends that "[m]any of the early studies of women's experiences in the Holocaust asserted that while men's efforts to survive were characterized by aggression, selfishness, and solitariness, women's efforts were marked by camaraderie, nurturing, and bonding" (p. 187), and argues that such a perspective provides a skewed view of what actually occurred. In doing so, she argues that it is critical not to impose one's own values on past experience. More specifically, she contends that concern for oneself as well as reaching out to others was a part of both genders' Holocaust experience.

## The State of Affairs Today

As evidenced by the above comment by Horowitz, a literary scholar, disciplines other than history have addressed the issue of women in the Holocaust and have been important factors in cross pollination. One early work representing multidisciplinary approaches to the Holocaust was Carol Rittner and John K. Roth's edited volume *Different Voices: Women and the Holocaust* which was published in 1993 and included both personal narratives as well as scholarly articles. In the late 1990s, works on Jewish women and other female victims began to appear with more frequency. Probably the most notable of these was Dalia Ofer and Lenore Weitzmann's 1998 edited volume *Women in the Holocaust*. This work took a comprehensive look at Jewish and non-Jewish women's experiences. It included twenty one essays covering a broad range, including scholarly works and victim testimony on the pre-war lives of Jewish women, life in the ghettos and concentration camps, as well as resistance and hiding.

There are multiple explanations for the late arrival of gender questions in Holocaust research. One theory posited that there was a reluctance among scholars to differentiate between women and men's experiences during the Holocaust, rejecting a notion of comparative victimhood or creating unequal victims (Langer, 1998, p. 351; Ringelheim, 1990). However, there are experiences during the Holocaust which are particular to gender. Another theory claims that questions about women were seen as being of secondary importance. Connected to this, some scholars have pointed out the fact that male voices have been privileged over women's testimonies as evidenced by the dominance of Elie Wiesel, Primo Levi, and other male memoirs despite the large number of women's memoirs created, particularly immediately after the war. One scholar noted that, "Traditionally, men have claimed war memories as their possessions....Women's war memories have been neglected and have played no role or at best a secondary role in war-related matters. Until recently, this also applied to the Holocaust" (Doerr, 2000, p. 71). Another reason for the lack of material on women's experience during the Holocaust is a problem within the field in general in which perpetrator's actions and motives are privileged as research topics while victim experience are deemed less important. Although this is beginning to change, the bulk of scholarship on the Holocaust focuses on the policies and actions against the victims rather than on specific experiences.

Scholarship on women and the Holocaust continues to develop. Researchers focused on women or gendered research questions have looked at individual categories of women victims, including Germans, Jewish, Roma, and other groups as well as the experiences of female victims at various stages of the destruction process and varying geographical locations. Country studies written from a gendered perspective during the Holocaust have begun to emerge or be proposed such as Laura Palosuo's project on Hungary and the Holocaust but more often a gendered perspective is utilized as one of many research tools in the more recent country studies such as for example Tim Cole's forthcoming work on Hungary and Alexander Korb's forthcoming work on Croatia. Experiences such as resistance, hiding, and forced labor have also been means by which researchers have examined women during the Holocaust.

## German Women

Work on German women's experiences during the war have often been linked with questions of sexism and Nazi ideology which makes the targeting of women possible. One explanation proffered by a number of scholars has been sexism or Nazi misogyny. Some of the earlier work in this area is George L. Mosse's (1985) theory of modern development of masculine identity that holds that the *Männerbund* identity, a male collective whose interrelationship was a source of power and strong masculinity defined in opposition to women, Jews, and homosexuals, reached its apex under Nazi Germany. Still others have looked at the misogyny of the Nazi regime as a logical extension of their racial theory which called for women to be breeders for the nation and saw Weimar era feminism as an obstruction to motherhood.

Scholars examining German women have also focused on questions about German women's roles in the National Socialist state. Various scholars have portrayed German women as perpetrators, bystanders and victims. Some important examples of this include Claudia Koonz's (1987) *Mothers in the Fatherland: Women, the Family and Nazi Politics*, Gundrun Schwarz's (1997) work on SS wives, and more recently Elizabeth Harvey's (2005) *Women in the Nazi East: Agents and Witnesses of Germanization.*

In 1986, Gisela Bock made the controversial claim that women's lack of reproductive autonomy made women, as a group, victims of Nazism by forcing desirable women into the forced labor of childbearing and mandating sterilization for those deemed by the regime to be racially undesirable.[2] Even if one accepts Bock's thesis that lack of control over their reproduction rendered German women victims, German women were also perpetrators of the Holocaust. For the purposes of this chapter, however, the focus will remain on those women the regime targeted for extermination or removal of their reproductive abilities.

Probably the most well-known category of "Aryans" subject to extermination and sterilization under the Nazi regime includes the mentally and physically handicapped. These men and women were subjected to starvation, brutal treatment, and as part of the T-4 killing operations, the Nazi program to exterminate the disabled, murder most often perpetrated through gas chambers or lethal injection. At present, there are only general studies on the T-4 killing operations. Scholars have yet to examine women as victims of the German euthanasia policy in depth though some have suggested that women were particularly vulnerable. Gendered examinations have been thus far focused on the perpetrators, particularly on nurses as killers.

In addition to the possibility of being labeled physically or mentally disabled, German women could be labeled "undesirables" for being sexually promiscuous and persecuted as "asocials" or "feebleminded." These labels carried serious consequences. The feebleminded and asocials were liable to face sterilization or concentration camp incarceration. This type of persecution was particular to women as men were not persecuted for multiple sexual partners. On the contrary, the regime created both military and civilian brothels for German men as well as male foreign workers, and even, male concentration camp inmates. In this respect, there was a particular crime which women alone could be convicted of within the Nazi regime.

Connected with women's sexuality was the persecution of prostitutes. Ironically the punishment meted out by the regime not only included incarceration in concentration camps but also often compelled them to engage in the occupation for which they had been prosecuted, as forced laborers in the various state controlled brothels.

Forced prostitution was not limited to German women. Rather, it most often was imposed on women from the countries occupied by Nazi Germany. Important work has been produced on forced prostitution by numerous individuals including Christa Paul's (1995) *Zwangsprostitution: Staatlich Errichtete Bordelle im Nationalsozialismus*, Christa Schikorra's (2002) work on female prostitution as slave labor, and more recently, the edited volume by Baris Alakus, Katharina Kniefacz, and Robert Vorberg (2006) *Sex-Zwangsarbeit in Nationalsozialist-ischen Konzentrationslagern*. Scholarship on sexual abuse during the Holocaust has largely been done by German scholars. Forced prostitution, rape, and other sexual abuse against women during the Holocaust has received little scholarly attention in the United States. The work of young scholars such as Annette F. Timm (2001) and Wendy Jo Gertjejanssen (2004) and the forthcoming work of Monika Flaschka (in progress) may represent a shift in the field towards more North American scholars examining sexual violence.

Another group of women subjected to persecution under the Nazi regime are lesbians. Research on Lesbians and persecution of them in Nazi occupied Europe remains limited. Claudia Schoppmann's 1991 work *Nationalsozialis-tiche Sexualpolitik und weibliche Homosexualität* remains the sole serious large scale scholarly work devoted to the topic. Schoppmann has also written in English on the topic, including her work co-written with Gunter Grau *Hidden Holocaust?: Gay and Lesbian Persecution in Germany, 1933-1945* (Schoppmann and Grau, 1995). Likewise, an excerpt from her work also appears in English: "National Socialist Policies towards Female Homosexuality" in *Gender Relations in German History: Power, Agency, and Experience from the Sixteenth to the Twentieth Centuries* (Schoppmann, 1997). She has also published an English language collection of testimonies of lesbian survivors which includes an overview of lesbians in the Weimar and Nazi period (Schoppmann, 1996). There is scant evidence on the experience of lesbians in Nazi Germany. This is, in part, because survivors were reluctant to come forward and additionally, because lesbianism, unlike male homosexuality which was prosecuted, was not against the law in Nazi Germany. Therefore, there are few court cases or police records that indicate someone was directly arrested for lesbianism. Without ample court records or testimonies, it is difficult to find material on the experiences of lesbian women in Nazi Germany.

## Jewish Women

While German women were encouraged to stay at home and produce children, those deemed by the Nazi regime to be racially undesirable were denied the right to reproduce through legislation, forced abortion, and forced sterilization. Ultimately, those at the lowest levels of the Nazi racial hierarchy, including Jewish and Roma women, were prevented from reproducing through the murder of children and the potential mothers.

Nazi policy against Jewish women progressed in different stages throughout the war and in different geographical locations. At the outset of the Nazi rise to power, legislation in Germany was passed which curtailed Jewish women's lives and freedoms. Marion Kaplan's work, particularly her monograph *Between Dignity and Despair: Jewish Life in Nazi Germany* (1998), provides a rich discussion of the effects of early Nazi policy on Jewish women. When the war expanded to encompass Poland and ghettos were established, Jewish women's circumstances were affected. Some research on gender and ghettoization have been undertaken by Michal Unger (1998) in her article, "The Status and Plight of Women in the Lodz Ghetto" and Helene J. Sinnreich (2005) in "...And We Eat Like on Yom Kippur": Women, Food, and the Struggle for Survival in the Lodz Ghetto." In his work *Holocaust City: The Making of a Jewish Ghetto,* Tim Cole (2003) includes gender analysis in his examination of daily life in the Budapest Ghetto. Another emerging topic has been family life within the ghetto as a means of uncovering gendered experience.

Concentration of women victims during the Holocaust did not always include the ability of families to stay together. In most concentration camps, women and men were separated. In this author's estimation, the most important work thus far on Jewish women in the concentration camps is Gisela Bock's recent *Genozid und Geschlecht: Jüdische Frauen im. nationalsozialistischen Lagersystem (Genocide and Gender: Jewish Women in the National Socialist Concentration Camp System).*

There has also been some research on women's experiences in specific concentration camps. Three books on Ravensbrück concentration camp have come out in the last few years, including Rochelle Saidel's (2004) recent work *The Jewish Women of Ravensbrück Concentration Camp.* Since the camp housed primarily women for most of its history, this is an important camp for studying women's experiences during the Holocaust. Other works have appeared on women in concentration camps, including the following works on women in Auschwitz: Lore's *Auschwitz—The Nazi Civilization: Twenty-three Women Prisoners' Accounts*; Lore's *Criminal Experiments on Human Beings in Auschwitz and War Research Laboratories: Twenty Women Prisoners' Accounts*; and Ofer's and Weitzmann's *Women in the Holocaust.*

Women's experiences in the camps varied but one theme which echoes through most testimonies and which has been commented on by various scholars is the dehumanization of the camps and the stripping of feminine markers from women. For many women this began upon arrival with the stripping of their clothing and hair, often in front of male guards and prisoners. Literary scholars, historians, sociologists, and others have all focused attention on this experience. For example, Anna Reading (1999) in her article "Scarlet Lips at Belsen," focuses on the linkages between femininity and feeling human for women during and after the Holocaust. Another aspect of feminine identity which runs through testimonies and scholarship is fear of loss of fertility including, for example, discussions of the cessation of menstruation and forced sterilization. Scholars, such as, for example, S. Lillian Kremer (1999) in *Women's Holocaust Writing: Memory and Imagination* and Nechama Tec (2003) in *Resilience and Courage: Women, Men, and the Holocaust* have commented on the absence of menstruation caused by the extreme conditions of the Holocaust. Shelly Lore's (1992) *Criminal Experiments on Human Beings in Auschwitz and War Research Laboratories: Twenty Women Prisoners' Accounts,* as well as a number of more general works on medical experimentation, deal with the physical destruction of Holocaust victims' ability to have children and medical experiments which mutilated breasts, genitals, and other body parts.

Not all women were interned during the war. Some spent the war or part of the war in hiding or in the resistance. Various edited volumes have chapters exploring the experiences of women in hiding and in the resistance and there are numerous testimonies of women in hiding and the resistance. Nechama Tec has written extensively on women in the resistance and hiding, including most notably in her book entitled *Resilience and Courage: Women, Men, and the Holocaust.* Work on women rescuers has included Eva Fleishner's and Michael Phayer's (1997) *Cries in the Night: Women Who Challenged the Holocaust.* However more work in that area could be done in both areas given the number of early memoirs and diaries produced by women in hiding (such as Anne Frank's [1952] *Diary of a Young Girl*) or the resistance (e.g. Adina Blady Szwajger's [1991] *I Remember Nothing More*).

## Women Survivors

Women survivors' memoirs and oral testimonies have been mined to answer a variety of questions, including how they construct gender specific memories of their experiences as well as to ascertain differences in women's experiences during the war. Various scholars have debated over factors of survival related to women, including discussions of biological attributes linked to survival and various notions that gender attributes and skills played a role in survival. For example, Marlene Heinemann (2002) identifies the female body's reproductive function as a factor in reducing women's survival rates because pregnancy and women with children were sent to the gas chambers. A number of scholars link gender specific roles such as nurturing qualities and passivity to female survival rates and victim experience.

Most work on women survivors have focused on their writing and the constructions of their memoirs. Sara Horowitz (1994) and S. Lillian Kremer (1999) were pioneers in the field of examining women's memoirs and Holocaust writings. They also focused on non-survivor writings and constructions of Holocaust memory. For example, Horowitz' (1997) focus on Jewish American women writing on the Holocaust is gender specific. And Kremer (1999) addresses female writings on the Holocaust and claims the focus is on motherhood and sexuality. Scholars such as Ellen S. Fine (1990) as well as R. Ruth Linden

(1993) have explored this aspect of writing as well. The notion of gender as an important aspect of memory construction is even further explored by the scholars in the edited volume *Gedächtnis und Geschlecht: Deutungsmuster in Darstellungen des nationalsozialistischen Genozids* (Eschebach, Jacobeti, and Wenk, 1993). Some scholars are beginning to look at women survivors in the immediate postwar period, including the experience of displaced persons as well as Jewish women and their integration into post-war European society. One important example of this is K. H. Adler's (2003) *Jews and Gender in Liberation France.*

## Critical Challenges Facing the Field Today

The most difficult challenge to researching the topic of women and the Holocaust is the current focus of Holocaust historiography in which victim experience is a peripheral rather than a central issue. One of the primary questions that needs to be addressed by Holocaust scholars is: What are the factors in survival (meaning everything from biological differences to gender behaviors)? For example, Sara Horowitz's (2000) contention that concern for oneself as well as reaching out to others was a part of both genders Holocaust experience needs to be proven or disproven with empirical evidence. To address this question, scholars will need to broaden the question to examining gender. Examining testimonies of women without comparative testimonies given by men fail to present a complete picture of what experiences are unique to women and which are more universal experiences of Holocaust victims.

Other challenges to the field of studying women and the Holocaust is the need for scholars to be willing to confront difficult issues such as sexual abuse during the Holocaust; to utilize gendered approaches both in scholarship in which gender questions are central as well as peripheral, looking at both men and women as a means to understanding women's experience; and an openness to appreciating that a focus on unique experiences is not an attempt to compare the suffering of men and women.

## The Real Probabilities of Progress in the Field

There are ample primary source materials to create a rich history of women during the Holocaust. Diaries, letters, memoirs, written testimonies, and oral testimonies were created by women during and/or after the war. There are also numerous sources written by men which discuss women's experiences or can be used as comparison material. Much of this material is accessible in archives as are other historical sources such as pre-war and wartime communal records and documents, and material cultural resources such as photographs, albums, and other objects from the war period. Additionally, there has been a move in the field of Holocaust studies to place greater emphasis on pre-war victim life as a means of understanding Holocaust era experiences. To that end, Karen Auerbach's (2005) "Bibliography: Jewish Women in Eastern Europe" in *Polin: Jewish Women in Eastern Europe* is an importance source, as is the volume itself.

In terms of published resources, there are more memoirs and collections of testimonies by women than personal diaries and oral testimonies given by women. Although there were a large number of diaries produced during the war by women which exist in archival collections, there are few which appear in print. The few well-known diaries written by women other than Etty Hillesum's (1996) diary, *An Interrupted Life*, are those of children and young teenagers such as Anne Frank's diary, and the diary of Eva Heyman, a thirteen-year-old Hungarian girl.

Not only victim-produced materials but also perpetrator and bystander materials exist which can assist in telling the story of women during the Holocaust. Nazi documents, including those written by various agencies concerned with women and victim groups, medical and court records, and other sources, contain a plethora of information about women during the Holocaust.

All of these sources can be used to provide histories of understudied victim groups such as Roma and Sinti women, African and Afro-German women, Slavic women, and lesbians, among others. They can also be employed to provide a fuller picture of women's experiences (e.g., at the hands of the *Einsatzgruppen*, those residing in various countries occupied by Nazi Germany, and women's experiences in countries such as Romania which had their own process of persecution and extermination).

There were numerous labor camps with large or even exclusively female labor forces and although there are a large number of testimonies on women's labor during the Holocaust, the field is lacking in synthetic histories of women's labor. One early work, Christian Bernadac's (1978) *Women Kommandos,* presents testimonies and other materials of women laborers. Similarly, Lore Shelley (1992) presented testimonies of women who worked in various parts of Auschwitz. However, other than a few specialized articles such as Christa Schikora's (2002), which argues that forced prostitution be examined as a form of slave labor, there is not much recent work on women's labor. Both Jewish and non-Jewish victim groups could be examined in such works.

## Conclusion

As new scholars have emerged in the field, research which employs a gendered approach has increased knowledge about the experiences of women and men during the Holocaust. A variety of scholars ranging from historians to sociologists, anthropologists, and literary scholars have utilized a wide range of methods resulting in a rich understanding of women during this time period. There are, though, numerous questions still unanswered. Recent developments in the field have pointed to the necessity of utilizing gender analysis and demonstrated that scholarship in this area is increasing.

## Notes

1.  Jehoshua Eibeshitz and Anna Eilenberg-Eibeshitz (Eds.) *Women in the Holocaust* (New York: Remember, 1993), p. ix
2.  Elizabeth Heinemann. "Sexuality and Nazism: The Doubly Unspeakable?" *Journal of the History of Sexuality,* vol. 11, January/April 2002, p. 43. See footnote on pp. 44 for list of people engaged in debate with Bock's thesis.

## References

All works in the above article not cited below are in the annotated bibliography.

Adler, K. H. (2003). *Jews and Gender in Liberation France.* Cambridge, UK: Cambridge University Press.

Auerbach, Karen (2005). "Bibliography: Jewish Women in Eastern Europe," pp. 273-303. In Chaeran Freeze, Paula Hyman and Antony Polonsky (Eds.) *Polin: Jewish Women in Eastern Europe.* Oxford: Littman Library.

Cole, Tim (2003). *Holocaust City: The Making of a Jewish Ghetto.* New York: Routledge.

Doerr, Karin (2000). "Memories of History: Women and the Holocaust in Autobiographical and Fictional Memoirs." *Shofar: An Interdisciplinary Journal of Jewish Studies*, 18(3): 71-90.

Horowitz, Sara (2000). "Gender Genocide, and Jewish Memory." *Prooftexts*, 20(1 and 2): 158-190.

Koonz, Claudia (1987). *Mothers in the Fatherland: Women, the Family, and Nazi Politics.* New York: St. Martin's Press.

Langer, Lawrence (1998). "Gendered Suffering? Women in Holocaust Testimonies," pp. In Dalia Ofer and Lenore Weitzmann (Eds.) *Women and the Holocaust.* New Haven, CT: Yale University Press.

Mosse, George L. (1985). *Nationalism and Sexuality: Respectability and Abnormal Sexuality in Modern Europe.* New York: H. Fertig.

Shelley, Lore (Ed.) (1992). *Auschwitz—The Nazi Civilization: Twenty-three Women Prisoners' Accounts.* Lanham, MD: University Press of America.

Ringelheim, Joan (1990). "Thoughts About Women and the Holocaust," pp. 141-150. In Roger S. Gottlieb (Ed.) *Thinking the Unthinkable: Meanings of the Holocaust.* Mahwah, NJ: Paulist Press.

Szwajger, Adina Blady (1991). *I Remember Nothing More.* New York: Pantheon.

Unger, Michal (1998). "The Status and Plight of Women in the Lodz Ghetto," pp. 123-143. In Dalia Ofer and Lenore J. Weitzmann (Eds.) *Women in the Holocaust.* New Haven, CT: Yale University Press.

## Annotated Bibliography

Alakus, Baris; Kniefacz Katharina; and Vorberg, Robert (Eds.) (2006). *Sex-Zwangsarbeit in nationalsozialistischen Konzentrationslagern.* Vienna: Mandelbaum, 212 pp.

This work describes the origins, emergence and functioning of the brothel system in the National Socialist Concentration camps. Includes discussion of prisoner selection and condition as forced prostitutes.

Allen, Ann Taylor (1997). The Holocaust and the modernization of gender: A historiographical essay. *Central European History*, 30 (3), 349-364.

Critiques the absence of gender as a category in various Holocaust writings despite the abundance of developed theory.

Altbeker Cyprys, Ruth. (1997) *A Jump for Life: A Survivor's Journal from Nazi-Occupied Poland.* New York: Continuum, 243 pp.
Memoir of woman who survives Holocaust in Nazi occupied Poland and its aftermath.

Baer, Elizabeth R. and Goldenberg, Myrna (eds.). (2003). *Experience and Expression: Women, The Nazis, and the Holocaust.* Detroit, MI: Wayne State University Press, 321 pp.
Multi-disciplinary study of women in the Holocaust. Comprised of a collection of essays written from a feminist perspective and stresses the importance of women in the Holocaust.

Baumel, Judith Tydor. (1998). *Double Jeopardy: Gender and the Holocaust.* Portland, OR.: Vallentine Mitchell, 292 pp.
A collection of seven essays discussing various aspects of gender (e.g., women's reactions to Nazism, their efforts in hiding and resistance, the unique horrors awaiting them in the camps and ghettos) and identity (women's roles in the ghettos) during the Holocaust.

Bendremer, Jutta T. (1997). *Women Surviving the Holocaust: In Spite of the Horror.* Lewiston, ME: Edwin Mellen Press, 118 pp.
Collection of testimonies of ten female Holocaust survivors who lived in the area of Akron, Ohio.

Berg, Mary (1945) *Warsaw Ghetto: A Diary.* New York: L. B. Fischer Publishing Corp., 253 pp.
Wartime diary of young girl in Warsaw ghetto.

Bergen, Doris L. (2001). Sex, blood and vulnerability: Women outsiders in Nazi-occupied Europe, pp. 273-293. In Robert Gellately and Nathan Stoltzfus (Eds.) *Social Outsiders in Nazi Germany.* Princeton, NJ: Princeton University Press.
While arguing for the primacy of race as a factor in victimhood and acknowledging the sexism of Nazi Germany, the author examines the intersection of race and gender in National Socialism.

Bernadac, Christian (1978). *Women's Kommandos.* Geneva, Switzerland: Ferni Publishing House, 296 pp.
Collection of testimonies and other materials relating to women's labor in various women's concentration camps.

Blady Szwajger, Adina (1990). *I Remember Nothing More: The Warsaw Children's Hospital and the Jewish Resistance.* New York: Pantheon, 184 pp.

Memoir of medical student who worked in the Children's Hospital in the Warsaw ghetto and then escaped the ghetto and while living on false papers became a courier for the resistance.

Bock, Gisela (1986). *Zwangssterilisaation im Nationalsozialismus: Studien zur Rassenpolitik und Frauenpolitik.* Opladen: Westdeutscher Verlag, 494 pp.
Study of forced sterilization in Nazi Germany

Bock, Gisela (2005) Genozid und Geschlecht: *Juedische Frauen im. national- sozialistischen Lagersystem.* Frankfurt/Main: Campus, 276 pp.
Edited volume on Jewish women in the concentration camps.

Brenner, Rachel (1997). *Writing as Resistance: Four Women Confronting the Holocaust.* University Park: Pennsylvania State University Press, 216 pp.
Discusses four women's writings as a form of spiritual resistance.

Bridenthal, Renate, Grossmann, Atina, and Kaplan, Marion (Eds.) (1984). *When Biology Became Destiny: Women in Weimar and Nazi Germany.* New York: Monthly Review Press, 364 pp.
Important collection of essays chronicling the transition of women's political, economic, and social lives as well as the evolution of their political and reproductive rights from Weimar Germany to Nazi Germany.

Costa, Denise de. (1998). *Anne Frank and Etty Hillesum: Inscribing Spirituality and Sexuality.* New Brunswick, NJ: Rutgers University Press, 275 pp.
Discussion of the two Dutch diaries from the perspective of the narra- tives as constructions by Jewish women writers.

Crane, Cynthia (2000). *Divided Lives: the Untold Stories of Jewish-Christian Women in Nazi Germany.* New York: St. Martin's Press, 372 pp.
On the experiences of Christian women of Jewish origin in Nazi Ger- many.

De Gaulle Anthonioz, Genevieve (1999) *The Dawn of Hope: A Memoir of Ravensbruck.* New York: Arcade Publishing, 83 pp.
Memoir of the niece of Charles de Gaulle who was held at Ravensbruck concentration camp as a political prisoner.

De Silva, Cara (Ed.) (1996) *In Memory's Kitchen: A Legacy from the Women of Terezin.* Northvale, NS: Jason Aronson, 110pp.
Collection of recipes collected at Terezin.

Delbo, Charlotte (1995) *Auschwitz and After.* New Haven, CT: Yale University Press, 354 pp.
Memoir of French woman's experience of the Holocaust and its after- math.

Disch, Lisa, and Morris, Leslie (2004) Departures: New Feminist perspectives on the Holocaust. *Women in German Yearbook*, 19, 9-19
Explores ethical and theoretical debates about representation of women in the Holocaust. Challenges the common notion of representation as standing for an absent object, event, or experience.

Distel, Barbara (2001) *Frauen im Holocaust*. Gerlingen: Bleicher Verlag, 428 pp.
Collection of essays on women in the Holocaust, including articles on the experiences of women from a diversity of geographical locations and experiences as well as essays by survivors.

Eibeschitz, Jehoshua, and Eilenberg-Eibeshitz, Anna (1993). *Women in the Holocaust: A Collection of Testimonies*. Brooklyn: Remember, 247 pp.
Collection of twenty women's testimonies covering the ghettos, concentration camps and experiences while in hiding. Published for a general audience.

Eschebach, Insa; Jacobeit, Sigrid; and Wenk, Silke (1993). *Gedächtnis und Geschlecht: Deutungsmuster in Darstellungen des nationalsozialistischen Genozids*. New York: Campus Verlag, 426 pp.
Collection of essays from a conference focusing on gender and memory of the Holocaust. Most articles focus on women's experiences and creations and their relations to the creation of Holocaust memory.

Fine, Ellen S. (1990). Women writers and the Holocaust: Strategies for survival, 79-97. In Randolph L. Braham (Ed.), *Reflections of the Holocaust in Art and Literature*. New York: Columbia University Press.
Discusses categories of women's experience during the Holocaust as expressed in their writing. Focuses on sexual abuse and issues related to motherhood and fears of future infertility.

Fleishner, Eva and Phayer, Michael (1997). *Cries in the Night: Women Who Challenged the Holocaust*. Kansas City, MO.: Sheed and Ward, 143 pp.
Story of seven Catholic women who were rescuers of Jews during the Holocaust.

Frank, Anne (1978) *The Diary of a Young Girl*. New York: Modern Library, 285 pp.
Diary of young girl in hiding in Nazi-Occupied Netherlands. Edited by her father Otto Frank. More complete scholarly versions available: *The Diary of Anne Frank: The Critical Edition* (New York: Doubleday, 2003); and *The Diary of a Young Girl: The Definitive Edition* (New York: Doubleday, 1995).

Frederiksen, Elke P., and Wallach, Martha (2000). *Facing Fascism and Confronting the Past: German Women Writers from Weimar to the Present*. Albany: State University of New York Press, 320 pp.

Presents writings from the 1920s through the 1990s of both Jewish and non-Jewish women writers from German-speaking countries who were silenced during the Nazi era. Discusses themes of gender, patriarchy, and fascism present in the works by these authors. Also includes an autobiographical account of a Holocaust survivor's experience.

Fuchs, Esther (Ed.) (1999). Women and the Holocaust: Narrative and representation. *Studies in the Shoah*, Vol. XXII. Lanham, New York, Oxford: University Press of America, 148 pp.

Interdisciplinary volume of scholarly essays and survivor accounts as well as other materials, including an article on lesbians and the Holocaust, discussion of various women's memoirs, as well as discussions of representations of women in film and literature.

Gertjejanssen, Wendy Jo (2004) *Victims, Heroes, Survivors: Sexual Violence on the Eastern Front during World War II.* Doctoral Dissertation. University of Minnesota, 401 pp.

Examines sexual violence against Jewish and non-Jewish women on the Eastern Front. Includes discussion and analysis of interviews of non-Jewish victims of sexual violence conducted by the author.

Goldenberg, Myrna (1990). Different horrors, Same hell: women remembering the Holocaust, pp. 150-167. In Roger S. Gottlieb (Ed.), *Thinking the Unthinkable: Meanings of the Holocaust.* Mahwah, NJ: Paulist Press. Compares and contrasts men's Holocaust experiences, including gendered approaches to survival.

Goldenberg, Myrna (1995) Testimony, narrative, and nightmare: The experiences of Jewish women in the Holocaust, pp. 94-109. In Maurice Sacks (Ed.) *Active Voices: Women in Jewish Culture.* Urbana: University of Illinois Press.

Analyzes and gives examples of women's accounts of their Holocaust experiences.

Gunter Grau (1995). *Hidden Holocaust? Gay and Lesbian Persecution in Germany, 1933-1945.* Chicago: Fitzroy Dearborn, 308 pp.

History of German policy towards homosexual men and lesbians during the Third Reich.

Gurewitsch, Brana (Ed.) (1998). *Mothers, Sisters, Resisters: Oral Histories of Women who Survived the Holocaust.* Tuscaloosa: University of Alabama Press, 396 pp.

Twenty-five testimonies of women focusing on women's relationships as factors in their Holocaust experiences.

Heineman, Elizabeth (1996). The hour of the woman: Memories of Germany's "crisis years" and West German national identity. *American Historical Review*, 101, 354-95.

Essay focuses on late 1940s and 1950s and explores the universalization in West German collective memory of crucial aspects of the stereotypically female experience of Germany at the end of the war and during the immediate postwar years. Reflects on the effects of this on the development of West German national identity and on the status of women in the Federal Republic.

Heineman, Elizabeth (1999). *What Difference Does a Husband Make? Women and Marital Status in Nazi and Postwar Germany*. Berkeley and Los Angeles: University of California Press, 374 pp.

Examines the role marital status played in the lives and experiences of women during the Nazi period and its aftermath.

Heinemann, Marlene (1986). *Gender and Destiny: Women Writers and the Holocaust*. New York: Greenwood Press, 149 pp.

Focuses on the Holocaust with regards to gender issues and women writers. Most of analysis focuses on five memoirs and one novel by women authors. Includes male memoirs as a basis for comparison of specific female experiences in the camps, what characterizes the texts, male and female relations within the camps, and considers the credibility and authenticity of these Holocaust texts.

Herz, Gabriele (2006). *The Women's Camp in Moringen: A Memoir of Imprisonment in Germany, 1936-1937*. New York: Berghahn Books, 183 pp.

Memoir of Gabriele Herz. Includes an extensive introduction by Jane Caplan which provides the history of the former women's camp as well as the individual experience of Mrs. Herz.

Heyman, Eva (1987). *The Diary of Eva Heyman*. New York: Sure Sellers, Inc., 124 pp.

Diary of a thirteen-year-old Hungarian girl who perished in Auschwitz.

Hillesum, Etty (1996). *An Interrupted Life*. New York: Holt, 226 pp.

Diary of young Dutch woman Etty Hillseum recording her life in Nazi occupied Netherlands and her letters to friends and family from Westerbork transit camp.

Horowitz, Sara R. (1997). 'The pin with which to stick yourself': The Holocaust in Jewish American women's writing, pp. 141-160. In Jay Halio and Ben Siegel (Eds.), *Daughters of Valor: Contemporary Jewish American Women Writers*. Newark: University of Delaware Press.

Argues that Jewish American women writers on the Shoah centers on three issues. First, the Holocaust and its impact on Jewish continuity, practice, and community. Second, the construction of identities—American, Jewish, female—as Jewish-American women writers imagine the unimaginable.

Third, as Jewish-American women construct their identities, the Holocaust becomes the means by which to explore other issues. Further claims that as women develop theoretical and pragmatic approaches to specifically Jewish feminism, they claim the historical experience of Jewish victimization as their own and utilize it to acknowledge define, and resist other types of victimization.

Hutton, Margaret-Anne (2005). *Testimony from the Nazi Camps: French Women's Voices*. New York: Routledge, 255 pp.

Testimony and rich analysis of testimony of French women deported during the Holocaust. Multi-level analysis of identity questions.

Kaplan, Marion (1998). *Between Dignity and Despair: Jewish Life in Nazi Germany*. New York: Oxford University Press, 290 pp.

Draws on memoirs, diaries, interviews, and letters of Jewish women and men to give the first intimate portrayal of Jewish life in Nazi Germany. Provides a detailed account of how Jewish men and women lived and fought for survival during the Holocaust.

Karay, Felicja (2002). *Hasag-Leipzig Slave Labour Camp for Women: The Struggle for Survival, Told by the Women and Their Poetry*. London: Vallentine Mitchell, 261 pp.

Describes the cultural, social, hierarchical, conditions at Hasag camp for women, a sub-camp of Buchenwald attached to the munitions plants Aktiengesellschaft-Leipzig-Schonefeld in Germany owned by Hugo Schneider. It includes poetry by women prisoners, providing an analysis for the psychological implications of imprisonment.

Katz, Esther and Ringelheim, Joan Miriam (1983). *Proceedings of the Conference on Women Surviving the Holocaust*. New York: Institute for Research in History, 196 pp.

Transcript of 1983 conference, "Women Surviving the Holocaust." Includes presentations on ghettos, camps, resistance, and major questions in the field, summaries of panels, panelist comments, and audience discussions.

Klein, Gerda (1957) *All But My Life*. New York: Hill and Wang, 246 pp. Memoir of woman who survives Nazi-occupied Poland as a slave laborer and death march. She marries an American GI, her liberator.

Koonz, Claudia (1987). *Mothers in the Fatherland: Women, the Family, and Nazi Politics*. New York: St. Martin's Press, 556 pp.

History of relationship between women and the Nazi party seeking to address how and why women were supportive of a party which removed women from political and economic power and returned them to the domestic sphere.

Kremer, Lillian (1999). *Women's Holocaust Writing: Memory and Imagination.* Lincoln: University of Nebraska Press, 278 pp.

Examines the ways in which seven women address Holocaust themes in their writings. Arguing that women's voices and experiences are absent from the largely male dominated field of Holocaust Studies, the author goes on to focus on feminine aspects such as motherhood and sexuality.

Laska, Vera (Ed.) (1983). *Women in the Resistance and in the Holocaust: The Voices of Eyewitnesses.* Westport, CT.: Greenwood Press, 330 pp.

Presents various women's testimonies about their experiences during the Holocaust. Deals with a wide range of topics (Nazi brutality within the camps, women's experiences in the camps, Nazi female overseers in the camps, resistance movements).

Leitner, Isabella (1978). *Fragments of Isabella: A Memoir of Auschwitz.* New York: Thomas Y. Crowell, 112 pp.

Memoir of woman entering Auschwitz with her sisters and their experiences.

Linden, R. Ruth (1993). *Making Stories, Making Selves: Feminist Reflections on the Holocaust.* Columbus: Ohio University Press, 191 pp.

Sociologist R. R. Linden explores her own life, Jewish women's narrative, identity, and survivors' coping strategies in the concentration camps, through broad (e.g., her own experiences and oral testimonies given by Holocaust survivors) and focused studies (sociological studies focusing on the epistemological issues facing scholars). Also included are subchapters describing the author's self critique and struggle with writing the texts.

Linke, Uli (1997). Gendered difference, violent imagination: Blood, race, nation. *American Anthropologist, New Series,* 99(3), 559-573.

Examines intersection between race and gendered conceptions of the Jew.

Miller, Joy Erlichman (2000). *Love Carried Me Home: Women Surviving Auschwitz.* Deerfield Beach, FL: Simcha Press, 227 pp.

Presents sixteen survivor testimonies and an analysis of the specific experiences of women during the Holocaust and their coping strategies.

Morrison, Jack G. (2000). *Ravensbruck: Everyday Life in a Women's Concentration Camp, 1939-45.* Princeton, NJ: Markus Wiener, 367 pp.

History of the Ravensbruck concentration camp including a detailed discussion of prisoner categories, daily experience and the liberation of the camp.

Nyiszli, Miklos (1993) *Auschwitz: A Doctor's Eyewitness Account.* Foreword Bruno Bettelheim. New York: Arcade Publisher, 222 pp.

Memoir of Jewish doctor who was forced to serve as Mengele's assistant when he experimented on prisoners at Auschwitz.

Ofer, Dalia, and Weitzmann, Lenore J. (Eds.) (1998). *Women in the Holocaust.* New Haven, CT: Yale University Press, 402 pp.
    Twenty-one essays on Jewish and non-Jewish victims of the Nazis that address the pre-war period a wide variety of wartime experiences.

Owings, Alison (1993). *Frauen: German Women Recall the Third Reich.* New Brunswick, NJ: Rutgers University Press, 494 pp.
    Examines testimonies from German women who lived in Germany during the twelve year Nazi regime as a means of understanding their lack of resistance.

Paul, Christa (1995). *Zwangsprostitution: Staatlich errichtete Bordelle im Nationalsozialismus.* Berlin. Edition Hentrich, 141 pp.
    Scholarly monograph examining the forced prostitution system under National Socialism.

Philipp, Grit (1999). *Kalendarium der Ereignisse im Frauen-Konzentration-slager Ravensbruck, 1939-1945.* Berlin: Metropol, 350 pp.
    Brief history of Ravensbruck, supplemented with a year by year breakdown of events and transports at Ravensbruck. Also includes the document references for the information, and photographs.

Raphael, Melissa (2003). *The Female Face of God in Auschwitz: A Jewish Feminist Theology of the Holocaust.* New York: Routledge, 228 pp.
    Feminist post-Holocaust theology based on nurturing in women's Holocaust memoirs. The nurturing is not biologically defined but a gender trait seen as a manifestation of the feminine aspect of God.

Reading, Anna (1999). Scarlet lips in Belsen: Culture, gender, and ethnicity in the policies of the Holocaust. *Media, Culture, and Society,* 21(4), 481-502.
    This work examines National Socialist policy from a gendered perspective arguing that although women were victims of Nazi policy because they were Jewish, they experienced the Holocaust as women as well. Argues that women were stripped of their gender identity as part of the Nazi dehumanizing process and thus in the immediate post-war period sought to restore their gender identities as a means of restoring their humanity.

Ringelheim, Joan (1990). Thoughts about women and the Holocaust, pp. 141-150. In Roger S. Gottlieb (Ed.), *Thinking the Unthinkable: Meanings of the Holocaust.* Mahwah, NJ: Paulist Press.
    Critiques Holocaust scholars who see victims as an undifferentiated mass. Argues this leads to not allowing space for the unique experiences of victims, especially women.

Rittner, Carol (1998). Blind but not ignorant: German women during the Holocaust, pp. 47-53. In Zev Garber and Richard Libowitz (Eds.), *Peace, Indeed: Essays in Honor of Harry Cargas*. Atlanta, GA: Scholars Press.
    Short essay on wives of Nazi officers and their unwillingness to confront their husband's wartime deeds.

Rittner, Carol, and Roth, John K. (Eds.) (1993). *Different Voices: Women and the Holocaust*. New York: Paragon House, 435 pp.
    Edited volume containing victim testimonies, scholarly writings, and post-war observations. Compares and contrasts victim testimonies with scholarly interpretations and reflections on women's experiences in the Holocaust.

Ritvo, Roger A., and Plotkin, Diane M. (Eds.) (1998). *Sisters in Sorrow: Voices of Care in the Holocaust*. College Station: Texas A&M University Press, 314 pp.
    Collection of memoirs of women prisoners who served as medical care givers whether as doctors or nurses during the Holocaust.

Ronit, Lentin (2000). Expected to live: Women Shoah survivors' testimonials of silence. *Women's Studies International Forum*, 23 (6), 689-700.
    Discusses the silence of women survivors and attributes it to a tension between a desire to not discuss traumatic experiences and society's inability or unwillingness to listen to the experiences of female survivors, particularly if sexual abuse is part of the story.

Rosen, Ilana (2004). *Hungarian Jewish Women Survivors Remember the Holocaust: An Anthology of Life Histories*. Dallas, TX: University Press of America, 119 pp.
    The memoirs of seventeen Hungarian Jewish women who survived the Holocaust. As a group the women were young and unmarried at the time of the war.

Saidel, Rochelle (2004). *The Jewish Women of Ravensbruck Concentration Camp*. Madison: University of Wisconsin Press, 279 pp.
    History of the experience of specifically Jewish women prisoners in Ravensbruck Concentration camp. Discusses women specific attributes as playing an important role in uniquely women's Holocaust experience.

Schikorra, Christa (2002). Prostitution of female concentration camp prisoners as slave labor: On the situation of "asocial" prisoners in the Ravensbruck women's concentration camp, pp. 246-258. In Wolfgang Benz (Ed.)*Dachau and the Nazi Terror 1933-1945*. Vol. 2. Dachau: Dachauer Hefte.
    The forced prostitution of female concentration camp prisoners.

Schloss, Eva and Kent, Evelyn Julia (1999). *Eva's Story: A Survivor's Tale by the Step-sister of Anne Frank*. Edgeware, Middlesex, UK.: Castle-Kent, 224 pp.

Memoir of Eva Schloss describing her and her mother's experiences during the war. Her mother married Otto Frank, Anne Frank's father, after the war.

Schoppmann, Claudia (1996). *Days of Masquerade: Life Stories of Lesbians During the Third Reich*. New York: Columbia University Press, 158 pp.
Profiles of ten lesbian women who survived the Nazi era, including extensive material drawn from oral histories. Includes a thirty-page overview of lesbians in the Weimar and Nazi periods.

Schoppmann, Claudia (1997). National Socialist policies toward female homosexuality, pp. 177-189. In Lynn Abrams and Elizabeth Harvey (Eds.), *Gender Relations in German History: Power, Agency, and Experience from the Sixteenth to the Twentieth Century*. Durham, NC: Duke University Press.
Compact article describing persecution of lesbians by the Nazi regime. Discusses reasons for persecution, lack of research on such issues, and provides a few illustrative stories of lesbians under the Third Reich.

Schoppmann, Claudia (1999). *Verbotene Verhältnisse: Frauenliebe 1938-1945*. Berlin: Quer. 155 pp.
Drawing on court records and other sources, discusses the situation of Austrian lesbians who unlike their German counterparts were subject to the criminal code thus making lesbian sex illegal.

Schwarz, Gundrun (1997). *Eine Frau an seiner Seite: Ehefrauen in der "SS-Sippengemeinschaft."* Hamburg: Hamburger Edition, 268 pp.
Explores role of the wives of the SS.

Schwertfeger, Ruth (1989). *Women of Theresienstadt: Voices from a Concentration Camp*. Oxford: Berg, 152 pp.
Collection of poetry and memoirs of Theresienstadt survivors.

Shelley, Lore (Ed.) (1992). *Auschwitz—The Nazi Civilization: Twenty-three Women Prisoners' Accounts*. Lanham, MD.: University Press of America, 296 pp.
Testimonies of twenty-three women interred at Auschwitz focusing on their work in the camp in offices and as physical laborers. This book does not describe the dynamics of Auschwitz, but instead focuses on the individual personal experiences of the survivors.

Shelley, Lore (1991). *Criminal Experiments on Human Beings in Auschwitz and War Research Laboratories: Twenty Women Prisoners' Accounts*. San Francisco, CA: Mellen Research University Press, 402 pp.
Testimonies of women subjected to medical experiments at Auschwitz.

Sigmund, Anna Maria (2000). *Women of the Third Reich*. Richmond Hill, Ontario: NDE Publishing, 236 pp.
Examines the lives of eight women connected to the National Socialist Movement. These women were Carin Goering, Emmy Goering, Magda Goebbles, Leni Riefenstahl, Gertrude Scholtz-Klink, Geli Raubal, Eva Braun, and Henriette von Shirach. Focuses on their role in the public and private sphere.

Sinnreich, Helene (2005) "And we eat like on Yom Kippur": Women, food, and the struggle for survival in the Lodz Ghetto. *Lilith Magazine*, Fall, 30(3): 24-27.
Article discussing women's role in obtaining food for their families in the Lodz Ghetto.

Stephenson, Jill (2001). *Women in Nazi Germany*. New York: Longman, 212 pp.
Examines the role of women, particularly how that was shaped by their reproductive function in Nazi society and in comparison with the position of men in the Third Reich. Explores the lives of women in the workforce, in the domestic sphere and those persecuted in the camps.

Stoltzfus, Nathan (1996). *Resistance of the Heart: Intermarriage and the Rosenstrasse Protest in Nazi Germany*. New York: W. W. Norton, 386 pp.
German women who were married to Jewish men who protested the deportation of their husbands.

Strzelecka, Irena. (1994). Women, pp. 393-412. In Michael Berenbaum and Yisrasel Gutman (Eds.), *Anatomy of the Auschwitz Death Camp*. Bloomington: Indiana University Press, in association with the United States Holocaust Memorial Museum, Washington, DC.
Article discussing women at Auschwitz, including their unique living and workings conditions and treatment by the Nazis.

Tec, Nechama. 2003). *Resilience and Courage: Women, Men, and the Holocaust*. New Haven, CT: Yale University Press, 438 pp.
Gendered approach to the Holocaust which examines men and women's experiences during the Holocaust, including the powerlessness felt by men in the ghettos to provide for their families and the more traumatic implications of camp procedures (including the shearing of hair) on women.

Timm, Annette F. (2001). The ambivalent outsider: Prostitution, promiscuity, and venereal disease control in Nazi Berlin, pp. 192-211. In Robert Gellately and Nathan Stoltzfus (Eds.) *Social Outsiders in Nazi Germany*. Princeton, NJ: Princeton University Press.
Discusses National Socialist policies with regard to prostitution during the Third Reich.

Von Mahlsdorf, Charlotte (1995). *I Am My Own Woman: The Outlaw Life of Charlotte von Mahlsdorf, Berlin's Most Distinguished Transvestite*. San Francisco, CA: Cleis Press, 179 pp.

Memoir of the Holocaust experiences of a transgendered teenager. Includes discussions of lesbian transgendered relatives.

Waxman, Zoe Vania (2007) *Writing the Holocaust: Identity, Testimony, Representation*. New York: Oxford University Press, 240 pp.

Explores writing of women in ghettos, in the concentration camps, survivor testimony and explores the representation of memory in these writings.

# 3

# The Bangladesh Genocide:
# The Plight of Women[1]

*Angela Debnath*

## Historical Background

On 25 March, 1971, the, government of Pakistan initiated a genocidal campaign against Bengalis in the province of East Pakistan, ostensibly to suppress a Bengali nationalist movement. An attempt, initiated a quarter of a century earlier, to unify the ethnically and linguistically distinct populations of East and West Pakistan (separated by more than a thousand miles of Indian territory) on the basis of a common religion—Islam—had failed. The systematic violence and widespread destruction executed by the Pakistani army, with the assistance of local supporters, eventually displaced 30,000,000 people within East Pakistan, drove 10,000,000 into India, and resulted in the deaths of at least 1 million Bengalis.[2] Intellectuals, students, political groups, and the Hindu minority were specifically targeted. In response, the Bengalis formed an insurgency movement known as the *Mukti Bahini* (Liberation Army) which also ended up committing human rights violations during the course of the conflict. On 4 December, 1971, India intervened and, alongside Bengali guerrillas, forced Pakistani troops, following a two-week war, to surrender. Shortly thereafter, East Pakistan was officially recognized as Bangladesh.

## The Plight of Females

Despite the extreme and systematic violence that precipitated the creation of Bangladesh, the event is largely neglected by genocide scholars.[1] In fact, Bina D'Costa (2006) asserts that given Bangladesh's geopolitically marginal position and reputation as a financially destitute country, it has excited little interest in any discipline except development studies (p. 131). Hence, she declares, "the war of 1971 remains one of the most under-researched conflicts in the world, and the traumatic experiences of the civilians after the war remain virtually

47

unknown despite growing interest in nationalism and ethnic violence" (D'Costa, 2006, p. 131). Indeed, notwithstanding the extraordinary number of people killed during over a relatively short period, it is far from commonly accepted that the event was genocidal in nature.[3] Volumes on systematic violence which include Bangladesh 1971, such as this one, are therefore rare.[4]

The specific focus of this chapter is the impact of the Pakistani campaign on the lives of Bangladeshi females, not only during the violence itself but in the form of subsequent violence (the latter of which was more social and less physical in nature, but traumatic nevertheless), inflicted upon women by their own state, community leaders, and peers in the aftermath of the conflict. By doing so, it will examine how the dynamics of violent conflict frequently transfigure women from individuals of worth into a homogeneous terrain of conflict, an extension of the physical battlefield. Finally, it will consider what females' experiences in 1971 and afterwards reveal about Bangladeshi society and the state, the ideology of nationalism and of nation-building, and the crime of genocide.

This is no easy task given the remarkable shortage of relevant sources—an absence that in some ways speaks as eloquently to the plight of women in Bangladesh in 1971 (and after) as any form of documentation could. As Yasmin Saikia (in press) states, although 1971 "is considered one of the most intense cases of brutalization of women in twentieth-century wars, there is no history of the violence. Scholars...as well as gender studies internationally have overlooked and forgotten 1971"(n.d.).[5]

## Females' Experiences of 1971

### Direct/Indirect Participation

Only a small number of women appear to have directly participated in the conflict as insurgents, and fewer still were engaged in direct warfare (Mookherjee, 2003, p. 164). A limited number also worked as nurses and teachers in hospitals and refugee camps during the conflict (Jahan, 1975, p. 8). A much greater number participated indirectly as supportive mothers, wives, and daughters who sacrificed sons and husbands to the war, provided food and shelter to insurgents, and took care of children and the elderly. Many of these women lost their families, their property, and livelihood. Indeed, the number of "female-headed households" increased dramatically after the conflict (D'Costa, 2005, p. 244). Destitution and suffering were thus the potential consequences of women's "indirect" participation within the domestic sphere.[6]

### Victimization

It is victimization, though, which typifies female experiences in 1971. One of the most distinctive features of the period was the use of various forms of violence against females. Regardless of class, ethnicity, religious/social backgrounds, and age, females were "principal targets" of male aggression including killing, torture, beating, and dismemberment (Saikia, in press, n.d.).

Systematic rape was one of the chief weapons of the atrocity campaign. Anywhere from 200,000 to 400,000 women were raped. Susan Brownmiller (1975), who published one of the earliest analyses of the event in her pioneering work on the politics of sexual violence, reported the following: "Rape in Bangladesh had hardly been restricted to beauty. Girls of eight and grandmothers of seventy-five had been sexually assaulted during the nine-month repression. Pakistani soldiers had not only violated Bengali women on the spot; they abducted tens of hundreds and held them by force in their military barracks for nightly use. The women were kept naked to prevent their escape" (p. 82).

Isolated incidents of rape, gang rape, abduction, and forced prostitution in mass rape camps where captives were often deliberately malnourished, comprised only the first phase of these women's ordeal (Malik, 1972, pp. 154-155). Subsequently, victims were forced to endure what some have referred to as a "second rape" (Shartach, 2000, p. 90)[7] in which they suffered from widespread gynecological infections, intense feelings of shame and humiliation, social ostracism, the loss of familial relationships, and economic security (Brownmiller, 1975, pp. 83-84). To avoid such horrors and agony, many committed suicide (Brownmiller, 1975, p. 84).

The sexual violence also resulted in an acute pregnancy crisis during which scores of poorer victims underwent dangerous abortions, often inducing serious medical complications (Brownmiller, 1975, p. 84).[8] The exact number of women impregnated as a result of rape in 1971 is unknown. Brownmiller (1975) reports that 25,000 women suffered from unwanted pregnancies, while the Bangladesh government at the time claimed that over 70,000 women were impregnated (p. 84). The International Commission of Jurists' 1972 legal analysis of the conflict concludes that "whatever the precise numbers, the teams of American and British surgeons carrying out abortions and the widespread government efforts to persuade people to accept these girls into the community, testify to the scale on which raping occurred" (p. 14).

After traveling throughout the war-ravaged country between 1971 and 1972, Indian journalist Amita Malik (1972) observed that "the fate of the women of Bangla Desh was, indeed, the proverbial fate worse than death.... [It is] the story of one of the most savage, organized and indiscriminate orgies of rape in human history: rape by a professional army, backed by local armed collaborators" (p. 154).

In addition to direct victimization, hundreds of thousands of females in 1971 became refugees in 1971. The testimony of a nurse in a refugee camp along the Indo-Bangladesh border during the conflict readily attests to the grave situation of female refugees who, she reported, arrived at the camps suffering from severe malnourishment, unwanted pregnancies, and, in some cases, the loss of their entire families—husbands, children, and parents: "And then of course, when they come here," she added, "they are so ill that they again face death every day, every day they face death in some form.... Everything has been taken away from them" (quoted in Indian Council of World Affairs, 1972, pp. 55-56). Whether as indirect participants, victims of extreme systematic violence, or as refugees, Bangladeshi girls and women endured untold agonies during the 1971 genocide.

## National Responses

*1971-1973*

The new government of Bangladesh responded to victims of sexual violence in various ways. First, they declared rape victims were *birangonas* or war heroines, ostensibly to acknowledge their "sacrifice" for the country and facilitate their reintegration into society. Moreover, the government attempted to socially reinstate *birangonas* through marriage—either by returning them to their husbands or by pairing them off with *Mukti Bahini* (fighters). The initiative, however, was unsuccessful. As Brownmiller (1975) comments, "the 'marry them off' campaign never got off the ground. Few prospective bridegrooms stepped forward, and those who did made it plain that they expected....handsome dowries" (p. 83).

In response to the pregnancy crisis, the Bangladeshi government endorsed—in concert with various local and international nongovernmental organizations (NGOs)—an extensive abortion and international adoption scheme coordinated by the newly formed "National Central Women's Rehabilitation Board" (D'Costa, 2005, p. 233). Besides abortion and adoption, "rehabilitation" also consisted of furnishing rape victims and other war-affected females with traditional labor skills as "an earning woman ha[d] better prospects of marriage than others" (Brownmiller, 1975, p. 85).

Precise numbers of abortions and adoptions carried out during this period are unavailable, as many of the social workers, medical practitioners, and activists assisting the government refused to disclose (or did not retain) records of victims (D'Costa, 2006, pp. 143-144).[9] According to Amita Malik (1972), "the names of the girls raped are withheld so as not to jeopardize their chances of marriage and their acceptance back into normal life. In a conservative society trying very hard to readjust itself to a problem that has affected almost every family in the land, it is natural that there should be a cooperative effort to protect the honour and future of the girls concerned" (p. 93).

*1973-Today*

The apparent concern of the state and social leaders for the welfare of abused women in the immediate aftermath of the conflict, however, soon dissipated.

After 1973, the issue of mass rape was "relegated to oblivion in government and journalistic consciousness," replaced instead by an overwhelming silence on the subject (Mookherjee, 2006, p. 436). The issue reemerged only in the early 1990s when, owing to various political developments in Bangladesh and abroad, rape victims were once again celebrated as liberation fighters who had sacrificed for the nation.[10]

The excavation of the *birangona* was initially propelled by the "Peoples' Tribunal" held in Dhaka on 26 March 1992, a mock trial of local collaborators that featured the testimonies of victims of sexual violence. However, as D'Costa (2005) relates, the effort was inefficiently run, utilized poor quality reports, and participants were ill-informed as to procedure (p. 234). Moreover, the publicity given to rape victims who took part affected them negatively, dissuading others from speaking about their experiences (D'Costa, 2005, p. 234). Thus, apart from the initial highly publicized "rehabilitation" drive and intermittent breaches of silence such as the "People's Tribunal," Bangladesh has made little effort to address the sexual crimes committed against women in 1971 virtually from their commission to today.[11]

## Understanding the Silencing of Women's Voices

*Society*

One has to wonder why one of the most extreme cases of systematic violence against women in the twentieth century is not spoken of in the very country in which it occurred. Part of the answer, it appears, is the nature of Bangladeshi society itself. As previously stated, victims of sexual violence in 1971 not only endured the crime itself but a so-called "second rape" perpetrated by families and communities who shunned them, exiled them, or concealed their victimization after the conflict (Sharlach, 2005, p. 90). Indeed, many Bengalis did not accept wives or daughters back into the family who had been raped in order to avoid public disgrace (Brownmiller, 1975, pp. 79-80, and Shariach, 2005, p. 95). As Jahan (1975) remarked: "When a woman [in Bangladesh] is violated, the family is more concerned about the loss of face than her physical and mental health" (p. 22). This prolonged victimization, moreover, endures today as many of these women continue to live on the margins of society. Victims of 1971's sexual violence are thus still "pay[ing] dearly for [their] victimization.... The oppression is unending"[12] (Saikia, 2004, p. 281).

Mookherjee (2002, 2004, 2006) investigated the ongoing ostracism of rape victims in depth in the 1990s when she visited the Bangladeshi village of Enayetpur, home of three *birangonas* whose participation in the aforementioned "People's Tribunal" gained them national fame coupled with intense local disrepute. According to Mookherjee (2006), oppression of the three *birangonas* by their own community is enforced with constant *khota'* or "sarcastic/censorious remarks expressing scorn and evoking the unpleasant events" (p. 443). Tellingly, the villagers never openly speak about sexual violence during the war. A process of revelation (through implicit scorn) and concealment (through overt silence) is therefore at work in the village, indicating that rape is being treated as a "public secret" or a fact that is "known but not articulated" (Mookherjee, 2006, pp. 443).

One factor contributing to this phenomenon is the manner in which national recognition of the poor and landless *birangonas* directly challenges the economic/social ladder of the village. The interplay between revelation and concealment operating in the community is, therefore, "indispensable to the operations of power" as it acts as a "controlling mechanism" by reinforcing social norms and ensures the continued subordination of the women (Mookherjee, 2006, pp. 445,446). This means of control thus encapsulates the "enchanting potential of the public secrecy of rape" (Mookherjee, 2006, p. 445).

Another factor underlying local contempt of the victims is their perceived transgression of Islamic standards vis-à-vis gender. In Muslim society, Mookherjee contends, women are to keep *purdah*, a doctrine which prescribes keeping things "hidden, covered" through modest dress and conduct (Mookherjee, 2006, p. 441).

If sexually compromised, an "honorable" woman would suppress that experience. That is, silence is the sign of an "authentic raped woman and moral being" (Mookherjee, 2006, p. 440).

Thus, the main crime in the village is not the rape itself, but the women's disclosure of it[13] Closely related to this issue is Enayetpur's "feminine social code," in which female honor is directly linked to sexual modesty (engaging in sexual relations exclusively with one's husband, for example) which is, in turn, a reflection of family/community honor (Mookherjee, 2006, p. 439). Knowledge of the dishonor incurred by rape, therefore, not only brings shame upon the victim, but also her family and community.

A final factor contributing to local ostracism of the rape victims is their breach of the village system of secrecy. As Mookherjee (2006) explains (and as commented on earlier herein) villagers do not speak about incidents of rape in 1971—apart from those which occurred outside of the village. This selective or "disjunctive" memory appears to be based on a desire to avoid thorny issues related to possible local complicity (Mookherjee, 2006, p, 442).

Thus, for the villagers, openly addressing the issue of rape holds negative consequences. They, therefore, intentionally "remember what to forget; they know what not to know" in order to avoid the destruction of long-held normative codes (Mookherjee, 2006, p. 446).

Mookherjee's extensive exploration of memories of sexual violence in Bangladesh thus indicates that a given victim's socio-economic status, Islamic gender doctrine, feminine codes of honor and sexuality, and the phenomenon of "public secrecy" may all contribute to the ongoing shrouding of sexual crimes in 1971. These patriarchal societal pressures have, in turn, made women suppress their experiences and resort to "negotiated survival" in order to avoid further persecution (D'Costa, 2006, p. 143).

*The State*

Intimately connected to Bangladeshi society's unwillingness to address the sexual crimes of 1971 is the state's handling of the affair. As discussed above, the founding government of Bangladesh mounted an extensive campaign to "rehabilitate" rape victims by declaring them national heroines, endorsing abortions and international adoptions, and attempting to instate (or reinstate) them into marriage or traditional forms of labor. While this campaign may appear to have been a progressive and genuine attempt to assist the violated women, scholars argue to the contrary.

D'Costa (2006), for example, explains that the term *birangona* itself, instead of serving to encourage the larger society to accept rape victims as women who had struggled for the nation, became synonymous with "prostitute," thereby intensifying the isolation of the victims (p. 133). As a result, many victims did not assume the label as to do so would be to "risk a social death" (D'Costa, 2005, p. 229).

The abortion/international adoption scheme, D'Costa (2005) further contends, was never intended to improve the lot of abused women; rather, it was a ploy to erase evidence of the humiliation suffered by Bengali men as a result of their failure to protect women during the independence struggle. "As far as Bangladesh was concerned, the task of flushing out 'impure' Pakistani blood was necessary for the honour of the new nation" (D'Costa, 2005, p. 231). Thus, the government campaign was a response to the "challenge to Bengali nationalist and masculine identity" posed by the sexual violence, not an authentic effort to assist the women themselves (D'Costa, 2005, p. 227). This, D'Costa (2005) concludes, demonstrates the power of the state to "forcibl[y] appropriate[e]... women's bodies for the interest of the nation" (p. 232).

Saikia (in press) agrees, stating that national treatment of rape victims after 1971 represented a "politics of active national forgetting" (n.p.) The existence of such politics, aiming to obliterate evidence of 1971's sexual violence, is further suggested by the fact that none of the nation's public institutions currently hold records of women's experiences during the conflict (Saikia, 2004). Thus, "silence enters at the source of making history...and makes us aware how power works even before a narrative is made" (Saikia, 2004, p. 284).

The national "marry them off" campaign was ostensibly another ploy to silence women by confining them to the private sphere. Mookherjee (2003), in fact, contends that women's *overall* participation in the liberation movement was restricted by the state itself and it was restricted to their domestic relational positions to men. Women's contribution to Bangladesh's independence struggle was, Mookherjee (2003) states, a form of "agency by invitation only" as "only a respectable, self-sacrificing mother and wife, and hence...an idealized woman [could]...be admitted into the dominant nationalist view as a model for society's women" (p. 164). The implication for rape victims who did not conform to such a model was, therefore, their "necessary appropriation" into traditional domestic roles which denied their much more ambiguous reality as living examples of the state's failure to protect its citizens. This, she concludes, demonstrates how the state constructs gender identities and "employ[s] women instrumentally to legitimize nation-building projects and consolidate sovereignty" (Mookherjee, 2003, p. 169).

As with the government "rehabilitation" program, scholars contend that both the ensuing silence about women's experiences in 1971 and the periodic reemergence of the issue are products of national political exigency; in other words, the treatment of violated women has depended on who has power in Bangladesh—pro-independence parties or coalitions of former collaborators and extremist religious parties. Each group appears to propagate a competing version of national history that either endorses a (very limited) recovery of women's experiences or vies against it. *Neither* version, however, accurately reflects nor responds to the needs of female victims of 1971.[14] Thus, scholars like D'Costa conclude that Bangladesh exists in "separate and parallel histories": a "macro-narrative" or state-endorsed history versus a "micro-narrative" history based on individual memories and experiences (D'Costa, 2005, p. 227).

Why does the Bangladeshi state—regardless of which party is in power — desire to avoid unearthing women's actual experiences of 1971? As discussed earlier, there is a need to erase evidence of the humiliation and de-masculinization Bangladeshi men suffered during 1971. This is related to the country's attempt to subsume women into its patriarchal national project by constructing idealized gender roles for them that confine them to the private sphere. Yet there is more to the state's manipulation of abused women than the avoidance of humiliation: there is also the denial of complicity. According to Saikia (2004), females in 1971 were victimized not only by Pakistani perpetrators, but also by *Bengalis*. More specifically, she asserts that women's testimonies expose the disturbing fact that many were brutalized by men they knew to revenge local enmities and spread terror. "Perpetrators were the Pakistani 'others,' so the state tells people in Bangladesh. It is an easy, uncomplicated story, until we start investigating. Then the picture becomes convoluted, murky and muddy" (Saikia, 2004, p. 285). Thus, Bangladesh appears to be suppressing a past in which powerful males, regardless of ethnicity, brutalized powerless women in the name of the state. "1971 was a nightmare; the violence was relentless," Saikia (2004), argues. 'The enemy...was *within,* not outside. This is why women have been forced to remain silent" (p. 283).

## Conclusion: Nationalism, Gender, and Genocide

Women's experiences in 1971 Bangladesh and the subsequent suppression of these experiences provide telling insights into how violence inflicted upon women in times of war and genocide are far from restricted to the "enemy" or to the period of conflict. In many cases, painful and long lasting traumas are also those inflicted by their "own side," through direct violence, and later, through mechanisms more subtle than the fist or the gun—that is, through social ostracism, the denial of suffering by the victim, the reinforcement of oppressive social structures, and the co-opting of women's experiences by those in power.

Bangladesh thus vividly attests to the power of the state and how "nation-building," the creating of social power structures and prevailing myths, takes place both during the horrors of war and afterwards, amid the rubble of lives, communities, and homes. It is, we are reminded, the state alone that can monopolize women's bodies to perpetuate national myths, repress historical truth to exclude the multifaceted experiences of its citizens, and ultimately, make men commit atrocities against the opposite gender. "Viewed as a disposable and killable group," Saikia (in press) concludes, "women are sexualized and constructed as bodies for killing, raping, and brutalizing in order to anchor the sovereign power of the state" (n.p.).

The plight of women in Bangladesh also tells us something of the nature of genocide and of the role of rape within it. Rape in 1971, as in other periods, was not for sexual gratification or a random act of desire, it was enacted within a specific historical context in which women's bodies were employed as political vehicles to sow terror, humiliate, inflict racial slander, and consolidate control of the "enemy."[15] In the words of Catherine MacKinnon (1994), it was

> Rape as a method of extermination: It is also rape unto death, rape as massacre, rape to kill and to make the victims wish they were dead. It is rape as an instrument of forced exile, rape to make you leave your home and never want to go back. It is rape to be seen and heard and watched and told to others: rape as spectacle, it is rape to drive a wedge through a community, to shatter a society, to destroy a people. It is rape as genocide. (pp. 8-9)

As the case of Bangladesh demonstrates, systematic violence has deeply disturbing gendered dimensions, which to date, remain all too neglected by scholars.

### Notes

1.  I extend my sincere thanks to Michael Berkowitz, Luca Bernardinetti, Silvia Esposito, Anders Lustgarten, and Falguni Parsons for their valuable comments on earlier drafts of this chapter.
2.  While scholars generally agree on the number of refugees and displaced persons resulting from the violence, estimates of the death toll vary between 1-3 million victims.

3.   The 1948 United Nations Convention on Genocide defines genocide as an act carried out with "intent to destroy, in whole or in part, a national, ethnical, racial or religious group, as such" (United Nations, *Convention on the Prevention and Punishment of the Crime of Genocide,* 1948; available from www.unhchr.ch/html/menu3/b/p_genoci.htm). This chapter contends that under the UNCG, genocide-in-part was committed against Bengalis in East Pakistan, given their status as a distinct ethnic-linguistic group (and in the case of Hindu-Bengalis, also a distinct religious group). For, while certain groups were indeed special targets of the Pakistani army, the majority of victims were poverty-stricken Bengalis killed or brutalized *because* they were Bengali (Rounaq Jahan, "Genocide in Bangladesh," in *Century of Genocide: Critical Essays and Eyewitness Accounts,* 2d ed., Eds. Samuel Totten, William S. Parsons, and Israel Charny, (New York and London: Routeledge, 2004), 302.

     Alternatively, the International Commission of Jurists' 1972 legal study of the event found that as political groups and Hindus were specially targeted, this "mitigate[d] against the finding that the intent was to destroy in whole or in part the Bengali people as such" (The International Commission of Jurists, *The Events in East Pakistan, 1971: A Legal Study* (Geneva: ICJ, 1972), section IV "Legal Position under International Penal Law"). Nevertheless, they noted, "this does not mean... that *particular acts* may not have constituted genocide against part of the Bengali people" on the occasions in which "the intent was to kill Bengalis indiscriminately as such....There would seem to be a *prima facie* case to show that this was the intention on some occasions" (ibid.; emphasis added).

4.   For a detailed analysis of these issues, see Donald Beachler, "The Politics of Genocide Scholarship: The Case of Bangladesh," *Patterns of Prejudice,* forthcoming.

5.   Yasmin Saikia, "Overcoming the Silent Archive in Bangladesh: Women Bear Witness to Violence in the 1971 'Liberation' War," in *Women and the Contested State,* Eds. Monique Skidmore and Patricia Lawrence (South Bend, IN: Notre Dame University Press, 2007 n.p. ). Further investigation, nevertheless, reveals that a few academics in the West are indeed seeking to understand the plight of women in 1971. These scholars, weary of the informational abyss both in Bangladesh and abroad, are pioneering new research to recover women's voices and integrate them into recorded history. Consequently, most of the works listed in the annotated bibliography are theirs. The limited diversity of sources is entirely reflective of how little academic interest the traumatic birth of Bangladesh has incited thus far. More information has been written in Bengali, an un-annotated sample of which appears at the end of the bibliography.

6.   For details about the diverse experiences of some "war affected" women, see "Women of 1971: Drishtipat Campaign to Assist Seven War-Affected Women," *Drishtipat Website',* available from http://www.drishtipatorg/1971/index.htm.

7.   Equating the experiences and treatment of rape victims afterwards with the original crimes perpetrated against them is, nevertheless, problematic as it poses the danger of "sensationalizing" stages of victimization.

8.   Nayanika Mookherjee points out that, according to many middle-class Bangladeshis, women in 1971 were *intentionally* impregnated to dilute the Bengali race. They theorize that "Bengali Muslims were considered as 'Indianized/Hinduized'.. rape was seen as a means to 'improve the genes of the Bengali Muslims' and to populate Bangladesh with a new breed of 'pure' Pakistanis" (Nayanika Mookherjee, "Gendered Embodiments," 160).

9.   D'Costa, on the other hand, considers this source of silence the "most dangerous kind" where those aiming to assist rape victims by concealing their experiences

ended up unwittingly cementing the government's campaign to eliminate evidence of the crimes committed against them (see below) (ibid., 144).

10. Adequate examination of these important developments is not permitted here. Instead, see Mookherjee's (2006) analysis in "'Remembering to Forget.'"

11. Another rupture in the silence was Nilima Ibrahim's *Ami Birangona Bolchi* (1994), a rare collection of rape victim testimonies (D'Costa, "Coming to Terms," 235). The preface to the 1998 edition, however, revealed that no further volumes would be produced partly because of their damaging impact on victims. Ibrahim blamed "the present society's conservative mentality. They [society] do not hesitate to call the Birangona sinners. Therefore, I don't want to insult those women all over again who were not allowed to live an easy and normal life even 25 years ago" (translated in ibid.).

13. Jahan agrees, stating that shame in Bangladeshi society is used as a controlling mechanism to repress women and, therefore, "it is not raping *per se,* but the... knowledge about it that brings disrepute" (Jahan, "Women in Bangladesh," 1975, 22).

14. For a detailed analysis of the misrepresentation of rape victims in the national media, see Mookherjee, "Ethical Issues Concerning Representation of Narratives of Sexual Violence of 1971," *Drishtipot Website,* 2003; available from http://www.drishtipat.org/1971.

15. D'Costa notes how recent investigations by Indian feminist scholars into violence against women during the 1947 partition of South Asia conclusively demonstrate how "women's bodies are charged with metaphorical meanings profoundly rooted in a social and cultural structure that is beyond the physical control of individual women. In times of conflict and violence, women's bodies often become the carriers of violent messages between different ethnic groups" (D'Costa, "Coming to Terms," 2005, 242). See, for example, Urvashi Butalia, *The Other Side of Silence: Voices from the Partition of India.* India: Penguin Books, 1998.

## References

Beachler, Donald (Forthcoming). "The Politics of Genocide Scholarship: Tthe Case of Bangladesh." *Patterns of Prejudice.*

Brownmiller, Susan (1975). *Against Our Will: Men, Women and Rape.* New York: Simon and Schuster.

Butalia, Urvashi (1998). *The Other Side of Silence: Voices from the Partition of India.* India: Penguin Books.

D'Costa, Bina (2005). "Coming to Terms with the Past in Bangladesh: Forming Feminist Alliance across Borders," pp. 227-247. In Luciana Ricciutelli, Angela Miles, and Margaret McFadden (Eds.) *Women, Power and Justice: Global Feminist Perspectives, Volume I: Politics and Activism: Ensuring the Protection of Women's Fundamental Human Rights.* London: Zed Publishers.

D'Costa, Bina (2006). "Marginalized Identity: New Frontiers of Research for IR?" pp. 129-152. In A. Brooke, Maria Stern Ackerly, and Jacqui True (Eds.) *Feminist Methodologies for International Relations.* New York: Cambridge University Press.

Indian Council of World Affairs (1972). *How Pakistan Violated Human Rights in Bangladesh: Some Testimonies.* New Delhi: Author.

The International Commission of Jurists (1972). *The Events in East Pakistan, 1971: A Legal Study.* Geneva: Author.

Jahan, Rounaq (2004). "Genocide in Bangladesh," pp. 295-319. In Samuel Totten, William S. Parsons, and Israel W. Charny (Eds.) *Century of Genocide: Critical Essays and Eyewitness Accounts,* 2nd Edition. New York: Routledge.

Jahan, Rounaq (1975). "Women in Bangladesh," pp. 5-30. In Ruby Rohrlich-Leavitt (Ed.)*Women Cross Culturally: Change and Challenge.* The Hague: Mouton Publishers.

MacKinnon, Catherine (1994). "Rape, Genocide, and Women's Human Rights," *Harvard Women's Law Journal.* 17:8-9;

Malik, Amita (1972). *The Year of the Vulture.* New Delhi: Orient Longman Limited.

Mookherjee, Nayanika (2003). "Ethical Issues Concerning Representation of Narratives of Sexual Violence of 1971." *Drishtipat Website,* 2003; available from http://www.drishtipat.org/1971; Internet.

Mookherjee, Nayanika (2003). "Gendered Embodiments: Mapping the Body-Politic of the Raped Woman and the Nation in Bangladesh," pp. 157-177. In Nirmal Puwar and Parvati Raghuram (Eds.) *South Asian Women in the Diaspora.* New York and Oxford: Berg.

Mookherjee, Nayanika (2002). '*A Lot of History': Sexual Violence, Public Memory in the Bangladesh Liberation War of 1971.* Ph.D. dissertation, University of London, School of Oriental and African Studies.

Mookherjee, Nayanika (2006). *"Muktir Gaan* [Songs of Freedom], the Raped Woman and the Migrant Identities of the Bangladesh War," pp. 72-96. In N. C. Behera (Ed.) *Gender, Conflict and Migration.* London and New Delhi: Sage.

Mookherjee, Nayanika (2004). "'My Man (Honour) is Lost but I Still have my Iman (Principle)': Sexual Violence and Articulations of Masculinity," pp. 131-159. In R. Chopra, C. Osella and F. Osella (Eds.) *South Asian Masculinities.* New Delhi: Kali for Women.

Mookherjee, Nayanika (2006). "'Remembering to Forget': Public Secrecy and Memory of Sexual Violence in the Bangladesh War of 1971." *Journal of the Royal Anthropological Institute,* 12:443-450.

Saikia, Yasmin (2004). "Beyond the Archive of Silence: Narratives of Violence of the 1971 Liberation War of Bangladesh." *History Workshop Journal,* 58:275-287.

Saikia, Yasmin (in press). "Bodies in Pain: A People's History of 1971." In Anne Feldhaus and Manu Bhagawan (Eds.) *Essays in Honor of Eleanor Zelliot.* New Delhi: Oxford University Press.

Saikia, Yasmin (forthcoming). "Lost in Violence: History, Memory and Humanity in 1971, East Pakistan." In Manali Desai, Piya Chatterjee, and Parama Roy (Eds.), *States of Trauma.* New Delhi: Zubaan.

Saikia, Yasmin (in press). "Overcoming the Silent Archive in Bangladesh: Women Bear Witness to Violence in the 1971 'Liberation' War." In Monique Skidmore and Patricia Lawrence (Eds.) *Women and the Contested State.* South Bend, IN: Notre Dame University Press.

Sharlach, Lisa (2000). "Rape as Genocide: Bangladesh, the Former Yugoslavia, and Rwanda" *New Political Science,* 22(1): 89-102.

"Women of 1971: Drishtipat Campaign to Assist Seven War-Affected Women," *Drishtipat Website',* available from http:/AAWw.drishtipat.org/1971/«ndex.htm; Internet.

## Annotated Bibliography

Brownmiller, Susan (1975). *Against Our Will: Men, Women and Rape.* New York: Simon and Schuster, 472 pp.

   This classic feminist text was one of the first to attest to the systematic nature of sexual violence in Bangladesh involving "hit and run rape," abduction, and forced prostitution in mass rape camps. The account also highlights the crisis-ridden aftermath during which many rape victims faced unwanted pregnancies and social ostracism suggesting that their physical ordeal was but the "first round of humiliation."

While Brownmiller is concerned with the sexual crimes committed against Bengali women, she points out that systematic rape of women in war is not new. Rather the uniqueness of Bangladesh, she argues, is that for the first time in history, the international community recognized that sexual violence in war could be a deliberate military strategy to further terrorize and subjugate an enemy population.

D'Costa, Bina (2005). "Coming to Terms with the Past in Bangladesh: Forming Feminist Alliance across Borders," pp. 227-247. In Luciana Ricciutelli, Angela Miles, and Margaret McFadden (Eds.) *Women, Power and Justice: Global Feminist Perspectives, Volume 1. Politics and Activism: Ensuring the Protection of Women's Fundamental Human Rights*. London: Zed Publishers.

According to this article, two histories of 1971 exist simultaneously in Bangladesh: a "macro-narrative" (or official version) versus a "micro-narrative" (based on individual memories and experiences). The official history, which excludes victims of wartime sexual violence, the author explains, was initially facilitated by the state-endorsed abortion and adoption programs run during the war's aftermath. These programs operated under the guise of addressing victims' needs, but in reality, aimed to conceal the troubling evidence that Bangladeshi men were unable to protect their women in 1971. Official state responses to the plight of raped of women were, therefore, not concerned with the victims themselves, but rather with the "challenge to Bengali nationalist and masculine identity."

In order to subvert this national scheme, D'Costa insists that the micro-narratives of women's experiences in 1971 must be incorporated into public consciousness through a coordinated national feminist/activist network linked to other South Asian groups. Such an initiative, she concludes, may not only result in justice for rape victims, but also assist Bengali society to deal with "a past that affects its present and future so strongly."

D'Costa, Bina (2003). "The Gendered Construction of Nationalism: From Partition to Creation." Ph.D. Dissertation. Australian National University, 387 pp.

This thesis examines to what extent Bangladeshi women's experiences in 1971 were conditioned by the larger processes of state-building, nationalism, and gender identity construction. Nation-state building, it concludes, requires that women's voices and experiences be suppressed, especially during periods of conflict, in order to consolidate legitimacy. The thesis attempts to counter this process by incorporating women's experiences of 1971 into Bangladesh's official history and, in doing so, offers not only a revised interpretation of the country's independence struggle, but also of nationalism and the practice of state-building itself.

D'Costa, Bina (2006). "Marginalized Identity: New Frontiers of Research for IR?" pp. 129-152. In Brooke A. Ackerly, Maria Stern and Jacqui True (Eds.) *Feminist Methodologies for International Relations*. New York: Cambridge University Press.

D'Costa challenges the discipline of international relations to incorporate the study of marginalized groups, particularly women, into more traditional studies of nationalism, state power, and international security. Examining marginal subjects, she argues, can be extremely revealing as in the case of Bangladesh, where the silence surrounding sexual violence of 1971 is inextricably linked to the Bangladeshi nation-building project. This case thus proves that until international relations starts "centering the marginalized subject," its understanding of nationalism and state power will remain restricted.

D'Costa's article further details the background of her research, her methodology and fieldwork, the conceptual challenges she encountered, and her use of oral history to undermine the suppression of Bangladeshi women's memories of 1971.

Indian Council of World Affairs (1972). *How Pakistan Violated Human Rights in Bangladesh: Some Testimonies*. New Delhi: Author, 63 pp.

Contains three first-person accounts of women's experiences of 1971 based on interviews conducted by Indian journalists in refugee camps along the Indo-Bangladesh border. "Neutral observers...and independent organizations were present at the time of the interviews," the introduction states, "and have authenticated these accounts as they were written."

One testimony given by a camp nurse entitled, "The Fate of Women," attests to the grave situation of female refugees, many of whom arrived suffering from severe malnourishment, unwanted pregnancies, and in some cases, the loss of their entire families—husbands, children and parents. The other testimonies relating to women are entitled "Escape from Rape" and "Tales of Village Women."

Jahan, Rounaq (1975). "Women in Bangladesh," pp. 5-30. In Ruby Rohrlich-Leavitt (Ed.) *Women Cross Culturally: Change and Challenge*. The Hague: Mouton Publishers.

An inclusive overview of women's lifestyles, socio-economic statuses, and level of emancipation in Bangladesh after 1971. References to women's direct experiences of the war, while brief, are informative. Jahan contends that "shame" in Bangladeshi society is used as a controlling mechanism to repress women. This is particularly evident in how victims of the "shameful" crime of rape during 1971 were forced to be silent about their experiences or face intense ostracism. Thus "it is not raping *per se*," states Jahan, "but the...knowledge about it that brings disrepute." This socially engineered regime of suppression, she concludes, indicates the highly vulnerable position of Bangladeshi women during and after 1971.

Kabir, Shahriar (Ed.) (1999). *Tormenting Seventy One: An Account of Pakistan Army's Atrocities During Bangladesh Liberation War of 1971*. Dhaka: Dana

Printers Limited. Accessed at: http://www.secularvoiceofbangladesh.org. Tormenting_71.

A publication by the *Ekatturer Ghatak Dalal Nirmul Committee* ("Committee for Resisting Killers & Collaborators of the Bangladesh Liberation War of 1971"), established by Bangladeshi political activist, Jahanara Imam, in 1992 to coordinate a national war crimes tribunal movement. The book, which seeks to document atrocities committed by the Pakistani army in 1971, includes a fairly detailed overview of women's experiences in its introduction and several graphic testimonies detailing the sexual crimes inflicted on them. Among the latter is that of prominent sculptor, Ferdousi Priyobhasini, the first Bangladeshi women to speak publicly about her experience as a rape victim during the conflict. The impartiality of this source is questionable.

Malik, Amita (1972). *The Year of the Vulture*. New Delhi: Orient Longman Limited, 159 pp.

Amita Malaik, an Indian journalist, traveled through Bangladesh from 1971-1972 gathering first-hand accounts of the conflict and its complex aftermath. Her description of women's experiences is partly based on her visit to the Bangladesh Central Organization for Rehabilitation of Women, an organization of professional and volunteer social workers founded to assist female victims of the war. The organization, the author relates, divided victims into four categories: "(1) Married women who were dishonoured; (2) Unmarried mothers whose babies resulted from rape by Pakistanis; (3) Pregnant women who [were] mentally disturbed; and (4) Women widowed and raped." Malik's account also includes several case histories of such women.

Mookherjee, Nayanika (2002). "'A Lot of History': Sexual Violence, Public Memory & the Bangladesh Liberation War of 1971." Ph.D. Dissertation. University of London, School of Oriental and African Studies, 324 pp.

This comprehensive socio-anthropological examination of how Bangladesh remembers the sexual violence of 1971 contends that national and societal conceptualizations of rape differ significantly from the actual experiences of violated women. This deficiency in public memory provides numerous insights into Bangladeshi society and how its turbulent relationship with 1971 denies rape victims the possibility of genuine rehabilitation and prevents understanding the gendered nature of the conflict. The thesis is based heavily on the author's fieldwork in the Bangladeshi village of Enayetpur, home of three rape victims who gained national fame in the 1990s as *birangonas* ("war heroines"), and contains numerous visual representations of victims of sexual violence featured in Bengali literary sources as well as a useful bibliography.

Mookherjee, Nayanika (2003). *Boundaries of Blood: Genealogies of "War-Babies" and the Bangladeshi Nation*. Paper presented at the Association of Social Anthropology Decennial Conference, Manchester UK, July 14-18.

Part of the author's ongoing inquiry into the subject of "war-babies" or babies of mixed Pakistani/Bengali origin who were born as a result of the systematic rape in 1971 and later placed in state-endorsed adoption programs. The paper examines the perceived "hybrid" nature of these children in contrast to officially crafted notions of racial "purity" and thus explores "constructions of 'blood', 'genes' and 'kinship'" in Bangladesh and their relationship to the racial identity of the nation.

Mookherjee, Nayanika (2003). "Ethical Issues Concerning Representation of Narratives of Sexual Violence of 1971." *Drishtipat.* Accessed at: www. drishtipat.org/1971.

Based on excerpts of Mookherjee's 2002 Ph.D. dissertation (see above), this essay contends that while oral history can help to recover women's experiences of sexual violence in 1971, it harbors potential ethical pitfalls. Mookherjee explores this argument by examining how the Bengali press inaccurately depicted the experiences of one rape victim to fit a preconceived image of the "authentic oppressed, violated woman" in need of national assistance. This image contrasts sharply to the victim's complex and ambiguous situation, as revealed in a direct conversation with Mookherjee. This disjunction between official and individual narratives caused by the "politics of remembrance" in Bangladesh thus denies the genuine experiences of rape victims and prevents their needs from being met. Oral history should therefore, the author declares, "reflect first and foremost the desires and wishes of the women whose narratives are being highlighted," not "a macro, national objective."

Mookherjee, Nayanika (2003). "Gendered Embodiments: Mapping the Body-Politic of the Raped Woman and the Nation in Bangladesh," pp. 157-177. In Nirmal Puwar and Parvati Raghuram (Eds.) *South Asian Women in the Diaspora.* New York and Oxford: Berg.

Mookherjee reveals the specific historical and political contexts within which systematic rape took place in Bangladesh 1971 by exploring the complex ways in which state-building projects use women instrumentally to generate support. In Bangladesh, she explains, this was done by fusing popular middle-class notions of femininity with idyllic conceptions of nature, the nation and motherhood. The Bangladesh state thus enforced "essentialist gender roles for women" which encouraged women's participation in the nationalist movement as nurturing and sacrificing mothers, wives, and daughters who symbolized the honor of the nation. Victims of sexual violence, who clearly contradicted these essentialized domestic roles, therefore, either had to be reintegrated into the private sphere through "rehabilitation" or left out of the national narrative entirely. Thus, the author concludes, "national historiography.... defines cultural identity for the nation by excluding the experiences of many from its fold; it grants citizenship to some, while others are confined to eschewed dimensions."

Mookherjee, Nayanika (2003). "Mapping Violent Narratives: War-Memorials in Dhaka and their Embodied Recallings" (audio recording). *City One Conference Proceedings on Urban Ethnographies*. New Delhi: Centre for the Study of Developing Societies. NOTE: Audio recording available from http://www.sarai.net/cityone/mp3/018-CO1D3-A/03_Talk-NayanikaMookherjee.mp3.

The author analyses some of Bangladesh's major war memorials in order to probe how the state and society remember 1971. Her examination of the few monuments featuring women reveals that the "heroic female" is typically depicted as a strong mother, wife, or nurse. Women are, in other words, only commemorated as *agents* actively participating in the independence struggle alongside males and thus worthy of acceptance and respect. This representation of the dynamic woman, Mookherjee asserts, is embedded in middle class notions of gender and heroism which, by definition, exclude (supposedly passive) victims of rape. Hence, memorialization in Bangladesh, located in a "middle class subjectivity and aestheticism," contributes to the veiling of women's experiences in 1971.

Mookherjee, Nayanika (2006). "*Muktir Gaan* (Songs of Freedom), the Raped Woman and the Migrant Identities of the Bangladesh War," pp. 72-96. In N. C. Behera (Ed.) *Gender, Conflict and Migration.* London and New Delhi: Sage.

This article focuses on the 1996 release of *Muktir Gaan*, a documentary film that follows a musical troupe of male and female Bengali migrants who toured India in 1971 providing moral support to other refugees and Bengali insurgents. The film's emphasis on the agency of middle class migrants during the war, Mookherjee asserts, challenges migration studies' exclusive focus on poor female war refugees and allows a deeper understanding of class and gender relations during the period. Consequently, it incited strong emotive responses from Bangladeshi audiences. "We were always told that women had been victims," stated a young female viewer, "This shows that women did do things during *Muktijuddho* [the Bangladesh war of 1971]. My legs are shaking."

Mookherjee, Nayanika (2004). "'My Man (Honour) is Lost but I Still have my Iman (Principle)': Sexual Violence and Articulations of Masculinity," pp. 131-159. In R. Chopra, C. Osella and F. Osella (Eds.) *South Asian Masculinities*. New Delhi: Kali for Women.

Here, Mookherjee focuses on the husbands of the three rape victims studied in her 2002 dissertation (see above) in order to explore gender identity construction and the different conceptualizations of masculinity promoted by Bangladeshi society and state. The article provides an intimate look into the lives of the violated women and their partners and reveals how constructs of masculinity "are located within the incessant everyday struggle and frustrations experienced by the *birangonas* ['war heroines'] and their husbands in their efforts to reclaim their social place in Enayetpur; as well [as] their place in the national history."

Mookherjee, Nayanika (2006). "'Remembering to Forget': Public Secrecy and Memory of Sexual Violence in the Bangladesh War of 1971." *Journal of the Royal Anthropological Institute* (N.S.) 12, (2): 433-450.

Another examination of the complex ways in which Bangladesh remembers the sexual violence of 1971. It is based, again, on the three rape victims of the Bangladeshi village of Enayetpur (see Mookherjee 2002 and 2004) who were recognized by the state in the 1990s for having "fought with their bodies" for the independence of the nation. This countrywide recognition, the author relates, contrasts sharply with the public contempt they were later subjected to by other villagers who spewed *khota* or "sarcastic/censorious remarks expressing scorn and evoking the unpleasant events."

The villagers' public evocation of the incident through snide gestures, she continues, deviates from the secrecy which they normally accord sexual crimes committed in their locality during the conflict. Consequently, it appears that Enayetpur's history of sexual violence is treated as a "public secret" or a fact that is "known but not articulated" except through contempt. This manner of dealing with the conflictual past ensures the women's continued subordination and upholds existing village power structures and normative codes related to economic status, gender, and religion.

By exposing how memories of sexual crimes in 1971 are often concealed in silence and alternately revealed through scorn, the article proposes a connection between memory, secrecy, revelation, and trauma. The paradoxical phenomenon of the "public secret," the author suggests, is therefore an apt methodological tool with which to examine societal memories of sexual violence in war.

Saikia, Yasmin (2004). "Beyond the Archive of Silence: Narratives of Violence of the 1971 Liberation War of Bangladesh." *History Workshop Journal*, 58 (1): 275-287.

This is a compelling account of the author's journey to Bangladesh in search of information on women's experiences in 1971 and her ensuing discovery that while numerous women of differing age, ethnicity, and religious/social background suffered extreme violence during the war, their stories were absent from official accounts. Further investigation into this "institutional silence" soon reveals, moreover, that not only are women's experiences missing, but their "voices are actively silenced."

*Who* is silencing female victims of wartime violence and *why* become the focuses of Saikia's investigation which ends by severely undermining Bangladesh's official version of its independence. In order to overwrite this distorted national discourse, the author insists, *all* voices who experienced the war—victims, perpetrators, and bystanders—must be taken into account to understand the true nature of liberation violence replacing the skewed official history with a "people's history of 1971."

Saikia, Yasmin (2004). *Bodies in Pain: Voicing a People's History of 1971.* Paper presented at the Seventh Sustainable Development Conference, Islamabad, December 8-10.

This paper deals with themes similar to those in Saikia's "Beyond the Archive of Silence" (see above). Again, the author is interested in documenting the memories of *all* survivors of the 1971 conflict (males and females; perpetrators, victims, and bystanders) to better understand gender violence and produce a humanistic "public biography" of the event as it unfolded in Bangladesh, Pakistan and India. Saikia is thus encouraging a revision of South Asian history which defies the conventional categories of perpetrator/victim and emphasizes instead the unexplored "common suffering of people in war" and the possibility of transnational reconciliation.

Saikia, Yasmin (2007). "Bodies in Pain: A People's History of 1971," n.p. In Anne Feldhaus and Manu Bhagawan (Eds.) *Essays in Honor of Eleanor Zelliot*, New Delhi: Oxford University Press.

Here, Saikia develops her December 2004 essay (see above) in her ongoing mission to write a "human biography" of 1971 by excavating the gender violence at its core. The article provides a succinct overview of the limited historiography of 1971, extended excerpts of oral testimonies from female rape victims and male perpetrators, and a summary of the role of state leaders—the ultimate "architects of violence." Inspired by Hannah Arendt, Saikia continues to challenge South Asians to consider how women's narratives of 1971 destabilize official histories of the conflict (promoted distinctly in Pakistan, India, and Bangladesh) and provoke complicated questions about postcolonial identities, nation-state building, and the overriding forces that transform ordinary men into criminals.

Saikia, Yasmin (Forthcoming). "Lost in Violence: History, Memory and Humanity in 1971, East Pakistan." In Manali Desai, Piya Chatterjee and Parama Roy (Eds.) *States of Trauma.* New Delhi: Zubaan.

This lengthy essay is yet another component of Saikia's biographical project documenting the memories of female and male survivors of 1971. Here, the author highlights how survivors' memories reveal the loss of *insâniyat*/humanity caused by the violence and refute the "anti-humanist project[s] of nationalism" perpetuated on the South Asian subcontinent. The essay concludes with a poignant exploration of cultural texts on humanism which, the author believes, offer avenues to recover the humanity destroyed by the brutality of 1971.

Saikia, Yasmin (2007). "Overcoming the Silent Archive in Bangladesh: Women Bear Witness to Violence in the 1971 'Liberation' War," n.p. In Monique Skidmore and Patricia Lawrence (Eds.) *Women and the Contested State.* South Bend, IN: Notre Dame University Press.

Saikia continues to unravel the silence masking sexual violence in 1971 through theoretical analysis and survivor testimonies. Once again, she explores the terrifying power of the state to make men commit violence against women and their effort to enforce a "politics of active national forgetting." To resist this process, the author encourages women to speak about their experiences—difficult as communicating them may be—to reveal the common suffering endured by all on the subcontinent in 1971. Saikia is, in other words, promoting female agency through language as a means of fighting state tyranny and moving beyond the barriers separating groups in Pakistan, Bangladesh, and India. "1971 was a shared trauma of the subcontinent," she writes. "The recognition of women's sufferings, 'ours' and 'theirs,' by women in Bangladesh can generate a new sense of an *unpartitioned* community."

Saikia, Yasmin (Forthcoming). "'They were Human': Men, Women and Memories of Violence in 1971, East Pakistan." In Elizabeth Heineman (Ed.) *The History of Sexual Violence in Conflict Zones/*. Philadelphia: University of Pennsylvania Press Human Rights Series.

Saikia delves even further into the loss of *insâniyat*/humanity in 1971 attested to by survivors' testimonies which she weaves together here to present an extended "polyversal narrative" of South Asia. Survivors' voices, she insists, not only intrude upon the silence cloaking sexual violence during the conflict, but they provide us with a means of interrogating nationally-constructed identities, the practice of modern warfare and, crucially, encourage "ethical and humanistic thinking in our era of global violence."

Sharlach, Lisa (2000). "Rape as Genocide: Bangladesh, the Former Yugoslavia, and Rwanda." *New Political Science*, 22 (1): 89-102.

This comparative study argues that sexual violence was employed as a military strategy to systematically destroy targeted groups during conflicts in the Balkans (1990s), Rwanda (1994), and Bangladesh (1971). Rape is therefore a form of genocide, the author declares, and the 1948 UN Convention on the Prevention and Punishment of the Crime of Genocide should be altered to reflect this reality.

Sharlach's brief but detailed survey of sexual violence in Bangladesh highlights how females and female chastity in Bengali society represent communal honor and "ethnic purity." As a result, Bengali victims of rape—not perpetrators—are subjected to extreme ostracism. This link between female sexuality and female honor, also present in the Balkans and Rwanda, leads Sharlach to conclude that "rape as genocide appears to occur to ethnic groups that strongly stigmatize rape survivors rather than rapists." Victims of sexual violence in these three societies are, consequently, "the invisible living casualties of the genocide" that must endure both the extreme trauma of the assault *and* a "second rape" perpetrated by their own hostile communities.

# 4

# Death, Shattered Families, and Living as Widows in Cambodia

*Judy Ledgerwood*

## Introduction

After the 1975 defeat of the U.S.-backed Cambodian government of Lon Nol, following a five-year civil war, the victorious Khmer Rouge or "red Khmers" renamed Cambodia, Democratic Kampuchea (DK). For the next four years, the Khmer Rouge instituted a reign of terror and socio-economic engineering aimed at uprooting the existing social fabric. The consequences were the deaths of 1.7 million Cambodians out of a prewar population of between seven and eight million people.

The specific plight of women in this period has not been the focus of research, though there are data available on aspects of social change, women's physical and mental health, sexual violence, and women's roles in the revolution. There is more research on women in the post-revolutionary years, including that which addresses the social effects of large numbers of widows, changing social patterns in the wake of widespread death and displacement, and new economic roles for women – new forms of labor in the 1980s, and migration to work in garment factories and the sex industry in the 1990s.

## Democratic Kampuchea 1975-1979

With the fall of Phnom Penh on April 17, 1975, Khmer Rouge leaders began evacuating approximately three million people from cities throughout the country. Former high-ranking government officials, businessmen, religious, intellectuals, leaders, and military officers were immediately executed; the key to survival in this first purge during the evacuation was to hide one's background, though even those who escaped initially were often ferreted out later in subsequent purges.

Under DK the Cambodian people were divided into different social categories; "new" people were those who had not lived in Khmer Rouge-controlled territory prior to April 17, while those who had were considered "base" people. Base people enjoyed more privileges, though their lives were also tightly controlled and transformed by the restructuring of society. New people were used as labor to clear new agricultural land from malaria-infested forests, to dig vast irrigation projects, and to grow rice alongside peasants. The new people were not accustomed to long, backbreaking hours of labor; moreover, they were considered "politically incorrect," so they were the last to be fed and the first to fall under suspicion. Peasants who had fled to the cities to escape the war were also labeled as new people despite their prior class status, since they had betrayed the revolution by fleeing rather than joining the communist war effort.

Living conditions varied from district to district and over time throughout the regime (Vickery, 1984, Heder, 1980), but there were important patterns. DK leaders viewed individualism and capitalism as the primary enemies of the revolution; thus, money, markets, and private property of all sorts were abolished. Basic resources could only be obtained through the newly established labor camps. DK leaders were confident that rice harvests could take place twice or three times per year with new irrigation schemes, and yields per hectare could be tripled through collectivization and revolutionary will. When regional leaders failed to meet these unrealistic goals, they too were purged as the paranoid central leadership searched for the saboteurs of their "perfect" revolution (Chandler, 1999).

People were organized into communes with militarized discipline; men and women were forced to work from dawn to dusk and often into the night. Food rations were low as the rice surplus was stored to feed the army and hoarded by a divided and fearful leadership. Over time there was a shift to collective dining, people were not allowed to cook or eat individually or as families. Hundreds of thousands of people died of starvation and diseases related to malnutrition. Buddhism, the religion of more than 90 percent of Cambodians, was viewed by the Khmer Rouge as reactionary, exploitative, and feudalistic; all monks were defrocked or killed, Buddhist temples were destroyed or used for profane purposes such as detention centers or warehouses (Harris, 2005). Though extended bilateral kinship ties had formed the core of Khmer society, DK practice recognized only the union of husband and wife and separated extended kin units. Work teams were organized by age and sex, with young adults often sent off as mobile work teams. Basic social networks of kinship and community were shattered; all loyalty was to be redirected to the *Angkar* (the organization, as the shadowy leadership was known).

## Women during Democratic Kampuchea

During Pol Pot's genocidal regime, more women than men managed to survive; women are better able to survive severe malnutrition (Ledgerwood, 1992, pp. 7-8; Banister and Johnson, 1993, pp. 83-87), and fewer women were targeted for execution and killed in fighting. DK's assault on traditional Cambodian society and, in particular, the family was devastating for women. Women tried desperately to stay in touch with family members as they were scattered across different work camps. The central roles for women in society as mothers, market sellers, holders of property, cooks for family meals, and as the key link in larger kinship networks were all shattered. It was now the *Angkar* who provided food, raised one's children, decided who would marry whom and where and how one would live.

The first person narratives that describe this era are first and foremost stories of families desperately trying to stay together. Many women interviewed about their experiences said they survived those years of horror because they had to care for their children—that if they had been alone, they just would have given up and died.

## Women's Health

Hard labor with little food caused terrible health problems; doctors had been summarily executed with other elites and western medicines were not available. Normally preventable diseases added to the death toll; people suffered blindness, hair loss, rotten teeth and other symptoms of malnutrition. Many women ceased to menstruate and pregnancy rates declined dramatically (Banister and Johnson, 1993). Some babies that were born in this period died from lack of breast milk as mothers were too malnourished to lactate. Haing Ngor (1987), for example, tells the heartbreaking story of his own wife dying in childbirth, while he, a trained doctor, had no way to perform the cesarean section that could have saved her life (pp. 293, 331-333). As a consequence of multiple births and extreme heavy labor, many women suffered prolapsed uteruses.

Obviously mental health problems also developed under the strain of suffering and seeing those one loved suffer and/or be killed. Several studies of Khmer refugees have documented high levels of anxiety and depression. A study by Carlson and Rosser-Hogan (1993) report the level of depression as high as 80 percent (p. 229). (For a summary of this literature, see Nou, 2006.) Up through today, women elders in particular often complain that they "think too much" or that their "brain is broken." There are no accurate statistics on the numbers of Cambodians who suffer mental health problems, though some have suggested that those who fled as refugees may have suffered at a higher rate as they had the added trauma of life in refugee camps and adjustment to a new social world (see Mortland, 2002, who makes this argument drawing on long-term ethnographic evidence).

## Sexual Violence

In the historical works on the DK regime, the Khmer Rouge are described as puritanical about sex. In fact, sexual misconduct was punishable by death.

On the issue of rape therefore, these reports are largely silent. If anything, they imply or say outright that it would have been impossible. Vickery (1984) even argues that given the tight restrictions on sexual activity between cadre and evacuees, "it might be safe to assert that women were in less danger of sexual molestation than at any time before 1975, which is not to claim that their situation, even as women, had improved" (p. 175). The first-person narratives by urban males published in the 1980s are also largely silent on the issue; and in one account by a woman, Theeda Mam (1987) writes, "rape was beyond comprehension" (p. 100).

However, among the first person narratives written by younger women and published twenty years later (or some twenty years after the initial accounts were written) by those who would have been children during DK, there are direct references to sexual assault – as indeed there are more eyewitness accounts of other forms of violence including executions (see for example Ung, 2000, pp. 71-72; Him, 2000, pp. 246-247). This could be a distortion of memory, as the authors say that they are in part reconstructing stories that they have been told by relatives. But given this author's interviews with women survivors and patterns of intergenerational change among Cambodians in the U.S., it seems that women who have grown up in Western societies are more likely to talk about the issue (Ledgerwood 1990, Smith-Hefner, 1999). For women raised in Cambodia the subject remains too shameful to discuss. And we now know, from interviews with guards/interrogators at the infamous S-21 torture and execution center, that even there, at the center of DK's "Panopticon," there were cases of rape (Panh/First Run Icarus Films, 2003). In situations where cadre and soldiers were given absolute power over life and death and ruled by terror, abuses occurred. Rape, however, was not a weapon wielded against one's enemies as has been the case in other regions of the world.

*Women and Social Status*

The DK period is often described by the Khmer as a time of social reversals, when rich elites, royalty, monks, and educated people were made low and peasants rose to power. Similarly, in a society where elders were held in highest esteem, the Khmer Rouge trained children to be cadre, saying that only they were pure enough to complete the revolution. These included girls as well as boys. From the first-person narratives we have descriptions of life in the camps where girls were separated and told they were "Daughters of Pol Pot," a new base upon which society would be built (Szymusiak, 1986). But the *"neary"* (female) cadre were only at the lowest levels; up the chain of command, higher authorities in the *angkar* were men. At the very top of the DK regime, there were two women cabinet members, Ieng Thirith, wife of Foreign Minister Ieng Sary and Yun Yat, wife of Defense Minister Son Sen. The rhetoric of gender equality was a part of DK communist ideology, but except for the young *neary* who had higher food rations and some protection, equality largely meant equal suffering.

During the DK period, women lost their sources of prestige and authority: as those who controlled household finances and small-scale trader, as mothers raising children, as wives who did the cooking and ran the household, and as central figures in bilateral kindred that were the center of communities. Even women who had lived as peasants before the revolution complained bitterly about the lack of food, the extreme levels of violence, the separation of families, and the practice of communal dining.

## The Legacy of DK for Women

The Khmer Rouge regime was overthrown in January 1979 by the Vietnamese army; the new government they installed and supported for a decade was the "People's Republic of Kampuchea" (PRK). With the collapse of DK, hundreds of thousands of people took to the roads, mostly on foot, to return to their native villages and towns. Death tolls as a result of the Khmer Rouge violence varied around the country. In the village where Ebihara had conducted ethnographic research in 1959-1960 only half of the people she had known survived the regime, and some 40 percent of adult women were widows (Ebihara, 1993a, pp. 58-59).

*Widows, Agriculture and Wage Labor*

Chanthou Boua (1982) was among the first to document the sexual imbalance in the post-revolutionary population; 55 percent of the overall population, but up to two-thirds in some areas, were women (p. 45). Her research focuses on the aftermath, women taking on the burden of extra physical labor, particularly in agriculture, but also in industry and commerce. She details how difficult it was to eke out a living in a country still in tatters. "Women in Today's Cambodia" also quotes women as expressing support for the system of "*krom samaki*" or solidarity groups, the agricultural collectives that the PRK established, in part to assist widows and orphans by establishing larger production units (Boua, 1982, pp. 48-49). As time passed, the solidarity groups became decidedly less appealing to the population, even to widows; peasants quietly returned to farming private plots by the mid-1980s.

Because of a lack of male labor, women engaged in agricultural tasks usually reserved for men, including plowing. There were new opportunities for women across a range of fields; for example, they staffed the mid-levels of the government bureaucracy where they had been little represented before the war. Women returned to running small-scale trade, but in the 1980s they also managed some large-scale trade (these operations were often run by the wives of government officials) (see Kusakabe, 2003). By the mid-1990s, such large-scale trading firms were once again largely in the hands of ethnic Chinese families.

Women in post-revolutionary Cambodia also went to work in factories; according to Ministry of Industry statistics, there were 7,137 women among the

10,693 employees in factories in 1992 (Ledgerwood, 1992, p. 22). After 1993 this would rise dramatically; there were seven garment factories in 1994 and 220 in 2001. The value of garment exports was 985 million U.S. dollars in 2000, 70 percent of total Cambodian exports that year (Derks, 2005, p. 96).

*The Return of Peace and Relative Stability*

In 1989, the Vietnamese military withdrew from Cambodia and in 1991 the PRK, the remnants of the Khmer Rouge, the royalists led by the former King Sihanouk and another non-communist resistance faction, the Khmer People's National Liberation Front (KPNLF), signed the Paris Peace Agreement, ending a civil war (which was also a proxy Cold War conflict). In 1992-1993, the United Nations peacekeeping mission in Cambodia (the Transitional Authority in Cambodia or UNTAC) organized general elections, the return of refugees from the Thai border, and rebuilt some the country's infrastructure. From the 1993 election emerged a shaky coalition that included the rulers of the PRK and the royalist FUNCINPEC party now led by Sihanouk's son Norodom Rannaridh. Subsequently, Rannaridh was ousted in a 1997 coup, and although he and his party members returned to a new coalition government a year later, the real power for the last ten years has been in the hands of Hun Sen, the leader of the Cambodian People's Party (the former ruling party of the PRK). The Khmer Rouge, who signed the peace accord, but later withdrew, were finally defeated and completely pacified after Pol Pot's death and the final disintegration of the movement in 1998.

By the late 1990s and early twenty-first century, as young men born of the post-1979 baby boom reached adulthood, they again dominated in white-collar employment, particularly government service. But as was the case in the U.S. after World War II, women did not revert completely to their prewar roles. The 1993 constitution of the new Kingdom of Cambodia provides some of the most liberal protections for women's rights in the world, including full political rights, the right to ownership of property, and the right to equal pay for equal work. While not all of these rights are protected, there are now women's activist groups who lobby to enforce the new laws. The post-1993 rise of non-governmental organizations has included a significant number of women's organizations that provide direct assistance to poor women, job training, advocacy, and media attention to women's issues (see GAD, 1999). The rhetoric of some of these organizations on equal rights for women is a unique hybrid of Western feminist ideas and PRK socialist ideology on the equality of women (Ledgerwood, 1996).

*Increased Freedom and Declining "Value"*

While women have faired better in the economic sphere, one can also argue that there has been a symbolic loss of status for women in Cambodia. In the immediate aftermath of DK, when the sex ratio was so unbalanced, there were many women with no one to marry. There was a decline in bridewealth value; and some women were willing to enter into marriages as second wives rather than live alone. With increased economic activity and mobility, visible most clearly among the hundreds of thousands of young women who came from the countryside to work in the garment factories, comes the accusation that women are now sexually promiscuous. Indeed, Tarr (1996) and others have documented increased sexual activity among young people. Young women go to the city as dutiful daughters, hoping to send money back to their families in the countryside, but they also seek the excitement and freedom that comes with urban life (Dirks, 2005). Any suspicion that a girl is not a virgin damages her chances for marriage and endangers the social status of her family.

The UN period also saw a dramatic rise in commercial sex workers, who were visited both by UN personnel and Cambodian men suddenly wealthy from UN salaries. The sex trade has remained a significant problem, with women trafficked to and from Cambodia, and through Cambodia to neighboring countries. Cambodia reopened to the outside world just as HIV/AIDs infection rates had soared in neighboring Thailand and the epidemic spread quickly in Cambodia. By 2003, Cambodia had an estimated adult prevalence rate of 2.6 percent, though there were signs by then that the rate of new infections had begun to stabilize due to aggressive education programs and condom distributions (Brown, 2003).

The post-revolutionary era has also seen an apparent rise in the levels of domestic violence though the research in this area is very limited (Zimmerman, 1994). This violence is in part the legacy of demobilized soldiers returning from years of warfare, a pattern found in many post-conflict societies.

Finally, the vast majority of women and men in rural areas (still 85 percent of the population) suffer crushing poverty fourteen years after an official end to the war. Development aid has disproportionately benefited those in the cities; the education and health care systems are under funded and have limited reach. The average life expectancy is only 54, the infant mortality rate is 97 per 1,000 live births, maternal mortality is 470 per 100,000 live births, one in eight children die before their fifth birthday, and 56 percent of childhood deaths are associated with malnutrition (Coates, 2005, p. 176).

## Critical Challenges Facing the Field Today

Cambodians have benefited from the years of peace; women are again central to kinship networks, though these are fragmented from the loss of life in the DK years. An argument ensued in the academic literature in the 1990s on the issue of social reciprocity. Ovenson et al. (1996), and other scholars, argued that social relationships were so fractured by the violence of the DK years that communities, even families, no longer aided one another. In several subsequent publications this discussion was refined (Ledgerwood, 1998, Ledgerwood and Vijghen, 2003, Kim, 2001, Marston, n.d.). In part, the researchers were looking at different kinds of villages in different parts of the country, seeing stability on the southern and central plains where life had largely returned to normalcy after 1979, and conflict in the north and northwest that had seen fighting into the late 1990s, where many residents were not returning members of prewar communities, but newcomers from other regions and/or factions. There is great need for additional ethnographic research in more remote areas of the country to understand these variations.

As the thirty-year mark since the end of the DK regime approaches, it is important to realize that many survivors are beginning to pass away. The limited number of published, first-person accounts of the period are nearly exclusively from urban elites, and thus there is a critical need to record additional first-person narratives now. There are a number of projects underway to do this, the most important being the work of the Documentation Center of Cambodia (DC-CAM) which is helping to assemble evidence for a tribunal for the surviving leadership of the DK regime.

One of the most exciting challenges is raised by Anuska Dirk's new thesis on Cambodian women and migration. She explores the lives of women factory workers, street venders and prostitutes, arguing that the process of migration for these three groups is parallel and overlapping (2005). The ramifications for Cambodian kinship and gender roles, marriage patterns, social status, and a host of other issues raised by this massive migration have barely begun to be researched and understood.

## The Real Probabilities of Progress in the Field

It is certainly much easier to conduct research in Cambodia today than it was in the 1990s as one can now get permission to live and conduct research in rural communities. With the reconstruction of highways and other infrastructure it is now easier and safer to travel. Among the younger scholars undertaking this work are increasing numbers of Khmer. The university system, which was restarted in the 1980s, has now expanded rapidly with the opening of private universities since the turn of the century. Postwar baby boomers are turning eighteen at a rate exceeding 200,000 per year; with the colleges being flooded, a new educated middle and upper class will emerge. As has been the case with many countries, local scholars will begin to dominate academic analyses of their own society.

There are, however, limits on what can be researched and published, with a general unwillingness to criticize government leaders or policies openly for fear of accusations of "defamation" (a tactic used several times in 2005-2006 to silence people from labor unions, the independent media, and human rights organizations) or of direct violence.

## Conclusion

For an overarching analysis of the Khmer Rouge period, there are several standard works, including most importantly those of Chandler (1991, 1992,

1999), Kiernan (1985, 1996), Vickery (1984), Etcheson (1984), and Hinton (2005); but the limited information specifically on women must be gleaned from general sources, most importantly the first person narratives of survivors. More research has been conducted on women in post-conflict Khmer society, focusing on the dramatic shifts in social life and labor and migration patterns, but except for Dirk's thesis (2005), (soon to be published as a book), much of the work is narrowly focused and geared to an audience of development specialists.

## References

Banister, Judith, and Johnson, Paige (1993). "After the Nightmare: The Population of Cambodia," pp. 65-139. In Ben Kiernan (Ed.), *Genocide and Democracy in Cambodia. Monograph Series 41*. New Haven, CT: Yale University Southeast Asia Studies.

Boua, Chanthou (1982). "Women in Today's Cambodia." *New Left Review*, 1(31): 45-61.

Brown, Tim (2003). "HIV/AIDS in Asia." *Asia Pacific Issues*, 68: 1-8.

Carlson, E., and Rosser-Hogan, E. (1993). "Mental Health Status of Cambodian Refugees Ten Years After Leaving Their Homes." *American Journal of Orthopsychiatry*, 63 (2): 223-231.

Chandler, David P. (1992). *Brother Number One: A Political Biography of Pol Pot*. Boulder, CO: Westview Press.

Chandler, David (1999). *Voices from S-21: Terror and History in Pol Pot's Secret Prison*. Berkeley and Los Angeles: University of California Press.

Coates, Karen (2005). *Cambodia Now: Life in the Wake of War*. Jefferson, N.C.: McFarland & Co.

Criddle, Joan D. and Mam, Theeda Butt (1987). *To Destroy You Is No Loss: The Odyssey of a Cambodian Family*. New York: Atlantic Monthly Press.

Dirks, Annuska (2005). *Khmer Women on the Move: Migration and Urban Experiences in Cambodia*. Amsterdam: Dutch University Press.

Etcheson, Craig (1984). *The Rise and Demise of Democratic Kampuchea*. Boulder, CO: Westview Press.

Gender and Development Program (GAD) (1999). *Looking Forward, Looking Back: The First National Conference on Gender and Development in Cambodia*. Phnom Penh: The Gender and Development Program.

Harris, Ian (2005). *Cambodian Buddhism: History and Practice*. Honolulu: University of Hawaii Press.

Heder, Stephen (1980). *From Pol Pot to Pen Sovan to the Villages*. Bangkok: Institute of Asian Studies.

Him, Chanrithy (2000). *When Broken Glass Floats: Growing up Under the Khmer Rouge*. New York and London: W.W. Norton and Company,

Hinton, Alexander Laban (2005). *Why Did They Kill? Cambodia in the Shadow of Genocide*. Berkeley and Los Angeles: University of California Press.

Kiernan, Ben (1985). *How Pol Pot Came to Power: A History of Communism in Kampuchea, 1930-1975*. London: Verso.

Kusakabe, K. (2003). "Market, Class, and Gender Relations: A Case of Women Retail Traders in Phnom Penh." *International Feminist Journal of Politics*, 5 (1): 28-46.

Ledgerwood, Judy L. (1992). *Analysis of the Situation of Women in Cambodia*. Phnom Penh: UNICEF.

Ledgerwood, Judy L. (1990). *Changing Khmer Conceptions of Gender: Women, Stories, and the Social order*. PhD Dissertation, Cornell University. Ann Arbor, MI:

University Microfilms.

Ledgerwood, Judy L. (1996). "Politics and Gender: Negotiating Conceptions of the Ideal Woman in Present Day Cambodia." *Asia Pacific Viewpoint*, 37(2): 139-152.

Marston, John (Ed.) (n.d.). *Village Community and the Transforming Social Order in Cambodian and Thailand: Essays in Honor of May Ebihara* (unpublished manuscript).

Mortland, Carol A. (2002). "Legacies of Genocide for Cambodians in the United States," pp. 151-175. In Judy Ledgerwood (Ed.) *Cambodia Emerges from the Past: Eight Essays*. DeKalb, IL: Center for Southeast Asian Studies Publications.

Ngor, Haing (1987). *Haing Ngor: A Cambodian Odyssey*. New York: Macmillan Publishing Company.

Nou, Leakhena (2006). "A Qualitative Examination of the Psychosocial Adjustment of Khmer Refugees in Three Massachusetts Communities." *Journal of Southeast Asian American Education and Advancement*. http://jsaaea.coehd.utsa.edu/index.php/JSAAEA.

Panh, Rithy/ First Run Icarus Films (2003). *S-21: The Khmer Rouge Killing Machine*. New York: First Run Icarus Films.

Smith-Hefner, Nancy (1999). *Khmer Americans: Identity and Moral Education in a Diasporic Community*. Berkeley and Los Angeles: University of California Press.

Szymusiak, Molyda (1986). *The Stones Cry Out: A Cambodian Childhood, 1975-1980*. New York: Hill and Wang.

Tarr, Chou Meng (1996). *People in Cambodia Don't Talk About Sex, They Simply Do It! A Study of the Social and Contextual Factors Affecting Risk-Related Sexual Behavior Among Young Cambodians*. Phnom Penh: UNAIDS.

Ung, Loung (2000). *First They Killed My Father: A Daughter of Cambodia Remembers*. New York: Harper Collins Publishers.

Vickery, Michael (1984). *Cambodia 1975-1982*. Boston, MA: South End Press.

Zimmerman, Cathy (1994). *Plates in the Basket Will Rattle: Domestic Violence in Cambodia*. Phnom Penh: Asia Foundation.

## Annotated Bibliography

Banister, Judith, and Johnson, Paige (1993). "After the Nightmare: The Population of Cambodia," pp. 65-139. In Ben Kiernan (Ed.), *Genocide and Democracy in Cambodia. Monograph Series 41*. New Haven, CT: Yale University Southeast Asia Studies.

This piece is a demographic analysis of the loss of life during the DK years. The authors estimate a prewar population of 7.3 million people, with a decline to approximately 6.36 million by the end of 1978; given that the population of the country could have been expected to rise with births, they estimate a total loss of 1.8 million people in four years.

Becker, Elizabeth (1998). *When the War Was Over: Cambodia and the Khmer Rouge Revolution*. New York: Public Affairs, 502 pp.

Elizabeth Becker, a journalist, has given us one of the most readable accounts of the Cambodian revolution and the devastation of the DK period. She provides descriptions of life under DK by using first person narratives from interviews, memoirs, and the "confessions" extracted under torture at the S-21 prison facility in Phnom Penh (known after the war as the Tuol

Sleng Museum of Genocidal Crimes).

Boua, Chanthou (1982). "Women in Today's Cambodia." *New Left Review*, 1 (31): 45-61.

Chanthou Boua offered the first in-depth look at the lives of Cambodian women in the aftermath of DK, including documenting the sexual imbalance in the post-revolutionary population. She describes some of the hardships of the DK era, including the psychological trauma of seeing family die, the separation of family members, and forced marriages. The article focuses on women's additional physical labor in the aftermath of DK, particularly in agriculture, but also in industry and commerce.

Chandler, David (1991). *The Tragedy of Cambodian History: Politics, War and Revolution Since 1945*. New Haven, CT: Yale University Press, 398 pp.

David Chandler provides a detailed, readable discussion of Cambodian history since 1945, including the DK period. He does not focus on women, but does note that the Khmer Rouge enforced strict regulations regarding sexual morality.

Coates, Karen (2005). *Cambodia Now: Life in the Wake of War*. Jefferson, N.C.: McFarland & Co., 375 pp.

A journalist's account of contemporary Cambodian society across a wide range of topics including women's lives, health care, pollution, the environment and development.

Criddle, Joan D. and Mam, Theeda Butt (1987). *To Destroy You is No Loss: The Odyssey of a Cambodian Family*. New York: Atlantic Monthly Press, 289 pp.

Theeda Mam's first person narrative is from the perspective of a young woman. She confirms the puritanical nature of the regime, including the fact that male cadre were not allowed to search women by touching them, and sexual misconduct was punishable by death. She notes that no one had the energy for sexual encounters, people were so exhausted they only wanted to eat and sleep.

Dirks, Anuska (2005). *Khmer Women on the Move: Migration and Urban Experiences in Cambodia*. Amsterdam: Dutch University Press, 287 pp.

Dirks describes and analyzes the patterns of migration of young women from the Cambodian countryside into the cities, primarily to work in the garment factories that sprang up in the 1990s. While her focus is contemporary, she notes the roots of changing gender roles and new "modern" subjectivities in the changes of the DK and PRK periods.

Ebihara, May M. (1993b). "Beyond Suffering": The Recent History of a Cambodian Village, pp. 149-166. In Borje Ljunggren (Ed.), *The Challenge of Reform in Indochina*. Cambridge, MA: Harvard Institute for International Development, Harvard University Press.

Herein, May Ebihara extends her discussion of the DK period in Sobay village to include life under the PRK regime and the State of Cambodia (the renamed government that ruled from 1989 until UN elections in 1993). This piece contains a discussion of the dissatisfaction that villagers felt towards the *"krom samaki"* or solidarity group system of organized agricultural cooperatives.

Ebihara, May M. (1993a). "A Cambodian Village under the Khmer Rouge, 1975-1979," pp. 51-64. In Ben Kiernan (Ed.), *Genocide and Democracy in Cambodia. Monograph Series 41.* New Haven, CT: Yale University Southeast Asia Studies.

May Ebihara writes about the experiences of the people of a single village under the DK regime, a village she had studied first in 1959-1960 for her doctoral dissertation. The horrors of the period (e.g., exhausting labor, lack of food, illness, and executions) are described here on a personal scale; she writes that half of those that she had known from before the war survived, that the village was now some 80 percent women (though she would question the accuracy of these numbers in later publications), and some 40 percent of adult women were widows.

Ebihara, May M. (1974). "Khmer Village Women in Cambodia," pp. 305-347. In C. Matthiasson (Ed.), *Many Sisters: Women in Cross-Cultural Perspective.* New York: Free Press.

This classic piece explores the lives of women in prewar society by following women through their life cycle, describing women as: babies, young girls, pubescent women, married women and mothers, and as grandmothers.

Ebihara, May M. (1977). "Residence Patterns in a Khmer Peasant Village." *Annals of the New York Academy of Sciences,* 293, 51-68.

Discussion of prewar kinship, marriage and residence patterns among the Khmer --Khmer kinship is bilateral, tracing kin ties through both men and women; marriages were arranged and include bride wealth payments; and while there was an ideal preference for post-marital matrilocal residence, Ebihara found that in fact residence was usually decided based on a range of practical considerations, including where the couple was most likely to inherit land.

Ebihara, May M. (1968). *Svay, a Khmer Village in Cambodia.* PhD dissertation, Columbia University. Ann Arbor, MI: University Microfilms.

May Ebihara's two-volume, 600 plus-page thesis is now the standard reference on prewar Cambodia. It is a classic ethnographic description of life in a rural village, including extended discussions of kinship patterns, social organization, agricultural production, and Buddhism.

Ebihara, May M., and Ledgerwood, Judy (2002). "Aftermaths of Genocide: Cambodian Villagers," pp. 272-291. In Alexander Laban Hinton (Ed.), *An-*

*nihilating Difference: The Anthropology of Genocide.* Berkeley and Los Angeles: University of California Press.

This short piece summarizes some of the changes in Khmer rural villages in the aftermath of the DK regime, including: an overview of mortality statistics, the reconstitution of kinship and other social networks, the gender imbalance, the revival of Buddhism and the long term consequences of living under constant fear and threats of violence.

Gorman, Shioban (1999). *Gender and Development in Cambodia: An Overview.* Phnom Penh: Cambodia Development Resource Institute, 65 pp.

This is a NGO report on gender issues in the fields of education, health and labor/employment.

Him, Chanrithy (2000). *When Broken Glass Floats: Growing up Under the Khmer Rouge.* New York and London: W.W. Norton and Company, 330 pp.

Chanrithy Him was only eleven years old when she and her family were forced into the countryside. She describes watching people being executed; and she tells of her sister's forced marriage to a "base" person. Like the other first person narratives, hers is primarily a story of family trying to stay together and survive.

Jackson, Karl D. (Ed.) (1989). *Cambodia 1975-1978: Rendezvous with Death.* Princeton, NJ: Princeton University Press, 334 pp.

This collection of essays emphasizes some of the key ideas behind the DK regime, both in terms of foreign influences and Khmer historical and ideological roots. There are several essays that mention Khmer social hierarchy, family patterns and the role of women in society.

Kiernan, Ben (1996). *The Pol Pot Regime: Race, Power and Genocide in Cambodia Under the Khmer Rouge, 1975-1979.* New Haven, CT: Yale University Press, 477 pp.

Kiernan's fine grained descriptions of life under the DK regime are necessary reading for understanding details of what occurred; his argument that the regime was primarily driven by racism (rather than class based) is controversial but important to the overall analysis of DK.

Kumar, Krishna; Baldwin, Hanna; and Benjamin, Judy (1999). *War, Genocide and Women in Post-Conflict Cambodia.* Washington, DC: Center for Development Information and Evaluation, United States Agency for International Development, 46 pp.

The report is an overview of all of the Women's organizations in Cambodia, what activities they are engaged in and their social impact.

Ledgerwood, Judy L. (1992). *Analysis of the Situation of Women in Cambodia.* Phnom Penh: UNICEF, 161 pp.

Using interview data from three villages near Phnom Penh, this report discusses the place of women in Khmer society and provides a picture of village level economics in the post-war era. It includes data on family composition, education levels, resources, expenditures, and the sexual division of labor.

Martel, Gabrielle (1975). *Lovea: Village des environs d'Angkor—Aspects démographiques, economiques et sociologignes du monde rural Cambodgien dans la province de Siem-Riep.* Paris: Ecole Française de'Extrême-Orient, 359 pp.
Besides that of May Ebihara, this work is the only other ethnography of prewar village life in Cambodia.

May, Sameth (1986). *Cambodian Witness: The Autobiography of Someth May.* New York: Random House, 287 pp.
Sameth May's first person account of life before the war and during the DK period documents many of the key social aspects of the regime, including the break-up of families, extreme deprivation, and the high death toll.

Ngor, Haing (1987). *Haing Ngor: A Cambodian Odyssey.* New York: Macmillan Publishing Company, 478 pp.
Haing Ngor's first person narrative of the DK period is perhaps the most well-known of the books in this genre. Ngor, a medical doctor in Cambodia, was the actor who starred in the movie *The Killing Fields.* He is particularly insightful in describing the social breakdown that occurred in Khmer society. The book is highly graphic in detailing the physical violence that Ngor endures.

Ovenson, Jan; Trankell, Ing-Breitt; and Ojendal, Joakim (1996). *When Every Household Is an Island: Social Organization and Power Structures in Rural Cambodia.* Uppsala: Uppsala University, 99 pp.
The authors present the argument often assumed among development workers that Cambodian society was so damaged by the disasters of the Khmer Rouge regime that in the aftermath families only looked after themselves and there was no operating sense of community in rural villages. This work sparked an extended exchange on the issue.

Secretariat of State for Women's Affairs (1994). *Women: Key to National Reconstruction.* Phnom Penh: The Secretariat of State for Women's Affairs, 78 pp.
This is Cambodia's country report prepared for the 1995 Beijing Conference on Women. It provides an overview of the, then, recent history, levels of poverty, social inequities (including lack of access to credit, unequal access to education and health care, violence against women and the effects of continuing armed conflict) in some parts of the country.

Szymusiak, Molyda (1986). *The Stones Cry Out: A Cambodian Childhood, 1975-1980.* New York: Hill and Wang, 245 pp.

This first person narrative is one of only two of the early works that were written by women. Molyda is only twelve years old when the story begins; through her eyes we can see the working of the young women's mobile work teams, the harsh rule of the female cadre, the constant hunger, and the struggle for her and her sisters to stay together.

U, Sam Oeur (2005). *Crossing Three Wildernesses*. Minneapolis, MN: Coffee House Press, 367 pp.

U, a poet; provides one of the most detailed and well-written, first-person narratives of his life before, during and after DK.

Ung, Loung (2000). *First They Killed My Father: A Daughter of Cambodia Remembers*. New York: HarperCollins Publishers, 239 pp.

Luong Ung was only five years old in April 1975; the story she tells is partly her own and partly reconstructed from the memories of her family members. From her child's eyes we see the workings of a children's work camp.

UNICEF (1990). *Cambodia: The Situation of Children and Women*. Phnom Penh: United Nations Children's Fund, Office of the Special Representative, 189 pp.

This book is one of the first good postwar overviews of the social situation, including the few statistics that were available at that time on education, health and nutrition, agricultural production, and women in development.

Vickery, Michael (1984). *Cambodia 1975-1982*. Boston, MA: South End Press, 361 pp.

This book is an important source on the details of the regional variations in conditions under the DK regime. That said, the interpretations that Vickery draws from these data are controversial, particularly among Khmer survivors. He argues, in part, that the conditions were, at least initially, not so bad, and that it was the city people's weakness and inability to accept the living conditions of peasants that made the period difficult to bear. He argues that a single narrative, what he calls the "standard total view" (STV), developed by journalists and outside researchers, assumed the same conditions nationwide and exaggerated the worst features of the regime.

Yathay, Pin. (1987). *Stay Alive, My Son*. New York: The Free Press, 240 pp.

Pin Yathay's first person narrative account of the DK period begins April 17, 1975 when the new regime comes to power. Pin Yathay was an engineer, and, like Haing Ngor and Sameth May, he was from among the urban elite. He lost seventeen members of his family.

# 5

# The Plight and Fate of Women During the Crisis in the Former Yugoslavia

*Ivana Macek*

## Introduction

Women are often portrayed as peaceful and passive victims in situations of political mass violence such as that which afflicted the former Yugoslavia in the 1990s. It is true, of course, that during periods of war and genocidal violence women experience (much as men do) poverty and starvation, damaged and destroyed homes, forced exile, the splitting up of families as members are wounded and killed, and the loss of social networks, jobs and health—not to mention the fact that they are also frequently shot, tortured, and killed as well as perceived as sexual and cultural "objects" and used as such when they are sexually assaulted. It is equally true, though, that during such periods of violent upheaval and mass killing, women also struggle to protect human rights, organize politically, work within war economies to provide for their families, and serve as physicians, teachers, journalists, aid workers, soldiers, and politicians. And while women are frightened, depressed, and disillusioned when faced with such cataclysmic violence, it is also true that some actually become clear-minded and energetic political visionaries of a better future.

Women, though, are frequently not recognized as political subjects. Women's agency in supporting and promoting national causes and violent solutions is frequently overlooked or ignored; the same is true, of course, of those women who struggle against nationalistic politics that result in war and genocide. Indeed, accounts and traditional (male) analyses of war's effects on a society often ignore the vast domains of women's activity and gender-specific experiences. Thus, vast expanses of a society's very ontology and epistemology go unacknowledged—as do women as social subjects. By not seeing women as active subjects in their own right, their suffering is diminished. On one level this was true of the mass rapes perpetrated against females in former Yugoslavia. While such rapes were the first rapes in history to be recognized as war crimes (and consequently prosecuted within an international court of law—the International Criminal Tribunal for the former Yugoslavia (ICTY)), it is also true that the women were recognized only in their role as members of a nation *and* as the means for men of the other nation to humiliate and conquer the men of the raped women's nation. As a result, the multilayered shame and the bodily harm that the women actually experienced was not truly accounted for.

What is also not readily recognized is that what transpires in peacetime is "played out" all over again, though on a larger and broader scale, during periods of violent conflict. For example, when a woman is raped during peacetime, she is often shunned and looked at askance by her fellow citizens, if not certain (often male) family members. In light of this, it is no surprise when genocidal rape results in both personal and cultural shame. Indeed, the politicized shame of genocidal rape in the name of nation is not really possible without its peacetime corollary.

---

### Overview of the Seeds of the Crisis in the Former Yugoslavia

As is true of any political crisis, the causes, evolution, and ramifications of war and/or genocide are complex. That was certainly the case in regard to the former Yugoslavia. At work were "a cluster of factors, including economic instability, the rise of nationalistic leaders after Tito's death, the deliberate revival and exploitation of historical traumas from World War II, and the barbaric war in Croatia that preceded war in Bosnia" (Mennecke and Markusen, 2004, p. 420).

As Mennecke and Markusen (2004) note:

[D]uring the 1980s, Yugoslavia began to experience worsening economic problems. Its productivity declined due to mismanagement and technical obsolescence in many industries and loans from international lenders that helped support Yugoslavia's growth and standard of living had created a massive national debt. After Tito's death in 1980, unemployment increased, and many Yugoslavs worried about their economic futures.

....As the national economic condition deteriorated, tensions within and among the constituent republics developed and escalated. In 1981, less than a year after Tito's death, armed confrontations occurred by Albanians and Serbs in the Serbian province of Kosovo. By 1986, prominent academics in Belgrade warned of potential genocide against Serbs in Kosovo by the Albanian majority. Moreover, the relatively rich republics of Slovenia and Croatia increasingly resented the fact that tax monies they contributed to the federal government in Belgrade were being invested in what they perceived as pro-Serbian projects and services.

Tito's death created a dangerous political vacuum. No leader emerged to replace his commitment to discouraging ethnic politics and promoting "Brotherhood and Unity." Indeed, just the opposite occurred. In May 1989, Slobodan Milosevic became president of Serbia and quickly consolidated power by purging the government and Yugoslav military of potential critics or rivals and assuming control of the powerful Serbian secret police....

In 1990, Franjo Tudjman was elected president of the Croatian republic.... Tudjman, the leader of the right-wing, nationalistic Croatian Democratic Union (HDZ) quickly instituted changes in the Croatian constitution that greatly increased his presidential powers and pushed through laws that were openly discriminatory against the Serbian minority in Croatia. Like Milosevic, Tudjman exploited the Croatian media to arouse tensions between Serbs and Croats.

[At one and the same time,] Milosevic was resurrecting traumatic memories of Serb victimization under the Ustasha [during World War II] and Croatian President Tudjman was "rehabilitating" the Ustasha regime. [Thus, it was] not "ancient hatreds'" [as some claimed,"] but the deliberate exploitation of the recent past by two skillful, power-driven leaders [that] helped push Yugoslavia into atrocious conflict.

...Yugoslavia's descent into war and genocidal violence began in 1991, when the republic of Slovenia and then the republic of Croatia declared their independence, with the republic of Bosnia-Herzegovina following in 1992. While the war in Slovenia, where very few Serbs lived, lasted only ten days and caused fewer than 50 deaths, the conflicts in Croatia and Bosnia were vastly more deadly and destructive. ...The war in Bosnia-Herzegovina (Yugoslavia's most ethnically diverse republic, with approximately 40 percent Muslims, 33 percent Serbs, and 12 percent Croats) began only a few months after the war in Croatia ended. It was a complex, vicious conflict that lasted more than three years and resulted in the death of as many as 200,000 people, including many civilians. Among the armed factions engaged in the conflict were Bosnian Serbs, Bosnian Muslims, Bosnian Croats, regular army and paramilitary forces from Croatia and Serbia, mercenaries, United Nations troops, and NATO soldiers (pp. 420-421, 424, 415-416).

## Overview of the Plight and Fate of Females as the
## Former Yugoslavia Crumbled

Women of former Yugoslavia shared a common socio-political background of living in the same one-party communist and socialist state for at least forty-five years, even though cultural specifics between different parts of the country, and between urban and rural surroundings, varied. Educational levels and the standard of living, in fact, varied considerably between rural and urban areas, and consequently so did women's roles and possibilities. Urban women had generally better living standards, were better educated and were to a larger extent employed outside of their homes, earning salaries.

The presence of women in politics was a legacy of World War II where Partisan and Communist women joined the struggle in the hope and promise of gaining equality—not only between social classes and Yugoslav nations, but also between men and women. The promise of equality versus the reality of equality were two different matters, though, and this was true because the country was mostly rural and patriarchal.

Apart from the differences between urban and rural areas, there was also a geographical difference, with more favorable conditions in the Northwest of the county and less favorable in the Southeast. Although this was primarily due to historical differences, the issue of natural resources also came into play. The Northwest parts of the country developed more industry and infrastructure due to the vicinity of strong Central European empires, which after the Second World War became modern and relatively powerful states. The Southeastern parts had more natural resources in the form of water, coal and various metals, but were further away from European centers of economic and political power.

As the crisis began to unfold in the former Yugoslavia in the 1990s, women faced increasingly dangerous and demanding life circumstances. Physical dangers had to be dealt with, basic subsistence had to be provided in a situation of increasing poverty, new social relations had to be forged and managed, and new political ideologies closely connected to nationalistic warfare had to be assessed. Everything was rapidly changing and demanded a reconsideration as to how one had lived one's life in the past and how one was going to do so in the present and future. *Everything*—the worth of life; relationships with family members, neighbors and friends; and the Scylla and Charybdis of political ideology, national identity, religious beliefs and world views. Of course, the latter was also true for men. Generally, though, a woman's situation during this period was also characterized by the additional responsibility of caring for the children and elderly members of their family. The latter influenced, in a decisive way, their strategies for tackling perilous day-to-day life during the 1990s.

The crisis became most pronounced with the first multiparty elections in 1990. The nationalists won in all the federal republics, and this is when the move towards establishing the various republics' sovereignty began. The first (during the summer of 1991) to attempt separation was Slovenia. The attempt was met by a short, one-week armed conflict, the short duration mostly due to the retreat of the Yugoslav Federal Army (JNA).

Both the make-up and the goals of the army began to change. Initially composed of young men from all parts of the former Yugoslavia whose duty was understood as protecting the people and borders of the entire Federation, it increasingly concerned itself with protecting the regions where the Serbian population was in majority. This "Serbification" of the army was due to the predominance of Serbian nationals in the ranks of officers and generals.

Tellingly, and significantly, beginning at this point in time, the women of former Yugoslavia became a major political force. They organized in various groups that opposed the militarization and demanded that their sons who were serving their obligatory army service be sent home. Within a relatively short period of time, though, this opposition split into anti-nationalistic and nationalistic factions.

As war broke out in neighboring republics, society as a whole became militarized and more patriarchal. As a result, domestic violence increased, job opportunities diminished, and women, children, and the elderly found themselves living in increasingly dire circumstances.

*The Impact of War on the Daily Lives of Women*

Even if they were not marked by horrible experiences of rape, exile, personal and/or material losses, all women during this period in former Yugoslavia faced daily survival in radically different living conditions from which they were accustomed. This was true whether the women were primarily attempting to protect and provide for themselves and their families or politically involved (either as supporters of their national causes and defenders of violence or as anti-nationalist and anti-war activists).

All women had to face the problems of supplying food and energy (wood, gas, electricity) for their families; losses of people close to them and changed social relations, either through death or flight; changes in their political ideology once the post-World War II notion of "brotherhood and unity" of former Yugoslav nations was taken over by nationalistic fear-and-hate ideology; and a reevaluation of their ethno-religious background that was forced upon people by the new nationalistic idiom (for more about this, see Bringa, 1993); and as a consequence of this, re-evaluation of their religiosity. Complicating matters was the fact that these problems were closely and indivisibly interconnected. Material interests and nationalist propaganda informed social relations. The case in point is the distribution of basic means of subsistence through religious humanitarian organizations. This meant that on the basis of their family's ethnoreligious background (sometimes obvious due to one's name, but not always) people went to a Muslim, Catholic, or Orthodox humanitarian organization where they were also required to more or less comply with the organization's religious customs and identity. As the religious identity was the basis of politicized national identities, this also positioned people on different sides in the war with all the conflicting moral implications of guilt and victimhood. Thus, in order to provide subsistence, women were forced to re-evaluate their religious "positioning," if not beliefs, as well as their national and politico-military allegiance. Again, women throughout the now fractured former Yugoslavia were faced with such problems. (For the case of Serbia see Nikolic-Ristanovic, 1999 and 2000; Mrsevic, 2000; Korac, 1998 ;and Hughes et al., 1995. For Croatia see Boric 1997, and for Bosnia and Hercegovina see Bringa 1993; Bringa and Christie 1993; and Macek 2000.)

Women were often left alone to support their families, while their men were drafted. In Sarajevo, for example, while men were not allowed to leave the country because of their duty as soldiers, women were not allowed to leave because of the so-called "working duty" ("working duty" was an obligation for all adults fit for work, and thus they were required to remain in place so they could continue to keep on working. If they did not have a job, they had to be readily available for work assignments by the authorities). In spite of the "working duty" requirement, there were very few jobs available—and even fewer that paid a decent wage. When men returned from the frontlines, they would bring with them some wood and food, and take over some of the physically more demanding duties such as fetching water. Tellingly, some of the returning soldiers observed that the dangers of living in the town were often much larger than at the frontlines.

To attempt to assist people, various humanitarian organizations were established, but the most helpful ones were based on religious belonging: Muslim Igasa, Catholic Caritas, Belgrade-based Adra, and Jewish Benevolencia. While Benevolencia provided warm meals for the homeless and helped a number of Sarajevans leave the town regardless of their nationality, the other organizations were more prone to only helping their own. For example, Caritas was relatively well equipped for providing food (and, at times, to help with travel), but only did so for members of the Catholic Community. That said, anybody who wanted to convert to Catholicism or could provide a certificate of some ancestor being Catholic was, ultimately, helped by Caritas. Choosing the pragmatic approach, many women searched for a Catholic ancestor or sometimes even opted to convert (which, in both cases, meant that they had to accept having a Catholic priest enter into and bless their home)—and that was true despite the fact that the entire affair was often perceived as a repetition of the Croatian attempt at Christianizing Bosnian Muslims during World War II.

Igasa, on the other hand, primarily assisted the medical sector by providing salaries for the medical staff. Many women accepted medical-related jobs, even though it meant covering their hair with a shawl (at least while at work).

In actuality, employment in a foreign organization was the best way of earning a salary. Mostly young people, though, were offered such jobs for they were the most fluent in different languages and/or knew how to operate computers.

In the war economy, it was enough that one member of a household (and households increased in size throughout the duration of the war as people moved in together for practical reasons) had such an employment. For young women, this meant an immense increase in status and self-assurance, something that has been difficult to maintain in the postwar period (which has been characterized by a return to the prewar norms, aided by religiously re-enforced patriarchal social values).

As the war progressed, families were split asunder. When possible, in order to protect the children, the latter were often sent away. In other cases, women with children and elderly family members were forced to relocate.

Many so-called mixed marriages, marriages where spouses were of different nationalities, faced overwhelming challenges when people of one nationality were portrayed and treated as villains. Even the strongest marriages could crack, which often resulted in split ups. Spouses, of course, were not the only ones forced to negotiate their relationships in terms of new national identities and the war's destruction; indeed, relationships between and amongst friends, neighbors, and colleagues also had to be negotiated. Many uprooted themselves and left their old lives behind; some offered farewells and explained the reasons behind their departure, others just disappeared. Some bonds were kept, but many were destroyed. And, of course, new ones were established and strengthened by similar choices and destinies as a result of the war.

## The Plight and Fate of Women as a Result of Genocidal Actions within the Former Yugoslavia

*Women in Exile*

Other than in Bosnia and Hercegovina, most women remained in their villages, towns and cities throughout the war. As for the case of Bosnia and Hercegovina, it is estimated that approximately half of the female population was driven from their communities or fled from their homes—in certain cases, several times.

Women in both groups—those who remained and those who left—frequently lost everything they owned. Those who remained had their homes and other material goods either destroyed or damaged as a result of warfare and/or looting. As for the women who became refugees, their situation was often worse. Not only were they forced to leave much behind but life in their new surroundings was almost unimaginably difficult due to the fact that they were largely bereft of officially recognized status, without which they could not obtain normal social security and employment opportunities. Such women were not only in need of help with mere subsistence, but also in need of health care for their health was often damaged by the years of war (e.g., the lack of proper nutrition, lack of medical care, etc.). Exacerbating the entire situation was the fact that these women were virtually bereft of any type of social network. And since women were frequently the only providers for their families, they ended up being greatly dependent on the local peoples' will to understand and support them.

Although not always officially recognized, refugees nevertheless were "stamped" as being refugees, the "others," and thus not perceived as part of the local population but a second-rank people. Those who had relatives were better off, but as it turned out, even those who fled from Bosnia to the country that was now the national home of their group were discriminated against—this was true in both Croatia and Serbia. The only other significant group of refugees, Croatian Serbs who fled to Serbia in 1995, met the same destiny. It seems that being a refugee was the paramount identification, stronger than the alleged homogeneity and solidarity among the members of the same national group.

Still, it is also true that in Bosnia and Hercegovina, Croatia, and Serbia, women's organizations such as *Medica Zenica*, The Women's Infotek in Zagreb, The Centre for Women War Victims in Zagreb, Women in Black in Belgrade, and Centre for Women Studies in Belgrade not only provided humanitarian assistance, but employment opportunities and human understanding. In countries outside of former Yugoslavia, so called "third countries," where institutions were more entangled in bureaucratic red tape, refugees had to rely on help and support—at least until they were granted permanent residence and employment permits or sent back to former Yugoslavia—from each other, private individuals, and various NGOs.

One might think that leaving behind the nationalist battlefields of former Yugoslavia would free women of at least the turmoil and agitation of the forced religious and national re-evaluation and re-identification processes. But the latter was far from true. In the "diaspora," nationalistic and religious revival was often even stronger than in the home-countries, and people were faced with a choice of either joining or being left adrift and all but totally alone. Of course, those with a network of friends could better resist such pressure.

Apart from losing their homes, families and friends, and of being confronted with extremely difficult economic, health and social situations, women in exile constantly worried about family members and friends they had left behind. Concomitantly, they often felt deep shame and guilt for leaving their people and their country. This was a price that is not really appreciated by those who stayed, and is also a situation that makes a return home almost impossible for some of the women.

*Women as Anti-War Activists*

The first opposition to the war came from the mothers of former Yugoslav recruits doing their army service in the former Yugoslav People's Army (Jugoslavenska narodna armija [JNA]). As most of young men serving in Slovenia and Croatia were from Serbia, the strongest organizations of Mothers Against War were in Belgrade.

In Zagreb, the women organized within the anti-war campaign, which was at the time the only real opposition to nationalistic and militaristic policies of the Croatian Democratic Community (Hrvatska demokratska zajednica [HDZ]). They organized to help women from Bosnia and Hercegovina when they were no longer recognized by the Croatian government due to the fact that Croatian and Muslim troops in Bosnia and Hercegovina started fighting each other in early 1993. The primary goals aimed to help women become active, get jobs, and earn money to support themselves, *as well as to help them heal their trauma and to move on with their lives, to make their own choices and not to fall into the victimhood of a helpless refugee.* They also set out to help women rebuild trust in themselves and regain a modicum of dignity that had been bleached out of them. One way in which they went about this was to make it possible for those who suffered to provide support for new refugee women. (The structure, aims and work of these NGOs has been well described by, for example, Lindsey 2002; Kesic, et al., 2003; Boric, 1997; Korac, 1998; and Hughes et al., 1995).

### A Change of Heart: Women Working for the National Cause

Initially, in NGOs such as Medica Zenica, The Women's Infotek in Zagreb, The Centre for Women War Victims in Zagreb, Women in Black in Belgrade, and the Centre for Women Studies in Belgrade, women combined their humanitarian work with anti-war efforts and, consequently, with anti-nationalistic, anti-patriarchal and broader gender activism. Such NGOs were for equality no matter one's gender, sexual orientation, political ideology, nationality, religion, occupation or age. However, as Morokvasic (1998) observes, in the case of Serbia, following the disintegration of former Yugoslavia into successor states, some of the women in the original movement of Mothers Against War chose to form new organizations that aligned themselves with the interests of their new nation-states (see also Lindsey 2002). The same thing happened in Croatia and Bosnia and Hercegovina. Organizations such as the Women's Movement for Yugoslavia in Belgrade and Bedem Ljubavi in Zagreb were founded. Mothers who wanted their sons out of the Yugoslav army offered them willingly to join the Croatian fighting formations that were soon to become the Croatian Army (HV) in Croatia and the HVO in Bosnia and Hercegovina. Their initial reason for wanting their sons out of the Yugoslav Army (JNA) was that soldiers had shot at civilians in 1991. Ultimately, though, the reason changed and turned into an objection that the army shot at Croats. Joining an army that would shoot at non-Croats was for these women permissible.[1] Not surprisingly, the local propaganda had it that Croats had to fight in order to protect themselves, nothing else. Subsequently, the Muslims followed suit.

So, to arms they, the women of the former Yugoslavia, took—or at the least, they gravitated to supporting the symbols of war and actual bloodshed. Indeed, they supported their compatriots and discriminated against others. They sent their sons, husbands and brothers to war. More powerful and insightful women, though, sent them abroad.

Women can and do, of course, support and promote violence, even if they are not the primary bearers of weapons. The general picture of women in the former Yugoslavia as victims and as persons of peace has been enforced by the almost exclusive focus on women as refugees and victims of rape. That said, there were women who took to arms during the crisis, and while they were rather limited in number they did exist.

Some years before the war, the former JNA[2] started accepting women as recruits and their numbers would have probably been larger had it not been for the revival of traditional patriarchal values and the proliferation of religious practice and propaganda in the public sphere that went hand-in-hand with new nationalistic sentiments. As the latter increased in intensity, women were increasingly objectified into bearers of the nation's reproductive power, as well as of its purity and thus "had to be" increasingly controlled and protected (Morokvasic, 1998 and Olujic, 1998). While before the war the objectification of women made it possible for men to compete with each other, assert their identity as men ("manliness"), secure the reproduction of the kin, and assert their honor, in war these individual and kin interests turned into national interests (Olujic, 1998). Subsequently, women's bodies became battlefields for the nation's dignity, purity, and continuity.

Before the war, women as subjects had certain cultural channels of resisting and counteracting male objectifications of their femaleness (Olujic, 1998, pp. 36, 47). Professional, mostly urban, women also had certain economic independence, as well as the opportunity to choose how they wanted to live their family life. In war, the objectification in the name and interest of the nation was counteracted by anti-war activism and feminist-grounded healing methods.

Tellingly, and significantly, from a nationalistic perspective, a raped woman was and is a disgrace for men, and pollutes the nation. It also signals the male's inability as a protector and an able fighter. Thus, the female no longer is "simply" an individual who has suffered severe physical and emotional injuries.

Again, from the nationalistic perspective, a woman who lost a son, husband, brother, or father was a victim of the enemy's cruelty, but also a hero of the nation. She was no longer considered a person suffering sorrow due to the loss of a loved one or one who was in need of economic, social, and/or emotional support. Furthermore, a female was perceived as a traitor if she did not remain and suffer on the behalf of her nation. She was not considered a person who had lost her social context or one who could never hope to feel truly at home anywhere ever again, which is exactly what many women felt. Some women chose to attempt to heal by embracing the locally served nationalistic interpretations, others tried to find more individual (and cosmopolitan) ways of reestablishing their emotional, professional and economic well-being. The nationalistic road was probably hardest for the raped women, because of the "shame" that their suffering induced upon the nation, that is, the nation's men. Tellingly, the international recognition of rapes and historically unique treatment of rapes as war crimes did not seem to affect the local jurisdiction and opinion in a significant way.

*Rape*

The Bosnian Ministry of Interior estimates that between 20,000 and 50,000 females were raped. Most were Muslim, but also included in that number are Serbians and Croatians.[3] The numbers are an approximation drawn from testimonies by women in the ICTY and based on information provided by various humanitarian workers and journalists. According to these sources, many females were raped in their homes, while others were taken prisoner and held in different houses or cafés that served as brothels. Still others were taken to "camps," some of which were labeled and served as "rape camps." Names such as Trnopolje, Doboj, Hotel "Vilina vlas" in Visegrad, Miljevina near Foca, an oil refinery in Slavonski Brod, and Dretelj near Capljina are just some of the many that served as rape camps. Witnesses from some of these places report that women were often kept until they became pregnant and frequently up to the point at which it was impossible to end the pregnancy.

Information on rape in wars and genocidal violence is difficult to obtain because rapes are often considered to be a constituent part of politico-military violence. But, as previously noted, in the case of former Yugoslavia, rape was also used as a means of nationalistic war and as such it has attracted immense international attention. For the first time, rape was prosecuted at an international court of justice (in this case, the International Criminal Court for the former Yugoslavia or ICTY), as a war crime, crime against humanity, and as an act of genocide.

Unfortunately, such rapes have often been treated within the former Yugoslavia as a way men of one nation could hurt, humiliate and defeat the men of the other nation. The point is, the horror suffered by the females, both during the egregious act, as well as in the aftermath, is often largely overlooked.

Rape, of course is *not*, in the first place, an act of men against other men. Rape is in, the first place, an act of harm by men against women. Raped women hurt physically, and they hurt emotionally. Their shame is double because their most intimate identity as sexual beings is violently taken away from them. To this shame, the cultural shame of being cast from their group of kin due to their "sexual impurity" is added, no matter how innocent the women are. In the case of former Yugoslavia, this cultural shame was also purposely extended for political purposes, and thus the rape of a woman was perceived as shame for the whole nation.

In the aftermath of the crisis, there were some attempts to restore the dignity of raped women by declaring them the victims of war and a nation's heroes, but to date the deeply rooted feelings of shame are still there—now in a triple way: personal, cultural, and political. The personal and cultural shame is not taken into account in the court of law where women are seen only as members of their nations and as the means for men to humiliate and triumph over each other.

This author finds Lindsey's (2002) plea for a broader and situated scholarship about the fate of women who were raped most helpful and hopeful. Instead of focusing on evidence, numbers and ethnicity, the focus should be on the socio-cultural context in which rape is an accepted part of gendered life, and how that was so prior to, during, and following (through today, in fact) the crisis. Only then can we start to understand the socially embedded and culturally pregnant picture of gender relations, roles and symbols: of male dominance and activity, political as well as sexual—and of female support and passivity, political as well as sexual. Only then can we also begin to better understand rape as an act of hatred and violence against women. Indeed, rape as a part of inter-ethnic conflict can be properly understood only against this socio-cultural background. In the case of former Yugoslavia, a number of authors such as Silva Meznaric (1994), Mirjana Morokvasic (1998), Maria Olujic (1998), and Sabrina Ramet (1999) have already attempted such an analysis.

## The Post-Crisis Period

The legacy of the crisis in the former Yugoslavia vis-à-vis women's engagement in political issues can still be seen, perhaps most vividly, in capitals like Belgrade, Sarajevo and Zagreb. Although activist organizations against nationalism and war are not as strong in postwar Bosnia and Hercegovina as they are in Croatia and Serbia, many women are still politically active as a direct result of the war. In Croatia and Serbia, the anti-war activists, fighters for democracy and human rights, as well as feminist organizations for gender equality, were all formed during the war and, one could say, still are the only real opposition to mainstream nationalistic politics.

## Critical Challenges Facing the Field

The real challenges in this field are the struggle for political empowerment of women in this region as well as for a de-traditionalization of the society and culture. As opportunities increase for women to work outside of their homes, greater economic independence and more freedom of choice should follow. The symbolic value of women is still a far cry from international standards for gender equality and human rights. Cultural gender stereotyping and religiosity play a major role in this, but the more modern institutions such as those that deal with health care and the legal system are still not gender-sensitive and thus continue to largely acknowledge and promote, respectively, male experiences and values.

Another challenge lies in how societies and politico-military crises are por-trayed in the international media, scholarship and the world of politics. The need to account for and understand women's experiences of every day life during such crises is largely ignored and seemingly passed off as that which is only important to women and not the larger society. In other words, what we need is a "thick description" (to borrow Geertz' term) of women's lives in war and during periods of genocide. Rapes are gruesome and thus important to recognize, of course, but women also need to be understood as family members, social beings, professionals and, in some cases, those who are politically active.

## The Real Probabilities of Progress in the Field?

As long as nationalists and traditionalists (be they in the political, religious, education or media spheres) remain in all but absolute power in former Yugosla-via, the prospects for women do not look good. The extremely difficult economic climate that accompanied the crisis and wars in the former Yugoslavia continues to this day and prevents women from more actively entering the labor force. It also seems easier for employers to offer worse work-conditions (e.g., lower salary, less leave, no bonuses, and no social or health insurance) to women than to men, which further devalues the place of women in society. Currently, the conditions for women in Croatia, for example, are still much worse than they were before the war. Female Croatians are encouraged by current social poli-cies to breed children rather than work as professionals—and this attitude and position goes hand-in-hand with the church and nationalist rhetoric.

Be that as it may, the crisis did open the door for a redefinition and new self-understanding for women. How women will use this situation is yet to be seen. Primarily through various NGOs and private initiatives, the international community has thus far played an important role in supporting women to find their own way and establish their own values privately as well as publicly. It seems that closer contact with the international arena of female intellectuals and activists could provide significant assistance to former Yugoslav women in achieving the post World War II goals of equality.

If international policy makers would only choose to make an effort to in-clude and make use of existing feminine ideology and experiences, as well as alternative ideas for inclusive and non-violent policies and way of life (such as, for example, promoted in Mertus 2000 and Cullberg Weston 2002) that comes out of the latter, this could result in real and positive progress, not only for the women of former Yugoslavia, but internationally. The basic view of feminine ideology, which is an alternative to traditional ideology, is that male violence against women and gender inequality, misogyny and other forms of discrimi-nation lies in facing the fact that it is not possible to stop war and violence in general without striving for basic change in society. This would include, for example, public consciousness raising about violence against women through documentation, legal analysis and changes in the law, and campaigning in the public space to address the systemic issues behind such—as well as, of course, the actual stanching of the violence.

## Notes

1.  I remember walking in Zagreb's largest park Maksimir in autumn 1991, the time when Croatian propaganda about Serbs being prone to violence while Croats were peaceful people was at its peak. I found it very hard to understand how and why a mother could dress her young, perhaps three year-old, son, in a camouflage uniform. The uniform that resembled the ones that many irregular units in Croatia wore at that time. What was she doing? Did the child enjoy dressing in imitation of his father, or uncle? What happened to the supposed Croats' love of peace?
2.  "Former" is used here due to the fact that with the dissolution of former Yugoslavia, the JNA ceased to be the army of all former Yugoslav people.
3.  These numbers do not include the domestic rapes that increased in numbers as a direct consequence of military violence, nor do they include the drastic increase of women forced into prostitution, misused also by the international personnel among others.

## References

Boric, Rada (1997). Against the war: Women organizing across the national divide in the countries of the former Yugoslavia, pp. 36-49. In Ronit Lentin (Ed.) *Gender and Catastrophe*. London: Zed Books.

Bringa, Tone (1993). Nationality categories, national identification and identity formation in "multinational" Bosnia. *Anthropology of East Europe Review*. Special Issue, 11(1-2): 69-76.

Bringa, Tone and Christie, Debbie (1993) *We are All Neighbours*. Granada Television.

Cullberg Weston, Marta (2002) *War is Not Over with the Last Bullet: Overcoming Obstacles in the Healing Process for Women in Bosnia-Herzegovina.* Stockholm: Kvinna till Kvinna Foundation, 80 pp.

Geertz, Clifford (1973) Thick description: Toward an interpretive theory of culture, pp. 3-30. In Clifford Geertz, *The Interpretation of Culture*. New York: Basic Books, Inc.

Hughes, Donna M.; Mladjenovic, Lepa; and Mrsevic, Zorica (1995). Feminist resistance in Serbia. *European Journal of Women's Studies*, 2, 509-532.

Kesic, Vesna; Jankovic, Vesna; and Bijelic, Biljana (Eds.) (2003). *Women Recollecting Memories. The Center for Women War Victims Ten Years Later.* Zagreb: The Center for Women War Victims.

Korac, Maja (1998). *Linking Arms. Women and War in Post-Yugoslav states*. Uppsala: Life and Peace Institute.

Lindsey, Rose (2002). From atrocity to data: Historiographies of rape in Former Yugoslavia and the gendering of genocide. *Patterns of Prejudice* 36(4): 59-78.

Macek, Ivana (2000) *War Within: Everyday Life in Sarajevo under Siege.* Uppsala Studies in Cultural Anthropology 29. Uppsala: Acta Universitatis Upsaliensis.

Macek, Ivana (2005). Sarajevan soldier story, pp. 57-76. In Paul Richards (Ed.) *No Peace, No War: An Anthropology of Contemporary Armed Conflicts*, Athens: Ohio University Press.

Mennecke, Martin, and Markusen, Eric (2004). Genocide in Bosnia and Herzegovina. In Totten, Samuel; Parsons, William S.; and Charny, Israel W. (Eds.). *Century of Genocide: Critical Essays and Eyewitness Testimonies.* 2nd ed. New York: Routledge, pp. 415–447.

Mertus, Julie A. (2000) *War's Offensive on Women: The Humanitarian Challenge in Bosnia, Kosovo, and Afghanistan.* Bloomfield, CT: Kumarian Press Inc.

Meznaric, Silva (1994). Gender as an ethno-marker: Rape, war, and identity politics in the former Yugoslavia, pp. 76-97. In Valentine M. Moghadam (Ed.) *Identity, Politics and Women. Cultural Reassertions and Feminisms in International Perspective.* Boulder, CO: Westview Press.

Morokvasic, Mirjana (1998). The logics of exclusion: Nationalism, sexism and the Yugoslav war, pp. 65-90. In Nickie Charles and Helen Hintjens (Eds.) *Gender, Ethnicity and Political Ideologies.* London: Routledge.

Mrsevic, Zorica (2000). Belgrade's sos hotline for women and children victims of violence: A report, pp. 370-392. In Susan Gal and Gail Klingman (Eds.) *Reproducing Gender. Politics, Publics, and Everyday Life after Socialism.* Princeton, NJ: Princeton University Press.

Nikolic-Ristanovic, Vesna (1999). Living without democracy and peace: Violence against women in former Yugoslavia. *Violence Against Women* 5(1): 63-80.

Nikolic-Ristanovic, Vesna (Ed.) (2000). *Women, violence and war: Wartime Victimization of Refugees in the Balkans.* Budapest: Central European University Press.

Olujic, Maria B. (1998). Embodiment of terror: Gendered violence in peacetime and wartime in Croatia and Bosnia-Herzegovina. *Medical Anthropological Quarterly,* 12(1):31-50.

## Annotated Bibliography

*Books and Reports*

Allen, Beverly (1996). *Rape Warfare: The Hidden Genocide in Bosnia-Hercegovina and Croatia.* Minneapolis and London: University of Minnesota Press, 180 pp.

This volume portrays war-rapes as a part of nationalistic projects rather than as a complex socio-cultural phenomenon based on gender role inequality existing already prior to the war.

Cale Feldman, Lada; Prica, Ines; and Senjkovic, Reana (Eds.) (1993). *Fear, Death and Resistance. An Ethnography of War: Croatia 1991-1992.* Zagreb: Institute of Ethnology and Folklore Research, Matrix Croatica and X-Press, 257 pp.

This volume by mainly female Croatian ethnologists sets out to document and analyze the impact of war on Croatian society. Based on a series of interviews with refugees and steeped in contemporary academic theory of identity building and violence, it highlights the otherwise marginalized perspective of the everyday impact of violence–a perspective that is sensitive not only to male, but also to female experiences of mass political violence.

Cullberg Weston, Marta (2002). *War Is Not Over with the Last Bullet: Overcoming Obstacles in the Healing Process for Women in Bosnia-Herzegovina.* Stockholm: Kvinna till Kvinna Foundation, 80 pp.

A report evaluating the Swedish NGO Kvinna till Kvinna's involvement in Women's Centres located mainly in Bosnia and Hercegovina. The psychologist who wrote the report comes to conclusions similar to other researchers: the lives of women are destroyed in many ways, mainly involving the loss of family, homes, social circles and job opportunities. The nature and level of traumatization are accessed though a line of semi-structured interviews and a questionnaire. At the end of the report recommendations are made for both international as well as local Bosnian and Herzegovian authorities and organizations: war affects women in a gender-specific way different to men, and involvement of women in the after-war politics and reconstruction is crucial in order to restore the vitality and capacity of a society.

Jambresic Kirin, Renata and Povrzanovic, Maja (Eds.) (1996). *War, Exile, Everyday Life: Cultural Perspectives.* Zagreb: Institute of Ethnology and Folklore Research, 305 pp.

This volume resulted from an international conference with the same title, held in Zagreb in 1995. It includes contributions by a number of renowned researchers and humanitarian aid workers such as Barbara Harell-Bond, Ger Duijzings, Herman Bausinger, Peter Loizos, Ina-Maria Greverus and Paul Stubbs. The articles are based on field work and include valuable first hand interview material. Negotiation of identities (national and in exile) is examined in a contemporary academic and humanitarian perspective. Chapters tackle questions of aid strategies, narratives, experience and memory, therapy and art, as well as future challenges facing anthropological research and humanitarian aid.

Kesic, Vesna; Jankovi, Vesna; and Bijeli, Biljana (Eds.) (2003) [1994]. *Women Recollecting Memories: The Center for Women War Victims Ten Years Later.* Zagreb: The Center for Women War Victims, 212 pp.

The second edition (in both English and Croatian language) of the original volume edited by Martina Beli, Rada Boric and Vesna Kesi. The work of the Centre is presented through its members' analyses, reports and personal reflections. Also included herein are the accounts by some of the women who found social and psychological refuge in the Centre. It is a tribute to women's political, anti-war and anti-nationalist organizing and activity that started with the war and continues up to this day.

Korac, Maja (1998). *Linking Arms. Women and War in Post-Yugoslav States.* Uppsala: Life and Peace Institute, 75 pp.

This report is based on interviews done mainly with women in Serbia, and thus addresses mostly women's organization in anti-war and solidarity groups in Serbia (e.g., Women in Black). Corroborating other gender sensitive research, the report points to the different and marginalized experiences of war that women share. It highlights women's political struggle for non-nationalist civil society of gender and human rights equality, marginalized by the mainstream male, patriarchal and nationalist discourse and politics.

Lentin, Ronit (Ed.) (1997). *Gender and Catastrophe.* London: Zed Books, 272 pp.

A collection of essays by academics and activists with the ambition to bridge the gap between the experience of violence of a (female) body, and the representation and/or use of this experience later on in (male) theory and politics. The volume also sets out to attempt to bridge the gap also between victimhood and "actorship" by situating gendered violence during a genocide into a wider socio-cultural and historical context of gendered power relations.

Among the many issues the various articles address are: black female slaves' birth-control strategies in America, Brazil and West Indies; women activist organizations during the war in former Yugoslavia; and the struggle for female memories of the Holocaust as well as the genocide in Guatemala in the 1980s. Of special interest are two articles: Rada Bori's "Against the War: Women Organizing Across the National Divide in the Countries of the Former Yugoslavia," and Euan Hague's (1997) "Rape, Power and Masculinity: The Construction of Gender and National Identities in the War in Bosnia-Herzegovina." (Both are included in this annotated bibliography as separate entries.)

Macek, Ivana (2000) *War Within: Everyday Life in Sarajevo under Siege.* Uppsala Studies in Cultral Anthropology 29. Uppsala: Acta Universitatis Uppsaliensis, 313 pp.

The everyday life is portrayed through all its ethnographic aspects – subsistence, social relations, psychological survival, formation of new national identities and politics, the role of religion and belief, as well as individual strategies for survival. The analysis is based on original material from first hand interviews with Sarajevans during the war. The theorizing, based on informants' perspectives as well as on contemporary anthropological theory of identity formation and mass political violence, promotes the usually marginalized view of the war, the one that often most significantly influences and portrays the female experience of war.

Mertus, Julie; Tesanovic, Jasmina; Metikos, Habiba; and Boric, Rada (Eds.) (1997). *The Suitcase: Refugee Voices from Bosnia and Croatia.* Berkeley and Los Angeles: University of California Press, 238 pp.

An invaluable document of the impact and consequence that this war has had on the population of former Yugoslavia, in particular the ones that have left their homes. Written accounts from over seventy-five refugees and displaced people are organized around themes of leaving, dreams of home, everyday life in refuge, children's voices and ways of starting new lives in places of their final refuge. Contributions vary in style mirroring the individualities of their authors. They are powerful in their straightforwardness and poignant honesty. With introductory and closing chapters by internationally renown scholars, writers and activists such as Cornel West, Dubravka Ugresic, Marieme Helie-Lucas, Judith Mayotte, and the editors.

Mertus, Julie A. (2000) *War's Offensive on Women: The Humanitarian Challenge in Bosnia, Kosovo, and Afghanistan.* Bloomfield, CT: Kumarian Press Inc., 157 pp.

A gender-based overview of situation in three different cases. The author, with help of Judy A. Benjamin in the Afghan case, uses her knowledge of legal procedures and experience of how humanitarian aid works, in order to give a valuable assessment and recommendations for future aid workers as well as policymakers.

Nikolic-Ristanovic, Vesna (Ed.) (2000). *Women, Violence and War.* Budapest: Central European University Press, 245 pp.

Grounded in the understanding that women's experiences of war have roots in their position in the pre-war society, the authors of the essays in this volume explore: the imbalance between sexes; the aftermath of war abuses; women's struggle as professionals, family providers and primary caretakers; and the impact of physical, sexual and psychological violence on victims of war. The research was done by a group of Belgrade-based criminologists and sociologists whose data was based on interviews with women mainly from Bosnia and Herzegovina in their refuge in Serbia and Montenegro. The theory is formed on the basis of women's experiences, rather than molding the experiences into hegemonic theories and discourses of others.

Ramet, P. Sabrina (Ed.) (1999). *Gender Politics in the Western Balkans: Women and Society in Yugoslavia and the Yugoslav Successor States.* University Park: Pennsylvania State University Press, 343 pp.

The pre-war socio-cultural background of gender relations is presented in a rich collection of articles. The volume is organized in two chronological parts, starting with the between the two world wars period and continuing with the period of the post-socialist states. It concludes with articles on literature and religion. Among other themes, the volume explores gendered power relations in traditional Yugoslav families, feminist movements in different former federal republics and different historical periods, political marginalizing, nationalism, feminism, homosexuality, and rape.

Stiglmayer, Alexandra (Ed.) (1994). *Mass Rape: The War against Women in Bosnia-Herzegovina.* Lincoln: University Press of Nebraska, 232 pp.

Authors of the volume have been criticized for graphic descriptions of war-rapes. This evidence-collecting approach narrowed the otherwise rich female experience of war. For the most serious and well informed critique of this volume see Lindsay (2002). (The latter is included in this annotated bibliography under "Essays, Articles, Chapters.")

*Essays, Articles, Chapters*

Boric, Rada (1997). Against the war: Women organizing across the national divide in the countries of the Former Yugoslavia, pp. 36-49. In Ronit Lentin (Ed.) *Gender and Catastrophe.* London: Zed Books.

This article by an academic and activist describes female experiences of war mostly in Serbia, Croatia and Bosnia and Herzegovina. The author contextualizes female war-experiences within female role and the realities of both before and after the war as politically and sexually passive as well as supportive of male politics and warfare. Women's destinies as refugees, but also as activists and survivors are described. As an example, the work of the Centre for Women Victims of War in Zagreb is given. The latter focuses on women creating real opposition to war and nationalist politics of "ethnically cleansed" states, by integrating local women and refugees (often illegal) into multiethnic teams of humanitarian aid and self-support groups.

Hague, Euan (1997). Rape, power and masculinity: The construction of gender and national identities in the war in Bosnia-Herzegovina, pp. 50-63. In Ronit Lentin (Ed.) *Gender and Catastrophe*. London: Zed Books.
This article provides an analysis of the inequality of male and female, casting the male as dominant over female. The example under discussion is the imagery of the Serbian and Bosnian Serb nationalist (para)military male, construed as dominant, powerful, aggressive and violent. The "enemy" is imagined and treated as a female, the case in point being rapes against non-Serb women, but also men who in this way ostensibly became reduced to "female-like subordination" and thus no longer constituted a threat as enemy soldiers.

Hughes, Donna M.; Mladjenovi, Lepa; and Mrsevic, Zorica (1995) Feminist resistance in Serbia. *European Journal of Women's Studies*, Volume 2, 509-532.
A good overview of women's groups in Serbia up through 1994. It is intertwined with personal histories and motivations. Valuable first-hand material.

Jambresic Kirin, Renata (1996). On gender-affected war narratives. *Narodna umjetnost*, 33/1.
The article tackles problems of memory, empowerment of female experiences of war and verbal violence from a gender perspective. The analyzed materials are various written records of this war by women authors. The problems of testimonial literature are also touched upon (see more about this under Lindsey 2002). It is an ambitious article though in parts hard to follow (over-theorized).

Jones, Adam (1994). Gender and ethnic conflict in ex-Yugoslavia." *Ethnic and Racial Studies,* 17(1), 115-134.
This article that has been much debated because its critique of feminist approaches highlighted war-rape of men and also posited that men are the primary victims of war-violence. As a consequence, the significance of war-rapes against women was diminished as well as the gender-specific suffering of women in war.

Jones, Adam (2002) Gendercide and genocide. *Journal of Genocide Research* 2(2), 185-211.
In this article, Jones reconciles the research and activism on war-violence against men on the one hand, and women on the other, thus altering the position he took in an earlier article where, various critics argued, he had minimized the significance of war-rapes against women and diminished the gender-specific suffering of women in war.

Lindsey, Rose (2002). From atrocity to data: Historiographies of rape in former Yugoslavia and the gendering of genocide. *Patterns of Prejudice, 36(4), 59-78.*

An important discussion of the way the mass rapes in the former Yugoslavia were perceived as a result of how they were reported and discussed in West, along with a rich and critical analysis of the relevant literature. Lindsey sees two main tendencies: one that focuses on testimonies, evidence, numbers, proving the rapes and waking the opinion in the West, and the other that tries to explain the rapes, rather than to prove them. The latter perspective she finds in Morokvasic (1998), Meznaric (1994), and Ramet (1999), who all integrate their analysis with a profound knowledge and analysis of the socio-cultural background of gender roles in former Yugoslavia. While the first perspective treats war rapes as a crime of one nation against the other, and moreover as a means for men to hurt men of the other nation, the second perspective treats rapes as crimes of men against women. The women are seen as subject, not only as symbols of men's, kin's and nation's honor and strength. Lindsey is critical of the first approach because its evidence is based on the collection of data, a categorization into types (e.g., types of rape: multiple rape, mutilation; types of violence: abuse and then murder; types of spaces where violent practice occurs: rape in a camp, rape during military attacks; and types of perpetrators) and then theorizing of this data, all of which, she asserts, diminishes the richness contained in the witnesses' own words. She finds that some Western authors (such as Allen, 1996; MacKinnon, 1994; and Stiglmayer, 1994) tapped into this impoverished and often ethnicizing and nationalizing identity discourse, which sounds very much like a national government's nationalistic discourse.

Lukic, Jasmina (2000). Media representations of men and women in times of war and crisis: The case of Serbia, pp. 393-423. In Susan Gal and Gail Klingman (Eds.) *Reproducing Gender: Politics, Publics, and Everyday Life After Socialism.* Princeton, NJ: Princeton University Press.

The reproduction of the patriarchal gender imagery of "mythic mothers" and "brave patriotic sons" in Serbian media, and its centrality to the forming of the nationalist war, is analyzed. While the independent anti-nationalistic press used the same type of traditional gender stereotypes, it was the feminist organizations that produced an alternative and critical rejection of stereotyped "mythic mothers" that willingly offered all of their sons to the war for their nation's survival. The feminist organizations are also the ones who rejected stereotypes of "brave patriotic sons" who, likewise, willing went to death. Such rejections opened the space for women and men to reconsider other possible (and honorable) attitudes towards the war and national belonging.

Meznaric, Silva (1994). Gender as an ethno-marker: Rape, war and identity process in the former Yugoslavia, pp. 76-97. In Valentine M. Moghadam (Ed.) *Identity Politics and Women: Cultural Reassertions and Feminism in International Perspective.* Boulder, CO: Westview Press.

Describes how men wage war and measure power between themselves through contesting the power and violence over women. The Serbian nationalist discourse in Kosovo is analyzed as well as the atrocities in Bosnia and Herzegovina. The author also discusses the importance of understanding the basic peacetime gender inequality of a patriarchal society in order to understand the process of nationalization of gendered roles and promotion of rape as a means of defeating the enemy.

Morokvasic, Mirjana (1998). The logics of exclusion: Nationalism, sexism and the Yugoslav war, pp. 65-90. In Nickie Charles and Helen Hintjens (Eds), *Gender, Ethnicity and Political Ideologies*. London: Routledge.

An important contribution to understanding women's experiences in this war. It begins by providing the political background to the ethnic and national division in former Yugoslavia. The author concludes that women's position in the new post-communist democracies has deteriorated due to militarization, impoverishment and an increase of traditional patriarchal values. More importantly, the author provides a concise and solid overview of the position of women in former Yugoslavia prior to the war, noting importantly that the socialist project of women's emancipation was the basis for women's war experiences. Thereafter, the author describes everyday violence and humiliation of women, women that organized themselves either against the war or for the national causes of their new states, the plight of displaced and refugee women, and women victims of sexual violence. She points out that although the war-rapes in former Yugoslavia are the first historical case of rape to be prosecuted as a war crime, this promotes the already culturally dominant view that rapes are crimes against a national/ethnic group—a perspective that made the mass rapes in this war a meaningful act. The fact that war-rapes are also crimes by men against women is overlooked, which makes the healing of women harder.

Mrsevic, Zorica (2000). Belgrade's SOS hotline for women and children victims of violence: A report, pp. 370-392. In Susan Gal and Gail Klingman (Eds.) *Reproducing Gender, Politics, Publics, and Everyday Life after Socialism*. Princeton, NJ: Princeton University Press.

An article about the Belgrade SOS hotline and the problems of marginalizing domestic violence. With a gender perspective, the patriarchal male dominated legal system and cultural values are analyzed.

Nikolic-Ristanovic, Vesna (1999). Living without democracy and peace: Violence against women in former Yugoslavia. *Violence Against Women* 5(1), 63-80.

An overview and discussion of the types of violence that women in former Yugoslavia have been subjected to as a result of war, lack of democracy, nationalism, militarization, the return to a more traditional and patriarchal gender roles, and the criminalization and impoverishment of society in general.

Oluji, Maria B. (1995). Sexual coercion and torture in former Yugoslavia. *Cultural Survival* 19/1: n.p.

A short discussion of political, juridical and individual aspects to war-rapes in Bosnia and Croatia. Rapes are seen as just one of the war crimes that should be prosecuted in order to heal the victims.

Olujic, Maria B. (1998). Embodiment of terror: Gendered violence in peacetime and wartime in Croatia and Bosnia-Herzegovina. *Medical Anthropological Quarterly* 12(1):31-50.

A feminist critique of Balkan gender roles and the culture supporting them. Rich with folkloristic material and grounded in the author's interviews with refugees in Croatia.

*Blogsites*

*Radio 92 Blogsite* (http://blog.b92.net/blog/22 )

This blogsite was initiated by Belgrade's independent Radio 92. It contains up-to-date information and debates on the current political alternative activism in Serbia. Among others, the Belgrade based writer and activist Jasmina Teanovic writes about her and other women's situations.

*Television Program*

Bringa, Tone and Christie, Debbie (1993). *We Are All Neighbours*. Granada Television.

A prize-winning documentary about an anthropologist (Tone Bringa) who had a unique opportunity to witness the escalation of mistrust and destruction of everyday lives, including cross-national relations, in a typical Bosnian village. Gender roles are portrayed from within the society thanks to anthropologist's personal relations with the villagers and knowledge of the socio-cultural milieu before the war. The documentary follows step-by-step the tearing of social fabrics through politicized violence in the lives of the nine women featured herein.

*Homepages*

*Belgrade Centre for Women Studies Homepage* (http://www.zenskestudie.edu.yu/)

This center promotes gender research, education and publishing in general, and follows the situation of women in Serbia in particular.

*The Centre for Women War Victims in Zagreb Homepage* (http://public.carnet. hr/czzzr/info.htm).

This homepage provides a history of the Centre's joint activities with women from Bosnia and Herzegovina, Croatia and those across the globe. The Centre runs a refuge for women (Rosa House), supports women's groups in Croatia and Bosnia and Herzegovina, organizes training in counseling and political organization skills, does advocacy work on women's issues, and has a broad international network with joint projects.

*Medica Zenica Homepage* (http://www.medica.org.ba)

An organization founded in 1993 for women victims of war. Initially, it provided psychological and medical support, mostly to victims of rape. Today, it provides psychological and medical support to women and children dealing with consequences of various war traumas. It is also active in educating and organizing women in the struggle to lead non-violent lives and gain equality personally, economically and politically.

*Women in Black Homepage* (http://www.zeneucrnom.org/)

An international NGO organizing women to carry out continuous silent demonstrations against all forms of violence, particularly political violence. The Belgrade branch (which this is the homepage for) was active in anti-war protests from the beginning of hostilities in former Yugoslavia, and continues its work through today by addressing various issues germane to women and human rights and women and civil society.

*The Women's Infotek in Zagreb Homepage* (http://www.zinfo.hr/)

This is the first information and documentation centre of this type in Croatia which promotes women's questions and history. Apart from managing data bases, the Centre also acts as a publishing house, a public library as well as an organizer of education, seminars and conferences.

# 6

# The Plight and Fate of Females During and Following the 1994 Rwandan Genocide

*Samuel Totten*

> *"For some victims, there is no life after rape; they lost their health and happiness. Women raped during the 1994 genocide in Rwanda lead a uniquely troubled existence and many feel their survival is its own form of torture. They are desperately impoverished, commonly infected with HIV/AIDS[1] and are responsible for several children. They see their lives as 'finished' or 'another form of martyrdom'; one woman described herself as a 'living dead person'" (African Rights, 2004, p. 1)*

## Introduction

Between April 6 and July 4 , 1994, an estimated 500,000 to 1,000,000 Tutsis and moderate Hutus were brutally slain in Rwanda by extremist Hutus and those who joined or were forced to join them in the genocidal slaughter.[2] Hutu family members murdered Tutsi family members, neighbors killed neighbors, colleagues (educators, business people, journalists) turned on one another, nuns and priests killed as well, and so and so forth throughout Rwandan society. Indeed, all components of society — including men, women, children, and the elderly — took part in the killing and were victims of it (even babies and fetuses in their mothers' wombs were purposely slain).[3] Schools, churches, hospitals, health centers, and maternity clinics were turned into places of mass slaughter. In certain cases, "wounded Tutsi women and girls were taken out of their hospital beds to be raped and violently abused in other ways" (e.g., "genital mutilation, having their breasts hacked off, [forced into] sexual slavery and forced to undergo abortion...") (Amnesty International, 2004, p. 6). Tutsi females of all ages (including little girls as young as six years old) were raped in front of their families, in their homes, along village paths, in the bush, and in roadways—indeed, in virtually in any and all places where they were caught. Other types of sadistic violence females were subjected to included "having arrows, spears or other objects pushed into their vaginas [and] being shot in the genitals" (Amnesty International, 2004, p. 6), which resulted in the deaths of some and serious injuries to those who survived (injuries that were not only unimaginably painful but resulted in numerous and severe health problems). Pregnant women, mothers who had just given birth, newborn babies and thousands of refugees "were macheted and blown apart by grenades inside maternity clinics" (Amnesty International, 2004, p. 208). After they were sexually assaulted and/or tortured in other ways, many were executed. Some perpetrators told their victims they weren't going to kill them just so they could suffer even greater torment by being alive and conscious as to what they and their loved ones suffered through. Ultimately, many females became pregnant with "rape babies." Many girls and women were left with internal injuries that not only continue to cause them physical and mental agony to this day, but which, in many cases, prevent them from ever having children (African Rights, 2006, p. 18).

Although the killers during the genocide were primarily men, the extent to which women took an active in role in a genocide was unprecedented (African Rights, 1995). In *The Order of Genocide: Race, Power, and War in Rwanda*, Scott Straus (2006), a political scientist at the University of Wisconsin, Madison, writes:

> To be clear, women did play important roles during the genocide. In particular, where women were in leadership positions at the national and local levels, they often were instrumental in organizing, promoting, and authorizing genocidal killing. Women participated in other ways during the genocide. Sometimes women looted, in particular after Tutsis were killed. Sometimes women told bands of killers where Tutsis were hiding. Sometimes women encouraged their husbands or sons to attack Tutsis. (p. 100)

Equally significant, "because men were the primary target of the genocide, women constitute a significant percentage of survivors"[4] (African Rights, 2006, p. 12).

The primary target of the killers was the Tutsi population, and the primary goal was the annihilation of the Tutsi population. Moderate Hutus, or those who opposed the policies and actions of the extremist Hutus and/or continued to consider Tutsis fellow Rwandans who deserved to be treated fairly, were also targeted by the extremists.

Tutsis were identified in various ways. To a large extent, the victims were either known by their killers or were pointed out to the murderers by their (the victims') former friends, fellow workers, employers, teachers, clergy members, among others. Still others were caught at roadblocks (as well as many other places, including their homes and churches) where they were forced to show their identity cards (which every Rwandan citizen was required to carry). A designation of Tutsi spelled certain death. In other cases, many (Tutsi and Hutu, alike) were killed by strangers who believed their victims looked like a Tutsi (tall and slim).

While many perpetrators of genocides in the last half of the twentieth century made use of various types of advanced technology to carry out their killings,[5] the killing process during the 1994 Rwandan genocide was "low tech." In fact, many have referred to the Rwandan genocide as "the machete genocide." That was largely due to the fact that the killers used machetes, a common farm implement in Rwanda, to carry out the killing. Along with the machetes, the killers used sharply pointed bamboo sticks, spears, and nail-studded clubs (*masus*). Many also used various types of farm tools, such as heavy hoes. Granted, certain killers used tear gas (to stun and temporarily "paralyze" people until they could be hacked with machetes or other weapons), grenades, pistols and rifles but, for the most part, a massive amount of the killing was done with the most rudimentary of weapons. Reportedly, victims who knew they were about to be murdered often begged (and, in certain cases, offered relatively large sums of money to) the killers to take pity and kill them in a "better way" – meaning by a shot to the head versus being hacked to death with a machete or beaten to death by a *masu*.

It is significant to note and recognize the fact that not all Hutus killed Tutsis or moderate Hutus; indeed there were those who refused to be coerced into killing and not a few were, themselves, murdered due to their refusal.[6]

## The 1994 Rwandan Genocide: An Overview

Space constraints preclude an extended discussion of the background, causes, major actors, and daily events of the 1994 Rwandan genocide, let alone the international reaction — or lack thereof to the genocide.[7] That said, in the following passage Lemarchand (1999) does an excellent job of providing a succinct overview:

> An estimated one million (out of 7.5 million) died at the hands of the Hutu militias, [along] with "auxiliary support" from the army, party activists, communal authorities and ordinary citizens who felt they had no choice but to kill their neighbors.... [As for the victims,] the vast majority belonged to the Tutsi minority, but thousands of Hutu from the south, identified with opposition parties, also perished....
>
> The 1994 Rwandan genocide has remote and proximate roots, but the two are intimately related. The watershed event was the 1959-1962 Hutu revolution. With substantial backing from the Catholic Church and the Belgian Trusteeship authorities, a radical shift of power took place in Rwanda preceding independence—resulting in the overthrow of the monarchy, the proclamation of a republican form of government, and the flight into exile of an estimated 200,000 Tutsis..., with the majority finding asylum in Uganda and Burundi. With the Tutsi minority excluded from participating in the political life of the country, the new Rwanda Republic was in fact if not in name a Hutu Republic. The Hutu revolution found its nemesis some

thirty years later when, on October 1, 1990, the RPF refugee-warriors proceeded to fight their way back into Rwanda. Most were sons of Uganda-based Tutsi refugees of the 1959 revolution....

The RPF invasion was a major factor behind [Rwandan President] Habyarimana's decision to accept the existence of opposition parties. Consistently accused by the RPF of behaving like a dictator, he had no option [but] to open up the countryto electoral democracy. Ready to challenge the ruling Mouvement Républicain National pour la Démocratie et le Dévelopement (MRNDD) stood the ethnically mixed Parti Libéral, the Parti Social Démocrate, and the Mouvement Démocratique Républicain.... All three parties...could conceivably be seen as potential allies of the RPF. To counter these threats, the MRNDD proceeded to recruit and train thousands of Hutu militias, most of them drawn from the unemployed youth of the capital. [They] numbered fifty thousand by the end of 1993. By then another party had appeared , the rabidly anti-Tutsi, violence-prone Coalition pour la Défense de la République, which soon joined hands with the MRNDD. No other party played a moredecisive role in driving a wedge between Hutu hard-liners and moderates, and in preparing the ground—through propa-ganda, political manipulation and the selective use of political assassination — for the genocide....

[M]onths before it came to pass, the genocide of the Tutsi population was already part of the strategy elaborated by members of Habyarimana's entourage to block the implementation of the Arusha accords and strengthen the hand of the hard-liners in dealing with the RPF.

The shooting down of Habyarimana's plane on April 6, 1994, [triggered the beginning of the killing]. In Kigali, the killing of opposition figures—Hutu and Tutsi—began moments after the crash. In a matter of hours scores of politicians suspected of RPF sympathies were butchered.... Some twenty thousand [civilians] were killed in Kigali in the [first] three weeks.... The bloodletting quickly spread from the capital city to the countryside. For days and weeks, in one locality after another, hundreds and thousands of Tutsi civilians (and civilians who looked like Tutsi), men, women, and children, were shot, speared, clubbed or hacked to pieces (pp. 508, 509, 511).[8]

Contrary to the assertions of many political leaders in Europe, the United States, and the United Nations, there were ample signs that the situation in Rwanda was heading towards mass, if not cataclysmic, violence. First, there were the ongoing small-scale massacres carried out by the extremists through-out the early 1990s. Then there were the editorials and articles in the extremist newspaper *Kangura*, and the screeds broadcast against the Tutsis over *Radio-Télévision Libre de Mille Collines* (RTLM). Finally, there were the warning signs that the UN Assistance Mission for Rwanda was picking up and relaying back to the United Nations headquarters on a regular basis.

Both in the pages of *Kangura* and over the airwaves of RTLM, the use of derogatory terms to refer to the Tutsis was commonplace. Some of the many degrading words/terms that were used to refer to Tutsis included the following: *"inyenzi"* (cockroaches), "snakes," and "dirt." While snakes are often considered dangerous, both cockroaches and dirt are, obviously, perceived as filthy and bad for one's health and thus constitute something that needs to be swept up, eradicated, discarded.

The extremists also used euphemisms to refer to their murderous actions —again, which were broadcast on RTLM. In addition to the frequent use of the word "work" to refer to the actual killing of someone and/or the killing process, the perpetrators used the term "liberate" for the rape of Tutsi girls and women.

## The Plight and Fate of the Female Victims

Like their male counterparts, females were killed in the most gruesome ways possible: beaten and shot dead, shot and then beaten to death, burned alive, stabbed repeatedly, slashed and hacked by machetes, blown up by grenades, trapped in churches and other buildings where they sought sanctuary and then slaughtered like cattle, forced from buildings in which they were hiding and then hacked to death, forced from hospitals and ambulances and then beaten and hacked to death, and forced to jump into rivers in which they drowned. In many cases, young girls were forced to undress and then made to march by militia to areas where they would be raped and/or killed. To heighten the cruelty and sadism of the killers, some mothers were forced to kill their own children.

In regard to the rape and murder of female victims during the genocide, African Rights (1995) has asserted that

> Unlike in the case of the killings, there is no evidence that the architects of the genocide had prepared lists of women they wanted to see raped, nor indeed that specific instructions went out to the *interahamwe* that they should rape women. But the exhortation to kill, destroy and humiliate the Tutsi, seize their property, slaughter and eat their cows and defile the churches where they sought refuge have a clear implication: rape their women. Women—and girls—were the "spoils of the genocide." (p. 83)

That said there were cases where local leaders, (including bourg estre) who encouraged their male counterparts to rape female victims.

The rapists came from all walks of life among the Hutu population: the educated and uneducated; soldiers; *gendarmes*; militia; peasants; and even the victims' own teachers and priests. Purportedly, "the interahamwe had purposely had those who were HIV-positive in their ranks rape the Tutsi women" (Temple-Raston, 2005, p. 155). There are documented cases where Hutu women encouraged, and, in some cases goaded, their neighbors and relatives (including their own sons) to rape Tutsi girls and women. In many cases, Tutsi girls and women were also forced to become chattel of Hutu men, in which they were forced to become slave laborers in homes and forced into the bed of their family's and friends' killers. Many of the men who enslaved their victims in order to rape them referred to the girls and women as their "wives."

In her book, *Justice on the Grass: Three Rwandan Journalists, Their Trial for War Crimes, and a Nation's Quest for Redemption*, Temple-Raston (2005) writes,

The exact number of women who were raped during the genocide is still uncertain. Figures compiled at the University of Rwanda at Butare indicate that more than half the Tutsi women who survived the genocide had been raped during the violence. Survivors confirmed that rape was wide-spread and that thousands of women were individually raped, gang raped, raped with objects, held in sexual slavery, or sexually mutilated. Many women were killed immediately after they were raped so they could not accuse their captors after the genocide ended. The women who were allowed to live were told they were spared so that they could, the *Interahamwe* said, "die of sadness," either because of the AIDs they had contracted or because they would be forced to raise a child conceived in a time of treachery....

Statistically, one hundred cases of rape give rise to one pregnancy. The United Nations determined that would mean there were at least 250,000 rapes, or at the high end, 500,000. The number is particularly stark when one realizes that in the wake of the genocide Rwanda has become a country of women: females make up about 70 percent of the population and lead more than half the households. (pp. 155, 156)

Straus (2006) questions the accuracy of those who claim the number of women raped reached 250,000:

The extent of sexual violence is unclear and may never be fully revealed. A commonly cited figure is 250,000 rapes committed during the genocide. The number is derived from the total number of "rape babies" reported after the genocide. However, according to the 1991 census, in Rwanda there were only 163,738 Tutsi women over the age of fourteen years old. Some Tutsi girls under the age of fifteen were surely raped, and some women were undoubtedly raped multiple times. However..., the killers quickly murdered most women, and they killed women at the same time as men. Thus, the figure of 250,000 rapes is probably too high, but a more accurate estimate is not currently possible. What can be said with certainty is that sexual violence was common and was an important dimension of the genocide. (p. 52)

Even if "only" half the generally estimated number of females were raped during the genocide (and nobody has or is making such a claim), the impact on the women, the babies born, and the Rwandan society is still nothing short of devastating.

### "Rape Babies"

Many of the girls and women who were raped became pregnant and had what many in Rwanda refer to as "rape babies." Without even considering the reality of what the phrase means, the juxtaposition of the words "rape" and "babies" is shocking. One can only imagine what it feels like to be referred to such, let alone how the individual children who have been deemed "rape babies" are treated by their mothers, family members and larger society.

Of the "rape babies," Temple-Raston (2005) writes,

The rape babies had arrived in the spring of 1995. The rapes were called *kubohoza*, which literally means, in Kinyarwanda, "to help liberate." The term was ironic and had its roots, like almost everything in Rwanda, in politics. When Rwanda first began its multi-party politics, political operatives used *kubohoza* to press people into changing their party affiliations. The term's meaning evolved. It came to describe the seizing of land, the robbing of cows or crops, and eventually it applied to the rape of women during the genocide....

The offspring of the 1994 violence were known as the *enfants non-désirés* (unwanted children), or *enfants de mauvais souvenirs* ("children of bad memories"). Others called them the "children of hate" or "little *Interahamwe*." There are between three and five thousand children in Rwanda today who are the result of the genocide. (p. 154)

There are a number of reported cases in which mothers of "rape babies" have said they can't stand being around the children they conceived, that they hate them, and wish they didn't exist. How prevalent such thoughts and ill-feelings are no one really knows. Temple-Raston (2005) relates the story of one women who told her that "there were many occasions when she would look at her son, Jean de Dieu, or Jean of God, and wish he were dead" (p. 156). Continuing, Temple-Raston (2005) reports that "When Jean would see his mother in the market, he would run up to her and throw his arms around her, calling her 'Maman.' She pushed him away. 'Call me your aunt, not your mother,' she would say. She wanted nothing to do with the little boy who was born of evil" (pp. 156-157).

Another woman, Berthilde, who lived in Taba in Gitamara, was gang-raped and subsequently became pregnant. About her child, she said, "At one point, I realized I was pregnant with a child I didn't want. I didn't know what to do. I even tried to bring about an abortion, but that didn't succeed. I gave birth when I was still in Zaire and the child was one more burden that I didn't know how to bear. I didn't have any affection for him" (African Rights, 2004, p. 8). Still another woman, Tabithe, said, "I wondered what I was going to do with this unwanted child, worse still, the unwanted child of an *Interahamwe*" (African Rights, 2004, p. 14). Equally sad is the following comment by another woman, Véréna, twenty-nine years old, who gave birth after being raped: "I love my child, but when I fall ill I hate her because it was the rape and genocide which is at the root of all my suffering, and then I hit her" (African Rights, 2004, p. 69).

Even where the mothers of such babies try to take care of their offspring, they face the prejudice of family members—many of whom the mother and child rely on for financial and other support (African Rights, 2004, p. 66). The husband of one young woman who was raped and gave birth to a "rape baby" reported that her husband (a widower of the genocide she met in a refugee camp) ultimately decided he wanted nothing to do with the child: "He told me that he didn't want the child of an *interahamwe*, so I should give her to the *interahamwe* and let them take care of her" (African Watch, 2004, p. 69).

## Female Collaborators and Killers

As alluded to earlier, females from all walks of life participated as collaborators and/or killers during the 1994 Rwandan genocide. These included, for example, uneducated peasant women and girls, school girls, teachers, nurses and doctors, local leaders, and even nuns. Tellingly, "many of the women…who participated in the killings in 1994…had also played an active role in the imprisonment of civilians in 1990, identified as RPF 'accomplices.' Some…are also said to have been active in the killings and purges of 1973" (African Rights, 1995, p. 61).

The roles the female perpetrators played were many, including the targeting of potential victims, overseeing the killing process, and, in certain instances, carrying out the killing. Some of the many types of collaborative activities with the killers undertaken by female Hutus included the following: identifying victims (by pointing out and/or developing lists of names of Tutsi and moderate Hutu for the killers); searching for documents in *cellules* in the various sectors, communes, and provinces that listed both the names and ethnicities of local residents; (teachers) handing over lists of their Tutsi students to the killers; providing information to the perpetrators concerning the homes and hiding places of the targeted population; handing people over – and this was particularly true of teachers, nurses and nuns— to the perpetrators; forcing Tutsis women from their homes and/or threatening the Tutsis women that their hiding places would be revealed to the *Interahamwe* if their (the Hutu women's) husbands continued to hide the Tutsis "or took any additional steps to assist them" (African Rights, 1995, p. 73); providing the *genocidaires* with petrol to burn people alive and/or burn down homes as well as churches and other buildings where people had sought sanctuary; distributing grenades and ammunition to the perpetrators; refusing to allow the targeted population to hide in churches, hospitals or other places where they might have had a chance of surviving; looting the dead and nearly dead; encouraging, if not ordering (depending on their role and position in society), men to rape girls and women and/or kill them; and, in some cases, even killing the victims themselves. Some, such as the infamous Rose Karushara (a councilor in the sector of Kimisagara, commune Nyarugenge in Kigali), even trained militia in preparation for the genocide.

As for the looting that took place, it has been reported that "throughout Rwanda thousands of women and young girls walked through churches, priests' rooms in parishes, schools, hospitals, maternity clinics, football stadiums and government buildings, snatching clothes from the dead, kicking over corpses and the seriously wounded as they searched for money, watches, and other materials. Almost invariably, there were wounded people and survivors hiding underneath corpses. Sometimes, the women and girls helped to finish them off before they robbed them" (African Rights, 1995, p. 81).

Just as the boys and men killed for various reasons, so did the female population. Some were extremists and true believers in the ideology of Hutu Power. Others were forced, often against their own will, to kill. Still others saw the deaths of fellow citizens (many of whom they had considered friends and colleagues only days before the mayhem was committed) as an opportunity to show their solidarity with the killers and/or to gain property and wealth at the expense of the victims.

Not surprisingly, women killed in much the same way as the men did: in some cases shooting or tossing grenades but more frequently slashing and hacking people with machetes and setting people on fire. Bizarrely, though, many of the women had their children in tow as they carried out their murderous acts.

Some of the women were especially vicious. For example, one woman, "an elderly grandmother in Gitamara was accused of having "murdered more than a hundred Tutsi baby boys" (African Rights, 1995, p. 58). Another woman, Solina Rwamakombe, "who compiled lists of Tutis to be killed in the *cellue*, including young children, said they [the perpetrators] should not spare a single baby, not even fetuses" (African Rights, 1995, p. 66). Similarly, Pauline Nyiramasuhuko, the minister for women and family affairs in the last government of Habyarimana as well as the interim government, who became notorious for the killings she oversaw and directed in Butare, ordered the militia "not to spare anyone, not even the foetus or the old" (African Rights, 1995, p. 91).[9]

### Rape, Genocide and a Monumental Finding at the International Criminal Tribunal for Rwanda (ICTR)

For centuries, both during and following violent conflict, rape was perceived by the perpetrators as "the spoils of war." In many parts of the world, that perverse attitude/stance remains in place today (Darfur, Sudan, being a classic example in the early part of the twenty-first century). Tellingly, despite the monumental attention that the international community focused on the issue of human rights throughout the twentieth century there remained no commonly accepted definition of rape in international law. That was, up and until the trial of one Jean-Paul Akayesu at the International Criminal Court for Rwanda (ICTR).[10]

Prior to and during the course of the 1994 Rwandan genocide, Akayesu served as the *bourgmestre* (mayor) of Taba, a rural community west of Kigali (the capital of Rwanda). A Hutu, he was the father of five children and had been trained as a teacher. For years he had been a highly respected local leader, and by most accounts his fellow community members perceived him as being a considerate and fair man. However, during the genocide he seemed to shed one skin and grow another—one that transformed him from a "peacemaker [to that of an] executioner" (Temple-Raston, 2005, p. 93). Temple-Raston (2005) writes that

> When Akayesu went on trial at the ICTR, in May 1997, he was not accused of being a mastermind of the genocide. He was, in many ways, something worse: he was the link between instigators and their followers. He was the highly effective middle management of the genocide. Without him, people in Taba said later, the massacres would not have happened. When he ordered them to kill, they did. When he ordered them to rape, they did that as well. (p. 94)

Continuing, Temple-Raston writes,

When one woman, who would later testify [at the ICTR] as Witness JJ, arrived in the [Taba] bureau's courtyard, she found sixty refugees already there, squatting in the mud outside the building. Most of the assembled were women and children. She noticed they were moving haltingly. When she got closer she realized something more horrifying: they had all been beaten. It was Akayesu, she said later, who had given the order....

Akayesu was also a party to something worse, the systematic rape of Taba's Tutsi women. The *Interahamwe* took young girls and women from the refuge near the bureau communal into the forest and ravaged them. It happened day after day. There were single rapes and gang rapes and violations of the most unspeakable kind. And while JJ never saw Akayesu rape anyone, she believed, as others did, that he could have prevented the rapes but never tried to do so.

The second time she was taken to the forest to be raped, she remembered seeing Akayesu standing at the entrance of the cultural center and heard him say loudly to the *Interahamwe*, "Never ask me again what a Tutsi woman tastes like." Then he grunted and said, "Tomorrow they will be killed." The Interahamwe stopped before Akayesu and told him they were taking girls away to "sleep with them," and he nodded approvingly. "Take them," he said. (pp. 94-95)

On September 2, 1998, Akayesu was found guilty of genocide and crimes against humanity. In announcing the verdict, the judges of the ICTR issued the first-ever judgment by an international court for genocide. While Akayesu had been indicted on fifteen counts of "genocide, crimes against humanity and violations of Article 3 common to the Geneva Conventions and Additional Protocol II thereto," he was unanimously found guilty of nine of the fifteen counts—and not guilty of six. More specifically, he was found guilty of "genocide, direct and public incitement to commit genocide, and crimes against humanity (extermination, murder, torture, rape and other inhumane acts)." In its finding of genocide, the Chamber stated that "There was an intention to wipe out the Tutsi in its entirety, since even newborn babies were not spared."

Significantly, during the course Akayesu's trial, Trial Chamber I of the ICTR defined the crime of rape:

The Chamber defines rape as a physical invasion of a sexual nature, committed on a person under circumstances which are coercive. Sexual violence, including rape, is not limited to physical invasion of the human body and may include acts which do not involve penetration or even physical contact....Threats, intimidation, extortion, and other forms of duress which prey on fear or desperation could be coercion (n.d.)

Further, the Tribunal asserted that rape and sexual violence under certain conditions and circumstances ("where they were committed with intent to destroy, in part or a whole, a particular group as such") could, and do, constitute genocide. Furthermore, the measures imposed can be physical or mental, "[f]or instance, rape can be a measure intended to prevent births when the person raped refuses subsequently to procreate, in the same way that members of a group can be led, through threats or trauma, not to procreate" (n.p.). Subsequently, the Tribunal found that sexual violence was an "integral part of the process of destruction of the Tutsi ethnic group," and thus constituted genocide. In so saying, the Tribunal asserted that "the rape of Tutsi women was systematic and was perpetrated against all Tutsi women and solely against them" (n.p.).

## The Challenges Faced by the Female Population of Rwanda in the Aftermath of the Genocide

Among the major challenges the female survivor population of Rwanda face in the post-genocide period are the following: (1) coping with ongoing and overwhelming sorrow (if not depression),[11] some fourteen years after the genocide, which is often the result of a combination of "illness, poverty, trauma and isolation"[12] (African Rights, 2004, p. 4); (2) eking out an existence (either as widows, alone or with children and/or husbands who are physically maimed or psychologically unbalanced as a result of the horrors they experienced and/or witnessed; as females with HIV/AIDS who are often too weak to work at all; as young females without family members to help support them); (3) coping with the mandatory attendance at *gacacas* (local tribunals hearing cases against alleged perpetrators who have been accused of having committed crimes in the very area where the tribunals are being held) during which they may be called to testify against the perpetrators, and thus forced to recall in vivid detail the horrors to which they were subjected (not to mention, possibly facing threats from those they testify against); and (4) dealing with HIV/AIDS that they contracted after being raped during the genocidal period. If debilitating and deadly health issues were not enough to contend with, "survivors of sexual violence [who contracted HIV/AIDS] frequently find that they and their families often face stigma, which can in turn lead to loss of employment, difficulty in asserting property rights, and a loss of civil and political rights" (Amnesty International, 2004, p. 2).[13]

## The Likelihood of Making Progress in Addressing the Challenges

There are so many females suffering from such terrible depression as a result of what they were subjected to during the genocide and so few resources (personnel with the expertise to serve as counselors and the funds to cover the cost of counseling, medication, and even as something as seemingly simple and cheap as transportation to and from health centers), it is unlikely that the vast majority of female survivors will ever be able to seek and receive the help they need. The words and insights of Rafiki Ubaldo, a survivor of the 1994 Rwandan genocide and now a genocide scholar, are enlightening in this regard:

> There are aren't enough counselors and this is because the number of those facing post-genocide trauma is immense. From the stories I've heard and what I've seen myself, the trauma becomes increasingly complicated over time and therefore very

difficult to, first, diagnose, and, second, treat. To do both, it requires highly trained practitioners and they simply don't exist. Added to that, it is difficult for many survivors to realize that they are facing trauma; many are under the impression that they have malaria, or other sicknesses, when, in fact, their physical weakness and recurring headaches are a result of trauma. And when they finally do go to the trauma centers, they present challenging cases that take hours and hours over days, weeks and even months of treatment. This means that the limited number of counselors spend long hours and days treating few cases.

Even though there are few professionals, I believe that they try their very best. But, as I said, they face extremely challenging cases. Let me tell you a story. A kid, a girl, was forced by *Interahamwe* to drink the blood of her mother they had just finished killing (after slashing her neck) at the church of Ntarama. They gave her the blood on a plastic plate (these plates are common in Rwanda, every common family uses them at the table). In 2006, she went to a boarding school hoping to spend some years there, but when she entered the refectory she discovered the plastic plates, same color that one she was forced to drink her mother's blood from in Ntarama. She went mad, screaming at all Hutus, and the director had no idea what was happening or why. Ultimately, the girl was forced to leave the school. So tell me, how does one treat the trauma of this girl? She has not yet met any counselor. Imagine if she meets a counselor: Do they start with the story of Ntarama? Or the story of the school ? Or...?

And remember trauma counseling is not only needed by survivors; perpetrators need it, too. What will happen if *gacaca* releases them [the perpetrators] without counseling? They may do the same thing all over again or may act in some other strange way. There is story of a man, a Hutu, who went to the place where he buried a Tutsi, and could only find the bones of the head [skull] as the rest were already broken into pieces and scattered. And so he took those bones, and he went around the village with the skull in his hands. He, of course, was arrested. Such cases, and there are many, of course, require the efforts, time, and skill of even more counselors.[14] (Personal correspondence)

The fact is, most of the organizations in place to help and assist survivors are stretched thin. For example, the Kigali-based office of Avega, the remarkable organization established by genocide widows in 1995 to provide various types of assistance to widows[15] has a grand total of twenty four women working as counselors, nurses and social workers to oversee such services as conducting tests for HIV, malaria and other illnesses, providing assistance with school fees, helping with the renovation of houses, meting out funeral payments, and giving legal advice. Significantly, though, Avega trains widows in trauma counseling in order to provide them with the skills to help others in need as well as themselves. Here is a situation where those nations, as well as the United Nations, that failed Rwanda so miserably as the genocide unfolded, could contribute some of their vast resources and do a world of good.[16]

The Genocide Survivors Assistance Fund (FARG) is another major organization in Rwanda that provides important assistance to the survivors. For example, through April 2007, FARG had spent 1.19 billion Rwandan Francs on school fees for genocide orphans, in both higher and lower institutions of learning (Agaba, 2007, p. 1). FARG also, in part, provides doctor and hospital care for survivors in need. Unfortunately, however, FARG's funding by the government has fallen short of what was initially promised. As a result, some survivors are suffering horribly. An orphan, Uwimana Solage, twenty-two, who lives with and cares for her brothers and sisters recently told a reporter, "I dropped out of school and joined a tailoring school so that I could take care of my siblings, one of whom has gone on the street in an effort to fend for himself. The local authorities have not helped us much. We have been left to fend for ourselves and it is not surprising to find that these orphans you see before you spend days without food" (quoted in Ntambara, 2007, p. 4).

Another organization whose express is to assist survivors of genocide is IBUKA, the umbrella organization of the survivors of the 1994 Rwandan genocide. But, it, too, is stretched thin and readily admits it needs all the financial help it can get.

Despite the good offices and serious efforts of the three aforementioned organizations, the Rwandan government (which is supposed to allocate 5 percent of the government's total budget to FARG), and international NGOs, much more help is needed to address the massive number of complex problems faced by the genocide survivors.

Coping with mandatory attendance at *gacacas*, where the female survivors may have to recount the horrors they experienced during the genocide, including the sexual assaults they endured (and/or listen to the testimony of others with similar stories), is likely to be almost overwhelmingly difficult —and that is true for at least three major reasons: (1) If they have to testify about what happened to them during the genocide, it is bound to bring back a swarm of devastating memories; (2) Listening to the horrific acts perpetrated against other females is likely to be just about as difficult, and is likely to trigger memories of the attacks they, themselves, suffered; and (3) If one has to testify against alleged perpetrators, there is always the chance that the witness may be attacked later by the perpetrator and/or his/her family members or friends. Such threats and attacks are not uncommon, and while the government asserts that it is concerned with such situations, the simple fact is that there are not enough police to adequately protect every one who is threatened or in need of assistance.[17] Unfortunately, the first two problems seem as if they are intractable. As for the third issue, in light of the great number of survivors who are presenting testimony at *gacacas* and the limited number of police available (compounded by the tight budget of local police departments), it seems as if it will remain a problem as long as the *gacaca* process exists.

The lives of a vast number of female survivors are incredibly difficult, and it doesn't appear as if they will improve dramatically anytime soon. Many returned to their villages to be greeted by destroyed homes, uprooted crops, land "littered" with dead bodies, and the families of the perpetrators who killed their (the victims') still living next door to them. Just about every configuration that constitutes "a bereft family" exists today in the hills of Rwanda: widows who lost their husbands and all of their children; widows who lost all of their immediate and extended family members (sometimes numbering in the seventies and eighties and more); widows with young children, some of the latter who are "rape babies" infected with HIV/AIDS; widows with so many young children that they (the women) cannot adequately care for them[18]; families in which husbands are so despondent they can no longer provide for their families and thus the total weight of responsibility falls on the shoulders of the wife and/or children; orphaned siblings living together in the very homes where their parents were slain; orphans totally alone in the world except for the other orphans with whom they reside in orphanages; and street children who fend for themselves. And that is just a sampling.

All of the aforementioned individuals need financial support (i.e., more than the meager amount they've received or, in many cases, the money due to them that they have not received). Many young female survivors are totally bereft of family members and thus must fend for themselves, and in doing so, they often risk their very lives: "[Many] children my age [early twenties] who lost their parents during the genocide could not continue with their studies, many have become cleaners, others are prostitutes to find the money to survive and are dying of AIDS"[19] (quoted in African Rights, 2006, p. 4).

As for those who have contracted HIV/AIDS and/or have children who have HIV/AIDS, there are efforts underway to assist such individuals but numerous complications have arisen that militate against reaching all who are in need. First, while funds are available for survivors to purchases the medication they need, not all female survivors seem to be cognizant of the fact that such funds are available from FARG (African Rights, 2004).[20] Second, many females who *are* aware of FARG live a fair distance from those medical centers that dispense such medication (in many cases, local village health centers do not serve as dispensaries for the anti-retroviral drugs, the key drug needed to attempt to control the ravages of AIDS[21]), and the cost involved in traveling to such centers is prohibitive. The latter speaks to just how destitute and impoverished many of the survivors are—that is, they cannot even afford the relatively inexpensive bus fare to reach a dispensary to obtain medication that may ease their pain and slow the progression of their illness. Third, many females are so ashamed and/or fearful of ostracism, that they refuse to acknowledge their rape to anyone, which they would have to do in order to obtain the anti-retroviral drugs. As a result of these reasons/situations, many are destined to die a slow, horrible death and/or watch their children do so as well. Again, this is where those nations, as well as the United Nations, that stood by and allowed the genocide to be perpetrated need to stand up and, while not make things right for that is virtually impossible, at least do the right thing and see to it that every woman and child who has HIV/AIDS as a result of rape during the genocide receive the medication they need to both slow down the illness and make their lives at least somewhat more comfortable.

Finally, on a different but related, it is critical to note that, at least in some respects, women in Rwanda *are* making significant headway vis-à-vis self-empowerment and gender equity in Rwanda (African Rights, 2004b). They have made most progress in the sphere, and the least in the social and economic spheres. Be that as it may, it is impressive that "women in Rwanda celebrated a substantial political victory in 2003, [when they] set a new global standard, winning 49% of seats in the legislative elections" (African Rights, 2004b, p. 4).

Such advancement has had a relatively positive impact in regard to prodding the Rwandan government and outside agencies to focus on the needs of the female victims of the genocide and their families:

> A number of legal and constitutional reforms in recent years have substantially improved women's *rights on paper*. The views of ordinary women were actively sought in the remaking of Rwanda's constitution and contributed to the arguments in favor of the introduction of 30% quotas for women in political institutions. Similarly, family law was reformed to allow women basic rights in relation to property ownership, inheritance and divorce that they had previously been denied. (Italics added, African Rights, 2004b, p. 6)

It is important to note, and recognize, the use of the phrase "on paper" in the above quote. More specifically,

> [t]he issue facing gender activists in Rwanda today is how to make these reforms meaningful for women, particularly in the rural areas where the majority of Rwandese people live and where women are most likely to be subject to discrimination. At present there are simply not adequate structures in place to make legal reforms operational....[And as for economic advances], change is still a long way off, especially for rural peasants for whom the "division of tasks between the sexes is so deeply ingrained that it's difficult to modify"[22] (African Rights, 2004b, p. 6).

## Recommendations

A host of Rwandan and international organizations, individual human rights activists, and scholars have made numerous recommendations in regard to what is needed to meet the various and serious needs of female survivors of genocide. Highlighted below is a mere sampling of the numerous recommendations, though they are among those that this author considers some of the most significant:

- "Implement the safeguards established by the 2004 *Gacaca* Law, which would permit a rape victim to give testimony before a single gacaca judge, confidential testimony in writing, or testimony to staff at the provincial prosecutor's office" (Human Rights Watch, 2004, p. 1);
- "Provide trauma counselors for women who report or testify to sexual violence to police, prosecutors, or *gacaca* judges" (Human Rights Watch, 2004, p. 2);

- "Ensure that at least one *gacaca* judge in each cell-level court has received timely and periodic training in investigation, prosecution, and witness protection in sexual violence cases" (Human Rights Watch, 2004, p. 2);
- "Once a reparations fund is in place, conduct nationwide campaigns to inform victims about the possibility of reparations and the procedures to obtain them" (Human Rights Watch, 2004, p. 3);
- "Provide assistance to genocide survivors, particularly rape victims, for:

  -- Outreach, medical services and trauma counseling for rape victims, with special attention to dissemination of information on voluntary HIV counseling and access to ARV therapy and treatment for opportunistic infection of AIDS (Human Rights Watch, 2004, p. 3)
  -- The primary and secondary education of children of HIV-positive genocide rape victims (Human Rights Watch, 2004, p. 3)
  -- Transport costs of victims who must travel to seek legal, medical, psychological or other assistance (Human Rights Watch, 2004, p. 3)
  -- Economic initiatives for female genocide survivors (Human Rights Watch, 2004, p. 3)
  -- The creation of counseling training programs (Human Rights Watch, 2004, p. 3)
  -- Survivors' organizations and counseling organizations to widen the network of legal assistance and counseling for genocide survivors, particularly those in rural areas (Human Rights Watch, 2004, p. 4)

- "The Government should, with the help of UN agencies, bilateral donors and other experts as appropriate, equitably enhance the provision of medical care to survivors of sexual violence. Programs should be constructed in such a way as to ensure equal access for both rural and urban populations" (Amnesty International, 2004, p. 31).
- "The Government, with the assistance of international donors, should expand psychological counseling programs for rape survivors and ensure that these constitute an integral part of the health care system" (Amnesty International, 2004, p. 31);
- "The Government should continue to press forward with the investigation and prosecution of reported cases of sexual violence, whether committed in the context of the genocide or by the Rwandan Patriotic Army..." (Amnesty International, 2004, p. 32);
- "The international community should continue providing funding and technical support to measures that contribute to the protection and fulfillment of the rights to health, food and education of PLWHA [people living with HIV/AIDS] and their families, including by supporting programs that provide assistance to children who are orphaned by HIV/AIDS or who are at risk of being orphaned" (Amnesty International, 2004, p. 34);
- The international community "must assist the government of Rwanda in establishing a systematic and comprehensive program of care for survivor of sexual violence" (Amnesty International, 2004, p. 34);

"The international community should assist and support the Government of Rwanda in establishing a compensation fund for victims of human rights abuse during the genocide and war" (Amnesty International, 2004, p. 34); and

- "The United States Government in particular must urgently recognize the extent of its humanitarian responsibilities as the major economic and political power and home to the major pharmaceutical manufacturers of anti-retroviral drugs" (African Rights, 2004, p. 1).

## Conclusion

More often than not, once a genocide ends and the initial (and generally, huge) surge of humanitarian activity in the post genocide period plays itself out within several years' time, the vast majority of the world tends to forget about the survivors and what they are forced to deal with on a daily basis. Fortunately, some humanitarian groups are in it for the long-haul, but they are too few in number. In light of the latter, it is good that so many (meaning, the survivors) are so resilient. Indeed, it is little short of astonishing how many survivors seem to fight through their nightmares, their daily sorrow and depression, their overwhelming losses, and do their utmost to forge a new life for themselves. Not having experienced such horror, such immense loss, such all-engulfing sorrow, all most of us can do is try to imagine what it would be like for the survivors — though most people across the globe seemingly do not really want to do that, and thus don't.

The female population of Rwanda is doing its best to eke out a new existence. In many cases, they are working together, remaining stoic in the face of continuing trials and tribulations, and doing so with few resources in hand. It seems as if the international community which largely looked on and watched as the 1994 genocide unfolded before its very eyes would want to make amends somehow, some way. There continue to be critical needs, and any serious help would certainly be most welcomed by the survivors.

While the international community has, in many ways, been extremely generous to Rwanda, the sad fact is that the very people who suffered horrendously as a result of the killing, mass rape and destruction—individual human beings — often are not the beneficiaries of the aid. That is, in many cases, due to the fact that Rwanda as a nation had to virtually start from scratch in forming a new government, building a new infrastructure, and rebuilding everything from the ground up, band-aids have been applied to the many gaping wounds that the survivors continue to suffer in Rwanda. Sadly, many in the international community, along with individual nations, have congratulated themselves for all they have done for Rwanda since 1994. The problem is: it is far too early to be self-congratulatory. Furthermore, the Rwandan people are so polite and sincerely appreciative of the help that they have received they are not likely to complain too loudly or to condemn the international community for the pittance it has provided to help the survivors attempt to begin to lead normal lives again. For the international community to be blind to these facts is nothing short of shameful, and it truly adds insult to injury following the international community's unconscionable silence and lack of action both prior to and during the onslaught of genocide in 1994.

## Notes

1.  "AVEGA, an association for genocide widows, carried out a study in 2000 of 1,125 women who survived rape during the genocide and found that 66.7% had HIV" (Amnesty International, 2004, p. 3).
2.  Some—including the current government of Rwanda—have placed the number of murdered as high as one million people. In his well-researched book, *The Order of Genocide: Race, Power, and War in Rwanda*, political scientist Scott Straus (2006) asserts that even the estimate of 800,000 dead is probably too high: "We may never know precisely how many civilians died in the genocide. The standard international estimate in journalist and United Nations reports is 800,000 killed. However, according to the last government census taken before the genocide (in 1991), Rwanda had only 600,000 Tutsis living in the country. Given Rwanda's population growth, there may have been as many as 660,000 Tutsis in Rwanda at the time of the genocide. It is possible that government officials or Tutsis themselves disguised the true number of Tutsis, but there is no concrete evidence of widespread fabrication, and the 1991 census data correspond to data in the last census conducted in the colonial period. The 800,000 figure is thus probably too high. The best aggregate estimate of the number killed during the genocide comes from historian and human rights activist Alison Des Forges, who has written the most comprehensive book documenting genocide at the national level. Des Forges triangulates data from three sources and estimates that at least 500,000 Tutsi civilians were killed in the genocide. That sum amounts to roughly three-quarters of Rwanda's pre-genocide Tutsi population" (p. 51).
3.  Strikingly, "more than any other profession, academics, teachers, school inspectors and the directors of schools, including primary schools, participated actively in the genocide. Throughout Rwanda, they helped to organize the killing squads and took a lead role in the hunt for victims and in carrying out the massacres" (African Rights, 1995, p. 196).
4.  "Certainly there are many examples of courageous women risking their lives to protect and save others. Others were silent bystanders, paralyzed by fear or because of indifference. But there is no evidence that women joined together to oppose the killings; nor did women's organizations take a stand against the genocide" (African Rights, 2004b, p. 10).
5.  For example, during the Holocaust, the perpetrators made use of a computer system (the Hollerith machine) used for census taking to track down people; machine guns; the railroad systems spanning the continent of Europe; gas chambers; and crematoria; the Iraq government used gas in its genocide of the Kurds residing in northern Iraq; the Serbs used various automatic weapons to carry out its genocide against the Muslim boys and men of Srebrenica in 1995).
6.  It has also been reported that "some local government officials resisted the call of mass murder and did their best to protect the vulnerable in their communities. Some, however, eventually relented and let the killers implement their programme; others fled after they were threatened.... But the majority were eager accomplices,

either because of their own extremism or out of political opportunism" (African Rights, 1995, p. 110).

7.  Among some of the key works readers may wish to consult for such information are the following: Alison Des Forges' *"Leave None to Tell"*: *Genocide in Rwanda* (New York: Human Rights Watch, 1999); Linda R. Melvern's *A People Betrayed: The Role of the West in Rwanda's Genocide* (New York: Zed Books, 2000); Michael Barnett's *Eyewitness to a Genocide: The United Nations and Rwanda* (Ithaca, NY: Cornell University Press, 2002): Romeo Dallaire's *Shake Hands with the Devil: The Failure of Humanity in Rwanda* (New York: Carroll & Graf Publishers, 2005); Straus' *The Order of Genocide*.

8.  For a detailed discussion of the causes and triggers of the 1994 Rwandan genocide and an analysis of how the killing process spread across the country, see Scott Straus' *The Order of Genocide: Race, Power, and War in Rwanda* (Ithaca, NY: Cornell University Press, 2006).

9.  The first woman to be charged by a UN criminal tribunal (the International Criminal Tribunal for Rwanda), Nyiramasuhuko was charged with numerous crimes, including: genocide, conspiracy to commit genocide, complicity in genocide, and rape as a crime against humanity. Allegedly, she ordered and cajoled members of the *Interahamwe* to rape Tutsi women and went so far as to encourage thousands of Tutsi females to gather in a sports arena where she then ordered and cajoled Hutu extremists to rape and murder them. In regard to the charge of rape, the ICTR has argued that under international law Nyiramasuhuko was responsible for the actions of her subordinates and thus can be charged with the crimes they committed.

10. The Akayesu case at the ICTR was notable, in part, for making the legal connection between rape and genocide. In doing so, it found that sexual violence was instrumental in attacking the very foundations of the Tutsi people as such.

11. For many, it is a sorrow that is perdurable. In this regard, one female survivor who had been raped during the genocide said: "Today I regret that I did not die that day. Those men and women who died are now at peace whereas I am still here to suffer even more. I am handicapped in the true sense of the word.... I regret that I'm alive because I've lost my lust for life. We survivors are broken-hearted. We live in a situation which overwhelms us. Our wounds become deeper every day. We are constantly in mourning (African Rights, 2004, p. 51).

12. Over and above that, many females also suffer from survivor's guilt in that they feel they should have perished with their families (African Rights, 2004, p. 50). Another female survivor remarked that "I always dream about my children, seeing them as the grown ups they would have been today. I also imagine the atrocities that they must have experienced during the genocide and it makes me feel like a living dead person" (African Rights, 2004, p. 57).

13. An example of such is the fact that "some widows lost their land when it was reclaimed by their husband's family or by Rwandese who returned in the months and years following the RPA victory, or during the 'villagization' process that sometimes forcibly attempted to group dispersed rural inhabitants into villages. During a decade of refugee returns, displacement, 'villagization' programs and seizures of land by powerful individuals, land has changed hands frequently; women's claim to land, even if codified in law, has been particularly difficult to enforce." (Amnesty International, 2004, p. 8)

14. Herein, Rafiki Ubaldo provides another stunning insight into the whole issue of providing counseling for survivors of the genocide, both women and men: "Often times people do not seek counseling for themselves; rather, it is often sought when

it is absolutely clear that the person has no other sickness than what could be related to madness, when the patient is losing his mind, with terrible headaches and crying jags, that is when family members bring them to counseling centers. It is also important to note that in Rwanda you do not say that you have trauma, especially when you are a man. That is the sickness of women and children. The weak sex. That tells you how people view that sickness."

15.  A nongovernmental, nonprofit organization, Avega-Agahozo's (Agahozo is a Kinyarwandan word that means "to dry one's tears") mission is, more specifically, as follows: promote the general welfare of genocide victims, promote solidarity among members of the association, carry out activities aimed at helping the widows; cooperate with organizations that have the same objectives; uphold the memory of the genocide victims and fight for justice, and participate in the national reconstruction and reconciliation process of Rwanda.

16.  "Although Avega is a national network, its HIV programmes do not cover members in all provinces of the country" (African Watch, 2004, p. 88).

17.  In fact, many female survivors who have been raped prefer not to provide testimony, and that is true due to the fact that "testifying even behind closed doors is traumatic and increases the chances that community members will find out about the rape" (Amnesty International, 2004, p. 16)

18.  Many of the women who are ill also worry constantly about what will happen to their children (who will feed them, house them, clothe them) when they (the women) die. As one female survivor who had been raped and now suffers from AIDS said, "Maybe after my death, my children will have somebody who will look after them. I can't be sure about that though, since it certainly won't be anyone from my family as they have all been killed" (African Rights, 2004, p. 38).

19.  Avega, the widows association, has various micro-credit schemes available, but many women are either not cognizant of such opportunities, do not know how to apply for such plans or lack the interest in pursuing such offers. Significantly, it is also true that the number of micro-credit opportunities is limited.

20.  This is in large part due to the fact that "women's diminished access to radios, community meetings and written information sources lessen their access to information and education about sexual health and contraception" (Amnesty International, 2004, p. 5).

21.  It is estimated by the Rwandan government that "the number of patients clinically in need of life-prolonging anti-retroviral (ARV) therapy is estimated at between 50,000 and 100,000. As of January 2004, only approximately 2,000 Rwandese were being treated with ARVs. Approximately 50,000 Rwandese per year died of AIDS. By the end of 2004, [it was] estimated 2,000 to 5,000 will receive ARVs" (Amnesty International, 2004, p. 4).

22.  For a detailed discussion of these issues and others related to the progress females in Rwanda have made since the end of the 1994 Rwandan genocide, see *Women Taking a Lead: Progress Towards Empowerment and Gender Equity in Rwanda* (Kigali: African Rights, 2004).

## References

African Rights (2004a). *Rwanda: Broken Bodies, Torn Spirits—Living with Genocide, Rape and HIV/AIDS*. Kigali: Author.

African Rights (2003). *Gacaca Justice: A Shared Responsibility*. Kigali: Author.

African Rights (1995a). *Rwanda: Death, Despair and Defiance*. London: Author.

African Rights (1995b). *Rwanda Not So Innocent: When Women Become Killers*. London: Author.

African Rights (2004b). *Women Taking a Lead: Progress Towards Empowerment and Gender Equity in Rwanda*. Kigali: Author.

Agaba, Godwin (April 8, 2007). "Rwanda: FARG Spends Frw1b on Survivors' School Dues." *The New Times*, p. 1. See: allafrica.com/stories/200704100406.html

Amnesty International (2004). "Rwanda: Marked for Death, Rape Survivors Living with HIV/AIDS in Rwanda." Accessed at: web/amnesty.org/library/index/en-gafr470072004

Des Forges, Alison (1999). *"Leave None to Tell the Story": Genocide in Rwanda*. New York: Human Rights Watch.

Hatzfeld, Jean (2005). *Into the Quick of Life: The Rwandan Genocide: The Survivors Speak*. London: Serpent's Tail.

Human Rights Watch (2004). *Rwanda: Struggling to Survive: II. Recommendations*. Accessed at: hrw.org/reports/2004/rwanda0904/3.htm

Lemarchand, René (1999). "Rwanda and Burundi, Genocide In, " pp. 508-513. In Israel W. Charny (Ed.) *Encyclopedia of Genocide*. Santa Barbara, CA: ABC Clio Press.

Ntambara, Paul (2007). "Varsity Students Reach Out to Child-Headed Families." *The New Times* [Kigali, Rwanda], p. 4.

Straus, Scott (2006). *The Order of Genocide: Race, Power and War in Rwanda*. Ithaca, NY: Cornell University Press.

Temple-Raston, Dina (2004). *Justice on the Grass: Three Rwandan Journalists, Their Trial for War Crimes, and a Nation's Quest for Redemption*. New York: Free Press.

## Annotated Bibliography

Adelman, Howard (2005). "The Rwanda Genocide," pp. 31-54. In Samuel Totten (Ed.) *Genocide at the Millennium —Genocide: A Critical Bibliographic Review*. New Brunswick, NJ: Transaction Publishers.

Adelman's essay and accompanying annotated bibliography provide readers with a solid sense of many of the key works on the Rwandan genocide published through 2003.

African Rights (1999). *Father Wenceslas Munyeshyaka: In the Eyes of the Survivors of Sainte Famille*. London: Author. 96 pp.

Many of the first-person accounts herein include information about how Father Wenceslas Munyeshyaka, a Catholic priest, had Hutu extremist toughs select girls for him to rape, his rape of the girls, his order to have a young teenager girl shot and killed because she repelled his advances, and how he provided those girls who "submitted" to his predatory behavior with presents, additional food, and safe transfer to the Hotel des Mille Collines, where people were safe from attacks by the Hutu extremists.

African Rights (2003). *Gacaca Justice: A Shared Responsibility*. Kigali: Author. 51 pp.

An informative booklet about the formation, focus and process of the *gacaca* system, the reinvention of a precolonial method of handling conflict and reconciliation in order to try alleged perpetrators of genocide by local tribunals. It includes a very short section entitled "Rape Prosecutions: Insufficient Clarity" (pp. 38-39).

African Rights (1995). *Resisting Genocide: Bisesero, April-June 1994*. London: Author. 110 pp.

This book includes several short first-person statements about how the women of Bisesero helped the Tutsi men attempt to fight off the onslaught of attacks undertaken by the Hutus extremists during the course of the genocide. Not only did women collect rocks for the men to throw at their attackers, but some of the women actually took part in the hand-to-hand combat against their assailants.

African Rights (2004). *Rwanda: Broken Bodies, Torn Spirits — Living with Genocide, Rape and HIV/AIDS*. Kigali, Rwanda: Author. 96 pp.

This is a detailed and highly informative (and moving) report based on interviews with 199 female survivors and two male survivors of the 1994 Rwandan genocide. The analysis of the plight and fate of those women who were raped is extremely detailed, informative and moving. It is also packed with excerpts from the interviews conducted with the survivors who were sexually assaulted.

The report is comprised of the following thirteen chapters: 1. Introduction; 2. Records of Rape: Violation Upon Violation; 3. Broken Bodies: The Physical Impact of Rape; 4. Facing a Demon; 5. In the Dark: Fear and Powerlessness; 6. Fragile Health; 7. Torn Spirits: The Emotional Impact; 8. The Primary Concern: The Future of Children; 9. On the Margins: The Price of Isolation; 10. Elusive Justice; 11. Patching Wounds: Assistance for Rape Survivors; 12. Creating Communities: The Critical Support of Women's Organizations; and 13. Future Hopes.

African Rights (1995). *Rwanda: Death, Despair and Defiance*. London: Author. 1200 pp.

This major report includes a section (pp. 748-797) that provides a detailed account of the rape and abduction of women and girls during the 1994 genocide.

African Rights (1996). *Rwanda: Killing the Evidence—Murder, Attacks, Arrests and Intimidation of Survivors and Witnesses*. London: Author. 105 pp.

This report presents findings about the violence perpetrated in Rwanda in the post-genocide period. It presents first-person accounts of intimidation, attempted murder and actual murder against both survivors and witnesses of the genocide. It also includes first-person accounts about the fact that attacks against the latter also included the destruction of their homes, the theft of their crops, and the looting of their other materials goods. Some people, it reports, were driven from their homes and forced to move to other areas of Rwanda, leaving them with no homes or jobs.

African Rights (1995). *Rwanda Not So Innocent: When Women Become Killers*. London: Author. 255 pp.

This book/report explores the issue of why and how certain females took an active part in the killing process during the 1994 Rwandan genocide. It provides detailed stories of various individuals and in doing so discusses what motivated the women as well as the exact roles they played (sometimes actually carrying out the killing, other times ordering others to kill and rape).

In addition to addressing the above issues/information, this work also includes a great deal of information on the fate and plight of Tutsi girls and women during the 1994 genocide. Ultimately, it is an invaluable source of information on the role of women as collaborators and killers as well as first-person insights about both the perpetrators and the victims.

The book is comprised of the following parts: Summary; Introduction; Background; Lending a Big Hand in the Massacres and Killing; Ministers in the Interim Government; Administrators of Death: Local Government Officials; Messengers of Death: Journalists Who Preached Genocide; The Unthinkable: Nuns Who Joined the Killers; Teachers and School Inspectors; and When Healers Become Killers: Doctors, Nurses & Employees of Medical Institutions.

African Rights (2004). *Women Taking a Lead: Progress Towards Empowerment and Gender Equity in Rwanda*. Kigali: Author. 49 pp.

The authors of this booklet delineate the various ways in which women have both gained numerous and significant rights in Rwandan society that they previously had been denied, as well as numerous and significant opportunities to take leadership positions throughout society (including the national government). The authors also discuss how reforms have created opportunities for women in every sphere of society, but the dramatic gains they've made in the political sphere have not yet been matched by those in the social and economic spheres.

African Rights (2006). *A Wounded Generation: The Children Who Survived Rwanda's Genocide*. Kigali, Rwanda: Author. 28 pp.

One section (pp. 15-18) of this powerful and thought-provoking report/booklet is entitled "Raped as a Child." First-person statements by rape victims are interwoven throughout the section.

Amnesty International (2004). "Rwanda: 'Marked for Death,' Rape Survivors Living with HIV/AIDS in Rwanda." Accessed at: web.amnesty.org/library/index/engafr470072004

This is a major report that addresses, in part, the following issues: ongoing discrimination against females who were raped during the 1994 genocide; poverty and its implications in regard to obtaining proper medical care; rape as a tool of genocide; legacies of the genocide (psychological trauma, guilt and ostracism); the differential impact on women and girls; land and inheritance issues; legacies of the genocide and war that contribute to HIV transmission; international and domestic legal issues germane to the plight and fate of females who were subjected to sexual violence during the genocide; issues of justice, impunity and redress; stigma and discrimination related to HIV status; and children of people living with HIV/AIDS. It concludes with two sets of recommendations, one aimed at the Rwandan government and one at the international community in regard to the aforementioned issues.

Balint, Jennifer (1999). "Rape as a Tool of Genocide," pp. 491-492. In Israel W. Charny (Ed.) *Encyclopedia of Genocide*. Santa Barbara, CA: ABC Clio Press.

Balint, a lawyer and a professor of law at Monash University in Melbourne, Victoria, Australia, discusses how the mass rape of women constitutes genocide: "rape as a weapon of genocide results in killing members of the group, causing serious bodily and mental harm to members of the group, imposing measures intended to prevent births within the groups, as well as deliberately inflicting on the group conditions of life calculated to bring about its physical destruction in whole or in part; all acts which constitute genocide as defined in the Genocide Convention" (p. 491). Balint goes onto to discuss the fact that Jean-Paul Akayesu was found guilty of nine out of fifteen counts of genocide, and that the ICTR found that the acts of rape and sexual violence constitute acts of genocide (p. 491).

Campanaro, Jocelyn (2001). "Women, War, and International Law: The Historical Treatment of Gender-Based War Crimes." *The Georgetown Law Journal*, 89(8):2557-2592.

In this "Note," Campanaro, a J.D. candidate at Georgetown University Law Center, examines how gender-based war crimes (e.g., sexual assaults against women) have been treated historically in war-crimes tribunals from World War II through the international criminal tribunals for the former Yugoslavia and Rwanda in the 1990s. In the last part of the piece, she addresses the Rome Statute of the International Criminal Court and assesses "its progress, limitations and implications for creating greater recognition of gender-based crimes and the increased possibilities for future prosecution of sexual violence" (p. 2559).

Des Forges, Alison (1999). *"Leave None to Tell the Story": Genocide in Rwanda*. New York: Human Rights Watch, 789 pp.

This massive volume addresses a host of key issues vis-à-vis the genocide, including but not limited: to the historical and political context of the genocide, the genocide at the national level, the genocide at the local level, the international response to the genocide, and "ending the genocide." It provides detailed accounts of the special targeting of women, the rape of Tutsi women, and Tutsi women forced into "sexual servitude." Also discussed is how some women and girls were mutilated during the course of being raped or just before they were murdered.

The book also includes a section entitled "Hutu against Hutu" and a subsection entitled "Property and Women." There are at least eighteen references to rape in this book, which address the issue of rape prior to and during the genocide.

In part, it is noted that "During the genocide, tens of thousands of women and girls were raped, including one who was only two years old. The assailants raped as part of their attempt to exterminate Tutsi, some of them incited by propaganda about Tutsi women disseminated in the period just before the genocide.... Some women [were kept] for weeks or months in sexual servitude" (p. 215).

Durham, Helen (2001). "Women and Civil Society: NGOs and International Criminal Law," pp. 819-843. In Kelly D. Askin and Dorean M. Koenig (Eds.) *Women and International Human Rights Law*, Volume 3. Ardsley, NY: Transnational Publishers, Inc.
    In her introduction, Durham, Australian Red Cross Manager for International Humanitarian Law, writes that "This chapter examines the role women's nongovernmental organizations (NGOs) play in international criminal law. Using case studies of the development of the Statute for an International Criminal Court [ICC] and the proceedings of the ad hoc international criminal tribunals both in the former Yugoslavia and Rwanda, the chapter argues that women's groups have had a significant impact on the creation and enforcement of this area of law" (p. 819).

Flanders, Laura (2000). Rwanda's Living Casualties," pp. 95-100. In Anne Llewellyn Barstow (Ed.) *War's Dirty Secret: Rape, Prostitution, and Other Crimes Against Women*. Cleveland, OH: The Pilgrim Press.
    A short piece on the extent of rape during the 1994 Rwandan genocide and the ongoing impact of such atrocities on the survivors and their children.

Hatzfeld, Jean (2000). *Into the Quick of Life: The Rwandan Genocide: The Survivors Speak*. London: Serpent's Tail, 176 pp.
    This book is comprised of fourteen first-person accounts, ten of which are by female survivors of the 1994 Rwandan genocide.

Hogg, Nicole (2001). *"I Never Poured Blood": Women Accused of Genocide*. M.A. thesis, Faculty of Law, McGill University, Toronto, Canada. November, 76 pp.
    An examination of women's participation in the 1994 Rwandan genocide, with an emphasis on the major ways in which the women took part in the process of the genocide.

Human Rights Watch/Africa and Human Rights Watch Women's Project (1996). *Shattered Lives: Sexual Violence during the Rwandan Genocide and its Aftermath*. New York: Human Rights Watch. 120 pp. Also available at: www.hrw.org/reports/1996/Rwanda/htm
    Based on a wide range of interviews and in-depth research in Rwanda, this major report addresses the following issues vis-à-vis sexual violence perpetrated during and following the 1994 Rwandan genocide: Background (The Genocide, Genocide Propaganda Against Tutsi Women, and The Status of Women in Rwandan Society); Problems Documenting Gender-Based Crimes; International and National Legal Protections Against Gender-Based Violence (Sexual Violence as a War Crime, Sexual Violence as a Crime Against Humanity, Sexual Violence as an Act of Genocide, and Rape as a

Crime Under Rwandan Law); Gender-Based Violence Against Rwandan Women (Sexual Violence Against Tutsi Women, Rape by Militia, Rape by the Military, Collective Sexual Slavery, and Individual Sexual Slavery and Forced "Marriage"); and Ongoing Problems Facing Rwandan Women (Stigma, Isolation and Ostracization; Discriminatory Treatment Under the Law; and Property and Inheritance Rights).

It also includes a set of recommendations to the Rwandan government, the International Criminal Tribunal for Rwanda, the United Nations Human Rights Field Operation in Rwanda, and such international donors as the UN, the U.S., the European Union, the Netherlands, Belgium, Germany, among others including international humanitarian groups.

International Criminal Tribunal for Rwanda (1998). *Judgement: The Prosecutor Versus Jean-Paul Akayesu. Case No. ICTR-96-4-T*. Arusha, Tanzania: The Office of the Prosecutor, ICTR. 155 pp. Also available at: http://69.94.11.53/ ENGLISH/cases/Akayesu/judgement/akay001.htm

This document presents key information about the arrest, trial and conviction of Jean Paul Akayesu for the crimes he committed during the 1994 Rwandan genocide. The Akayesu case is notable due to the fact that it involved the first judgment by an international court for the crime of genocide.

Akayesu was arrested in Zambia on October 10, 1995, indicted by the International Criminal Tribunal for Rwanda (ICTR) on February 16, 1996, and transferred from Zambia to Arusha on May 26, 1996, where he was detained at the ICTR's detention facility. His trial began January 9, 1997.

Akayesu, former *bourgmestre* (mayor) of Taba, was indicted on fifteen counts of "genocide, crimes against humanity, and violations of Article 3 common to the Geneva Conventions and Additional Protocol II thereto." In its judgment, the ICTR judges — unanimously — found Akayesu guilty of nine of the fifteen counts, and not guilty of six of the counts. More specifically, Akayesu was found guilty of "genocide, direct and public incitement to commit genocide, and crimes against humanity (extermination, murder, torture, rape and other inhumane acts).

During the course of the trial, the crime of rape, for which there is no commonly accepted definition in international law, was defined. More specifically, the judges stated that "the Chamber defines rape as a physical invasion of a sexual nature, committed on a person under circumstances which are coercive. Sexual violence, including rape, is not limited to physical invasion of the human body and may include acts which do not involve penetration or even physical contact." The court further stated that coercive circumstances did not need to be evidenced by a show of physical force. "Threats, intimidation, extortion and other forms of duress which prey on fear or desperation could be coercion."

In their judgment, the judges emphasized the fact that rape and sexual violence constitute genocide when they are committed with the "intent to destroy a particular group targeted as such." In doing so, the judges found that sexual violence was an "integral" part of the process of destruction of the Tutsi ethnic group: "The rape of Tutsi women was systematic and was perpetrated against all Tutsi women and solely against them."

Lemarchand, René (2004). "The Rwanda Genocide," pp. 394-412. In Samuel Totten, William S. Parsons, and Israel W. Charny (Eds.) *Century of Genocide: Critical Essays and Eyewitness Accounts*. Second Edition. New York: Routledge.

This chapter includes a short but very powerful account by a seventeen year old Tutsi girl who was repeatedly raped by her assailants in "lieu" of their killing her.

Lyon, Michelle S., and Drumbl, Mark A. (2005). "International Criminal Tribunal for Rwanda," pp. 547-555. In Dinah L. Shelton (Ed.) *Encyclopedia of Genocide and Crimes Against Humanity*. New York: Thompson Gale.

In part, the authors discuss the ICTR's contribution to international law and in doing so note the significance of the Akayesu case. More specifically, the authors state that

The ICTR's most significant contribution is to the development of international criminal law. Its decisions build a jurisprudence that informs the work of other international criminal tribunals, such as the ICTY, other temporary institutions, and prospectively the permanent ICC....

Several of the ICTR's decisions highlight these contributions. One of these is the Trial Chamber's groundbreaking 1998 judgment in the Akayesu case (subsequently affirmed on appeal), which provided judicial notice that the Rwanda violence was organized, ethnically motivated, and undertaken with the intent to wipe out the Tutsi (the latter element being a prerequisite to genocide). The Akayesu judgment marked the first time that an international tribunal ruled that rape and other forms of systematic sexual violence could constitute genocide. Moreover, it provided a progressive definition of rape. (p. 554)

Magnarella, Paul J. (2000). *Justice in Africa: Rwanda's Genocide, Its Courts, and the UN Criminal Tribunal*. Burlington, VT: Ashgate Publishing Company, 154 pp.

Magnarella, Professor of Anthropology and Affiliated Professor of Law and African Studies at the University of Florida, discusses the rape of girls and women during the 1994 Rwandan genocide in a short section (pp. 100-103) entitled "Sexual Violence and Rape as Crimes Against Humanity and Genocide."

Mazurana, Dyan; Raven-Roberts, Angela; and Parpart, Jane (Eds.) (2005). *Gender, Conflict, and Peacekeeping*. Lanham, MD: Rowman & Littlefield Publishers, 321 pp.

The authors in this book explore how gender has become a central factor in shaping current thinking about the causes and consequences of armed conflict, complex emergencies, and reconstruction. Presenting a rich array of examples from Bosnia Herzegovina, East Timor, the former Yugoslavia,

Guatemala, Kosovo, Rwanda, Serbia, as well as others, the authors offer significant insights for future peacekeeping and humanitarian missions.

The book is comprised, in part, of the following chapters: "Gender, Conflict, Peacekeeping" by Dyan Mazurana, Angela Raven-Roberts, Jane Parpart, with Sue Lautze; "Gender and the Causes and Consequences of Armed Conflict" by Dyan Mazurana; "Gender Mainstreaming in United Nations Peacekeeping Operations: Talking the Talk, Tripping over the Walk" by Angela Raven-Roberts; "Prosecution of Gender-based Crimes in International Law" by Valerie Oosterveld; "The Renewed Popularity of the Rule of Law: Implications for Women, Impunity, and Peacekeeping" by Barbara Bedont; "Peacekeeping Trends and Their Gender Implications for Regional Peacekeeping Forces in Africa: Progress and Challenges" by Heidi Hudson; and "Les Femmes Aux Milles Bras: Building Peace in Rwanda" by Erin K Baines.

Quénivet, Noëlle, N. R. (2005). *Sexual Offenses in Armed Conflict and International Law*. Ardsley, NY: Transnational Publishers, Inc., 210 pp.

Discusses the case of sexual assaults during the course of the 1994 Rwandan genocide throughout the book, particularly in relation to the Akayesu case at the International Criminal Tribunal for Rwanda (ICTR).

Schabas, William A. (2000). *Genocide in International Law*. New York: Cambridge University Press, 624 pp.

Schabas, Director of the Irish Centre for Human Rights and holder of the chair in human rights law at the National University of Ireland, Galway, discusses, in part, the Akayesu case in a fair amount of detail, noting how the ICTR's defining rape as genocide "constitutes a major contribution to the progressive development of the law of genocide" (p. 164). He also discusses the cases of Kayishema and Ruzindana in which the ICTR asserted that "'the conditions of life' include 'rape, the starving of group of people, reducing required medical services below a minimum, and withholding sufficient living accommodations for a reasonable period, provided the above would lead to the destruction of the group in whole or in part'" (p. 167).

Sellers, Patricia Viseur (2005). "Rape," pp. 862-869. In Dinah L. Shelton (Ed.) *Encyclopedia of Genocide and Crimes Against Humanity*. New York: Thompson Gale.

Sellers briefly discusses, in part, the Akayesu trial at the ICTR. She notes that "in finding Mr. Akayesu guilty, the Trial Chamber, for the first time in international law, undertook to define rape" (p. 867).

Straus, Scott (2006). *The Order of Genocide: Race, Power and War in Rwanda*. Ithaca, NY: Cornell University Press, 273 pp.

Throughout this well researched and written book, the plight and fate of women are briefly addressed. Among the issues addressed are: the rape of Tutsi females, the number of Tutsi girls and women who were raped, "rape babies," those perpetrators who took the Tutsi victims "as wives," the case of Jean-Paul Akayesu, and the participation of Hutu women in the genocide.

Temple-Raston, Dina (2005). *Justice on the Grass: Three Rwandan Journalists, Their Trial for War Crimes, and a Nation's Quest for Redemption.* New York: Free Press, 302 pp.

   Various sections of this book address the issue of rape during the 1994 Rwandan genocide. Certain sections discuss actual rapes during the genocide, the role played by Jean-Paul Akayesu vis-à-vis his encouragement of the rape of Tutsi women, and the plight and fate of the children resulting from the rapes. One entire chapter is entitled "The Rape Babies Arrived in the Spring" (pp. 141-159).

Zawati, Hilmi M., and Mahmoud, Ibtisam M. (Eds.) (2004). *A Selected Socio-Legal Bibliography on Ethnic Cleansing, Wartime Rape, and Genocide in the former Yugoslavia and Rwanda.* Lewiston, NY: Edwin Mellen Press, 612 pp.

   Comprised of more than 6,000 entries of key socio-legal materials, this bibliography addresses, in part, the sexual violence perpetrated during the crisis in the Former Yugoslavia during the 1990s and the 1994 Rwandan genocide. It includes pieces that were published in English and other European languages. Among the materials it includes are books, collections of essays, periodical articles, addresses, interviews, proceedings, dissertations, encyclopedia entries, treaties, national agreements, decisions, declarations, government documents, NGO documents, professional associations' documents, audio-visual materials, and press releases.

# 7

# The Darfur Genocide: The Mass Rape of Black African Girls and Women

*Samuel Totten*

### Introduction

The first acknowledged genocide of the twenty-first century[1]—the Government of Sudan (GOS) troop's and *Janjaweed* [2](Arab militia) mass killing of black Africans of Darfur in the Sudan—has involved widespread sexual assault and rape against the females (ranging in age from eight years old to their late forties and early fifties) of the victim group. The sexual assaults have been perpetrated (a) against black African females as they go about their chores inside and outside their villages; (b) during the course of attacks on the black African villages by GOS troops and the Janjaweed; (c) in the mountains and desert areas into which the victims of the aforementioned attacks flee; and (d) outside internally displaced persons (IDPs) camps (where the black Africans have sought sanctuary) when females go out to forage for wood which they need in order to cook meals for their families.

Furthermore, for the past several years (2005-through today, December 2007), sexual attacks have also become common occurrences outside the refugee camps in Chad, where black African females are attacked by a broad spectrum of males (i.e., local Chadian men, Chadian rebels fighting against the Chadian government, Chadian military and police officials, and Janjaweed who periodically carry out cross border attacks against the black Africans in the refugee camps). Just as in Darfur, the women are generally attacked as they are out foraging for wood (and, in certain cases, fetching water).

The sexual attacks of the black African females in Darfur are frequently accompanied by taunts such as "You're going to have an Arab baby!" and "No *zuregs*[3] belong here [within Sudan]." Both the threat and intent to impregnate

137

black African females by the Arab soldiers and Janjaweed to create Arab babies constitutes a genocidal act under Article 2b and 2c of the United Nations Convention on the Prevention and Punishment of the Crime of Genocide (UNCG). Likewise, the fact that the assailants know that any black woman who is raped will be considered a pariah within her own family and larger community, thus cutting off, especially for young females, the possibility of having children in the future with a man of her own people, constitutes genocidal intent under Article 2d of the UNCG.

### Overview of Darfur and the Genocide of the Black Africans in Darfur

Darfur, a region in west Sudan, is comprised of three states (Northern Darfur, Western Darfur and Southern Darfur). The three-state region is roughly the size of France, and shares borders with Libya, Chad, and the Central African Republic. The vast majority of the people of Darfur, both the so-called "black Africans" and the Arabs, are Muslims. There are scores of black African tribal groups in Darfur, though those who have seemingly suffered the greatest grief and loss at the hands of the GOS and Janjaweed are the Massaliet, Fur, and Zaghawa.

Darfur is one of the most under-developed and isolated regions of Sudan, the latter of which constitutes one of the twenty-five poorest countries in the world. More specifically, over 90 percent of Sudan's citizens live below the poverty line, barely eking out an existence.

While much of the Darfur region consists of large swaths of burning desert (except during the rainy season when *wadis* swell with water), it also has lush grasslands where herds graze and areas where crops are cultivated. Up until recently, the most productive land was largely occupied by sedentary farmers and cattle owners who tended to be non-Arabs. At certain times of the year, though, the pasture land was used, as a result of mutual agreement between the sedentary black Africans and Arab semi-nomadic and nomadic peoples. This resulted in a symbiotic relationship; that is, while the Arabs' animals were allowed to feed and be watered, the herds fertilized the ground owned by the black Africans, thus renewing the soil for subsequent growing seasons.

When conflicts erupted in the not too distant past amongst individuals and/or groups (be it among individuals in the same village, different black African tribal groups, or between black Africans and Arabs), the disagreements were generally resolved by the intervention and mediation of local leaders (*umdas* or *sheiks*). Neither conflict nor violence were uncommon, but it rarely resulted in wholesale violence that went on for months, let alone years. When called for, some sort of "blood money" was paid to the victim, be it for kin who were killed, animals stolen, or for some other transgression. The handing over of the blood money by the "guilty party" to the "victim" generally settled the grievance, and life went on as usual.

Notably, there was some intermarriage amongst and between the various peoples of Darfur, and as a result non-Arabs and Arabs married and vice versa.

Thus, different groups of people cohabited as neighbors, friends and even relatives, and not as sworn enemies due to ethnic, racial, or any other type of classification/category.

The causes and effects of any case of genocide are, of course, extremely complex. Any act of genocide is never the result of a single factor; indeed, genocide results from a synergy of trends, issues, and events that influence the thinking and actions of potential perpetrators who, ultimately, intend to extirpate, in one way or another, those it perceives as enemies, dangerous and/or loathsome in some way (and thus "outside their universe of obligation"). In the case of Darfur (2003-present), the issues/events that combined to make genocide possible were the following: extreme drought; increased desertification; Arab supremacism; authoritarianism; extreme nationalism; an ever-increasing bellicosity in the region (within Sudan, Darfur, and beyond its borders); and the disenfranchisement of black Africans at the hands of the Sudanese government.

### Extreme Drought and Desertification

Since the early 1970s, numerous droughts (including the "great drought" of 1984-1985), resulted in ever-increasing desertification. As a result of a severe drought in the 1970s, sections of the Sahara Desert reportedly crept south by as much as sixty miles.

The desertification of the land in Darfur, accompanied by fierce stand storms, resulted in a dramatic decline in the yield of produce, loss of pastureland, and a loss of livestock. Increasingly, this caused conflict between the nomadic/semi-nomadic Arab groups and the sedentary/farming group of non-Arabs. All of the latter, along with famine (some caused by nature, some by man—and some lasting much longer than those of the past), increased tensions over land usage and access to water and, ultimately, resulted in ever-increasing conflict and violence.

Exacerbating the situation was the fact that drought affected other countries in the region as well, and nomads from Chad and Libya migrated to Darfur in extremely large numbers in search of grazing land, which put further pressure on the available resources.

Nature thus forced nomadic groups to sweep lower south to locate sustenance for their herds. It also resulted in their grazing their herds for longer than usual. At one and the same time, farmers became evermore protective of their land. Some even resorted to putting up fences and establishing fees for land and water usage. What constituted protective efforts by the sedentary peoples/farmers were perceived as being stingy and unfair by the nomads.

### Arab Supremacism

Arab supremacism is an ideology that preaches, promotes, and sustains—in certain situations, at all cost—the notion that Arab beliefs and way of life are superior to all others. In that regard, it is an ideology that perceives all those who are not Arab as inferior. In Sudan, it has led to the demonization of certain groups who are perceived as "different" and, consequently, inferior to Arabs. Essentially, and, ultimately, it calls for Arab dominance in all aspects of life—culturally, politically, economically, judicially, and socially.

The origins of Arab supremacism "lay in the Libya of Colonel Gaddafi in the 1970s" and "the politics of the Sahara" (Flint and De Waal, 2005, p. 50). Gaddafi, in fact, fantasized about establishing an "Arab belt" across Africa. To accomplish this goal, he created, with his oil riches, various mechanisms, including "the Faliq al Islamiyya (Islamic Legion), which recruited Bedouins from Mauritania to Sudan; the Munazamat Da'awa al Islamiyya (Organization of the Islamic Call), which fostered Islamic philanthropy and evangelization; and sponsorship of the Sudanese opposition National Front, including the Muslim Brothers (or Muslim Brotherhood) and the *Ansar* (the *umma's* military wing).

Any mention of Arab supremacism and Sudan is incomplete that neglects to comment on the role of Hassan Abd al Turabi. Turabi—an Islamist, former law professor at the University of Khartoum, and a government official under Jaafar Nimeiri and then Omar al Bashir—was a major figure for decades in the Muslim Brotherhood. The Brotherhood, which originated in Eygpt, had been active in Sudan since 1949. The group's primary goal in Sudan was to "institutionalize Islamic law" (Mertz, 1991, n.p.). In 1964, Turabi became the secretary general of the Muslim Brotherhood, which was the year that the Brotherhood established its first political party. Turabi was closely involved with the Islamic Charter Front, which proposed that Sudan adopt an Islamic Constitution. The latter basically established that those Sudanese who were not Muslim would, from that point forward, be considered and, treated, as second-class citizens.

Over time, the Brotherhood established a close relationship with young Darfurians, convincing the latter that the Brotherhood's headlong push for the establishment of Islamic law was positive and that, as an organization, it was bereft of the prejudice and discrimination that was so rife within the Sudanese government when it came to ethnic and tribal differences. Understandably, these same young people came to trust and support Turabi.

Beginning as a peaceful civilian movement, the Brotherhood gradually morphed into a powerful and radical rebel group. More specifically, following a *coup d'état* in 1969, in which Colonel Jaafar Nimeri became prime minister of Sudan, Turabi's Islamist Party was dissolved. Immediately, though, the Islamists began planning its own rebellion. The planned rebellion, however, was quashed by the Sudanese military in March 1970. The combined effort of the Sudanese air force and ground troops resulted in the deaths of hundreds of Islamists fighters. Many survivors sought exile in Libya, where they established military-like camps in preparation for a later attempt to dislodge the Nimeri (who eventually became president) government. As Flint and De Waal (2005) note, "Their [the Islamists'] plan [while undergoing training] was an armed invasion of Sudan from bases in Libya, crossing Darfur and Kordofan to storm the capital. [Ultimately,] in July 1976, the Ansar-Islamist alliance very nearly succeeded... but the army counterattacked and the rebels were defeated" (pp. 22-23).

Turabi, a master at Machiavellian politics, found a way to disassociate himself from the failed invasion and to ingratiate himself with Nimeiri. In fact, Turabi became so close to Nimeiri he became his attorney general in 1977. At one and the same time, in his quest to establish an Islamic state, "[Turabi] infiltrated Islamist cadres into the armed forces, including elite units such as the air force" (Flint and De Waal, 2005, p. 23).

Always intent on imposing his Islamist vision on Sudan, Turabi, in 1983, led the way in implementing *shari'a* (Islamic law) in Sudan. The imposition of *shari'a* resulted in a slew of amputations and hangings. Due to a combination of disgust over (and, no doubt fear) the brutality meted out by the government as a result of its *shar'ia*-induced legislation and actions, Nimeiri was overthrown in 1985. Parliamentary rule was subsequently reinstated. Almost immediately, Turabi helped to establish the National Islamic Front (NIF), a political party that was controlled by the Muslim Brotherhood.

For a short while, Sudan returned to parliamentary rule. However, in 1989, with Turabi in the shadows but playing an integral role as a power broker, the military overthrew the elected government, and Omar al Bashir was installed as president of Sudan. As Sudan entered a period of increased turbulence, Turabi is said to have served as the real power behind the scenes.

In the early 1990s, the Sudanese Islamists began to inculcate Islamist thought throughout Sudan. At the forefront of the effort were Turabi and Ali Osman Mohamed Taha, an ardent Islamist and an on-and-off government figure. As part and parcel of this effort, Turabi, in 1990, established the Popular Arab Islamic Conference (PAIC), which was basically a regional organization for political Islamist militants. In his position as secretary general of PAIC, Turabi induced the Sudan government to create "an-open door policy for Arabs, including Turabi's Islamist associate Osama bin Laden, who made his base in Sudan in 1990-1996" (Human Rights Watch, 2002, p. 1). In order to accomplish their goals, "Islamist cadres were dispatched to foment a new Islamist consciousness in every village. Islamist philanthropic agencies were mobilized to open schools and clinics, and to support the Popular Defence Forces. A raft of programs aimed at building an Islamic Republic was launched" (Flint and De Waal, 2005, p. 28). Ultimately, though, Turabi concluded that if he was to succeed in gaining power through the elective process, he needed to part ways with the Brotherhood. That was true for the Brotherhood perceived Islamism and Arabism as one and the same, and many of those residing in Darfur were not Arab; and since Turabi believed he needed the votes of those in the West who were not Arab, he, calculatingly, cut his ties with the Brotherhood.

In 1999, Turabi set out to become the major power in Sudan. But, once again, his grand plans came to naught. Not only did Ali Osman break with Turabi as a result of looking askance at Turabi's ploys, schemes and intrigues, but al

Bashir—not about to be pushed aside—announced a state of emergency and removed Turabi from office (thus, wiping out Turabi's powerbase within the government). The ramifications were immense for Darfur: "The Bashir-Turabi split lost Darfur for the government, but made it possible to make peace in the South" (Flint and De Waal, 2005, p. 41).

## Authoritarianism

For nearly twenty years (1989-present), Sudan has been under the authoritarian rule of Omar al Bashir. His government controls virtually every aspect of Sudanese life. And when al-Turabi was a power behind the scenes, it meant that the Islamists were, like puppeteers, largely directing all aspects of Sudanese life. Those living in what is commonly referred to as the "peripheries" in Sudan (that is, those areas far from Khartoum, the "center" or powerbase in Sudan), were (and are) perceived and treated as second class citizens.

As soon as the new al-Bashir government, with its Islamicist focus, took power in 1989, it began dictating what was and was not acceptable in the way of behavior, dress, speech, and association with others. Furthermore, individuals were arrested for any and all dissent, individuals "disappeared" into secret prisons, torture was meted out regularly and viciously, and the judicial system answered only to al-Bashir and his cronies.

## Disenfranchisement

First, it is important to recall that Darfur is one of the poorest regions in all of Africa. Second, a single region of Sudan, the North (where Khartoum, the capital, is located), which comprises just over five percent of the population of the country, virtually controls all of Sudan—including its powerbase and its wealth. It is also the seat of advanced education in the nation. Almost all of those who hold major posts within the country have come from the North. Indeed, all of the presidents and prime ministers have come from the North, along with the vast majority of those who head up such important positions as those dealing with development, the infrastructure of the country, and banking. Third, for years on end, the black Africans of Darfur have requested the establishment of more schools, medical facilities, and roads—all of which are minimal in number, sorely under-funded, or, as is true in the case of roads, largely nonexistent. Fourth, most, if not all, of the black Africans' requests largely fell on deaf ears in Khartoum.

For many years, the black Africans of Darfur decried the hegemony of the North, as well as the fact that they (those residing in the West) have suffered prejudice, discrimination and disenfranchisement. Numerous examples of such disenfranchisement could be cited, but three shall suffice. First, "infant mortality in the West (at 122.5 boys and 104.2 girls dying per 1000 births) is strikingly different from infant mortality in the North (100.1 boys and 88.8 girls per thousand births)" (Cobham, 2005, n.p.). This difference is undoubtedly due in large part to the fact that adequate medical facilities and qualified medical personnel are available in the North but not in the West. In fact, "The entire State of Western Darfur has two medical specialists in the field of obstetrics and gynaceology, one in Geneina and the other in Zalengay. They are to serve a population of 1,650,000 aided by [a] few medical students who visit the area for training and for escaping mandatory military service" (Justice and Equality Movement, 2000, p. 53).

Second, "water development is currently reserved for the ever-expanding capital Khartoum. The rest of the country is left out, dying of thirst as well as diseases like malaria, kalazar, bilharsiasis, and other water-borne diseases" (Justice and Equality Movement, 2000, p. 41).

Third, the development of the country (the construction of roads, bridges, water systems, hospitals, schools) is largely limited to the North. Even those other areas that have seen development largely benefit those who are from the North. As for the West, "the entire Western region now lacks a single developmental scheme which could support one province for a single week" (Justice and Equality Movement, 2000, p. 5).

In May 2000, *The Black Book* (whose complete title is *The Black Book: Imbalance of Power and Wealth in Sudan*) mysteriously appeared in Khartoum. Copies were handed out outside major mosques following Friday prayers. Many are said to have even been placed, brazenly, on the desks of key Sudanese officials, including that of al Bashir. As photocopies of the book were "spontaneously" produced, the *Black Book* began to appear throughout the country and abroad. The *Black Book,* which was the work of the Islamicists in the country, was dedicated, in part, to "To the Sudanese people who have endured oppression, injustice and tyranny."

*The Black Book* argues that ever since Sudan's independence those who control the political and economic power within the Sudanese government (frequently referred to as "the elite," or, variously, "the ruling elite"), and by extension, the entire country, are from northern Sudan. More specifically, it asserts that the vast majority of posts in the government, the judiciary, the military, and the police all come from the North (and primarily from three tribal groups, the Shaygiyya, Ja'aliyiin and Danagla), and/or are appointed by the "centre" or the ruling elite. It also states that the "peripheries" of the country (those in the West, South and East) have been purposely denied fair representation in the government, and have been forced to lead a life of impoverishment. In the authors' introduction, it is asserted that at the turn of the millennium, Sudan remains "steeped in poverty, illiteracy, disease and lack of development" (Justice and Equality Movement, 2000, p. 1).

As De Waal (2004b) asserts, *The Black Book* essentially "condemned the Islamist promise to Darfur as a sham. *The Black Book* was a key step in the polarization of the country along politically constructed 'racial' rather than religious lines, and it laid the basis for a coalition between Darfur's radicals, who formed the SLA, and its Islamists, who formed the other rebel organization, the Justice and Equality Movement" (p. 8). In light of the ongoing attacks since the early 1990s by various Arab groups (nomads, semi-nomads and then, collaboratively, by Arab herders and GOS troops) against black African villages it seems that De Waal's assertion is not a little overblown. Indeed, the "racial divide" was certainly evident, and being acted up, many years prior to the appearance of *The Black Book.*

### Ever-Increasing Insecurity and Bellicosity in the Darfur Region

Beginning in the early- to mid-1990s, Arab herders began carrying out attacks against entire villages of sedentary black African farmers. Over time, such attacks began to involve both GOS troops and the Arab herders working in tandem. While vicious, such attacks were certainly not as systematic as the scorched-earth attacks that became increasingly common in 2003 and beyond (the attacks ebbed and flowed over the years, up through today, or December 2007).

The initial increase in violent conflict within the region was due to a host of issues. For example, in the 1980s, the GOS, under President Nimeri, abruptly replaced the tribal councils, the traditional bodies that helped solve and bring an end to conflicts, with government oversight of the region. Nimeri, however, failed to provide adequate resources to the regional government offices in order to carry out their work, and, as a result, the offices and expected services largely became hollow shells.

Making matters even more volatile, since riverine Arabs held the vast majority of positions in the government posts (including those as police and court officials), the black Africans of Darfur were automatically put at a distinct disadvantage. That is, disputes that were once dealt with, for the most part, fairly and equitably, by traditional authorities and/or a combination the latter and governmental authorities, were now handled by officials partial to the Arab sector of the population.

Furthermore, as certain groups of nomads increasingly bought into the beliefs of Arab Supremacism, they began to act as if they were superior to the black Africans. (Arab nomadic groups were and are not, of course, of a single mind and thus should not be painted as a monolithic group or movement.) Along with the huge influx of weapons into Darfur (resulting, in part, due to the various wars in the region, three of which were the Libya/Chad conflict, the prolonged war in southern Sudan, and a war in Eritrea), more and more herders began carrying weapons—no doubt, as a means of protection, but also because they had become accustom to carrying them as a result of their having fought in one or more of the violent conflicts in the region. As the Arab herders increasingly engaged in conflicts with the black Africans over land and water usage, they (the Arabs) made it known that they were ready and willing to use their weapons. Thus, with the difficulties presented by the droughts and desertification of pasture land, the influence of Arab Supremacism, and the Arab herders' experiences as mercenaries, it is not surprising that many of the Arab nomadic groups became increasingly cavalier and aggressive in their use of the sedentary people's lands in the early- to mid-1990s.

Not only did the Arab nomads purposely neglect to seek permission to use the land, but they refused to apologize for trespassing when confronted by the black African farmers. And when confronted by the farmers, it was not uncommon for the nomads to threaten the lives of the farmers – and, in many cases, they carried out their threats.

Out of fear and anger over the constant assaults and attacks on their villages and a lack of protection from local and regional governmental authorities, along with the gradual realization that the Arab marauders had tacit approval from the local government officials to do as they wished, the black Africans began to form self-defense groups.

## The Initial Rebel Attacks and the Response by the Government of Sudan

By the early 1990s, traditional dispute resolution approaches were proving to be inadequate. Arab nomadic attacks against black Africans were becoming more brazen, more frequent, more vicious and more costly in terms of lost lives and destroyed villages, farm land, et al. In August 1995, for example, Arab raiders attacked and burned the non-Arab village of Mejmeri in West Darfur, stealing 40,000 cattle and massacring twenty-three civilians. By late 1998, more than 100,000 non-Arab Massalit had fled to Chad to escape the violent attacks (Flint and De Waal, 2005, p. 69).

A great many of these attacks on villages were not one-time affairs. In fact, in the early to late 1990s, some villages were attacked up to three to four and more times. In certain cases, African villages were partially burned down by the marauders; in others, villages were utterly destroyed. Almost always, first, the villages were pillaged, and then, the herds were stolen. Black Africans were often forced out of their village only to be chased down in the desert and beaten and/or killed.

Still, desirous of remaining on their land, the black Africans more often than not returned to their villages once the marauders had left, rebuilt those sections destroyed, and carried on with life. However, as these attacks continued unabated, the black Africans began to look askance at the government. In light of the way the black Africans were being treated (a frustrating combination of being ignored and/or ill-treated by the government), it is not surprising that the following statement/critique of the Sudanese government made it into *The Black Book*:

> Conditions for accepting the authority of the ruler/ governing *power*: The authority must demonstrate its commitment to maintain sovereignty of land against foreign intruders; treat its citizens equally; afford them peace and protection;

guarantee dignified life; spread freedom and dignity, and must enable its citizens to fully participate in conducting their public affairs. All that is to take place within an environment that is conducive for participation of all without religious, ethnic, skin colour and gender discrimination.

The state authority cannot implement that without commitment to its national laws that regulate and divide powers among different state organs. Most important here is the separation between state powers, and in particular the political, the judicial and the legislative. (Justice and Equality Movement, 2000, p. 6)

In 2001 and 2002, before the current conflict became widely known to the outside world, a rebel movement comprising non-Arabs in Darfur emerged. The first rebel group to appear called itself the Sudanese Liberation Movement/Army (SLM/A), and on March 14, 2003, issued the following political declaration: "The brutal oppression, ethnic cleansing and genocide sponsored by the Khartoum government left the people of Darfur with no other option but to resort to popular political and military resistance for purposes of survival. This popular resistance has now coalesced into a political movement known as the Sudan Liberation movement and its military wing, the Sudan Liberation Army (SLM/SLA)" (The Sudan Liberation Movement and Sudan Liberation Army, 2003, pp. 1-2). Within a relatively short period of time, the group splintered, and from the split emerged a rebel group that called itself the Justice and Equality Movement (JEM). According to Flint and De Waal (2005), within JEM there are "two main tendencies that dwarf all others: one is tribal, the other Islamic" (p. 89).

In addition to providing local security for the black African villagers of Darfur, the two rebel groups issued protests against the economic and political marginalization of Darfur. The aforementioned *Black Book*, the brainchild of the leaders of JEM, was one such protest; indeed, it constituted the most detailed critique of the government to date, as well as the protest that reached the greatest and most diverse audience (from the top officials of the country all the way to the illiterate population who learned about the contents of the *Black Book* as a result of having it read to them). Members of both rebel groups came primarily (but by no means exclusively) from three non-Arab tribes—the Fur, Massalit, and Zaghawa—that had been attacked by nomadic Arab groups and GOS troops.

By late 2003, a flood of black Africans had either been forced from their homes as a result of GOS and Janjaweed attacks or had left out of sheer fear. By September 2003, the United Nations (UN) reported that some 65,000 refugees from Darfur had fled to Chad. By December 9, 2003, the United Nations estimated that there were up to 600,000 internally displaced people (IDP) in Darfur as a result of the attacks on the black Africans' villages. In November 2004, Médecins Sans Frontieres (Doctors Without Borders) estimated that some 1.8 million Darfurians had been displaced from their homes, with 200,000 of them in refugee camps in Chad (with the rest were in internally displaced (IDP) camps in Darfur) (Médecins Sans Frontieres, 2004, p. 1).

At one and the same time, the leaders of both rebel groups seemingly followed the ongoing peace negotiations between the GOS and the rebel groups in southern Sudan and realized that armed insurrection in the south had eventually led to important concessions by the GOS, including power-sharing and access to major economic resources. Whether such knowledge was the catalyst or trigger for the rebel initial attacks against the government only the leaders of SLM/A know for sure.

Popular accounts have it that the GOS, alarmed by the rebel attacks and with its own military forces stretched thin by the north-south civil war, decided to recruit, train, and equip Arab militias (the so-called Janjaweed) to help suppress what it purportedly perceived as a black African rebellion in Darfur.[4]

Any government whose military bases and/or other government facilities are attacked is to going to retaliate and attempt to suppress future attacks. Governments will either arrest the perpetrators or, if the situation degenerates into violence, shoot and then apprehend them, or, outright kill them. What the GOS did, however, was something vastly different and, ultimately, criminal. Using the argument that it believed that black African villagers were harboring rebels, the GOS (along with the Janjaweed) began attacking village after village after village of black Africans. Thus, instead of solely tracking down and attacking the black African rebel groups, the GOS and Janjaweed began carrying out a widespread and systematic, scorched earth policy against non-Arab villagers. In doing so, the GOS troops and the Janjaweed slaughtered men and boys (including infants), rape, mutilated, and often killed females, looted household goods and animals, and then burned the homes and villages to the ground (Physicians for Human Rights, 2005; UN Commission of Inquiry into Darfur, 2005; U.S. State Department, 2004). The attacks comprised bombings by aircraft, helicopter gunships, and four wheel vehicles with mounted machine guns, as well as hundreds of Janjaweed on camels and horses. In a report of its findings, the UN Commission of Inquiry on Darfur (2005) stated that "...the large majority of attacks on villages conducted by the [Janjaweed] militia have been undertaken with the acquiescence of State officials" (paragraph 125). The attacks led to the forcible displacement of, at first, ten of thousands, then hundreds of thousands and, ultimately (or at least through today, November 2007) over two and a half million people in Darfur alone (and more than another 250,000 in Chad).

As early as spring 2002 (May 1, to be exact), a group of Fur politicians complained to Sudanese President Omar al Bashir that 181 villages had been attacked by Arab militias, with hundreds people killed and thousands of animals stolen (Flint and de Waal, 2005, pp. 77-78).

In what De Waal and Flint (2005) call a "pivotal point" in the conflict between the black African rebels and the GOS troops, the SLA and JEM forces struck the government air force base at El Fasher on April 25, 2003. In doing so, they killed at least seventy-five people, destroyed several airplanes and bombers, and captured the base's commander (Flint and De Waal, 2005, pp. 99-100). In quick succession, numerous other attacks were carried out. According to Flint and De Waal (2005) "The rebels were winning almost every encounter—34 out of 38 in the middle months on 2003. [At this point in time, the GOS purportedly] feared it would lose the whole of Darfur..." (p. 101).

Between 2003 and today, the GOS has repeatedly denied that its troops have taken part in the scorched earth actions against the black Africans of Darfur. Indeed, while the rest of the world asserts that at least over 200,000 have been killed in Darfur over the past four years (with certain activist organizations claiming that the number is closer to 400,000 or more), the GOS asserts that just 9,000 have been killed, mostly as a result of rebel actions. Ample evidence, though, from a broad array of sources (e.g., the black African survivors of the attacks, AU and VN troops that are deployed in Darfur as monitors, numerous humanitarian organizations attempting to meet the basic needs of the IDPs, numerous human rights organizations, including Human Rights Watch, Physicians for Human Rights, and Amnesty International, and the investigations conducted by the United States in 2004 and the UN in 2004 and 2005) have provided evidence that clearly and definitively refutes the GOS' denials. ADD NOTE: The largest estimate of the number killed seemingly includes both outright murders as well as deaths due to what genocide scholars have, of late, referred to as "genocide by attrition" (deaths as a result of starvation and/or dehydration while on the run, injuries incurred in attacks or during flight from the attacks, and a lack of proper medical care). It is argued, the latter deaths would not have happened had the victim group not been forced from their homes and villages into the stark deserts and the IDP camps bereft of adequate food, water and medical care.

By late 2003, as various NGOs (nongovernmental organizations) and the UN scrambled to help the IDPs and the refugees flooding across the Sudan/Chad border, and word got out about the escalating carnage in Darfur. Finally, in December 2003, Jan Egeland, UN Under-Secretary for Humanitarian Affairs, asserted that the Darfur crisis was possibly the "worst [crisis] in the world today" (United Nations, 2004, p. 1). That same month, Tom Vraalsen, the UN Security General's Special Envoy for Humanitarian Affairs for Sudan, claimed that the situation in Darfur was "nothing less than the 'organized' destruction of sedentary African agriculturalists—the Fur, the Massaleit and the Zaghawa" (quoted in Reeves, 2003, p. 1).

In early 2004, one activist organization after another in the United States, Canada and Europe began rallying around the Darfur issue, variously, decrying the lack of action to halt the atrocities against the black Africans of Darfur, preparing and issuing reports, calling on the United Nations and/or the U.S. government to be proactive in addressing the crisis, and issuing calls for citizen action. On June 24, 2004, the U.S. Holocaust Memorial Museum (USHMM) took the extraordinary measure of shutting down normal operations for thirty minutes to focus attention on the ongoing crisis in Darfur. U.S. senators Sam Brownback and Jon Corzine, U.S. congressman Donald Payne, as well as a Holocaust survivor and a member of the Darfurian community-in-exile, came together in a special program in the USHMM's Hall of Witness to highlight and discuss the unfolding conflict in Darfur. On the same day, the U.S. House of Representatives unanimously declared that the situation in Darfur constituted genocide.

On June 30, 2004, U.S. Secretary of State Colin Powell visited a refugee camp for IDP camps and a refugee camp in Chad. While visiting the IDP camp, Abu Shouk, where malnutrition was rife among the 40,000 or so black Africans, Powell said: "We see indicators and elements that would start to move you toward a genocide conclusion but we're not there yet" (quoted by the BBC, 2004, p. 2).

In July and August 2004, the United States—in a joint effort involving the U.S. State Department, the Coalition of International Justice (CIJ), and the United States Agency for International Aid (USAID)—sent a team (the Atrocities Documentation Team or ADT) of twenty-four investigators to Chad to conduct interviews with Sudanese refugees from the Darfur region of Sudan for the express purpose of collecting evidence to help ascertain whether genocide had been perpetrated by the GOS and the Janjaweed. The ADT, which was the first ever official field investigation of a suspected genocide by one sovereign nation into another sovereign nation's actions while the killing was underway, conducted more than one thousand interviews with Darfurian refugees in camps and settlements on the Chad side of the border with Sudan. Evidence collected by the ADT led U.S. Secretary of State Colin Powell, on September 9, 2004, in a hearing before the U.S. Senate's Foreign Relations Committee, to publicly accuse the GOS of genocide. This was the first time that a government ever accused another government of genocide during an ongoing conflict.

Ultimately, the U.S. State Department presented the findings of the ADT in an eight-page report, "Documenting Atrocities in Darfur." The analysis of the data collected in the 1,136 interviews by the ADT revealed "a consistent and widespread pattern of atrocities in the Darfur region of western Sudan" (U.S. State Department, 2004, p. 1). The data also suggested a "close coordination between GOS [Government of Sudan] forces and Arab militia elements, commonly known as the *Jingaweit* [Janjaweed]" (U.S. State Department, 2004, p. 2). Furthermore, the data indicated that there was a clear "pattern of abuse against members of Darfur's non-Arab communities, including murder, rape, beatings, ethnic humiliation, and destruction of property and basic necessities" (U.S. State Department, 2004, p. 3).

Sixteen percent of the respondents witnessed or experienced rape. Significantly, the report suggests that the rapes were probably "under-reported because of the social stigma attached to acknowledging such violations of female members of the family" (U.S. State Department, 2004, p. 7). What makes the under-reporting even more probable is the fact that all of the interpreters and half of the investigators on the team were males, and that there was likely a natural disinclination on the behalf of the woman to mention such assaults in the company of males (strangers or otherwise).

During the course of his report on the ADP findings to the Senate Foreign Relations Committee on September 9, 2004, Powell remarked that the findings did not mean that the United States needed to do anything other than what it had already done. What he meant was that the finding of genocide did not obligate the United States government to carry out an intervention on the behalf of the black Africans of Darfur.

With that said, under Chapter VII of the UN Charter, the United States referred the Darfur matter to the United Nations. Subsequently, on September 18, 2004, the UN established the UN Commission of Inquiry into Darfur (COI), whose express purpose, as outlined in UN Security Council Resolution 1564, was to conduct its own investigation into the Darfur crisis. The COI conducted its inquiry in December 2004 and January 2005, and submitted its report to the Security Council in late January 2005. In its final section, "Conclusions and Recommendations," the COI report states: "...the Commission concludes that the Government of the Sudan and the Janjaweed are responsible for a number of violations of international human rights and humanitarian law. Some of these violations are very likely to amount to war crimes, and given the systematic and widespread pattern of many of the violations, they would also amount to crimes against humanity" (UN, 2005, para 603). While many scholars agreed with the conclusions of the COI, others were taken aback that—based on its own findings—it had not concluded that genocide had been perpetrated (Fowler, 2006, pp. 127-139; Stanton, 1996, pp. 181-188; Totten, 2006, pp. 199-222).

## Talk, Talk, and More Talk by the International Community

Between the summer of 2004 and today (November 2007), the UN Security Council repeatedly issued resolutions (over twenty between 2003 and April 2007) vis-à-vis the ongoing crisis in Darfur. The resolutions addressed a host of issues, including but not limited to the following: the need by the GOS to halt the ongoing indiscriminate attacks on black African civilians and the forced displacement of tens and hundreds of thousands of the latter; the need for the perpetrators of the atrocities in Darfur to be brought to justice without delay; concern over the GOS's failure to meet its obligations in ensuring the security of the civilian population of Darfur; disappointment regarding the constant cease-fire violations by all actors; the threat to issue various types of sanctions; the issuance of actual sanctions, including the freezing of certain actors' (GOS officials, Janjaweed leaders; and a leader of a rebel group) assets; and the referral of the Darfur conflict to the International Criminal Court (ICC), along with the names of key actors to be investigated on suspicion of having perpetrated atrocities.

The results of the resolutions were, at best, mixed. Some were acted on, but most were not. Various resolutions were revised time and again, along with ever-increasing threats, but largely to no avail due to a dearth of action. Tellingly, in July 2006, a senior Sudanese government official was quoted as saying that "The United Nations Security Council has threatened us so many times, we no longer take it seriously" (cited in Nathan, 2007, p. 249).

After much debate, compromise, and dithering, the United States and the UN Security Council finally imposed some sanctions on Sudan. For example, on April 25, 2006, the UN Security Council passed a resolution imposing sanctions against four Sudanese individuals, all of whom have been accused of war crimes in Darfur. Those sanctioned were Gaffar Mohamed Elhassan, an ex-Sudan air force commander, Sheikh Musa Hilal, a Janjaweed militia leader Adam Yacub Shant, a rebel SLA commander, and Gabril Abdul Kareem Badri, and a rebel National Movement for Reform and Development field commander. All four were to be subject to a ban on foreign travel, and any assets they had in banks abroad were to be frozen.

As for the United States, in May 2007, President George W. Bush ordered the imposition of sanctions that prevents thirty-one Sudanese companies (many of them oil related) and three individuals (two high level government leaders and a black African rebel leader) from doing business in the United States or with U.S. companies.

*Realpolitik* was at the center of the dithering, the watering down of certain sanctions, and the decision not to follow through on numerous resolutions and threatened sanctions. More specifically, various members of the Permanent Five members (the United States, Great Britain, France, the Russian Federation and China) of the UN Security Council had vested interests in Sudan and wanted to protect them.[5] China has an enormous petroleum deal with Sudan, and engages in significant weapons sales to Sudan; Russia also has a major arms deal with Sudan; and the United States has, off and on, taken advantage of GOS's offers to help shut down terrorist cells within Sudan and prevent potential terrorists from traveling through Sudan on their way to Afghanistan and Iraq to battle the United States in the latter's efforts to, respectively, capture Osama Bin Laden (terrorist mastermind of the September 11, 2001, attack on the World Trade Center in New York City and the Pentagon in Washington, D.C.) and to stabilize Iraq following the U.S.'s overthrow of dictator Saddam Hussein, which resulted in internecine conflict that has ripped the fabric of Iraq apart.

In June 2004, Sudan allowed the AU to deploy a small ceasefire monitoring team in Darfur comprised of representatives from the African Union, the GOS, two (later, three) rebel groups, along with the European Union, the UN and the U.S. From a tiny force of 300 troops, the force slowly increased to—and eventually leveled off at—about 7,000 troops. "As violence against civilians continued, the African Union Mission in Sudan (AMIS) force's mandate was expanded in October 2004 to protecting 'civilians whom it encounters under imminent threat and in the immediate vicinity, within resources and capability" (Human Rights Watch, 2007, p. 5). The new mandate, though, for all intents and purposes constituted little more than a paper tiger. The AU had neither the resources nor the capability of truly protecting anyone, let alone themselves.

Between 2003 and the end of 2007, the international community worked in various, though hardly effective, ways to bring the Darfur crisis to a close; and as it did, it continually decried the GOS troops' and Janjaweed's attacks of innocent civilians, the GOS's support of the *Janjaweed* and its murderous behavior, and called on the GOS to reign in the *Janjaweed*. Throughout, the GOS vigorously and disingenuously protested the validity of the accusations made by the international community, but, periodically, also made lukewarm promises to bring the situation under control. Such promises, though, were quickly broken. In most cases, however, the GOS blithely ignored the international community's requests, demands and threats.

When it became obvious that the AU troops were outmanned and outgunned, various calls were issued by various actors to insert UN troops into Darfur. Initially, the AU adamantly rejected the offer, asserting that it wanted to operate an all-African operation As for al Bashir, he was vociferous in his rejection of the suggestion. Time and again, he asserted that any force that entered Sudanese territory without an invitation from the Government of Sudan would not only be a violation of Sudan's sovereignty but would be perceived and treated as an enemy invasion. More specifically, for example, on February 26, 2006, al Bashir asserted, and then warned, that "We are strongly opposed to any foreign intervention in Sudan and Darfur will be a graveyard for any foreign troops venturing to enter" (quoted in *Sudan Tribune*, 2006, p. 1).

Finally, after immense international pressure, Sudan, in mid-June 2007, agreed to allow the deployment of a special force into Darfur, the UN/AU Hybrid (UNAMID) force. Ultimately, that was followed, on July 31, 2007, by the passage of UN Security Council Resolution 1769 which authorized a combined AU/UN Hybrid force for deployment in Darfur. The resolution called for "the immediate deployment of the United Nations Light and Heavy Support packages to the African Union Mission in the Sudan (AMIS) and a [AU/UN] Hybrid operation in Darfur [UNAMID], for which back-stopping and command and control structures will be provided by the United Nations.... [The] UNAMID...shall consist of up to 19,555 military personnel, including 360 military observers and liaison officers, and an appropriate civilian component including up to 3,772 police personnel and nineteen formed police units comprising up to 140 personnel each." In addressing the mandate of the UNAMID, the resolution states that "Acting under Chapter VII of the Charter of the United Nations: ...UNAMID is authorized to take the necessary action, in the areas of deployment of its forces and as it deems within its capabilities in order to: (i) protect its personnel, facilities, installations and equipment, and to ensure the security and freedom of movement of its own personnel and humanitarian workers, (ii) support early and effective implementation of the Darfur Peace Agreement, prevent the disruption of its implementation and armed attacks, and protect civilians, without prejudice to the responsibility of the Government of Sudan." The hybrid force was partially deployed in December 2007.

## Talk, Talk, and More Talk About Peace

In early September 2007, U.N. Secretary General Ban Ki-moon asserted that a new round of peace talks, which were to begin on October 27, 2007, in Libya, must be "a final settlement of this issue" (quoted in the *International Herald Tribune*, 2007, p. 1). At best, that seemed wishful thinking. As the *International Herald Tribune* (2007) noted, "Darfur has a history of peace talks — their sheer numbers a testimony to their lack of success.... Since fighting began in 2003 between ethnic African rebels and the Arab-dominated Sudanese government, there have been over half a dozen cease-fires or peace deals of various formats — all quickly breached by both sides" (p. 1).

In fact, beginning in 2004 and continuing through today, peace talks between the GOS and various rebel groups have been on again, off again affairs, with agreements often being broken by various and/or both sides within days, if not hours, of the signed agreements. In various cases and at various points in time, the intransigence of the GOS and/or rebel groups has placed one barrier after in the way of finding a workable solution to the crisis in Darfur. The GOS has broken agreements both blatantly (attacking black African villages with Antonov bombers, helicopter gun ships and GOS troops and Janjaweed) and surreptitiously (whitewashing planes white, attaching UN insignias to the wings and sides of the plane and using them to transport weapons and personnel into Darfur). Various black African rebel groups have not only reneged on agreements, but purposely prevented other rebel factions from taking part in the peace talks. Throughout parts of 2007, some of the many rebel groups even began to treat their counterparts enemies and engage them in vicious battles. Not only that, but the various factions—as the UN estimates that there are up to 28 declared rebel factions (Gettleman, 2007, p. A6)—have even shot and killed civilians, raped black African women and girls, attacked and killed AU troops, and harmed and killed humanitarian aid workers.

Each rebel faction is eager to be involved in the peace talks and no doubt have their own motives for doing so. Undoubtedly, many, if not most, are anxious to have their say regarding the fate of Darfur. All are likely to be cognizant of the new-found wealth and power that those residing in the south garnered upon the signing of the Comprehensive Peace Agreement, which finally brought to an end the twenty year war between north and southern Sudan.[6]

A peace agreement in Darfur had been finalized in May 2006, but it was signed by only one of three negotiating rebel groups. Throughout the entire "peace process, though, the killing and mass rape continued unabated. The most current attacks (all of 2007 and most of 2008) have focused on both the relatively few remaining black African villages in Darfur as well as the IDP camps. Out of fear of being murdered should they venture outside the IDP camps, black African men insist that girls and women scavenge for wood needed to build fires to cook food even if it means (as it often does) that the females will be raped by GOS soldiers and *Janjaweed*.

Over time, and particularly from mid-2007 onwards, the lay of the land has gotten even more dangerous in Darfur. This is true for numerous reasons: the *Janjaweed* not only continue to attack black Africans but have begun fighting amongst and between themselves; the various rebel groups continue to battle GOS troops and *Janjaweed* but have also begun fighting between and amongst themselves and attacking black African people in their villages and IDP camps; and roaming the region are bandits who attack anyone and everyone, including IDPs and humanitarian workers. Interestingly—and if true, tellingly—in a report entitled *Chaos by Design: Peacekeeping Challenges for AMIS and UNAMID*, Human Rights Watch (2007) asserted that "the [GOS] continues to stoke the chaos, and, in some areas, exploit intercommunal tensions that escalate into open hostilities, apparently in an effort to 'divide and rule' and maintain military and political dominance over the [Darfur] region" (p. 1).

## Pervasiveness and Nature of the Sexual Assaults

The sexual assaults carried out by the GOS troops and *Janjaweed* against black African woman has been nothing short of ubiquitous. In a major report that Médecins Sans Frontières issued in 2005, it stated that 82 percent of the rapes (at least those committed in 2005) were perpetrated while were engaged in "daily activities" versus only four percent during the frontal attacks on villages by GOS troops and the Janjaweed (n.d.). In many, if not most, cases, rape has been perpetrated with the purpose of terrorizing the black African female population, shaming the women and making them pariahs, humiliating the black African men, tearing apart the seams of the black African community, and creating Arab babies. In its July 2007 report, "Laws Without Justice: An Assessment of Sudanese Laws Affecting Survivors of Rape," Refugees International asserted that "rape is an integral part of the pattern of violence that the GOS, [through the actions of its proxies, the *Janjaweed*] is inflicting upon the targeted ethnic groups in Darfur.... The raping of Darfuri women is inexorably linked to the systematic destruction of their communities" (n.p.). Furthermore, as the *Guardian* (2006) put it: "Sexual violence is aimed...at weakening tribal ethnic lines[, and] the brutal rape of women and children has become a weapon of war" (n.p.).

The sexual assaults by GOS troops and the Janjaweed against the black African females have run the gamut from forcing the latter to undress in front of hordes of men, individual rape, gang rape, and sexual slavery.[7] It is not uncommon for the females to be raped out in the open—in their fields, their villages, near *wadis*—and in their homes in front of family members. In a 2004 report,

Amnesty International reported that "Pregnant women have not been spared. Those who have resisted rapes were reportedly beaten, stabbed or killed.... Girls as young as eight years old have been abducted and held in sexual slavery, some for many months" (n.p.).

In July 2005, the United Nations issued a report that accused the GOS of ignoring the mass rapes being perpetrated by GOS troops and the Janjaweed, and berated it for taking absolutely no action to either halt the rapes or bring the perpetrators to account. Furthermore, the UN report asserted that GOS officials both threatened and even arrested rape victims in order to force them to recant their accusations/charges. In its report, the UN called on the GOS to abolish all laws, rules, regulations granting immunity from prosecution to those in the state's employ, and to provide in-depth training to police officials, prosecutors, and judges vis-à-vis sexual assault cases. Some two years later, in 2007, Refugees International reported that "Sudan's laws [continue to] grant immunity to members of the military, security services, police and border guard; many Janjaweed members have been integrated into the Popular Defense Forces, which also makes them exempt from prosecution" (Refugees International, 2007, n. p.).

Cognizant of the fact that both their community and closest family members may treat them as pariahs for having been raped, many females refuse to inform loved ones or authorities about such attacks. This is true for not only may married women be disowned by their husbands, but unmarried girls and women generally become unmarriageable as a result of their diminished status. Wishing to keep their assault a secret, many girls and women purposely avoid seeking medical assistance following a rape. This, of course, can (and often does) lead to additional medical complications.

In a 2004 report entitled *Darfur: Rape as a Weapon of War: Sexual Violence and its Consequences*, Amnesty International reported that

> [ra]pe will have a devastating and ongoing impact on the health of women and girls, and survivors now face a lifetime of stigma and marginalization from their own families and communities....Women who have become pregnant as a result of rape often suffer complications before, during and after giving birth, because of the physical injuries resulting from assault. When giving birth, women who have been raped are prone to fistula and lose control of the bladder or bowel functions. They become isolated as a result of their incontinence. (n.p.)

Furthermore, health problems such as infection or injuries to the genital area and reproduction system can result in the inability to have children. The latter could result in the rejection of the female victim by her husband. Of course, each female (and male, of course) who is raped is also in danger of contracting HIV/AIDS. Each infection and disease also has the possibility of causing serious health problems for those children born to the victims of rape. As time passes that is going to be a horrific problem that will, obviously, be insidious in its own way. Furthermore, "a child born as a result of rape may be considered a child of the 'enemy', a '*Janjawid* child' and women can feel forced to abandon the child born" (Amnesty International, 2004, n.p.). In fact, "huge numbers of abandoned babies are among the consequences of unwanted pregnancies resulting from rape in Darfur. An aid worker who spoke to IWPR (Institute for War and Peace Reporting) on condition of anonymity said, 'The women cannot deal with the stigma attached to babies born out of rape and often abandon the infants'" (Nieuwoudt, 2006, n.p.).

## Rape as Genocide

Contingent on the circumstances, rape committed during a violent conflict can be classified as a war crime, crimes against humanity and/or genocide. Indeed, rape is in contravention of the 1949 Geneva Conventions, the 1984 Torture Convention, and the 1998 Rome Treaty (the mechanism that established the International Criminal Court).

The systematic nature of the sexual attacks and the epithets, threats, and comments screamed at the black African females by the GOS troops and *Janjaweed* during their perpetration of the rapes strongly suggest that the attacks constitute a genocidal assault on the black Africans of Africa. Common epithets directed at the girls and women being raped are: slave, slave dogs, and *zurega* (which is roughly the equivalent of "nigger"). A seventeen year old black African, Aisha (a pseudonym), who was attacked by Arabs in military uniforms reported the following: "They called us 'abid' [slaves], and said they were going to make us their wives" (cited in Mariner, 2004, n.p.). Another rape victim reported that "They [those who raped her] told us that now we would have Arab babies; and if they would find any Fur woman, they would rape them again to change the colour of their children" (quoted in *Médecins Sans Frontières*, 2005, n.p.). Some human rights activists have "described rape of this kind [making different color babies] as a form of ethnic cleansing, a claim that goes to the heart of the allegation that 'rolling genocide' is slowly but surely taking place in Darfur" (Nieuwoudt, 2006, n.p.). Finally, a humanitarian aid worker told *Washington Post* journalist Emily Wax, "Everyone knows how the father carries the lineage in the culture [of Sudan]. They [the militiamen] want more Arab babies [by Darfur's African women] to take the land" (quoted in Wax, 2004, p. 2).

## Sudanese Law and Rape

Reportedly, those black African females who are raped in Darfur and report it (either to local health organization or the police) face insult to injury because they, the females, are often arrested. Despite having been horrifically violated, they can be (and often are) arrested for either having engaged in extramarital sex or sex out of wedlock. In an investigation carried out in Darfur, Médecins Sans Frontières (MSF) (2005) documented the fact of such arrests. In its report,

MSF provides first-person accounts by the victims, including the following one by a sixteen-year-old black African girl:

> One day, in March 2004, I was collecting firewood for my family when three men on camels came and surrounded me. They held me down, tied my hands and raped me one after the other. When I arrived home, I told my family what had happened. They threw me out of [our] home and I had to build my own hut away from them. I was engaged to a man and I was so much looking forward to getting married. After I was raped, he did not want to marry... because he said that I was now disgraced and spoilt.
>
> When I was eight months pregnant from the rape, the police came to my hut and forced me with their guns to go to the police station. They asked me questions, so I told them that I had been raped. They told me that as I was not married, I will deliver this baby illegally. They beat me with a whip on the chest and back and put me in jail. (n.p.)

In 2005, Human Rights Commissioner Louise Arbour also reported that rape victims in Darfur could face criminal charges if and when courts ruled that they were unable to prove their case, which, ultimately, discouraged women from making accusations (BBC, 2005, n.p).

Up until quite recently, under Sudanese law, in order for a female to prove she had been raped, she was required to have four male witnesses corroborate the fact that the crime had taken place. Jane Lindrio Alao, a psychologist working with victims of the genocide in Darfur, remarked that "All four [men must have] witness[ed] the actual penetration. So even if you could get two such witnesses, the accused could not be charged. How many women have the luxury of having witnesses to their rape?" (quoted in Nieuwoudt, 2006, n.p.).

And adding insult to injury, in 2006, an analyst with the International Crisis Group, reported that "women [who report they have been raped] are often...accused by police of waging war on the central government" (quoted in Nieuwoudt, 2006, n.p.).

## The Critical Challenges

There are numerous and serious challenges in the face of the relatively recent and ongoing rape of females in Darfur. First, there is the critical need to halt the killing and rape of all black Darfurians by bringing Darfur under control. Second, immediate and thorough medical care needs to be provided to those who have been raped. Third, adequate medical care must be provided for those babies who have been born as a result of their mothers having been raped. Fourth, psychological care must be provided for those women, men, and children who are suffering grievous mental harm due to either what they have experienced and/or witnessed. Fifth, there is a dire need to bring to justice those perpetrators who raped the black African Darfurian girls and women.

## The Likelihood of that the Critical Challenges Shall be Addressed

The likelihood that the aforementioned challenges shall be addressed any time soon, let alone at all, is extremely mixed. In regard to putting a stop to the killing, only time will tell if the international community is successful in deploying an effective hybrid African Union/UN force in Darfur. At this point in time (December 2007), it remains a question as to whether the AU/UN Hybrid force will be deployed on time, have a strong enough mandate to allow it to bring Darfur under control, and/or whether it will have the staying power, mandate, personnel, material resources, and support to see its plan to fruition. Even with the hybrid force's intended deployment, there is the looming question as to whether such a small contingent (an increase from 7,000 to between 19,000 to 25,000 or so troops) is going to be able to truly provide safety for some 2.5 million internally displaced peoples in such a large and violent region.

As for providing immediate and thorough medical care for those females who have been raped, as well as the babies who were conceived as a result of their mothers being raped, some (but, far from most) are currently receiving basic care by the International Red Cross and Doctors Without Borders. That said, the number of rape victims is so great that there is no way that more than a fraction can be helped; plus, the doctors and nurses face Herculean obstacles in providing what care they can, and that is due, in part, to the constant attacks by the GOS and *Janjaweed* (and, as of late, rebel groups). It is also due to the fact that the temporary medical facilities established by the latter are quite rudimentary. There is also the fact that if females do not seek medical assistance out of fear that their secret will be divulged to others in their community, then there is little to nothing that can be done for them.

Unfortunately, due to various extenuating circumstances, there is no hope that most of the sexual assault victims will receive any psychological care in the near future. In fact, in all likelihood, it is dubious that all but a fraction will receive such care, either in the near future or, for that matter, years from now. The primary focus vis-à-vis medical attention in the IDP and refugee camps is on taking care of physical injuries, illnesses and, in far fewer cases, complications due to rape. Over and above that, only a tiny number of psychologists are available in the numerous IDP and refugee camps. Complicating matters is the aforementioned fact that many, if not most, females refuse to divulge the fact they've been raped. Also, if the black Africans are ever allowed to return to their villages, psychological help will not likely be available in the remote areas where they live.

It is almost a certainty that at least some of the major alleged perpetrators of the crimes against humanity and genocide will be indicted by the ICC, but whether they will actually be tried is another question altogether. That said, it is painfully clear—based on the cases that have been tried at the International Criminal Tribunal for the Former Yugoslavia and the International Criminal

Tribunal for Rwanda—that very few, if any, of the common soldiers or militia members who murdered and raped black Africans will ever be indicted or be held responsible in anyway whatsoever for the crimes they committed. Generally, only the main leaders and planners of genocide acts are held accountable, and even that is not always a given. To end impunity, both upper *and* lower echelon mass murderers and rapists must be accountable for their actions.

## Recommendations

There needs to be a large deployment of a cadre of medical personnel (preferably women) knowledgeable about medical issues related to sexual assault to both the IDP camps in Darfur and the refugee camps in Chad. (Even those females who are willing to seek help are not accustomed to seeing male doctors (and many of the volunteers in Darfur are, in fact, male), and their customs and way of life militate against them (the females) seeing males about health matters, especially ones that are so personal. So, female medical personnel is critical to the success of such efforts. Why? As Amnesty International reported back in 2004. The consequences of this lack of medical support for rape survivors is severe" (n.p.). Unfortunately, this largely remains true today. It should go without saying that all medical personnel must be provided with ample support staff, resources, and adequate security in order to carry out their work.

* There is a critical need for the deployment of a large cadre of trained medical personal and psychologists (preferably women) who are not only knowledgeable about sexual violence but have the knowledge and skills to develop and implement educational and psychosocial counseling programs for sexual assault victims and others. Why? Médecins Sans Frontières (2005) reports that "Given the fact that sexual violence is often a taboo, it is important to have education activities in place to raise awareness about the issues" (n.p.), as well as about the fact that medical and psychosocial treatment is available. Such personnel will also need to educate about the dangers faced by those victims who choose not to seek such assistance (as well as the value in seeking it).

  A social services program in the IDP camps to specifically care for those babies (and/or children) who have been abandoned is desperately needed. Why? Because, as Nieuwoudt (2006) has noted: "According to a report ("Children Born Out of Rape/Wedlock") by the United Nations Children's Fund, UNICEF, "babies are brought to the police who take them to hospitals: but many are found too late to save their lives. For those who survive, there is no standard procedure or service offered after the hospital examination" (n.p.).

• A reliable, honest, upright police force (preferably women) from the international community is critically needed to accompany black African females as they continue to forage for wood outside the IDP and refugee camps (Kinnock, 2005, p. 1). This is likely to be the only way that such females will be protected from rape at the hands of the GOS soldiers, *Janjaweed*, rebel groups, bandits, and others.

Better yet, the international community should undertake a major effort to provide fuel-efficient stoves that consume far smaller amounts of wood, thus precluding the need for females to place themselves at risk foraging for wood. At one and the same time, it would be ideal to provide the camps with fuel for their stoves.

## Conclusion

As the international community dithers, innocent people in Darfur continue to be murdered, die as a result of malnutrition, dehydration and lack of medication attention, and suffer rape at the hands of the GOS troops and Janjaweed (and increasingly, members of some of the rebel groups). Four long years have gone by since the start of the crisis in Darfur, and the international community continues to engage in talk over real action to ameliorate the problems that beset Darfur. Unfortunately, Darfur is a stark reminder, as if the international community really needs such, that the world is no closer to solving, halting, let alone, preventing genocide than it was during the Ottoman Turk genocide of the Armenians (1915-1923), the manmade famine in Ukraine (1933), and the Holocaust perpetrated by the Nazis (1933-1945). The same is true, unfortunately, in regard to sexual assaults against girls and women during periods of violent conflict.

## Notes

1.    The phrase "the first acknowledged genocide" is used here for it is certainly possible that other genocides were and are being perpetrated in the early part of the twenty-first century but not detected yet by the international community. In fact, various scholars and political pundits have suggested that genocide could be underway in such varied places as the Democratic Republic of the Congo, and in far-flung areas where indigenous groups reside.
2.    Colloquially, according to the black Africans of Darfur, *Janjaweed* " means, variously, "hordes," "ruffians," and "men or devils on horseback."
3.    In Arabic, the word "zureg" is basically equivalent to the word "nigger" in English.
4.    Tellingly, in interviews with black African Darfurian refugees in Gaga and Forchana refugee camps in eastern Chad during the summer of 2007, this author was told that Arab nomads had been provided with weapons and trained by the GOS as early as the mid-1990s. Furthermore, the so-called *Janjaweed* had been used by the Sudanese leadership since the late 1980s to supplement government troops in the fight against southern rebels (Prunier, 2005, p. 97), and it is certainly possible, if not highly probable, that many of them had roamed throughout Darfur and even joined nomadic groups as the latter herded livestock.
5.    Each member of the Permanent Five of the UN Security Council can, alone, with a vote of "no" on any resolution defeat any motion or vote on an issue. The Permanent Five are the only members of the UN Security Council with such power.

6.  Following a series of complex of talks during 2002 and 2003, a Comprehensive Peace Agreement (CPA) was signed in Nairobi on January 9, 2005. The CPA provided for the sharing of power between the Government of Sudan (GOS) and leaders of the SPLM and determined that the main rebel leader, John Garang, would become the First Vice-President of Sudan. An important provision of the CPA called for the sharing of revenues from oil, which had begun to be pumped in 1999, between the north and the south of the nation. Six years after the signing of the CPA, the south will be permitted to hold a referendum for self-determination and, essentially independence.

7.  Some black African males have also been sexually assaulted by the *Janjaweed* during which the former have been gang raped.

    On a different note, it is also important to acknowledge the fact that throughout at least 2006 and 2007, members of various black African rebel groups have attacked black African woman as well and raped them. As horrific as the latter is, it does not, of course, constitute genocide.

## References

Amnesty International (2004). *Darfur: Rape as a Weapon of War: Sexual Violence and its Consequences*. London: Author. Accessed at: http://web.amnesty.org/library.

Anonymous (2000). *The Black Book: The Imbalance of Power and Wealth in Sudan*. Khartoum: Author(s).

Apiku, Simon (2007). "African Darfur Troops Must Meet UN Standards – Adada." *Reuters*. August 16. Accessed at: www.reuters.com/resources/archive/us/20070816.html

Baldauf, Scott (2007). "Sudan: Climate Change Escalates Darfur Crisis." *Christian Science Monitor*. July 27. Accessed at: www.cscomonitor.com/2007/0727/p01s04-woaf.html

Cobham, Alex (2005). "Causes of Conflict in Sudan: Testing the Black Book." *Queen Elizabeth House, University of Oxford, Working Paper Series*. Oxford, England: University of Oxford. Accessed at: ideas.repec.org/p/qeh/qehw.ps/qehw.ps

BBC (2005). "UN accuses Sudan over Darfur Rape." July 29, 2005, n.p. Accessed at: news.bbc.co.uk/2/hi/Africa/4728231.stm

BBC News (UK Edition) (2004). "Sudanese Refugees Welcome Powell." June 30, 4 pp. bbc.co.uk

De Waal, Alex (2004a). *Famine That Kills: Darfur, Sudan*. New York: Oxford University Press.

De Waal, Alex (2004b). "Tragedy in Darfur: On Understanding and ending the Horror." *Boston Review: A Political and Literary Forum*. October/November, n.p. Accessed at bostonreview.net/BR29.5/dewaal.html

Flint, Julie, and de Waal, Alex (2005). *Darfur: A Short History of a Long War*. New York: Zed Books.

Gettleman, Jeffrey (2007). "At the Darfur Talks in Libya, Rebel Unity Is as Scarce as the Rebels Themselves." *New Times*, October 31, p. A6.

Global News Monitor (2004). "Genocide Emergency in the Darfur Region of Sudan," p. 2, July 28. http://www.preventgenocide.org

The Guardian (2006). "The Rape of Darfur. Special reports." *Guardian Unlimited*. January 18, n.p. Accessible at: www.guardian.co.uk/sudan

Human Rights Watch (2007). Chaos by Design: Peacekeeping Challenges for AMIS and UNAMID. New York: Author.

Human Rights Watch (2002). "Biography of Hassan al Turabi." New York: Author. Accessed at: www.hrw.org/press/2002/03/turabi-bio.htm

Human Rights Watch (2007). "Q & A: Crisis in Darfur." New York: Author. Accessed at: www.hrw.org/english/docs/2004/05/05/darfur8536.htm

International Herald Tribune (2007). "Success Uncerrtain for New, U.N.-Sponsored Darfur Peace Talks." September 12. *International Herald Tribune*. Accessed at www.iht.com/articles/ap/2007/09/12/africa/AF-GEN-Darfur-Peace-Talks.php

Kevane, Michael (2005). "Was the Black Book Correct? Regional Equality in Sudan." Santa Clara, CA: Santa Clara University, Department of Economics. Unpublished paper. Accessed at: understandingsudan.org/darfur/Was%20the%black%book%correct.doc

Kinnock, Glenys (2006). "The Rape of Darfur." *Guardian Unlimited*. January 18. Accessed at: www.guardian.co.uk/sudan

Lumeya, Fidele (2004). *Rape, Islam, and Darfur's Women Refugees and War-Displaced*. Washington, DC: Refugees International. Accessed at: www.refugeesinternational.org/content/article

Mamdani, Mahmood (2007). "The Politics of Naming: Genocide, Civil War, Insurgency." March 8. Accessed at: www.wespac.org/WESPACCommunity/DiscussionMessages/tabid/124/forumid/7/postid/408

Malan, Mark (2007). "Africom: A Wolf in Sheep's Clothing?" Testimony Before the Subcommittee on African Affairs, Committee on Foreign Relations, U.S. Senate. August 1. Accessed at: www.senate.gov-foreign/testimoy/2007/MalanTestimony070801/pdf

Mariner, Joanne (2004). "Rape in Darfur.*" FindLaw's Writ - Mariner: October 27*. Accessed at: writ.news.findlaw.com/mariner/20041027.html

Médecins Sans Frontières (2005).*The Crushing Burden of Rape Sexual Violence in Darfur*. March 8. Paris: Author.

Médecins Sans Frontières (2005). "Persecution, Intimidation and Failure of Assistance in Darfur. *MSF Reports*. November 1. Paris: Author. Accessed at: www.msf.org/ms-finternationa/invoke.cfm?objectid

Nathan, Laurie (2007). "The Making and Unmaking of the Darfur Peace Agreement," pp. 245-266. In Alex De Waal (Ed.) *War in Darfur: And the Search for Peace*. Cambridge, MA and London: Global Equity Initiative, Harvard University, and Justice Africa, respectively.

Nieuwoudt, Stephanie (2006). "No justice for Darfur rape victims." NEED NAME OF PUBLICATION. October, n.p. Accessed at: iwpr.net/?p=acr&s=f&o=324842&apc_state=henpacr

Payne, Donald M. (2004). "Rep. Payne Urges Action at Congressional Black Caucus Press Conference on the Crisis in Darfur, Sudan—Press Release," June 23, p. 1. Washington, DC: U.S. Representative Donald M. Payne's Office.

Powell, Colin (2004). "Darfur." *Wall Street Journal*, August 5, p. 1.

Reeves, Eric (2007). "Darfur Betrayed Again: The UN/AU 'Hybrid' Force Steadily Weakens." August 24. Accessed at: www/sudanreeves/org/Article182.html

Reeves, Eric (2003). "'Ethic Cleansing' in Darfur: Systematic, Ethnically Based Denial of Humanitarian Aid Is No Context for a Sustainable Agreement in Sudan." SPLM-Today.com, the official website of the SPLM/A, December 30, p. 1.

Refugees International (2007). *Laws Without Justice: An Assessment of Sudanese Laws Affecting Survivors of Rap*e. Washington, DC.

U.S. State Department (September 9, 2004). *Documenting Atrocities in Darfur*. State Publication 11182. Washington, DC: Author.

The Sudan Liberation Movement and Sudan Liberation Army SLM/SLA) (2003). "Political Declaration." March 14. Accessed at: http://www.sudan.net/news/press/postedr/214.shtml

Sudan Tribune (2006). "'Darfur Will be Foreign Troops' Graveyard' – Bashir." *Sudan Tribune*, February 27, p. 1. Accessed at: www.sudantribune.com/spip.ph?

United Nations (2004). "Sudan: World's Worst Humanitarian Crisis—Press Release."
March 22. New York: Author, p. 2

United Nations Commission of Inquiry (2005). *UN Commission of Inquiry: Darfur
Conflict*. New York: Author.

UN News Centre (2003). "As Refugees Pour into Chad from Sudan, UN Announces
Plans for Safer Camps." *UN News Centre*. December 23. New York: United Nations, 2 pp.

Wax, Emily (2004). "'We Want to Make a Light Baby': Arab Militiamen in Sudan
Said to Use Rape as Weapon of Ethnic Cleansing." June 20. The Washington Post,
pp. A01-02. Accessed at www.washingtonpost.com/wp-dyn/ articles/A16001-
2004Jun29.html

## Annotated Bibliography

Amnesty International (2004). *Sudan—Darfur: Rape as a Weapon of War:
Sexual Violence and its Consequences*. London: Author, 46 pp.

This report, based on first-person accounts by some 250 black African
women, addresses how rape has been used as a weapon of war by Government of Sudan troops and *Janjaweed* against the black African population
of Darfur. In doing so, it also addresses such issues as such as the social
stigmatization of being raped; the economic, social and health ramifications as a result of having been sexually assaulted; and how and why sexual
assaults result in the destruction of the social fabric of the black African
peoples' communities.

Askin, Kelly Dawn (2006). "Prosecuting Gender Crimes Committed in Darfur:
Holding Leaders Accountable for Sexual Violence," pp. 141-160. In Samuel
Totten and Eric Markusen (Eds.) *Genocide in Darfur: Investigating Atrocities
in the Sudan*. New York: Routledge.

This chapter by a noted scholar on international law and sexual violence
addresses a host of key issues, including but not limited to the following: a
succinct historical overview of wartime rape in law and society, sexual violence in Darfur, rape as genocide and a crime against humanity, individual and
superior responsibility, and holding leaders accountable for sex crimes.

Bureau of Democracy, Human Rights and Labor and Bureau of Intelligence
and Research (2004). *Documenting Atrocities in Darfur*. Washington, DC:
United States Department of State, 8 pp.

This is the official report of the U.S. State Department's project to conduct
interviews of Sudanese refugees living in refugee camps in Chad along the
Chad/Sudan border in July and August 2004. The study/analysis was based
on semi-structured interviews with 1,136 randomly selected refugees. The
analysis of the findings were used by U.S. Secretary of State Colin Powell
to declare that genocide had been (and possibly still was being) perpetrated
in Darfur by Government of Sudan troops and the Janjaweed.

Sixteen percent of "the respondents said either that they had been raped
or had heard about a rape from a victim" (p. 4). A key caveat of the report
states that "it is very likely that rapes are underreported because of the social
stigma attached to acknowledging such violations" (p. 7).

Fricke, Andrienne L. with Amira Khair (2007). *Laws Without Justice: An Assessment of Sudanese Laws Affecting Survivors of Rape*. Washington, DC: Refugees International, 21 pp.

Laws Without Justice: An Assessment of Sudanese Laws Affecting Survivors of Rape "outlines a system of Sudanese laws that exposes rape victims to further abuse, shields perpetrators from prosecution, limits the ability for survivors to receive medical services and generally denies any access to justice. The report examines these laws and makes a series of recommendations on how the laws can be revised. The report also encourages international support of Sudanese civil society organizations and opposition members of Parliament who are calling for changes to these laws."

Gingerich,Tara, and Leaning, Jennifer (2004). *The Use of Rape as a Weapon of War in the Conflict in Darfur, Sudan*. Washington, DC: U.S. Agency for International Development with Physicians for Human Rights, 56 pp.

This report makes use of extensive interviews and published literature to qualitatively assess the nature, circumstances and context of rape as a weapon in Sudan's ongoing war against the black Africans of Darfur. It is comprised of the following parts: Overview of Darfur Conflict; Use of Rape as a Weapon of War (Historical Overview, Military Utility of Rape as a Weapon of War; The Strategic Use of Rape; Other Uses of Rape in Conflict; Codification as a Crime Under International Law); Use of Rape as a Weapon of War in the Darfur Conflict (Circumstances Under Which Rape Occurs; Prevalence of Rape in the Darfur Conflict; Strategic Use of Rape as a Weapon of War in Darfur; Other Issues Regarding Rape in the Darfur Conflict; Sexual Abuse of Males Participation of GOS Forces in Darfur Rape); Individual and Community Effects of Rape in Darfur (Short-Term Effects on Individuals; Physical Effects; Psychological and Psychosocial Effects; Short-Term Effects of Rape at the Community Level; Longer-Term Effects on Individuals and Communities); and Major Findings and Recommendations.

Human Rights Watch (2005*). Sexual Violence and Its Consequences Among Displaced Persons in Darfur and Chad*. New York: Author, 18 pp.

This report is based on two Human Rights Watch research missions in February 2005, one to displaced persons camps in South Darfur and one to refugee camps in Chad, to "conduct research on patterns of sexual and gender-based violence and the response of local and international actors." While the research does not constitute a comprehensive assessment of the numerous and complex issues related to sexual and gender-based violence or provide an evaluation of all of the humanitarian groups' efforts underway in Darfur and Chad, it does highlight some of the most significant "elements in the patterns of sexual and gender-based violence—including the urgent need for protection from ongoing violence—and stresses the need for an appropriate response."

Kristof, Nicholas D. (2005). "A Policy of Rape." *The New York Times*, June 5. Accessed at: www.nytimes.com/2005/06/05/opinion/05kristof

Herein, Kristof, a *New York Times* columnist, describes what he refers to as "a systematic campaign of rape to terrorize civilians and drive them from 'Arab lands'" [in Darfur, Sudan]. More specifically, he writes about how women in one "squatters" camp, Kalma, which holds some 110,000 people who had been driven from their homes by government of Sudan troops and the *Janjaweed*, "still face the risk of gang rape every single day as they go out looking for firewood." In doing so, he relates various women's stories, including one twenty-one-year-old woman, Nemat, who was gang-raped by men in uniforms who told her, "'You are black people. We want to wipe you out.'" Another woman who was raped by seven men in police uniforms was told, "We want to finish you people off."

Médecins Sans Frontières (2005). *The Crushing Burden of Rape: Sexual Violence in Darfur – A Brief Paper*. Paris: Author, 8 pp.
    Based on Médecins Sans Frontières' (MSF) work in Darfur between October 2004 and February 2005, this report addresses a host of issues related to sexual assault, including but not limited to the following: sexual assaults perpetrated against girls and women as they go about their daily activities (versus being sexually assaulted during an attack carried out on a village by GOS troops and/or the *Janjaweed*); multiple rapes and abductions; the medical and social effects of rape; how victims are treated as criminals; and how MSF provides assistance to those who have been sexually assaulted.

Physicians for Human Rights (2006). *Darfur: Assault on Survival—A Call for Security, Justice and Restitution*. Cambridge, MA: Author, 67 pp.
    Based on a series of interviews conducted between May 2004 and July 2005 with eyewitnesses from the villages of Furawiya, Terbeba, and Bendisi, Physicians for Human Rights investigators "randomly surveyed dozens of survivors and documented...compelling evidence of a destroyed way of life and means of survival." The report includes a section entitled "Rape," and while relatively short it is packed with significant information. The authors also delineate how the rape of the black African females constitutes genocide under the UN Convention on the Prevention and Punishment of Genocide.

Reeves, Eric (2005). "Genocidal Rape and Assault in Darfur" (Congressional Briefing.) July 21, 2005. Available from: www.sudanreeves.org/modules
    In his testimony to the U.S. Congress, Professor Eric Reeves of Smith College (Northampton, Massachusetts) addresses, in part, the following issues: how rape was being used, in a systematic manner, as a weapon of warfare in Darfur by Government of Sudan troops and the *Janjaweed*; the inadequacy and irresponsibility of the international community to leave the issue of security solely to the under-staffed, under-resourced African Union; how until Khartoum disarms and brings the Janjaweed under control, the brutality against the women will continue against black African girls and women at the hands of the *Janjaweed*; the haphazard and totally inept way in

which the UN Security Council dealt with the rape of black African girls and women; and two studies (one by Doctors Without Borders, "The Crushing Burden of Rape: Sexual Violence in Darfur," and one by Tara Gingerich and Jennifer Leaning of Harvard University) that suggest that tens of thousands of black African girls and women had already been raped by July 2005. He further argues that the rape of the black African females constitutes part of the genocidal process undertaken by the Government of Sudan troops and the *Janjaweed* against the black African tribal groups (especially the Massaleit, Zaghawa and Fur) in Darfur.

Refugees International (2005). "Sudan: Rapidly Expand the Use of Fuel-Efficient Stoves in Darfur." Washington, DC: Author, 4 pages.

This short but significant report provides information on the ongoing deforestation in Sudan as a result of using wood from forests for cooking fires. It also discusses the fact that black African females continue to suffer rape and gang rape as they (the females) go out and forage for wood. Refugees International recommends the expansion of fuel-efficient stoves as a way to assist with halting the destruction of valuable timberland as well as to alleviate the need for the females to forage for wood.

Totten, Samuel, and Markusen, Eric (Eds.) (2006). *Genocide in Darfur: Investigating Atrocities in the Sudan*. New York: Routledge, 284 pp.

Two chapters in this book discuss in a fair amount of detail the sexual assaults (including gang and mass rape, and sexual slavery) against black African females in Darfur: "Prosecuting Gender Crimes Committed in Darfur: Holding Leaders Accountable for Sexual Violence" by Kelly Dawn Askin, and "Moving into the Field and Conducting the Interviews: Commentary and Observations by the Investigators" by Samuel Totten and Eric Markusen.

Totten, Samuel, and Markusen, Eric (2006). "Moving into the Field and Conducting the Interviews: Commentary and Observations by the Investigators," pp. 85-107. In Samuel Totten and Eric Markusen (Eds.) *Genocide in Darfur: Investigation Atrocities in the Sudan*. New York: Routledge.

Numerous investigators involved in the U.S. State Department's Atrocities Documentation Project quoted in this chapter comment on their interviews with black African females who had been raped. In doing so, they provide a clear and horrific picture of the horror to which the females were subjected and continue to deal with in the aftermath.

UN Commission of Inquiry (2005). *Report of the International Commission of Inquiry on Darfur to the United Nations Secretary-General*, January 25, 2005. New York: United Nations, 176 pp. Also available at: www.un.org/News/dh/sudan/com ing.darfur.pdf

Following the United States declaration on September 9, 2004, that Sudan had committed genocide and the U.S.'s referral of the Darfur matter to the United Nations, UN Secretary General Kofi Annan authorized, under

Chapter VII of the UN Charter, a UN investigation into the crisis. During December 2004 and January 2005 a team of investigators conducted an inquiry that took them to Darfur, Khartoum, the refugee camps in Chad and other areas for the express purpose of ascertaining whether the atrocities amounted to the crime of genocide. In the final report issued by the Commission of Inquiry on Darfur it was stated that "There is no doubt that some of the objective elements of genocide materialized in Darfur.... Some elements merging from the facts including the scale of atrocities and the systematic nature of the attacks, killing, displacement and rape, as well as racially motivated statements by perpetrators that have targeted members of the African tribes only, could be indicative of the genocidal intent. However, there are other more indicative elements that show the lack of genocidal intent.... The Commission does recognize that in some instances, individuals, including Government officials, may commit acts with genocidal intent. Whether this was the case in Darfur, however, is a determination that only a competent court can make on a case-by-case basis..." (pp. 129, 130). Ultimately, though, the COI fund that the actions of the GOS troops and Janjaweed did not amount to a genocide but rather crimes against humanity.

The report includes reference after reference to the rapes perpetrated in Darfur against the black African girls and women. Over and above the latter, the report also includes a section entitled ""Rape and Other Forms of Sexual Violence (pp. 87-96). Part and parcel of the latter are short "case studies" that highlight actual rapes perpetrated in Darfur. The stories used in the case studies were collected by the COI investigators.

Ward, Jeanne, and Marsh, Mendy (2006). *Sexual Violence Against Women and Girls in War and Its Aftermath: Realities, Responses, and Required Resources: A Briefing Paper*. Brussels: UNFPA, 31 pp.

Addresses various conflicts, including Darfur. Comprised of three parts: Part I: The Nature and Scope of Violence Against Women and Children in Armed Conflict and Its Aftermath; Part II: Rising to the Challenge: Combating Violence Against Women and Girls During War and Its Aftermath; and Part III: Where Are We Now? Assessing Progress (the latter of which addresses the issue of ending impunity).

Wax, Emily (2004). "'We Want to Make a Light Baby': Arab Militiamen in Sudan Said to Use Rape as Weapon of Ethnic Cleansing." *Washington Post* (Foreign Service), June 20, p. A01.

This newspaper article relates the story of three young black African women who, while foraging for straw for their family's donkeys outside the internally displaced persons camp they reside in West Darfur, were raped by six Arab militia men. Calling the girls such Arabic slurs as "zurga" (black) and "abid" (slave), the men raped and beat them with a whip. One of the girls, Sawela Suliman, twenty-two, reported that one of the men screamed at her, "Black girl, you are too dark. You are like a dog. We want to make a light baby." They also told her, "You get out of this area and leave the child when it's made."

The article goes on to state that interviews with twenty-four women "at camps, schools and health centers in two provincial capitals in Darfur yielded consistent reports that the *Janjaweed* were carrying out waves of attacks targeting African women. The victims and others said the rapes seemed to be a systematic campaign to humiliate the women, their husbands and fathers, and to weaken tribal ethnic lines in Sudan, as in many Arab cultures, a child's ethnicity is attached to the ethnicity of the father."

An international health care worker (who refused to give her name out of fear of retaliation) stated that "The pattern is so clear because they are doing it in such a massive way and always saying the same thing." She showed the reporter a list of victims "from Rokero, a town outside of Jebel Marra in central Darfur, where 400 women said they were raped by the *Janjaweed*." Wax states that "Another international aid worker, a high-ranking official, said: 'These rapes are built on tribal tensions and orchestrated to create a dynamic where the African tribal groups are destroyed. It's hard to believe that they tell them they want to make Arab babies, but it's true. It's systematic, and these cases are what made me believe that it is part of ethnic cleansing and that they are doing it in a massive way.'"

# 8

# Rape as Genocide

*Frances T. Pilch*

## Introduction

The concept of rape as genocide began to emerge in the 1990s, when the systematic use of rape during the conflict in the former Yugoslavia was used as an instrument to attack both individual women and the groups to which they belonged. The combination of the rising importance of non-governmental organizations, enhanced communications through new technology, and the formation of the ad hoc tribunals created to address crimes in the former Yugoslavia and Rwanda also served to generate a deepened concern about the role of rape in the destruction of communities. This understanding of the role of sexual violence in genocide found legal expression in the groundbreaking Akayesu decision at the International Criminal Tribunal for Rwanda (ICTR).

## Current State of Affairs

The 1948 Convention on the Prevention and Punishment of the Crime of Genocide (UNCG) was adopted in response to the horrors of the Holocaust in the post-Nuremberg Years. Article I of the Genocide Convention provides that the contracting parties confirm that genocide "whether committed in time of peace or in time of war, is a crime under international law which they undertake to prevent and punish." Article II specifies the following acts, which constitute genocide when they are "committed with intent to destroy, in whole or in part, a national, ethnical, racial or religious group": (a) Killing members of the group; (b) Causing serious bodily or mental harm to members of the group; (c) Deliberately inflicting on the group conditions of life calculated to bring about its physical destruction in whole or in part; (d) imposing measures intended to prevent births within the group; and (e) forcibly transferring children of the group to another group. Article IV provides that "[p]ersons committing genocide or any of the other acts enumerated in Article III shall be punished, whether they are constitutionally responsible rulers, public officials, or private individuals." Article VI notes that international tribunals, duly constituted, as well as competent national tribunals of the territory wherein the crimes have been committed, may try these persons.

The statutes defining the jurisdiction of the International Criminal Tribunal for the Former Yugoslavia (ICTY) and the ICTR include the crime of genocide as within their purview. Article 4 of the ICTY Statute and Article 2 of the ICTR Statute gives those courts the power to prosecute persons committing genocide as defined in those articles. The definitions were taken virtually word for word from the UNCG.

The statutes of the ICTY and the ICTR reflect the differences between the conflicts in Yugoslavia and Rwanda, the former viewed as an international as well as an internal conflict and the latter as an internal conflict that involved the systematic attempt to exterminate an ethnic group. Therefore the statute of the ICTR listed genocide first among the prosecutable crimes and mentions Additional Protocol II of the Geneva Conventions, which extends the protection of certain provisions of the Geneva Conventions to non-international conflict. The statutes of both the ICTY and the ICTY explicitly listed rape as a crime against humanity.

In 1994, the United Nations Security Council established the ICTR under Chapter VII of the United Nations Charter. The tribunal has the competence to prosecute persons for serious violations of international humanitarian law committed in the territory of Rwanda and by Rwandan citizens in neighboring states, between 1 January 1994 and 31 December 1994. Under Article 2 of the ICTR statute, persons could be charged with genocide. Article 2, paragraph 2 lists the acts that constitute genocide when committed with the intent to destroy in while or in part a national,ethnical, racial or religious group. Article 3, paragraph 3 identifies genocide, conspiracy, incitement to genocide, attempt to commit genocide, and complicity in genocide as punishable acts. Article 3 of the ICTR statute identifies the crimes against humanity that can be charged as murder, extermination, enslavement, deportation, imprisonment, torture, rape, persecutions on political, racial, and religious grounds, and other inhumane acts when committed as part of a widespread or systematic attack against any civilian population.

While the legal treatment of sexual violence slowly evolved since its codification as a punishable offense under the Lieber Code during the American Civil War, it made a quantum leap in the 1990s. For example, while rape was not mentioned in the 179-page judgment of the Nuremberg tribunal, some rape charges were brought during the International Military Tribunal for the Far East. Be that as it may, international attention to the crime of rape was relatively negligible until the revelation of atrocities that occurred during the "rape of Nanking." Furthermore, the connection between rape and genocide was not made explicit until 1998 in actions taken by the ICTR.

Prior to the establishment of the ICTR and the ICTY, possible interpretations of the "meaning" of rape (symbolic connotations) had been increasingly articulated, particularly as a result of the widespread use of sexual violence during the Balkan Wars. The accounts of victims eventually led to a broader understanding of the many functions that rape and sexual violence can serve. To the original conceptualizations of rape as booty or reward and rape as a boost to soldiers' morale, were added rape as symbols of domination, rape as instrument of terror, rape as torture, rape as dehumanization, rape with intent to impregnate (thereby changing the ethno/racial composition of progeny), and rape with intent to destroy or dilute community and culture. All of these new understandings of the role of rape became important in making the connection between rape and genocide. Reports on rape in the former Yugoslavia during the Balkan Wars revealed its systematic use as a weapon of war, further reinforcing the idea of rape as genocide.

The ICTR case of Jean-Paul Akayesu—the first person ever to be convicted of the crime of genocide—established the legal connection between rape and genocide. The case was important for the broad definition of rape that was developed by the court, the concept of "command responsibility" that was reinforced by this judgment, and the legal link that was created between rape and genocide by the ruling of the court.

In a judgment delivered by the ICTR on September 2, 1998, Akayesu, the former mayor of Taba, a community in Rwanda, was found guilty of genocide and crimes against humanity. (See *Prosecutor* v. *Jean-Paul Akayesu*, Judgment No. ICTR-96-4-T, September 2, 1998.) According to the evidence, Tutsi women who had sought refuge at a Taba communal office had been systematically raped and subjected to acts of sexual violence at the hands of local militia. Akayesu was found to have encouraged these acts by his attitude and his utterances. The Court found that sexual violence was an integral part of the process of destruction of the Tutsi ethnic group. It was also determined that the rape of Tutsi women was systematic and was perpetrated against all Tutsi women and solely against them.

After establishing that Tutsis could be construed as an ethnic group, the Court proceeded to link several of the separate acts of murder and rape with genocide. The tribunal held that these crimes had taken place within the context of genocide, a genocide during which even newborn Tutsi babies or fetuses were not allowed to live. This made Akayesu's actions, in the determination of the Court, crimes with the intent to eliminate a particular ethnic group.

The notion of intent is critical to a conviction on genocide. The Chamber considered that it was possible to deduce genocidal intent from the general context of the perpetration of other acts systematically directed against the same group, whether those acts were committed by the same offender or by others. The scale of atrocities plus the targeting of victims on account of their membership of a particular group while excluding members of other groups enabled the Chamber to infer the genocidal intent of particular acts.

The ICTR acknowledged that rape and sexual assault constituted genocide in the same way as any other act, and described rape and sexual violence as among the "worst ways of inflicting harm on the victim, as he or she suffers both bodily and mental harm." Therefore, although rape is not explicitly listed in the UNCG as a specified act under the umbrella of the concept of genocide, the ICTR established that rape may—if supporting conditions of intent and context exist—constitute genocide.

The Akayesu judgment also addressed the definition of rape, for which there was no accepted definition in international law. The Court explicitly rejected a mechanistic definition, and stated that rape is a form of aggression that could not be captured in a mechanical description of objects and body parts. Rape was thus defined as a physical invasion of a sexual nature, committed on a person under circumstances which are coercive. Sexual violence, which includes rape, was also considered to be any act of a sexual nature committed on a person under circumstances which are coercive. The Court went on to say that sexual violence is not limited to physical invasion of the human body and may include acts which do not involve penetration or even physical contact. An example of sexual violence, for example, under this broad definition, might be the coercion of an individual by another individual to perform sexual acts upon a third party.

The ICTR also reaffirmed the principle that a public official could be held criminally responsible for genocide through "command responsibility"; that is, it could be assumed that the accused had facilitated criminal acts by failing to prevent them or verbally encouraging them, even if he had not himself perpetrated them. For example, Akayesu was not himself accused of personally raping Tutsi women; however, witnesses testified that he had verbally encouraged militias to do so.

The landmark Akayesu judgment might not have occurred had it not been for the pressure of women's groups to amend the original Akayesu indictment to include crimes of sexual violence. Chief Prosecutor Louise Arbour added charges of sexual violence to the indictment in June 1997. The Coalition for Women's Human Rights in Conflict Situations, which included both Rwandan and other international women's rights groups, presented an amicus brief concerning the Akayesu case, highlighting the relationship between genocide and rape.

Subsequent to the Akayesu judgment, the former Rwandan minister for family and women's affairs, Pauline Nyiramasuhuko, was indicted on charges of genocide, crimes against humanity and war crimes. She is charged with rape in addition to other crimes; it is alleged that she encouraged mass rape in the Butare prefecture during the 1994 genocide. The Akayesu judgment is expected to figure importantly as precedent in her case, if she is convicted of the charges against her.

Although the ICTY Statute permitted charges of genocide, crimes of a sexual nature have been linked in the ICTY primarily with crimes against humanity, violations of the laws and customs of war, and torture. The gravity and specificity of the crime of genocide and the necessity to show intent to destroy in whole or in part a specific group of people to prove genocide, in addition to the extremely high standard of burden of proof, have made it difficult to link rape and genocide in the former Yugoslavia. However, the Rule 61 decision concerning Karadzic and Mladic, Trial Chamber I of the ICTY, in addressing sexual crimes, acknowledged that forced impregnation may constitute genocidal intent. (A Rule 61 hearing is necessary when an accused eludes justice, when authorities where a warrant for arrest has been issued are unable to locate the accused, or where authorities refuse to cooperation with the tribunal. The hearing allows the prosecutor the opportunity to convince tribunal judges to issue an international arrest warrant, making the accused an international fugitive and obligating any member of the United Nations to arrest that fugitive. The Mladic and Karadzic Rule 61 hearing resulted in the issuance of such international arrest warrants; more importantly, however, the argument and evidence presented contributed substantially to the interpretation of rape as genocide.)

The General Assembly of the United Nations has established through resolution (see UN Doc. A/RES/50/192, para 3) that rape, under certain circumstances, can constitute genocide. The Resolution adds to the weight of customary international law in the recognition of a potential linkage between rape and genocide.

The Preparatory Commission of the International Criminal Court (ICC) also recognized that sexual violence may fall within the legal definition of genocide. Under the ICC statute, in order for someone to be convicted of the crime of genocide, he/she must have committed one of more of the acts mentioned in Article 6 of the statute, and it must be proven that the perpetrator had a specific intent to destroy in whole or in part a national, ethnical, racial or religious group.

## Critical Challenges Facing the Field Today

There are two major critical challenges facing the field today. The first concerns agreement on the legal definition of rape. The Akayesu judgment included a broad definition of rape that has not been accepted by the ICTY. The Furundzija judgment of the ICTY used a narrower definition of rape. More specifically, the ICTY Trial Chamber found that under international criminal law the offense of rape comprises the following elements: "the sexual penetration, however slight, either of the vagina or anus of the victim by the penis of the perpetrator, or any other object used by the perpetrator, or of the mouth of the victim by the penis of the perpetrator, where such penetration is effected by coercion or force or threat of force against the victim or a third person." (See Prosecutor v. Furundzija, Judgement, No. IT-95-17/lT. December 10, 1998.)

The second challenge concerns the progress of the ICC. The Rome Statute establishing the ICC gives the Court jurisdiction over the crime of genocide, the definition of which is taken from the UNCG. The Court will also look at precedents created by the Ad Hoc Tribunals for Yugoslavia and Rwanda, as acceptable sources of international law. The mixed tribunals of Cambodia, Sierra Leone, and perhaps Liberia, may also provide precedent. However, the United States is not party to the treaty establishing the ICC, and in particular circumstances has advocated alternatives to the ICC as the appropriate vehicles for criminal prosecutions of violations of international humanitarian law. Therefore, the judgments coming from the ICC may not have the same status in international law as those that have emanated from the Ad Hoc Tribunals, which were established by the United Nations Security Council.

The cases that the ICC is likely to take up, such as those involving crimes committed during conflicts in the Congo, Uganda, and the Central African Republic, undoubtedly will involve questions of sexual violence, and may involve genocide. Therefore, the ICC will have the opportunity to consider the link between the two. It remains to be seen whether ICC jurisprudence will incorporate the link established by the Akayesu judgment of the ICTR, and whether ICC jurisprudence will have universal stature.

## The Real Probabilities of Progress in the Field

Potential for progress in understanding the ubiquity of sexual violence during conflict, particularly conflict involving national, racial, ethnic, and religious groups, is promising. Potential for progress in the legal interpretation of rape and how it can comprise an act of genocide is also promising, given the legacies of the Ad Hoc Tribunals, particularly the ICTR. However, acts of sexual violence that target members of particular groups defined by the Genocide Convention continue relatively unabated.

There allegedly are hundreds, if not thousands, of victims of rape in the current conflict in the Darfur region of Sudan. There are reports that forcible impregnation is being used to Arabize the African population in Darfur. However, the appropriate venue for the prosecution of perpetrators of crimes in the Sudan (and elsewhere) continues to be debated in the international community. The debate concerns whether the venue should be the ICC, as preferred by the parties to the Rome Statute, or whether additional Ad Hoc Tribunal should be established by the Security Council, thus bypassing the ICC. In addition, the international community, in particular the Security Council of the United Nations, has not yet affirmed that the term genocide is appropriate to describe the conflict in Darfur.

Ultimately, then, what can be said is this: rape as a weapon against a specific population continues to occur in contemporary conflict and even in times of peace; in practice, prohibitions against the use of sexual violence are not universally accepted or observed.

## Conclusion

While rape and genocide have been linked in scholarly discourse, particularly in feminist interpretations of recent conflicts, the legal linkage did not appear until relatively recently (1998). Problems still remain in the acceptance of a definition of rape, and, as noted above, rape continues to be used as a weapon against specific populations in current conflicts, despite some advances in promoting culpability of perpetrators, both in international and domestic law. The fact that the ICC is not universally supported creates a problem for advancement of legal interpretations of rape and genocide. The strength of human rights advocacy groups should increasingly serve to discredit the use of sexual violence to destroy groups and their cultures and to raise awareness of continued use of rape as a weapon designed to break down community cohesiveness. Rape as genocide continues to be a problem in contemporary international affairs that will need to be addressed on multiple fronts, through the law, education, and advocacy.

## References

*Prosecutor* v. *Jean-Paul Akayesu*, Judgment No. ICTR-96-4-T, September 2, 1998), available on-line at www.un.org/ictr/english/judgements/akayesu

### Annotated Bibliography

Agosin, Marjorie (Ed.) (2001). *Women, Gender, and Human Rights: A Global Perspective.* New Brunswick, NJ: Rutgers University Press, 320 pp.
   This collection of essays presents a global perspective on women's human rights and the differences and commonalities of the female experience with regard to the attainment of those rights. It includes chapters specifically relevant to the topic of rape as genocide, including one on human rights and violence against women.

Allen, Beverly (1996). *Rape Warfare: The Hidden Genocide in Bosnia-Herzegovina and Croatia.* Minneapolis: University of Minnesota Press, 180 pp.
   This book is an account of the policy of rape as genocide as it occurred during the Balkan Wars. Through the accounts and testimony of survivors of death/rape camps, the author portrays the systematic use of rape to terrorize and destroy community in Bosnia-Herzegovina and Croatia in the 1990s.

Amnesty International (2004). *Sudan: Darfur – Rape as a Weapon of War: Sexual Violence and Its Consequences, AI Index: AFR 54/076/2004, 19 July 2004.* Available at http://web.amnesty.org/library/index/engafr540762004
   This report explores the incidence of rape in the Darfur conflict and raises the question of the relationship of rape to genocide.

Askin, Kelly D. (1997). *War Crimes Against Women: Prosecution in International War Crimes Tribunals.* The Hague: Kluwer Law International, 476 pp.
   This book surveys the historic treatment of women in wartime, with special emphasis on Yugoslavia. It discusses international tribunals and determines why they did or did not prosecute gender crimes. It assesses the

impact that domestic law has had on international law, and describes the evolving status of women in international law.

Askin, Kelly D. and Koenig, Dorean M. (Eds.) (1999). *Women and International Human Rights Law.* Ardsley, New York, Transnational Publishers, Inc., 3 Volumes, 1,013 pp.
    The indispensable resource for scholars and practitioners concerned with gender issues in international law. It contains chapters by noted scholars on numerous topics of relevance, including international law and organizations, regional issues, and common abuses against women.

Bassiouni, Cherif and McCormick, Marcia (1996). *Sexual Violence: An Invisible Weapon of War in the Former Yugoslavia.* Chicago, IL: International Human Rights Law Institute, Depaul University, 48 pp.
    A detailed study by eminent legal scholars on the role of sexual violence in the former Yugoslavia.

Brownmiller, Susan (1975). *Against Our Will: Men, Women, and Rape.* New York: Simon and Schuster, 472 pp.
    One of the seminal volumes of feminist literature, and one of the first explorations of the power calculus that underlies sexual violence against women.

Butegwa, Florence (1996). Women in conflict situations, pp. 139-144. In Chrisophe Mulei, Laketch Dirasse, and Marguerite Garling (Eds.) *Legal Status of Refugee and Internally Displaced Women in Africa.* Nairobi: UNIFEM/AFWIC.
    This report investigates the vulnerability of refugee and internally displaced women to crimes of sexual violence, particularly during periods of conflict.

Card, C. (1996). Rape as a weapon of war. *Hypatia, 11(4). 4-18.*
    This article discusses the use of rape during conflict as a weapon of war, power, and domination.

Chang, Iris (1997). *The Rape of Nanking: The Forgotten Holocaust of World War II.* New York: Basic Books, 283 pp.
    The research by Iris Chang on the Japanese occupation of Nanking during World War II, which involved thousands of rapes of Chinese women, is critical to understanding the development of the understanding of the use of sexual violence during war.

Chinkin, Christine (1994). Rape and sexual abuse of women in international law, *European Journal of International Law,* 1994, 5, 326-41.
    This article presents a legal approach to crimes involving violence against women prior to the Akayesu decision.

Copelon, Rhonda (1995). Gendered war crimes: Reconceptualizing rape in time of war, pp. 197-214. In J. Peters and A. Wolper (Eds.)*Women's Rights, Human Rights: International Feminist Perspectives*. New York: Routledge.

Rhonda Copelon's seminal work in feminist perspectives on violence against women is presented in this article.

Copelon, Rhonda (1995). Women and war crimes. *St-John's Law Review*, 69 (1-2), 61-69.

Rhonda Copelon delves into the relationship of war crimes against women and the social and cultural patterns that permit these crimes to take place.

Enloe, Cynthia (1987). Feminist thinking about war, militarism, and peace, pp. 526-547. In B. Hess (Ed.) *Analyzing Gender: A Handbook of Social Science Research*. Newbury Park, CA, Sage.

This volume laid a scholarly feminist foundation for thinking about relationships between gender and war.

Fisher, Siobhán K. (1996). Occupation of the womb: Forced impregnation as genocide. *Duke Law Journal,* 46(1): 91-133.

This article is one of the few that presents a legal approach to forced impregnation as an act of genocide.

Gardam, Judith G. (1997). Women and the law of armed conflict: Why the silence? *International and Comparative Law Quarterly*, 46 (1): 55-80.

This article is an attempt to understand why crimes against women were not taken seriously within the body of international humanitarian law prior to the 1990s.

Henkin, Louis; Neuman, Gerald; Orentlicher, Diane; and Leebron, David (Eds.) (1999). *Human Rights*. New York: Foundation Press, 1,228 pp.

This volume in the University Casebook series provides important information on the development of the term "genocide," and the interpretations of the International Court of Justice as to the universality of the convention, within a comprehensive framework of general human rights principles.

Human Rights Watch (1996). *Shattered Lives: Sexual Violence During the Rwandan Genocide and its Aftermath*. New York: Human Rights Watch, 103 pp.

This Human Rights Watch Report was instrumental in highlighting the sexual violence that was prevalent during the Rwanda genocide, and served to draw international attention to rape as an act of genocide.

International Committee of the Red Cross (1995). Protection of women in armed conflicts, n.p. In ICRC's *Protection of the Civilian Population in Periods of Armed Conflict: 26th International Conference of the Red Cross and Red Crescent, Geneva, 3-7 December 1995*, 95/C.I/3/1, http://www.icrc.ch/icrcnews/3926.htm.

The International Committee of the Red Cross, as the primary repository of information and treaties dealing with the laws of armed conflict, published this report on the protection of women during war.

International Committee of the Red Cross (1995). *Women and War*. Geneva: Author, 13 pp.

This report is one of the best compilations of data on the vulnerability of women during conflict and the laws that are designed to protect them.

Jones, Adam (1994). Gender and ethnic conflict in ex-Yugoslavia. *Ethnic and Racial Studies*, 17 (1): 115-134.

This article is an excellent analysis of the treatment of women during the Balkan Wars, and the relationship of such to ethnic cleansing.

Kalajdic, Jasminka (1996). Rape, representation, and rights: Permeating international law with the voice of women. *Queen's Law Journal*, 21 (2): 457-497.

This article presents an unusual approach to women's rights and international law, stressing the importance of a gender perspective in the representation of women's human rights.

Koenig, Dorean Marguerite (1994). Women and rape in ethnic conflict and war, *Hastings Women's Law Journal*, 5:129-140.

Dorean Koenig presents the legal perspective on the prosecution of the crime of rape during war, drawing heavily on the situation during the early 1990s within the former Yugoslavia.

Kuper, Leo (1982). *Genocide: Its Political Use in the Twentieth Century*. New Haven, CT: Yale University Press, 256 pp.

A general look at genocide and its manifestations in the twentieth century. A useful background book on the nature of genocide.

Loikkanen, Laura M. (2005). *Tortured Minds, Broken Bodies: How Rape Can Constitute Genocide*. Master's Thesis, University of Helsinki, November 2005, unpublished.

This master's thesis is a comprehensive look at feminist interpretations of sexual violence and genocidal rape. It includes an extensive discussion of the definition of genocide and the physical, psychological, and social effects of rape.

MacKinnon, Catharine A. (1994). Rape, genocide and women's human rights. *Harvard Women's Law Journal*, Spring 17: 5-16.

This article was one of the first to articulate the relationship between rape and genocide, and is fundamental to an understanding of the logic behind the connection of the two.

Meron, Theodore (1993). Rape as crime under international humanitarian law. *American Journal of International Law*, 87: 424-428. The eminent international law scholar writes on the evolution of the crime of rape in international law of armed conflict.

Morris, Virginia, and Scharf, Michael (1997). *The International Criminal Tribunal for Rwanda.* Ardsley, NY: Transnational Publishers, 743 pp.
    This volume describes the evolution of the Rwanda Tribunal, its statute, procedures, and legacy in international law.

Niarchos, Catherine N. (1995). Women, war and rape: Challenges facing the International Criminal Tribunal for the Former Yugoslavia. *Human Rights Quarterly,* 17, 649-676.
    Catherine Niarchos describes the legal challenges in dealing with crimes of sexual violence, including witness protection and attainment of evidence.

Nikolic-Ristanovic, Vesna (Ed.) (2000). *Women, Violence, and War: Wartime Victimization of Refugees in the Balkans.* Budapest, Hungary: Central European University Press, 240 pp.
    This book presents important scholarship on the incidence and importance of rape during the Balkan Wars, including its psychosocial consequences for women and their communities. A chapter on the International Criminal Tribunal for Yugoslavia discusses the interpretation of the crime of rape in jurisprudence to that time.

Nordstrom, Carolyn (1996). Rape: Politics and theory in war and peace. *Australian Feminist Studies*, 11 (23):147-162.
    This article is a theoretical treatment of the meaning of rape during conflict and peace.

Nyankanzi, Edward (1997). *Genocide: Rwanda and Burundi.* Rochester, VT: Schenkman, 250 pp.
    This book explores the reasons underlying the genocides in Rwanda and Burundi. It highlights the uses of rape and sexual violence as instruments of genocide.

O'Connell, H. (Ed.) (1993). *Women and Conflict.* Oxford, Oxfam, 58 pp.
    Although this report was written prior to the Rwanda genocide, it contains penetrating analyses of the vulnerability of women during war.

Orentlicher, Diane (2006). Genocide, pp. 77-82. In Richard P. Claude and Burns H. Weston (Eds). *Human Rights in the World Community: Issues and Action.* Philadelphia: University of Pennsylvania Press.
    This short article on the origin, meaning, and evolving interpretation of the term genocide, coined by Raphael Lemkin, also discusses the ambigui-

ties of various interpretations of the concept and the reluctance of some to apply the concept, which carries with it certain legal obligations, to real world cases.

Pilch, Frances (1998/1999). The crime of rape in international law. *Journal of Legal Studies*, 9: 99-119.
This article discusses the evolution of international law as it relates to gender crimes, particularly sexual violence during conflict. It highlights the jurisprudence of the International Criminal Tribunal for Yugoslavia and the International Criminal Tribunal for Rwanda.

Pilch, Frances (2001). Rape as genocide: The legal response to sexual violence. *Columbia International Affairs Online*. http://www.ciaonet.org/wps/pif01/
In this article, the changes in the legal interpretation of sexual violence are outlined and the impact of nongovernmental actors assessed. The proposed tribunal for abuses that occurred during the civil war in Sierra Leone is also discussed.

Power, Samantha (2002). *A Problem from Hell: America and the Age of Genocide*. New York: Basic Books, 610 pp.
This seminal work on genocide and U.S. foreign policy includes substantial discussion of ethnic cleansing in the Balkan Wars and the genocide in Rwanda, and provides detailed coverage of sexual violence in both instances.

Prunier, Gerard (1995). *The Rwanda Crisis: History of Genocide*. New York: Columbia University Press, 389 pp.
This thorough history of the Rwandan genocide provides an excellent background to the legal treatment of rape that emerged from the hearings at the ICTR.

Russell-Brown, S. L. (2003). Rape as an act of genocide. *Berkeley Journal of International Law*, 21 (2): 350-374.
Published prior to the Akayesu ruling, this article lays out the argument that rape can be an act that falls under the general category of an attempt to destroy in whole or in part a national, racial, ethnic, or religious community.

Schabas, William A. (2004). *An Introduction to the International Criminal Court, Second Edition*. Cambridge, UK: University of Cambridge Press, 481 pp.
This indispensable handbook on the International Criminal Court is useful to interpret the evolution of the conception of genocide within the new legal framework of the court.

Scharf, Michael and Williams, Paul. (2002). *Peace With Justice? War Crimes and Accountability in the Former Yugoslavia.* Lanham, MD. Rowman and Littlefield, 323 pp.

This examines the work of the International Criminal Tribunal for Yugoslavia. The jurisprudence of this tribunal laid an important foundation for the subsequent interpretations and definitions of the crimes of rape and genocide.

Schiessel, C. (2002). An element of genocide: Rape, total war, and international law in the twentieth century. *Journal of Genocide Research,* 4 (2): 197-210.

This article discusses the role of rape in the attempt to destroy entire communities.

Stiglmayer, Alexandra (Ed.) (1993). *Mass Rape: The War Against Women in Bosnia-Herzegovina.* Lincoln: University of Nebraska Press, 234 pp.

This volume of essays, written by a group of prominent scholars presents, a compendium of approaches to the problem of violence against women in the former Yugoslavia. Some of the chapters include interviews with both victims and perpetrators of rape. Cumulatively, the volume presents an indispensable introduction to the sociological, psychological, and medical effects of rape during conflict.

Taylor, Christopher C. (1999). *Sacrifice as Terror: The Rwandan Genocide of 1994.* New York: Oxford International Publishers, 197 pp.

Taylor presents an analysis of the Rwandan genocide, with a strong emphasis on sexual interpretations of the propaganda leading up to the genocide and the use of sexual violence in the extermination of the Tutsi population.

Thomas, Dorothy, and Regan, Ralph (1994). Rape in war: Challenging the tradition of impunity, *SAIS Review,* 14 (1): 81-99.

This article is an example of the arguments used to draw attention to rape as a crime of war in the considerations of international tribunals.

Tompkins, Tamara L. (1995). Prosecuting rape as a war crime: Speaking the unspeakable. *Notre Dame Law Review,* 70 (4): 845-890.

In this article, the evolution of the treatment of crimes of sexual violence in international humanitarian law is examined.

United Nations (1994) *Human Rights: A Compilation of international Instruments,* 2 Volumes. New York: United Nations Publications, 418 pp.

Comprehensive listing of human rights instruments, including the UN Convention on the Prevention and Punishment of the Crime of Genocide.

United Nations, Economic and Social Council, Commission on Human Rights (1994). *Preliminary Report Submitted by the Special Rapporteur on Violence Against Women, its Causes and Consequences*, Ms. Radhika Coomaraswamy, in Accordance to Commission on Human Rights Resolution 1994/45, E/CN.4/1995/42, 92.
    This report was seminal in the accumulation of evidence concerning crimes against women during armed conflict.

United Nations, Economic and Social Council, Commission on Human Rights (1996). *Report of the Special Rapporteur on Violence Against Women, its Causes and Consequences*, Ms. Radhika Coomaraswamy, Submitted in Accordance with Commission on Human Rights Resolution 1995/85, E/CN.4/1996/53, 50.
    A sequel to the 1994 report, the United Nations Special Rapporteur on Violence Against Women again drew attention to the continuing problem of crimes of violence perpetrated against women.

Van Den Herik, L. J. (2005). *Contribution of the Rwanda Tribunal to the Development of International Law*, Volume 53. The Hague: Brill Academic Press, 324 pp.
    A comprehensive and essential compilation of the essential contributions of the International Criminal Tribunal for Rwanda to jurisprudence on international law, including a detailed analysis of the important Akayesu judgment.

Wali, Sima (1995). Women in conditions of war and peace, pp. 289-303. In Margaret Schuler (Ed.) *From Basic Needs to Basic Rights: Women's Claim to Human Rights.* Washington, DC: Women, Law and Development International.
    This article is a general contribution to an understanding of the problems confronting women during both war and peace.

Zawati, Hilmi, and Mahmoud, Ibtisam (Eds) (2005). *A Selected Socio-Legal Bibliography on Ethnic Cleansing, Wartime Rape, and Genocide in the Former Yugoslavia and Rwanda.* Lewiston, NY: Edwin Mellen Press, 587 pp.
    This volume presents a useful and comprehensive bibliography on rape and genocide in Rwanda and the former Yugoslavia.

# 9

# The Evolution of Gender Crimes in International Law

*Nicole Hallett*

*"[T]hey brought her fourteen-year-old son and forced him to rape her.... On [another] occasion, I was raped with a gun by one of the three men...in the room.... Others stood watching. Some spat on us. They were raping me, the mother and her daughter at the same time. Sometimes you had to accept ten men, sometimes three.... I felt I wanted to die.... The Serbs said to us, "Why aren't you pregnant?".... I think they wanted to know who was pregnant in case anyone was hiding it. They wanted women to have children to stigmatize us forever. The child is a reminder of what happened."*
—Victim's testimony, Bosnia

## Introduction

The Bosnian War, which is remembered for its "manipulation and abuse of the female gender to commit ethnic cleansing and genocide" (Askin, 1997, p. 256), shocked the conscious of the international community. The universal euphoria and heady optimism that had overcome the world like a wave after the fall of the Soviet Empire evaporated. Reports of "ethnic cleansing" seemed unfathomable: How could another genocide occur in Europe almost fifty years after the continent had proclaimed "never again" after the Holocaust? But perhaps most terrifying was the fact the Serbians seemed to have invented a brand new tool of persecution – genocidal rape. This chapter details how sexual violence was used in Bosnia, and a year later in Rwanda, as a tool of genocide, and how the horror of those genocides transformed gender crimes from "the least condemned war crime[s]" to an emerging area of international criminal law.

The 1998 conviction of Jean-Paul Akeyesu for genocide by the International Criminal Tribunal for Rwanda (ICTR) was a double victory. Not only did it represent the first international prosecution and conviction for the crime of genocide, but it was also the first time that an international tribunal recognized that rape could serve as a tool of genocide. The conviction, based partly on charges of the systematic rape of Tutsi women, marked an important development in international criminal law. Yet, the focus on genocidal rape has not been without controversy, with some scholars arguing that it obscures gender and renders women invisible. This chapter explores that debate and future challenges for the field, including the development of gender crimes as *jus cogens* norms of customary international law.

## Historical Perspectives

*Early Evolution – Rape as a "Violation of Family Honor and Rights"*

For as long as human societies have engaged in armed conflict, women have been victimized by gender-based violence.[1] Yet for the first several millennia of human civilization, the laws of war did not prohibit rape. When rape was considered a crime at all, it was seen as a property crime against a woman's husband or father rather than a crime of violence against the woman herself. During war, rape was the right of the victor. As the customary laws of war developed over the centuries, sexual violence never achieved universal acceptance as a war crime, leading Grotius (1646), considered the father of the law of nations, to remark that wartime rape violated "the law not of all nations, but of the better ones" (p. 567). Legal protection for women improved in the nineteenth century. The 1863 Lieber Code, part of the U.S. Army regulations on the laws of land warfare, marked the first time that rape, or any other act of sexual violence, was classified as a war crime and was largely considered to reflect the customary laws of war at that time.[2] Rape was serious enough to warrant the death penalty, but it was rarely prosecuted, and legal protection for women remained in name only. Importantly, however, the Lieber Code became the template for other codes of warfare and represents the first clear prohibition of rape in customary international law.

Treaties and conventions concerning the laws of war proliferated in the nineteenth century, culminating with the 1907 Hague Conventions and Regulations. Only one article indirectly prohibited sexual violence as a violation of "family honour"[3] and nowhere does the word rape appear. Rape slowly evolved from a property crime to a crime of honor, but the emphasis was still placed on the injury suffered by the woman's family and husband. At the outbreak of World War II, rape was still categorized as it had been for thousands of years – as a crime by men against men with women as its silent victims.

*The Nuremberg and Tokyo Tribunals – Impunity for Gender Crimes*

The atrocities of World War II are hard to comprehend even today. Close to six million Jews died in the Holocaust in Europe, and some five million others, including Roma and Sinti (Gypsies), and the mentally and physically handicapped, among numerous other groups, also perished in that conflagration. In both Europe and Asia, millions also perished, many as innocent casualties of war. Civilian deaths outnumbered military deaths for the first time in recorded history. Sexual crimes, including rape and forced prostitution, were rampant. Gender violence did not play the central role in genocide that they would later play in the Bosnian and Rwandan conflicts, yet, the stories of tragedy that emerged were no less devastating.

The rape of Jewish women by the Nazis was illegal and discouraged by Nazi leaders who viewed such acts as corrupting the Aryan race. Nevertheless, widespread rape did occur as Nazi soldiers took advantage of the helpless and captive Jewish population. Sexual crimes became a torture device in concentration camps, where medical doctors performed medical experiments on women and guards sexually mutilated women as a method of torture. Incidences of forced sterilization and forced abortion were also well documented as tools of genocide. The advancing German army also committed systematic rape in Eastern Europe and the Soviet Union.

In Asia, the Japanese army committed widespread rape during the invasion and occupation of Korea, China, and the Philippines. In one particularly gruesome event, known colloquially as the "Rape of Nanking," over 20,000 women were raped in the first month of the occupation alone. No woman in the city was spared as women as old as eighty and girls as young as seven were assaulted by the Japanese. Additionally, the Japanese army forced over 200,000 "comfort women," mostly from Korea, into sexual slavery against their will to service the Japanese troops. Most of these women did not survive and those that did survive suffered permanently physical and psychological scars.

The Allied forces also committed their share of atrocities. The atomic bombs dropped on Hiroshima and Nagasaki and the firebombing of Dresden could both constitute war crimes or crimes against humanity under modern definitions. The sexual violence committed by the Allied forces is less well known, but equally shocking. It is estimated that 100,000 women were raped by Allied troops during the last two weeks of the war in Berlin alone. Predictably, these crimes went unpunished. The victorious nations were focused on punishing the war criminals on the other side, not looking inwards at their own conduct. Despite this "victors' justice," the Allies did show enlightened thinking on one front. Rather than summarily execute German and Japanese war criminals, the Allies made the unique decision to create international tribunals – the International Military Tribunals of Nuremberg (IMT) and for the Far East (IMTFE) – to deliver post-conflict justice. The result marked the first time individuals had been legally held accountable for crimes they had committed at the international level.

The IMT Charter did not include in its list of crimes any form of sexual violence even though such crimes were extensively documented in the evidentiary record. However, Article 6(b) of the IMT Charter defined war crimes as including, but "not limited to" the list of crimes enumerated in the Charter, which gave the tribunal the authority to prosecute charges of rape if it had chosen to do so. Evidence of sexual crimes was presented during the Nuremberg Trials, but neither the indictments nor the convictions referred to sexual crimes. Council Law No. 10, which governed the trials of lesser Nazi war criminals, did list rape as a crime against humanity, but did not enumerate other sexual crimes such as forced sterilization, forced abortion and sexual mutilation.

The Tokyo indictment did contain specific allegations of sexual crimes, although it classified them as "failure to respect family honour and rights" rather than crimes of violence. However, because the IMTFE Charter did not list rape as a separate "greater" crime, it was reduced to a minor infraction that could not be prosecuted separately from other war crimes. Perhaps the greatest oversight of the Tokyo trials was the total disregard of the sexual enslavement of the "comfort women."

Although sexual crimes were not entirely ignored in the Nuremberg and Tokyo Trials, they played at most a peripheral role in the prosecutions. And while a few individuals were prosecuted for sexual crimes, most acts of sexual violence went unpunished. Still, the groundwork was laid for later progress in the field.

*Case Study – General Yamashita*

General Tomoyuki Yamashita, a high-ranking Japanese general who led the assault on the Philippines, was not tried by the IMTFE, but his trial is nevertheless an important point in the development of gender crimes in international law. Since he was not charged with waging a war of aggression, he was not eligible to be tried by the IMTFE. Instead, he was tried by a U.S. Military Commission in Manila. The trial began on October 8, 1945, and he was convicted and sentenced to death by hanging on December 7, 1945, four years to the day from the Japanese attack on Pearl Harbor (United Nations War Crimes Commission, 1948). His conviction was later upheld by the U.S. Supreme Court (U.S. Supreme Court, 1946).

Of the many charges against General Yamashita, rape played a prominent role. The military commission convicted Yamashita of "torture, rape, murder and mass executions of very large numbers of residents of the Philippines, including women and children" (United Nations War Crimes Commission, 1948). While rape was considered only a constituent crime and not a separate offense, the Yamashita conviction marked the first time that rape appears in an indictment for war crimes.

Perhaps most importantly, however, is that Yamashita was convicted not for rapes he committed himself but of rapes committed by his soldiers under his command. The opinion concedes that "[i]t is absurd...to consider a commander a murderer or rapist because one of his soldiers commits a murder or rape." But "where murder and rape and vicious, revengeful actions are widespread offenses, and there is no effective attempt by a commander to discover and control the criminal acts, such a commander may be held responsible, even criminally liable, for the lawless acts of his troops, depending upon their nature and the circumstances surrounding them" (Lael, 1982, p. 95). The Yamashita judgment paved the way for subsequent criminal prosecutions by recognizing that rape in the context of war becomes political and tactical as well as personal and should be prosecuted as such.

## The 1949 Geneva Conventions and the 1948 Genocide Convention – Gender Crimes as Afterthought

After the conclusion of the Nuremberg and Tokyo trials, the newly formed United Nations set about codifying the laws of war and the crime of genocide into international instruments. The most important of these instruments—the 1949 Geneva Conventions and the 1948 UN Convention on the Prevention and Punishment of the Crime of Genocide (UNCG)—did not entirely ignore sexual crimes, but did not go far enough in recognizing their gravity.

The Fourth Geneva Convention provides comprehensive protection for civilians. Article 27 specifically addresses sexual crimes, stating that women "shall be especially protected against any attack on their honour, in particular against rape, enforced prostitution, or any form of indecent assault" (United Nations, 1949). The Convention retains the classification of rape as a crime of honor rather than a crime of violence. The Second Protocol to the Geneva Conventions similarly defines rape and forced prostitution as "outrages upon personal dignity."[4] However, the reference to sexual crimes at all represents a step forward and reflects the experience of the international community in the prosecution of gender crimes in the Nuremberg and Tokyo trials. Still, the Geneva Conventions do not list gender crimes among the "grave breaches" subject to universal jurisdiction, thus relegating them once again to minor status and not recognizing them as serious crimes in their own right.

Conversely, the UNCG does not explicitly reference gender crimes. The reason for this omission has its roots in the Holocaust itself. Genocide was defined largely in direct response to the tactics used by the Nazis:

Genocide means any of the following acts committed with intent to destroy, in whole or in part, a national, ethnical, racial or religious group, as such:

(a) Killing members of the group;
(b) Causing serious bodily or mental harm to members of the group;
(c) Deliberately inflicting on the group conditions of life calculated to bring about its physical destruction in whole or in part;
(d) Imposing measures intended to prevent births within the group;
(e) Forcibly transferring children of the group to another group.

Although sexual crimes were rampant during World War II, rape and other sexual crimes were not used systematically to exterminate the Jewish people and other persecuted groups, as they would later be used during the Bosnian and Rwandan genocides. Instead, the widespread rape that occurred during World War II was motivated by opportunity, which led the international community to classify it as a crime against humanity and a war crime rather than as a constituent crime of genocide.

International criminal law developed very little in the second half of the twentieth century. The Cold War prevented any international criminal prosecutions, despite conflict situations in Bangladesh (e.g., the 1971 genocide) and Southeast Asia (the 1975-1979 Khmer Rouge-perpetrated genocide) that had large gender crime components. The status of women in international law in general improved slowly. The 1979 Convention on the Elimination of All Forms of Discrimination Against Women attempted to rectify the historical discrimination against women, although sexual violence was not mentioned. Even the 1974 Declaration on the Protection of Women and Children in Emergency and Armed Conflict, more thematically related to gender crimes, does not mention rape and only contains one vague reference to sexual violence in the preamble, which states that women are "too often the victims of inhuman acts" (United Nations, 1974).

At the same time as international law developed broader protections for women, the international women's rights movement fought for equal treatment of women at the domestic level. Although this did not immediately translate into increased protection for women during armed conflicts, it set the stage for events that unfolded as the Cold War came to a close. By the time genocide broke out in Yugoslavia and Rwanda, the world was ready to listen.

## Gender and International Law Today

*The ICTY and ICTR Statutes*

The Bosnian and Rwandan conflicts were unique in their use of rape as a tool of genocide, a fact that was reflected in the prominence of gender crimes in the statutes of the International Criminal Tribunals for the former Yugoslavia and Rwanda (ICTY and ICTR, respectively). Article 5(g) of the ICTY Statute and Article 3(g) of the ICTR Statute explicitly list rape as a crime against humanity for the first time in the history of international criminal tribunals (United

Nations, 1993 and 1994, respectively). The Statutes do not enumerate rape or other sexual crimes under their lists of "grave breaches" and war crimes, nor do they list forced impregnation as a constituent crime of genocide.

Yet rather than reflecting contemporary prejudices, the decision not to include sexual crimes as constituent offenses under the war crimes and genocide provisions stems from the fact that unlike these other categories, crimes against humanity were not governed by pre-existing international conventions. While the ICTY statute had to imitate the definitions found in the Geneva Conventions and the Genocide Convention, no such restrictions existed when drafting the list of crimes against humanity, which provided the drafters with an opportunity to include rape on its list of crimes against humanity over which the tribunals had jurisdiction.

## Case Studies

Although the ICTY and ICTR Statutes marked the first explicit enumeration of rape as a crime against humanity, it remained to be seen how this development would play out in the trials themselves. Moreover, it remained to be seen how the tribunals would address the widespread use of genocidal rape, despite the fact that rape was not included as a constituent crime of genocide under the Statutes. What follows are largely considered the most important judgments from the ICTY and ICTR and reflect the evolving jurisprudence of the tribunals with respect to sexual violence and gender crimes.

*Jean-Paul Akayesu.* Akayesu, the former mayor of the Taba commune in Rwanda, was sentenced on September 2, 1998, to three consecutive life sentences and marked the first time an international tribunal concluded that rape and other forms of sexual violence were used as instruments of genocide (International Criminal Tribunal for Rwanda, 1998). Akeyesu was convicted of genocide and crimes against humanity for the systematic rape of Tutsi women during the genocide. As in the Yamashita case, Akayesu was convicted not of rapes he himself committed but rather of the instigation, facilitation, aiding, and abetting of sexual violence on a massive scale. The judgment affirmed that rape could constitute a constituent crime of genocide in certain circumstances, such as when sexual violence is used to cause serious physical and mental harm to a group.

*Dusko Tadic.* Tadic, a Serbian and a former café owner, was the first person tried by the ICTY and observers believed that he would be the first individual convicted of rape as a separate war crime for his participation in the rape, murder, and torture of detainees at several detention camps in Bosnia-Herzegovina. The independent rape crimes were subsequently dropped, however, when a witness became too frightened to testify. Although eventually convicted for sexual assaults and mutilation, the incidents upon which the conviction rested were committed against men, not women.

*Anto Furundzija.* Furundzija, the local commander of the Croatian Defense Council Military Police unit known as the "Jokers," was charged with and convicted of war crimes in December 1998 (ICTY, 1998b). The decision marks the first time that rape was recognized as an instrument of torture and the first time rape charges were brought under the standard set in Second Protocol to the Geneva Conventions as outrages upon personal dignity.

*Dragoljub Kunarac, Radomir Kovac and Zoran Vukovic.* Otherwise known as the Foca indictment, this case was the first that prosecuted rape as a crime against humanity at the ICTY (International Criminal Tribunal for the former Yugoslavia, 2001). The charges concerned the rape and sexual slavery of Muslim and Croatian girls in a Serbian detention center in the town of Foca. The judgment detailed the long-term sexual enslavement of women and girls, which included occurrences of forced prostitution and forced impregnation in addition to rape and sexual assault. Kunarac, Kovac, and Vukovic, who were leaders of the camp, were convicted of crimes against humanity on February 22, 2001.

*Pauline Nyiramasuhuko.* Nyiramasuhuko, the Rwandan minister of women and family affairs during the 1994 genocide, is the first woman to be charged with rape as a crime against humanity by an international tribunal (International Criminal Tribunal for Rwanda, 2004). She reportedly gave instructions to the *Interahamwe* militia to rape Tutsi women before killing them, at one point offering sanctuary to thousands of Tutsi women in a sports stadium before ordering Hutu soldiers to rape and slaughter them all.

## The International Criminal Court – Participation and Codification

The experience of the ICTY and ICTR informed the drafting of the Rome Statute of International Criminal Court (ICC). In addition to recognizing rape as a crime against humanity, Article 7(1)(g) explicitly names sexual slavery, forced prostitution, forced sterilization, forced pregnancy, and "any other form of sexual violence of comparable gravity" as well (United Nations, 2002). Although not specifically enumerated as grave breaches, sexual crimes can be prosecuted as war crimes under Article 8(2)(b), which provides jurisdiction for the prosecution of other serious violations of the laws of war. The Rome Statute marks the first time that sexual slavery has been recognized as an international crime.

Early drafts of the statute did not specifically enumerate the constituent crimes under each of the four main categories: war crimes, genocide, crimes against humanity, and crimes of aggression. As each of these categories became fleshed out, delegates began to lobby for the inclusion of sexual crimes. Early drafts reverted to framing sexual crimes as outrages to family honor and personal dignity, which many involved in the negotiations saw as a step backwards. In 1997, the decision was made to enumerate specific sexual crimes under the statute. Importantly, the Rome Statute departs from the traditional classification of rape as a crime of honor and instead clearly defines it as a crime of violence and a violation of the victim's agency.

A further breakthrough occurred in the ICC Elements of Crimes, which is the first international instrument to delineate the elements of rape and forced pregnancy. Rape under the ICC statute requires proof of two elements: (1) penetration of any part of the body by a sexual organ or of the anal or genital opening with any object or part of the body; and (2) force, threat of force, or coercion. While the Elements of Crimes are non-binding, they will be used by the Court to interpret the Rome Statute in future cases, and therefore added much needed clarity to the definition of gender crimes in international law.

For the first time in history, women were closely involved in the drafting of the international instrument. The Women's Caucus for Gender Justice, a coalition of women's groups from around the world, played an integral role in the drafting. The movement to include gender crimes in the Rome Statute received an additional boost from the overwhelming success of the 1995 World Conference on Women in Beijing. The decision to include the list of sexual crimes in 1997 can be traced partly to the efforts of the Women's Caucus and other groups. Allowing women to have a voice in the process contributed to this latest development in international criminal law.

### Legal Theories

While the classification of rape as a war crime and a crime against humanity dates to World War II, rape as a tool of genocide is a more recent invention and there is still some question as to how to conceptualize genocidal rape. Catherine MacKinnon (1993) explains the multitude of ways in which rape was used during the Bosnian War:

> Like all rapes, these rapes are particular as well as generic, and the particularity matters. This is ethnic rape as an official policy of war: not only a policy of the pleasure of male power unleashed; not only a policy to defile, torture, humiliate, degrade, and demoralize the other side; not only a policy of men posturing to gain advantage and ground over other men. It is rape under orders: not out of control, under control. It is rape unto death, rape as massacre, rape to kill or make the victims wish they were dead. It is rape as an instrument of forced exile, to make you leave your home and never come back. It is rape to be seen and heard by others, rape as spectacle. It is rape to shatter a people, to drive a wedge through a community. It is rape of misogyny liberated by xenophobia and unleashed by official command.... This is rape as torture and rape as extermination. Some women who are not killed speak of wanting to take their own lives. It is at once mass rape and serial rape indistinguishable from prostitution. It is concentration camp as brothel: women impounded to be passed around by men among men. It is also rape as a policy of ethnic uniformity and ethnic conquest, annexation and expansion.... Most distinctively, it is rape for reproduction as ethnic liquidation: Croatian and Muslim women are raped to help make a Serbian state by making Serbian babies. (p. 90)

*Rape as Destruction*

Sometimes sexual crimes "constitute genocide in the same way as any other act as long as they were committed with the specific intent to destroy, in whole or in part, a particular group, targeted as such" (International Criminal Tribunal for Rwanda, 1998). Rape, like murder, can be used to destroy. For instance, in Rwanda, many women and girls were raped to death, often with sharp objects. The *Interahamwe* also raped and then killed as a way of making death more gruesome. Women who survived were often faced with a slow, cruel death of HIV/AIDS, which they contracted as a result of rape. The use of HIV/AIDS to eradicate the Tutsis was deliberate—reports suggest that AIDS patients were released out of hospitals to form battalions of rapists. It is estimated that over seventy percent of women raped during the Rwandan genocide are now infected with HIV. Rape is a war crime when it is the spoil of the victors. Rape becomes genocide when "It [is] to ensure that the victory [is] secured" (Vranic, 1996, p. 26).

*Rape as Torture*

In addition to "killing members of the group," the 1948 Genocide Convention defines acts of genocide to include "causing serious bodily or mental harm" to members of the group. In some cases, rape is used to cause such serious harm. Although rape that rises to the level of torture has been prosecuted as a crime against humanity or a war crime, it can also constitute an act of genocide. The ICTY recognized that "rape causes severe pain and suffering, both physical and psychological" (International Criminal Tribunal for Yugoslavia, 1998a). Con-comitantly, in the Akayesu judgment, the ICTR found serious bodily or mental harm "to mean acts of torture, be they bodily or mental, inhumane or degrading treatment, persecution" (International Criminal Tribunal for Rwanda, 1998). Some scholars have expressed reservation, however, in defining genocidal rape as torture because it might seem to imply that rape alone, without additional physical harm, is not serious enough to constitute an act of genocide (Copelon, 1999, 332-360; Etienne, 1995, pp. 139-170).

*Rape as Social Ostracism*

Rape can also cause psychological harm by provoking the "destruction of the spirit, of the will to live, and of life itself" (International Criminal Tribunal for Rwanda, 1998). This harm is often accomplished through capitalizing on the social ostracism that often accompanies rape in traditional societies. The rape of Bosnian women is the perfect example. Because the consequences of rape are "particularly severe in traditional, patriarchal societies, where the rape victim is often perceived as soiled and unmarriageable," rape becomes a particularly effective way of dividing and destroying communities (Wing and Merchán, 1993, p. 25). Women are often killed by their families or commit suicide to avoid the shame of rape. If they survive, they are often viewed as unmarriageable, which effectively prevents the community from reproducing, which can constitute "measures intended to prevent births within the group" under the Genocide Convention.

### Rape as Forced Impregnation

In the Bosnian context, rape also served another purpose: forced impregnation. Because in the Muslim tradition, children take the ethnicity of their father, impregnating Bosnian women effectively created a generation of Serbians and at the same time preventing births within the Bosnian Muslim community. The Serbians were, in effect, occupying the wombs of the Bosnian women so as to prevent them from giving birth to Muslim children. The Serbians used other sexual crimes, including forced abortion and sterilization, to accomplish the same goal.

## Critical Challenges Facing the Field Today

### Balancing the Rights of Victims and Defendants in Gender Crimes Prosecution

One difficult question that arises in international prosecutions of gender crimes is the correct balance between protecting victims and securing a fair trial for defendants. The ICC Statute and Rules of Procedure and Evidence prioritize the rights of victims by protecting the safety, physical and psychological well-being, dignity, and privacy of victims and witnesses, particularly victims of gender-based violence. At the same time, procedural safeguards are in place to make sure that defendants are protected.

Significantly, victims' past sexual history is inadmissible, and consent cannot be a defense when the perpetrator took advantage of an inherently coercive environment, such as a detention center. Special rules apply to the introduction of evidence of consent in all other cases. The Statute and Rules also establish a Victims and Witnesses Unit to assist and protect victims of gender-based violence.

Perhaps most controversially, witnesses can testify anonymously in exceptional circumstances provided the decision is "consistent with the rights of the accused." A five-part test is used by the Trial Chamber to decide whether witness anonymity is warranted. First, the witness or his or her family must face an objective fear for their safety. Second, the testimony must be of critical importance to the prosecution. Third, there must be no *prima facie* evidence of the witness' untrustworthiness. Fourth, alternative measures intended to protect the witness, such as redaction of the record, suppression of witness identity or whereabouts, assignment of pseudonyms, and closed sessions, must be considered and rejected. And fifth, the measure must be undertaken only when strictly necessary.

The conflict between victims' and defendants' rights came to the forefront during the trial of Furundhaczija, in which the ICTY Trial Chamber found the prosecution guilty of misconduct for not disclosing a rape victim's psychiatric treatment and thus declared a mistrial. The rape charges were subsequently dropped because the victim did not want to go through the trauma of testifying again. The Trial Chamber decided that the defendant's right to a fair trial outweighed the victim's right to privacy. Such actions by courts have the effect of discouraging victims from seeking help or from testifying once they've sought help.

However, the effect of such victim protection measures on a defendant's right to a fair trial should not be discounted. They can have a profound effect on the defendant's ability to mount an effective defense. International tribunals will continue to try to balance these considerations.

*How Should Gender Crimes be Classified?*

A more fundamental debate within the field is whether genocidal rape should even exist as a constituent crime of genocide at all or whether rape is more appropriately classified as a crime against humanity or a war crime. Rhonda Copelon (1995) explains how treating genocidal rape as a special crime obscures the gender component of the crime:

> [T]o emphasize as unparalleled the horror of genocidal rape is factually dubious and risks rendering rape invisible once again. When the ethnic war ceases or is forced back into the bottle, will the crimes against women matter? Will their suffering and struggles to survive be vindicated? Or will condemnation be limited to this seemingly exceptional case? Will the women who are brutally raped for purposes of domination, terror, booty, or revenge in Bosnia and elsewhere be heard? (p. 61)

She compares the rape of Bosnian women to the rape of Korean, Chinese, and Filipino women during World War II, arguing that while ethnicity played no part in Japan's industrialized forced prostitution, it constituted a serious crime against humanity that should be viewed as no less serious than the "genocidal rape" perpetrated during the Bosnian War.

Catherine MacKinnon (1994), however, takes the opposite position—that there is something particularly egregious about rape committed to destroy a racial, ethnic, or religious group and that it should be recognized as such. She argues that the result of ignoring the intersectionality of gender and group identity is that

[T]hese rapes are grasped in either their ethnic or religious particularity, as attacks on a culture, meaning men, or in their sex specificity, meaning as attacks on women. But not as both at once.

Attacks on women, it seems, cannot define attacks on a people. If they are gendered attacks, they are not ethnic; if they are ethnic attacks, they are not gendered. One cancels the other. But when rape is a genocidal act, as it is here, it is an act to destroy a people. What is done to women defines that destruction. Also, aren't women a people?

Copelon and MacKinnon both argue that the other's viewpoint dehumanizes and disempowers women. The dialogue will likely continue as gender crimes begin to come before the International Criminal Court.

### What are the Real Probabilities of Progress in this Field?

The Rome Statute elevated gender crimes to well-established crimes under treaty law. Scholars have since begun to question whether they have become *jus cogens* norms of international law as well. A *jus cogens* norm is a fundamental principle of international law considered to have acceptance among the international community of states as a whole. Once a norm achieves *jus cogens* status, all governments are bound by it regardless of whether they have signed the relevant treaties or conventions. The achievement of *jus cogens* status is essential to ensure that this "less condemned war crime" becomes a serious crime with universal jurisdiction.

The Rome Statute itself provides the framework with which to evaluate the development of gender crimes as *jus cogens* norms. Because the crimes against humanity provisions were intended to reflect current *jus cogens* norms, the inclusion of rape and other sexual crimes gives strong support to their status as *jus cogens* norms. Likewise, their inclusion under the war crimes provision but not on the list of grave breaches implies that this, too, is a reflection of current customary norms. The reason to place so much emphasis on the Rome Statute in both cases is because the drafters went beyond the existing treaty law to elevate gender crimes.

The fact that the drafters did not similarly elevate rape to a grave breach is equally probative. Likewise, the fact that the definition of genocide was not expanded to include the concept of genocidal rape suggests that gender crimes have yet to achieve *jus cogens* status as genocide. However, the Preparatory Commission of the International Criminal Court did acknowledge that rape could constitute genocide under the "serious bodily or mental harm" prong, suggesting that the law is continuing to develop in this direction.

Other sources suggest that rape as a constituent crime of genocide is slowly achieving *jus cogens* status. In Kadic v. Karadzic, a U.S. court recognized that rape constituted a crime against humanity and genocide under customary international law (United States Court of Appeals for the Second Circuit, 1995). Therefore, at least in the United States, genocidal rape is a crime in customary international law. And while the ICTY's judgments do not themselves establish norms of customary international law, the Akayesu judgment provides strong support for the proposition that genocidal rape has been accepted, at least by a large part of the international community, as a *jus cogens* norm.

The issue of gender crimes has again resurfaced in some of the first cases referred to the ICC from the Democratic People's Republic of Congo, which will provide the court with a chance to continue to define the contours of the law. Sadly, however, the recent developments in international law have not prevented new incidences of genocidal rape from occurring. Recent reports from Sudan suggest that rape is being used as a tool of genocide against the people of Darfur. At the very least, the developments will make it harder for perpetrators to escape punishment for their crimes.

## Conclusion

The days of absolute impunity for perpetrators of gender crimes are over. It is no longer seen as a natural and unavoidable consequence of war, but a serious crime in its own right against women, communities, and humanity as a whole. Although such developments will not always prevent such atrocities from oc-curring, they provide valuable tools for bringing perpetrators to justice.

## Notes

1. This chapter focuses on sexual crimes committed against women and not men for several reasons. First, the book of which it is apart focuses on women. Second, although it is true that men are also the victims of sexual crimes, the vast majority of sexual crimes are committed against women.
2. See Lieber Code, Article 44. Instructions for the Government of the United States in the Field by Order of the Secretary," 24 April 1863 [Lieber Code; also known as General Orders No. 1000]
3. See Laws of War: Laws and Customs of War on Land (Hague IV); October 18, 1907, art. 46.
4. See *Protocol Additional to the Geneva Conventions of 12, August 1949, and Relating to the Protection of Victims on Non-International Armed Conflicts* (Protocol II, art. 4(2)(e)). The First Protocol likewise names women as "the object of special respect" and states that they "shall be protected against rape, forced prostitution, and any other form of indecent assault." Article 76(1) of Protocol I.

## References

Askin, Kelly (1997). *War Crimes Against Women*. The Hague: Kluwer Law International.

Copelon, Rhonda (1999). Surfacing gender: Reengraving crimes against women in humanitarian law, pp. 332-260. In Nicole Ann Dombrowski (Ed.) *Women and War in the Twentieth Century: Enlisted With or Without Consent*. New York: Garland.

Copelon, Rhonda (1995). Women's rights as international human rights: Women and war crimes. *St. John's Law Review*, 69, 61-68.

Etienne, Margaret (1995). Addressing gender-based violence in an international context. *Harvard Women's Law Journal*, 18: 139-170.

Grotius, Hugo (1646). *The Law of War and Peace* (Book III, Chapter IV, Point XIX). Translated by Francis W. Kelsey, 1925).

International Criminal Tribunal for the former Yugoslavia (1998a). *Prosecutor v. Delalic, Mucic, Delic, and Landzo*. The Hague: Author. November 16. IT-96-21-T.

International Criminal Tribunal for the former Yugoslavia (1998b). *Prosecutor v. Furundzija, ICTY Judgment*. The Hague: Author. December 10. IT-95-17/1-T.

International Criminal Tribunal for the former Yugoslavia (2001). *Prosecutor v. Kunarac, Kovac and Vukovic, ICTY Judgment*. The Hague: Author. February 22. IT-96-23 and IT-96-23/1.

International Criminal Tribunal for Rwanda (1998). *The Prosecutor v. Jean-Paul Akayesu, Trial chamber judgment of 2, September 1998*. Available at ww.ictr.org. [Summarized in International Legal materials, 37(6):1399-1410.] Note: Appeal chamber judgment published on June 1, 2001.

International Criminal Tribunal for Rwanda (2004). *Prosecutor v. Nyiramasuhuko*. ICTR-97-21-AR73 (July 2).Available at ww.ictr.org.

Lael, Richard L. (1982). *The Yamashita Precedent, War Crimes and Command Responsibility* . Wilmington, DE: Scholarly Resources. *95*.

MacKinnon, Catherine (1993). Crimes of war, crimes of peace in human rights. In Shute and Hurley (Eds.) *The Oxford Lectures*. London: Amnesty International.

MacKinnon, Catharine (1994). Rape, genocide, and women's human rights. *Harvard Women's Law Journal*, 17, 5-16.

United Nations War Crimes Commission (1948). *Trial of General Tomoyuki Yamashita, United States Military Commission, Manila. In Law Reports of Trials of War Criminals: Selected and Prepared by the United Nations War Crimes Commission*, Volume IV. London: HMSO.

United States Court of Appeals for the Second Circuit (1995). *Kadic v. Karadzic: Opinon of 2nd Circuit re: Subject Matter Jurisdiction. Nos. 1541, 1544*. Available at: www.yale.edu/lawweb/avalon/diana/karadzic/4298

United States Supreme Court (1946). *Application of Yamashita, 327 U.S. 1 (1946)*. Available at: law.findlaw.com/us/327/1

United Nations (1949). *Convention Relative to the Protection of Civilian Persons in Time of War*, 75 U.N.T.S. 287, August 12.

United Nations (1974). *Declaration on the Protection of Women and Children in Emergency and Armed Conflict*. New York: Author. U.N. Doc. A/9631.

United Nations (2002). *The Rome Statute of International Criminal Court* (ICC). New York: Author. U.N. Doc. 2187 U.N.T.S. 90.

United Nations (1993). *Statute of the International Tribunal for the Former Yugoslavia*. New York: Author. UN Doc. S/RES/1329.

United Nations (1994). *Statute of the International Tribunal for Rwanda*. New York: Author. UN Doc. S/RES/955.

Vranic, Seada (1996). *Introduction to Breaking the Wall of Silence: The Voice of Raped Bosnia*. Zagreb: Antibarbarus.

Wing, Adrien Katherine, and Merchán, Sklke (1993). Rape, ethnicity and culture: Spirit injury from Bosnia to Black America. 25 *Columbia Human Rights Law Review* 1(5):25.

## Annotated Bibliography

Abreu, Veronica (2005). Women's bodies as battlefields in the former Yugoslavia: An argument for the prosecution of sexual terrorism as genocide and the recognition of genocidal sexual terrorism as a violation of *jus cogens* under international law. *The Georgetown Journal of Gender and the Law*, 6, 1-20.

Abreu argues that genocidal sexual terrorism should be recognized as an international crime separate and distinct from other war crimes and crimes against humanity. She argues that this recognition should occur through an amendment to the Genocide Convention that explicitly names sexual violence as a tool of genocide.

Arbour, Louise (2003). Crimes against women under international law. *Berkeley Journal of International Law*, 21, 196-212.

Arbour, former head prosecutor of the International Criminal Tribunals for Yugoslavia and Rwanda, recounts the advances made by the tribunals in prosecuting gender crimes as crimes against humanity and genocide.

Askin, Kelly (2003). Prosecuting wartime rape and other gender-related crimes under international law: Extraordinary advances, enduring obstacles, *Berkeley Journal of International Law*, 21, 288-349.

Askin focuses on the development of gender crimes in international humanitarian law over the past fifteen years (roughly, 1988 and 2003) and provides an in-depth study of the jurisprudence of the International Criminal Tribunal for the Former Yugoslavia and Rwanda, including the designation of rape, sexual assault, sexual slavery, and forced prostitution as war crimes, crimes against humanity, and genocide.

Askin, Kelly (1997). *War Crimes Against Women*. The Hague: Kluwer Law International. 455 pp.

Askin presents a comprehensive discussion of the development of war, gender, and gender crimes from the Middle Ages to the Bosnian War. Her approach is unique because she does not immediately narrow her focus to gender crimes. Rather, she looks at each situation as a whole before focusing in on the gendered aspects of the conflict. She also compares gender crimes during conflict to crimes against women more generally, not to downplay the severity of gender violence during wartime but rather to put such violence into a social and historical context.

Boon, Kristen (2001). Rape and forced pregnancy under the ICC statute: Human dignity, autonomy, and consent. *Columbia Human Rights Law Review*, 32, 625-675.

Boon interprets the codification of rape and forced pregnancy in the Rome Statute of the International Criminal Court, specifically focusing on the elements of the crimes and their origin in international and common law.

Brownmiller, Susan (1976). *Against Our Will: Men, Women, and Rape*. New York: Bantam Books. 541 pp.

A history of rape during war in the twentieth century, including World War I and II, Vietnam, and Bangladesh.

Campanaro, Jocelyn (2001). Women, war, and international law: The historical treatment of gender-based war crimes. *Georgetown Law Journal*, 89,
2557-2592.
    Campanaro provides a historical overview of gender crimes in interna-
tional law from World War II to the creation of the International Criminal
Court.

Coan, Christin (2000). Rethinking the spoils of war: Prosecuting rape as a war
crime in the International Criminal Tribunal for the Former Yugoslavia.
*North Carolina Journal of International Law & Commercial Regulation*,
26, 183-237.
    Coan provides an overview of the procedural protections afforded to
victims of gender violence in the International Criminal Tribunal for the
Former Yugoslavia (ICTY) and discusses the precarious balance between
protecting victims and providing defendants with a fair and public trial. He
also reviews the ICTY's subject matter jurisdiction, evidentiary requirements,
victim compensation, and sentencing in the prosecution of gender crimes.
Finally, he turns to alternatives to the ICTY for victims of gender crimes,
including the possibility of prosecution in domestic courts under such statutes
as the Alien Torts Statute in the United States.

Copelon, Rhonda (1999). Surfacing gender: Reengraving crimes against women
in humanitarian law, pp. 332-360. In Nicole Ann Dombrowski (Ed.) *Women
and War in the Twentieth Century: Enlisted With or Without Consent*. New
York: Garland.
    Copelon argues that focusing on genocidal rape does not increase the
likelihood that the struggles and voices of women will be vindicated but
does increase the likelihood that victims of other kinds of gender violence
will go unheard. She argues that rape and genocide are separate crimes and
should be evaluated as such.

Copelon, Rhonda (1995). Women's rights as international human rights: Women
and war crimes. *St. John's Law Review*, 69, 61-68.
    Copelon argues that subsuming rape beneath the definition of genocide
makes gender invisible and instead argues that rape is a separate crime against
humanity, one that is based on gender.

Engle, Karen (2005). Feminism and its (dis)contents: Criminalizing wartime
rape in Bosnia and Herzogovina. *American Journal of International Law*,
99, 778-816.
    Engle differentiates "genocidal rape"—systematic rape utilized as a tool
of ethnic cleansing—and everyday rape or wartime rape. Feminist theorists
have clashed on how genocidal rape, as occurred during the Bosnian War,
should be viewed. On one hand—rape is always horrific and it seems perverse
to declare some rapes worse than others. On the other hand, genocidal rape
represents a particularly invidious threat that should be recognized—and
punished—as such.

Etienne, Margaret (1995). Addressing gender-based violence in an international context. *Harvard Women's Law Journal*, 18, 139-170.

Etienne criticizes the international community's acceptance of gender-based violence in conflict situations without also addressing the gender-based violence inflicted against women in all countries on a daily basis. She argues that failing to recognize all gender-based violence as a human rights violation has diverted attention to only a small subset of gender crimes while ignoring the larger threat to women.

Fisher, Siobhan (1996). Occupation of the womb: Forced impregnation as genocide. *Duke Law Journal*, 46, 91-133.

Fisher identifies forced impregnation as a crime distinct from rape which is, at its core, a crime of genocide, as became clear during the Bosnian War.

Gardam, Judith Gail, and Jarvis, Michelle (2001). *Women, Armed Conflict and International Law*. Boston, MA: Kluwer Law International 284 pp.

Garham and Jarvis provide a comprehensive overview of women in international humanitarian law, including the special protections afforded to women under the law, the institutional response to gender violence, and the international prosecution of gender crimes.

Jones, Adam (2004). Gendercide and genocide, pp. 1-38. In Adam Jones (Ed.) *Gendercide and Genocide*. Nashville, TN: Vanderbilt University Press.

Jones argues that the focus on femicide and gender crimes against women is curious, given the fact that men, not women have been traditionally targeted as victims of genocide. For instance, during the Bosnian War, while Bosnian women were subject to rape and sexual abuse in far greater numbers than men, the Serbian army purposefully killed greater numbers of men. The same is true for war in general as well, as men of "battle-age" are always the most numerous victims.

MacKinnon, Catharine (2006). Defining rape internationally: A comment on Akayesu. *Columbia Journal of Transnational Law*, 44, 940-958.

MacKinnon traces the definition of rape in the jurisprudence of the International Criminal Tribunal for the former Yugoslavia (ICTY) and the International Criminal Tribunal for Rwanda (ICTR), and argues that the ICTR, with its judgment in the *Akayesu* case, set forth the most progressive definition of systematic rape as genocide. The ICTY's utilization of the non-consent paradigm, as evidence in the *Furundzija* case, has caused it to lose credibility among female survivors and, according to MacKinnon, represents a backpedaling. The International Criminal Court's definition of rape attempts to straddle these two definitions and in doing so fails to resolve the dispute between them.

MacKinnon, Catharine (1994). Rape, genocide, and women's human rights. *Harvard Women's Law Journal*, 17, 5-16.

MacKinnon identifies the rape of Bosnian and Croatian women during the war as both inherently ethnic *and* gendered. She argues that all too often women's rights are subsumed under human rights more generally, and therefore not really recognized at all, or are considered individual, and therefore, private. MacKinnon wants genocidal rape recognized for what it is—a systematic attack on women as a tool of genocide to eradicate an ethnic group.

Meron, Theodor (1993). Rape as a crime under international humanitarian law. *American Journal of International Law*, 87, 424-28.

Meron details the development of gender crimes in international law from before World War I to the Bosnian genocide and celebrates the designation of rape as a crime under international humanitarian law by the U.N. Security Council as monumental.

Milne, Allison (2005). Prosecuting cases of gender violence in the international criminal tribunal for Rwanda. *Buffalo Human Rights Law Review*, 11, 107-128.

Milne presents a good overview of the use of gender violence during the Rwandan genocide and the efforts to bring the perpetrators to justice in the International Criminal Tribunal for Rwanda and argues that the precedent established will help bring future perpetrators to justice.

Mitchell, David (2005). The prohibition of rape in international humanitarian law as a norm of *jus cogens*: Clarifying the doctrine. *Duke Journal of Comparative and International Law*, 15, 219-257.

By looking at state law and practice, international conventions, and the decisions of international and regional judicial bodies, Mitchell argues that the prohibition of rape in international humanitarian law has achieved *jus cogens* status. In particular, he points to the decisions of the International Criminal Tribunal for the former Yugoslavia and the International Criminal Tribunal for Rwanda as evidence that rape is now prohibited under customary international law.

Obote-Odora, Alex (2005). Rape and sexual violence in international law: ICTR contribution. *New England Journal of International and Comparative Law*, 12, 135-159.

Obote-Odora focuses on the contributions of the International Criminal Tribunal for Rwanda to the development of gender crimes in international law, specifically the rejection of non-consent as an element of sexual violence and the recognition of rape as a tool of genocide.

Oosterveld, Valerie (2004). Sexual slavery and the International Criminal Court: Advancing international law. *Michigan Journal of International Law*, 25, 605-651.

Oostervald studies the inclusion of "sexual slavery" as a war crime and a crime against humanity in the Rome Statute of the International Criminal

Court and discusses some of the definitional and methodological problems that arose when defining the elements of the crime.

Ray, Amy (1997). The shame of it: Gender-based terrorism in the former Yugoslavia and the failure of international human rights to comprehend the injuries. *American University Law Review*, 46, 793-840.

Ray argues that the International Criminal Tribunal for the former Yugoslavia failed to understand the injuries inflicted on Croatian and Bosnian Muslim women during the Balkan War because it did not grasp that the physical violence inflicted on these women was only the tip of the iceberg in terms of the mental and psychological trauma they suffered. She rejects the view of rape as a crime of violence because in doing so rape becomes like any other crime inflicted on men. Instead, she argues, rape is always political—whether perpetrated in war or peacetime—and becomes an effective tool of genocide only because of preexisting male domination.

Russell-Brown, Sherrie (2002). Rape as an act of genocide. *Berkeley Journal of International Law*, 21, 350-74.

Russell-Brown reviews a major disagreement among feminist scholars in the aftermath of the Bosnian genocide concerning the treatment of genocidal rape. Feminist scholars such as MacKinnon have argued that genocidal rape is especially egregious because it targets women both because of their gender and because of their membership in an ethnic group. Scholars such as Copelon have argued the opposite—that treating genocidal rape as different than other forms of gender-based violence has the effect of rendering rape invisible. Russell-Brown points out that much of this debate occurred after the Rwandan genocide but before the Akayesu Judgment, which, according to Russell-Brown, emphasized the intersectionality of gender and ethnicity in genocidal rape and detailed the way in which genocidal rape becomes a tool of destruction.

Sackellares, Stephanie (2005). From Bosnia to Sudan: Sexual violence in modern armed conflict. *Wisconsin Women's Law Journal*, 20, 137-165.

Sackellares sounds an alarm on the emerging gender violence in Sudan and argues that international law, and in particular the International Criminal Court, provides all of the tools necessary to prevent and punish gender violence. She also discusses barriers to and strategies for enforcement in Sudan, using lessons learned from the International Criminal Tribunals for the Former Yugoslavia and Rwanda.

Sellers, Patricia Viseur (2002). Sexual violence and peremptory norms: The legal value of rape. *Case Western Reserve Journal of International Law*, 34, 287-303.

Sellers argues that while rape has become a constitutive element of many crimes under customary international law such as genocide, torture, and crimes and against, sexual violence as a separate crime has not attained *jus cogens* status. She points to the fact that states do not feel compelled to prevent and punish sexual violence except in the very narrow context of armed conflict or genocide.

*Statute of the International Criminal Tribunal for the Former Yugoslavia.* SC Res. 827, annex, Art. 5(g) (May 25, 1993), 32 ILM 1203 (1993).

Article 2 defines grave breaches of the 1949 Geneva Conventions, including "wilfully causing great suffering or serious injury to body or health," which has been interpreted to include rape and other sexual crimes. Article 4 defines genocide to include "causing serious bodily or mental harm to members of the group" and "imposing measures intended to prevent births within the group." Article 5 defines "rape" as a crime against humanity.

Wood, Stephanie (2004). Woman scorned for the "least condemned" war crime: Precedent and problems with prosecuting rape as a serious war crime in the International Criminal Tribunal for Rwanda. *Columbia Journal of Gender and Law*, 13, 274-327.

Wood looks at both the positive and negative developments for gender crimes at the International Criminal Tribunal for Rwanda (ICTR). She focuses specifically on the prosecution of two individuals: Jean-Paul Akeyesu and Pauline Nyiramasuhuko. The judgment against Akeyesu was historic—the first time rape has been prosecuted as a crime against humanity and as a tool of genocide. But the prosecution of Nyiramasuhuko, who was singled out among her male co-conspirators as a perpetrator of genocidal rape, is more troubling. Wood also identifies three systemic failures in the ICTR's prosecution of gender crimes—the failure to arrest perpetrators of gender crimes in the immediate aftermath of the genocide; the failure to indict for gender crimes from the outset, thereby diminishing the likelihood of an adequate historical and legal record of the gender-based violence that occurred during the genocide; and the failure to adequately protect the victims' rights at trial, preferencing the rights of the accused over the interests of the rape victims.

# 10

# Prosecution of Gender-Based Acts of Genocide under International Law

*Valerie Oosterveld*

### Introduction

"Gender" is not included in the list of targeted groups in the definition of genocide found in the 1948 Convention on the Prevention and Punishment of the Crime of Genocide ("Genocide Convention"), and that exclusion is replicated in the 1998 Rome Statute of the International Criminal Court (ICC). That does not mean, however, that gender is not a relevant consideration in the prosecution of genocide. Various gender-based acts clearly fall within the prohibited acts included in the genocide definition and gender interacts with the definition's list of targeted groups – national, ethnic, racial or religious – in a myriad of ways. Thus, the prosecution of genocide must take into account the fact that gender deeply informs how genocide is carried out.

Literature discussing the prosecution of gender-based acts of genocide tends to focus on two issues: how international criminal tribunals have addressed such acts as genocide, and how these tribunals (and international criminal law more generally) could address such acts as genocide in the future. This chapter and the accompanying annotated bibliography explore both approaches. While the World War II international tribunals barely considered the link between gender and genocide, the International Criminal Tribunals for the Former Yugoslavia (ICTY) and Rwanda (ICTR) have explored in some depth how gender and genocide are intertwined. Judgments in ICTR cases such as *Akayesu*, *Kayishema* and *Nahimana et al.* have examined how gender-based violence such as rape and twisted portrayals of Tutsi femininity in the media contributed to genocide in Rwanda. Judgments in ICTY cases such as *Krstic* and *Stakic* have concluded that sexual violence can qualify as serious bodily or mental harm and therefore as an act of genocide, and the *Blagojevic and Jokic* judgment found that the intent to destroy can be closely linked to gender-specific targeting for genocidal acts.

To date, the role of gender in genocide has been most thoroughly examined by the ICTR when considering cases involving sexual violence committed against women and girls. To a lesser extent, gender-based acts of genocide have been considered by the ICTY. The International Criminal Court (ICC) has not yet heard a case involving genocide, but its list of the elements of crime for genocide certainly provides the possibility of advancing the prosecution of gender-based acts of genocide beyond that of the ICTR and the ICTY.

## International Law and Gender-Based Acts of Genocide

While, the role of gender in genocide has largely been left unexamined within international treaty law, it is not entirely absent. During the drafting of the Genocide Convention's category of "imposing measures intended to prevent births," various gender-specific acts were considered to fall within this description: castration, sterilization, compulsory abortion, segregation of the sexes and obstacles to marriage (Schabas, 2000). Five decades later, during the drafting of the Rome Statute of the ICC, some nongovernmental organizations proposed a much wider incorporation of gender issues within the definition of genocide: they argued that the Statute's definition of genocide be drafted to include efforts to destroy particular groups based on gender (Women's Caucus for Gender Justice in the International Criminal Court, 1998). This suggestion was not followed because states were reluctant to alter in any way the definition found in the Genocide Convention, which they felt had entered customary international law (Steains, 1999, pp. 357-390). However, recognition of the link between gender and genocide came through a different route during the drafting of the ICC's non-binding "Elements of Crimes" document. Negotiations on the Elements of Crimes document opened in February 1999, only months after the release of the ICTR's Trial Chamber judgment in *Akayesu*. The Akayesu judgment set an important precedent by recognizing that the genocidal act of causing serious bodily or mental harm could include "acts of torture, be they bodily or mental, inhumane or degrading treatment, rape, sexual violence, persecution." France proposed that this case law be reflected in commentary accompanying the elements of crimes on genocide (Garraway, 2001, pp. 50-51). After some consideration, states later agreed to instead include a footnote to the first element of "genocide by causing serious bodily or mental harm" to indicate that such conduct "may include, but is not necessarily restricted to, acts of torture, rape, sexual violence or inhuman or degrading treatment" (United Nations, 2000). Thus, the ICC's Elements of Crimes directly recognize that rape and sexual violence can amount to serious bodily or mental harm within the crime of genocide. Quénivet (2005) argues that this also reflects customary international law.

The function of gender-based violence within the crime of genocide was not examined by international criminal tribunals until after the creation of the ICTY and ICTR in 1993 and 1994, respectively. The September 1998 *Akayesu* judgment of the ICTR was the first consideration of individual criminal liability for genocide by an international tribunal and the first such consideration of gender-based genocidal acts. The Akayesu Trial Chamber commented on the connection of almost every aspect of the genocide definition to gender-based violence, substantially advancing international legal understanding in this area and setting precedent followed in subsequent ICTR prosecutions. Most importantly, the judgment ended speculation as to whether rape could constitute a genocidal act. The Trial Chamber found that rape can be considered a genocidal act when, as with any other type of act, it fulfills the requirements of one or more of the list of prohibited acts and was committed with the specific intent to destroy, in whole or in part, a particular group, targeted as such. With respect to the overarching requirement of intent to destroy in whole or in part, the Trial Chamber noted that acts of sexual violence can form an integral part of the process of destruction of a group, as such violence results in the physical and psychological destruction of a group's women, their families and their communities. In the case of Rwanda, "[s]exual violence was a step in the process of destruction of the Tutsi group – destruction of the spirit, of the will to live, and of life itself." With respect to group identity, the Trial Chamber noted that sexualized portrayals of ethnic identity were directly linked to how Tutsi women were targeted for destruction: "sexualized representation of ethnic identity graphically illustrates that Tutsi women were subjected to sexual violence because they were Tutsi."

The Akayesu Trial Chamber also commented on the specific acts listed under the genocide definition. The Trial Chamber observed that many women who were subjected to rape and other forms of sexual violence were murdered afterward, and that therefore rape and killing were linked: "acts of rape and sexual violence...reflected the determination to make Tutsi women suffer and to mutilate them even before killing them, the intent being to destroy the Tutsi group while inflicting acute suffering on its members in the process." There is disagreement, however, as to whether this recognition means that crimes of sexual violence can be prosecuted under the category of killing members of the group.[1] The Trial Chamber also held that gender-based violence can inflict serious bodily or mental harm on members of the group: "rape and sexual violence certainly constitute infliction of serious bodily and mental harm on the victims and are even...one of the worst ways of inflicting harm on the victim as he or she suffers both bodily and mental harm."[2] According to the Chamber, imposing measures intended to prevent births within the group includes "sexual mutilation, the practice of sterilization, forced birth control, separation of the sexes and prohibition of marriages." As well, "[i]n patriarchal societies, where membership of the group is determined by the identity of the father, an example...is the case where, during rape, a woman of the said group is deliberately impregnated by a man of the other group, with the intent to have her give birth to a child who will consequently not belong to its mother's group." The measures imposed can be physical or mental, "[f]or instance, rape can be a measure intended to prevent births when the person raped refuses subsequently to procreate, in the same way that members of a group can be led, through threats or trauma, not to procreate."

To date, the judgments in *Akayesu* are the most detailed consideration of the intersection of gender and genocide in the ICTR's jurisprudence. That said, subsequent cases have simply tended to reinforce certain of the *Akayesu* findings.[3] For example, in *Gacumbitsi*, the ICTR found the accused guilty of causing serious bodily harm by instigating the rape of Tutsi women and girls. In *Muhimana*, the accused was convicted of causing serious bodily or mental harm by taking part in attacks in which he raped Tutsi women. Other judgments have gone further. In *Kayishema and Ruzindana*, the Trial Chamber found that the deliberate infliction on a group of conditions of life calculated to bring about its physical destruction in whole or in part includes the infliction of rape. The *Nahimana et. al.* judgment explored the role of the extremist *Kangura* newspaper and Radio Télévision Libre des Mille Collines (RTLM) radio station in promoting genocide through rape. The Trial Chamber found that the newspaper and radio station had relentlessly characterized Tutsi women as dangerous *femmes fatales* and seductive agents of the enemy: "By defining the Tutsi woman as an enemy in this way, RTLM and *Kangura* articulated a framework that made the sexual attack of Tutsi women a foreseeable consequence of the role attributed to them."

ICTY prosecutions have also led to Trial and Appeals Chamber findings on the link between genocide's intent to destroy and gender. With respect to the required specific intent to destroy, in *Krstic*, the ICTY's Appeals Chamber found that the Trial Chamber was entitled to consider the long-term impact that the elimination of 7,000 to 8,000 Bosnian Muslim boys and men would have on the survival of the Bosnian Muslim community in Srebrenica. The Trial Chamber found that, given the patriarchal character of the Bosnian Muslim society in Srebrenica and having that many males listed as missing within the overall community would result in spouses unable to remarry within their own community and thus unable to produce new children within their own community. The end result would potentially be the end of the Srebrenica Muslim community. This reasoning cast Srebrenica Muslim women as vessels of culture in a somewhat reductive manner. A more nuanced approach was used in *Blagojevic and Jokic*. In that case, the Trial Chamber found that the Bosnian Serb forces knew that the combination of the killing of the men and boys and the forcible transfer of the women, children and elderly out of the Srebrenica enclave would inevitably result in the physical disappearance of the Bosnian Muslim population of Srebrenica, and intended through these acts to physically destroy the group. In other words, the intent to destroy was intimately linked to the gendered choice of who to kill and who to transfer.

The ICTY has also commented on gender-based genocidal acts. For example, the *Blagojevic and Jokic*, *Brdjanin*, *Stakic* and *Krstic* ICTY judgments all note that acts of sexual violence, including rape, can be considered as causing serious bodily or mental harm for the purposes of the genocide definition. As well, in *Blagojevic and Jokic*, the ICTY found that the forced displacement of women, children and elderly was itself serious mental harm: "After their husbands, fathers and sons were taken from them, the Bosnian Muslim women felt even more vulnerable and afraid—afraid not only for their own safety, but especially that of their loved ones."

In sum, prosecutions before the ICTR and ICTY have led to a relatively rapid development in international criminal law's understanding of how certain gender-based acts, especially sexual violence, can contribute to genocide by amounting to serious bodily or mental harm, deliberately inflicted conditions of life calculated to bring about a group's destruction or measures imposed to prevent births within the group. In addition, the Tribunals' case law has also demonstrated how media vilification of a certain group of women can foresee-ably lead to genocidal sexual violence against women in that group, and how gendered acts of genocide when combined, such as killing men within a group and forcible transfer of women, can result in the destruction of a group.

This expansion of understanding with respect to gender and genocide, though, has been accompanied by critical challenges: a lack of clarity within prosecutions and judgments as to how sexual violence might be linked in other ways to the genocidal acts, a similar lack of clarity as to what gender-specific acts, apart from sexual violence, also constitute genocidal acts; and a lack of understanding within international criminal tribunals as to how deeply gender is intertwined with the definition of genocide. The ICC will undoubtedly, over time, be required to address these challenges.

## Critical Challenges Facing the Field Today

Clearly, international criminal law is still at an early stage of understanding how gender-based acts can contribute to, or amount to, a genocide and be prosecuted as such internationally and domestically. Certain prosecutions have raised, but not answered, specific questions about how sexual violence is linked to genocidal acts. For example, can rape that leads to death, whether directly through internal injury or indirectly (and perhaps over time) through disease, be considered under the genocidal act of "killing members of the group"? Rape unto death, killing preceded by rape and sexual mutilation, and transmission of HIV/AIDS was common during the Rwandan genocide (Des Forges, 1999).[4] For example, in *Gacumbitsi*, the accused was found to have instigated the death of a twenty-five-year-old woman, who was raped and then impaled through her genitals. However, the ICTR has not explored in any depth the answer to this question. De Brouwer (2005) outlines the possibility of intentional killing with a sexual component being prosecuted as genocidal killing. She differentiates between cases where sexual violence is the intentional mode of killing and cases where the intention of the perpetrator is to rape, but death is the indirect consequence of the rape. The former situation demonstrates the required *mens rea* (mental element) for genocide by killing, whereas it is much more difficult to prove the necessary *mens rea* for the latter. She argues, however, that the ICC's Elements of Crimes seem to leave room for covering unintentional homicide, such as the case where death is an indirect result of sexual violence. In contrast, Quénivet believes that regarding sexual offenses as "killing members of the group" is erroneous, but admits that numerous rapes leading to death through disease such as AIDS might be able to be prosecuted under this category.

Other gender-based acts of genocide that have yet to be fully explored within international criminal prosecutions and judgments are: sexual slavery as "serious bodily and mental harm" (de Brouwer, 2005); sexual violence in the context of "conditions of life calculated to bring about [the group's] physical destruction;"[5] the parameters of "measures to prevent births" beyond physical and mental harm created by sexual violence[6] (de Brouwer, 2005); and how the acts of "forcibly transferring children" might apply in cases of sexual violence (de Brouwer, 2005, and Quénivet, 2005).[7] In addition, the legal consequences of post-sexual violence harm such as mental and physical trauma and social and economic consequences for women who have suffered sexual violence (for example, those who bore children conceived through genocidal rape) have yet to be examined in depth in international jurisprudence (de Brouwer, 2005). As well, more examination is needed as to what gender-specific acts, apart from sexual violence, might fall within the parameters of genocidal acts, such as physical or mental coercion or violations related to culturally-defined roles of mothers and caregivers, or enslavement of women for non-sexual purposes.

Within international criminal prosecutions, much more consideration is needed of how "femaleness" and "maleness" as socially-constructed categories are linked to genocide. This is difficult because it forces investigators, prosecutors and judges to step away somewhat from the focus upon whether or not discrete elements of crimes have been proven. However, it is also worthwhile because it allows a much deeper conceptualization of societal roles in the context of those crimes. In the past, a lack of understanding of this larger picture has led to inadequate investigations, overlooked charges, dropped charges and acquittals (International Criminal Tribunal for Rwanda, 2004).[8]

## Real Probabilities of Progress in the Field

Forthcoming ICTR judgments present possibilities to further define how gender-based acts contribute to genocide. In several ICTR cases currently in progress or awaiting trial, the Prosecutor argues that rape and other forms of sexual violence formed part of the *modus operandi* of genocide (e.g. indictments in *Bizimunga et al., Karamera; Bikindi,* and *Gatete*). For example, in

*Bizimunga et al.,* the indictment alleges that, in furtherance of the genocide, Tutsi women and girls were abducted and raped or subjected to other forms of sexual violence, which resulted in serious mental and physical injuries, permanent disabilities, including destruction of reproductive organs, unwanted pregnancies and sexually transmitted diseases, including AIDS. In the future, the ICC is likely to be the institution that will advance international law's understanding of gender-based acts of genocide. In addition, the Extraordinary Chambers of the Court of Cambodia may consider gender-based genocidal acts (though this is not clear), and, due to the increasing number of countries that have enacted legislation criminalizing genocide, it is likely that domestic courts will also play an important role in developing this area.

## Conclusion

International understanding of the role that gender plays within genocide has advanced significantly since the drafting of the 1948 Genocide Convention. This understanding has largely developed through prosecutions before the ICTR and ICTY. The ICTR's *Akayesu* judgment has done the most to examine gender-based acts of genocide and the influence of gender in genocide. While pending ICTR decisions may take the opportunity to clarify these issues further, it is likely that, in the future, prosecutions before the International Criminal Court and domestic courts will need to address the many unanswered questions identified above about gender and genocide.

## Notes

1. While Quénivet argues against and de Brouwer argues for it, see, Anne-Marie L. M. De Brouwer (2005). *Supranational Criminal Prosecution of Sexual Violence: The ICC and the Practice of the ICTY and the ICTR.* Antwerp, Belgium: Intersentia, and Noëlle N.R. Quénivet (2005) *Sexual Offences in Armed Conflict & International Law.* Ardsley, NY: Transnational Publishers Inc.
2. See also judgments in *Kayishema, Musema, Rutaganda, Kajelijeli, Gacumbitsi* and *Muhimana.*
3. See also judgments in *Kayishema, Rutaganda,* and *Musema.*
4. On the transmission of AIDS, see the *Bizimunga et al.* indictment.
5. Quénivet does not believe that sexual offences can be deemed "methods of destruction," but de Brouwer and Schabas argue otherwise.
6. Quénivet supports the use of this category in circumstances where raped women are rejected (or killed) by their families and communities.
7. Forced impregnation or systematic rape may fall within the category of acts leading to the transfer of children to another group.
8. See the presentation by Binaifer Nowrojee, *We Can Do Better: Investigating and Prosecuting International Crimes of Sexual Violence.*

## References

De Brouwer, Marie L. M. (2005). *Supranational Criminal Prosecution of Sexual Violence: The ICC and the Practice of the ICTY and the ICTR.* Antwerp, Belgium: Intersentia.

Des Forges, Alison (1999). *"Leave None to Tell the Story": Genocide in Rwanda*. New York: Human Rights Watch.
Garraway, Charles (2001). Article 6(b) – Genocide by causing serious bodily or mental harm, pp. 50-51. In Roy S. Lee (Ed.),*The International Criminal Court: Elements of Crimes and Rules of Procedure and Evidence*. Ardsley, NY: Transnational Publishers.
International Criminal Tribunal for Rwanda (2004). *Report of Proceedings of the Colloquium of Prosecutors of International Criminal Tribunals on "The Challenges of International Criminal Justice."* Arusha, Tanzania: Author.
Quénivet, Noëlle N.R. (2005). *Sexual Offences in Armed Conflict and International Law*. Ardsley, NY: Transnational Publishers Inc.
Schabas, William A. (2000). *Genocide in International Law: The Crime of Crimes*. Cambridge, United Kingdom: Cambridge University Press.
Steains, Cate (1999). Gender issues, pp. 357-390. In Roy S. Lee (Ed.), *The International Criminal Court: The Making of the Rome Statute*. The Hague, Netherlands: Kluwer Law International.
United Nations (2000). *Report of the Preparatory Commission for the International Criminal Court, Addendum, Part II, Finalized Draft Text of the Elements of Crimes*. U.N. Doc. PCNICC/2000/1/Add.2.
Women's Caucus for Gender Justice in the International Criminal Court (1998). *Gender Justice and the ICC*. New York: Author.

## Annotated Bibliography

Askin, Kelly D. (2005). Gender crimes jurisprudence in the ICTR. *Journal of International Criminal Justice*, 3 (4), 1007-1018.

The ICTR's Trial Chamber judgment in *Akayesu* set important precedent for the recognition of rape and other forms of sexual violence as acts of genocide. Specifically, the *Akayesu* judgment formally recognized that rape and other forms of sexual violence cause serious bodily or mental harm, which results in harm inflicted far beyond the immediate victim to families, communities, associated groups and the public at large. This was confirmed in the *Kayishema and Ruzindana, Gacumbitsi* and *Nahimama* Trial Chamber judgments. Askin asserts that these prosecutions represent important achievements, but that the remaining cases should aim to further develop international law in this area.

Askin, Kelly D. (1999). Women and international humanitarian law, pp. 41-87. In Kelly D. Askin and M. Dorean Koenig, (Eds.), *Women and International Human Rights Law, Volume 1*. Ardsley, NY: Transnational Publishers, Inc.

In this chapter, Askin examines the various ways in which sexual violence may be prosecuted within the United Nations Convention on the Prevention and Punishment of Genocide's definition, assuming that the overarching elements (such as the required specific intent) are fulfilled. Sexual violence can be prosecuted within "killing members of the group" in cases where the victim dies as a result of excessively violent sexual violence, where sex offences committed against particularly young, old, weak or ill individuals result in death, when perpetrators infected with the HIV/AIDS virus sexually assault and infect their victims, who then die, or when pregnant women are sexually violated and either the women or their fetuses die. Sexual violence can amount to "causing serious bodily or mental harm to members of the group," especially when committed in public, before members of a victim's family, by multiple persons, with foreign objects or by anal or oral sex. Pregnancy resulting from rape would also increase the mental and physical harm, as would undergoing an abortion to terminate a pregnancy caused by such rape. Forced sterilization, forced abortion, sexual mutilation or sexual violence resulting in reproductive harm may be charged under "deliberately inflicting on the group conditions of life calculated to bring about its physical destruction." "Imposing measures intended to prevent births within the group" can be fulfilled through killing certain members of the group (especially women and girls), forced abortion, forced sterilization, severe punishment imposed for pregnancy, psychological damage that leads to refusal of future sex, and forced impregnation between different groups. "Forcibly transferring children of the group to another group" can be prosecuted where women are forced to bear children of different groups. Askin states that sexual violence can destroy a group just as completely and effectively as does killing members of a group. She argues that the term "gender" should be included within the list of target groups protected from genocidal acts, and that this must be done in order to appropriately identify gender as a pervasive basis of genocidal persecution.

Carpenter, R. Charli (2000). Surfacing children: Limitations of the genocidal rape discourse, *Human Rights Quarterly*, 22 (2), 428-477.

In Carpenter's view, the current legal understanding of forced impregnation as genocide is too limited in scope as it fails to consider the fate of children conceived from rape. She outlines how past international legal analysis of the act of forced impregnation as a distinct crime was framed in such a way as to marginalize the children as subjects of international law and to identify them with the perpetrators, rather than the victims, of genocide. She clarifies the linkage between forced impregnation and genocide: to function as genocide, the children (and the mothers who bore children of "the enemy") must be seen by *the group* (and not necessarily the perpetrators) as alien to the group. It is the rejection of these children and mothers that destabilizes and destroys the group. Carpenter critiques Copelon, Fisher, MacKinnon and others, claiming that feminist discourse on forced impregnation manipulated the categorization of the resulting child's identity to fit the UN Genocide Convention's requirements. She urges the use of precise terms within international law to focus on specific harms to women: "forced impregnation" for assault (usually rape) with conception; "enforced pregnancy" for prevention of abortion access to forcibly impregnated women; and "forced maternity" for forced childbirth as a result of forced impregnation. For recognition of the child as an individual being whose rights have been violated, she suggests "birth-by-forced-maternity." She claims that birth-by-forced-maternity is a genocidal act because it constitutes forcible removal of children from the group. However, how it accomplishes this is contrary to the traditional understanding of "forcibly transferring children of the group to another group" because it involves the targeted group itself classifying the child born of rape as outside of the group, thereby forcing that child out of the group.

Copelon, Rhonda (1994). Surfacing gender: Re-engraving crimes against women in humanitarian law. *Hastings Women's Law Journal*, 5 (2), 243-266.

Copelon argues that it is important to "surface" gender in international laws governing genocide, crimes against humanity and war crimes, by recognizing that rape is a crime of gender that also intersects with ethnicity, religion, and other identities. She fears that a focus on "genocidal rape" as a means of emphasizing the heinousness of the rape of Muslim women in Bosnia increases the likelihood that condemnation will be limited to this seemingly unique case, whether within the ICTY or within the broader international community. Copelon also stresses that considering forced impregnation only as a genocidal crime risks pushing all rape pregnancies to the periphery of legal consideration.

de Brouwer, Anne-Marie L. M. (2005). *Supranational Criminal Prosecution of Sexual Violence: The ICC and the Practice of the ICTY and the ICTR.* Antwerp, Belgium: Intersentia, 570 pp.

De Brouwer explores the connection between crimes of sexual violence and genocide in depth in a chapter entitled "Sexual violence as genocide." Drawing upon the jurisprudence of the ICTR, especially the judgements in *Akayesu*, *Gacumbitsi* and *Muhimana*, she posits that sexual violence can satisfy each of the five enumerated acts included within the genocide definition used by the UN Convention on the Prevention and Punishment of Genocide. She argues that sexual violence that directly or indirectly causes death can be charged under "killing members of the group." ICTR case law has convincingly held that sexual violence such as rape and sexual mutilation causes both serious physical and psychological harm, and therefore qualifies as "causing serious bodily or mental harm to members of the group." De Brouwer adds that sexual slavery should also be considered under this act, and that this act logically includes post-sexual violence harm, such as contracting HIV/AIDS, pregnancy and birth resulting from rape, lasting physical injury to reproductive organs, psychological trauma, and social stigmatization. The ICTR recognized that the "deliberate infliction on the group of conditions of life calculated to bring about its physical destruction in whole or in part" can include the infliction of rape, and, de Brouwer suggests, can also include slow death through contraction of HIV/AIDS. "Imposing measures intended to prevent births within the group" may include physical and mental acts relating to sexual mutilation, sterilization, forced birth control, separation of the sexes, prohibition of marriages and interruption of lineage in patriarchal societies. "Forcibly transferring children of the group to another group" could encompass, according to de Brouwer, abduction of children to serve in fighting forces to serve as, for example, sex slaves. She concludes that the Rome Statute of the International Criminal Court should be amended to include "gender" in the list of specific groups targeted for destruction.

Engle, Karen (2005). Feminism and its (dis)contents: Criminalizing wartime rape in Bosnia and Herzegovina. *American Journal of International Law*, 99 (4), 778-816.

Engle discusses the intense debate that emerged in the early 1990s over whether rapes committed during the conflict in Bosnia and Herzegovina should be seen as instruments of genocide or "genocidal rape." As she notes, some feminists argued that these rapes should be considered a tool for the systematic extermination of Bosnian Muslims, while others insisted that the rape of women in times of war was, unfortunately, nothing new and that a focus on rape as genocide shifted attention away from the gendered nature of rape. Engle concludes that, while this debate faded with the founding and operation of the International Criminal Tribunal for the Former Yugoslavia (ICTY), the issues underlying the debate are still being mediated by the ICTY in its judgments, rules, procedures and institutional organization. She is concerned that the "genocidal rape" debate may have resulted in the ICTY adopting problematic assumptions about ethnic identity and women's political and sexual agency during wartime. Concomitantly, she expresses concern that an unintended consequence of this debate is that the ICTY has shifted its focus from gender to sex in two ways: by finding ethnicity to be the sole reason for systematic rapes and by treating sexual violence against women and men under one rubric.

Fisher, Siobhan K. (1996-1997). Occupation of the womb: Forced impregnation as genocide. *Duke Law Journal*, 46 (1), 91-133.

Fisher argues that when forced impregnation (which she differentiates from rape) is part of a policy to destroy a group, it should be prosecuted as an act of genocide. Focusing on forced impregnation as it took place in the former Yugoslavia, she explains that this act can destroy a group in several ways. First, the experience of forced impregnation may psychologically traumatize or physically damage a group's women such that they cannot have normal sex and childbearing experiences within their own group, thus satisfying the Genocide Convention's act of causing serious bodily or mental harm to members of the group. Second, forced impregnation may deliberately inflict on the group conditions of life calculated to bring about its physical destruction in whole or in part by creating a group of reproductive-age women who are shunned or are considered unmarriageable. Third, women forcibly impregnated by one group cannot bear children from their own group while their wombs are occupied for nine months, resulting in measures intended to prevent births within the group. Fisher concludes that the International Criminal Tribunal for the Former Yugoslavia should prosecute forced impregnation as an act of genocide, to demonstrate that rape is a method of waging war and not simply a side effect of conflict.

Gardam, Judith, and Jarvis, Michelle (2001). *Women, Armed Conflict and International Law*. The Hague, Netherlands: Kluwer Law International, 290 pp.

Gardam and Jarvis argue that rape and other forms of sexual violence have often been mischaracterized as incidental acts occurring alongside genocide, as opposed to acts that form part of a genocide. When sexual violence occurs in the context of a genocidal attack, it is a manifestation of the same hatred toward members of the group that motivates other physically harmful acts. It is therefore artificial to separate sexual violence from other genocidal acts and to do so distorts the nature of the international crime of genocide and the nature of sexual violence. Gardam and Jarvis note that, within the Genocide Convention definition, rape and other forms of sexual violence can qualify as acts of serious bodily or mental harm. Rape and other forms of sexual violence can also contribute to conditions of life calculated to bring about the physical destruction of a group by forming part of oppressive living conditions, and can amount to measures intended to prevent births within a group through destruction of sexual and reproductive organs and child-bearing capacity. Gardam and Jarvis suggest that the International Criminal Tribunal for Rwanda's approach to sexual violence in genocide in *Akayesu* and *Musema* provides support for the proposition that targeting women exclusively on the basis of their gender falls within the existing definition of genocide.

MacKinnon, Catherine (2006). Defining rape internationally: A comment on *Akayesu*. *Columbia Journal of Transnational Law*, 44 (3), 940-958.

MacKinnon argues that, in the International Criminal Tribunal for Rwanda's (ICTR's) *Akayesu* Trial Chamber judgment, the crime of rape was defined in law as what it is in life: a sexual invasion under coercive circumstances. In particular, she notes that rape was recognized as an act that inflicted serious harm with intent to destroy an ethnic group as such, and therefore as an act of genocide. She argues that this groundbreaking approach, under which it is understood that an inquiry into individual consent is not relevant, has informed the ICTR's jurisprudence, but not that of the International Criminal Tribunal for the Former Yugoslavia (ICTY). The ICTR has held that rape and other sexual violence were integral components of the Rwandan genocide and that an examination of individual consent to sex for acts that took place in the clear context of mass sexual coercion is unnecessary. The jurisprudence of the ICTY, on the other hand, has developed in such a way as to focus on individual nonconsent and the interaction of discrete body parts between perpetrator and victim. As a result, the genocidal circumstances of rape recede into the background, resulting in a failure to successfully prosecute rape as an act of genocide. Where the ICTR has followed the ICTY's approach, a similar result has ensued. The *Akayesu* definition shifted the focus of proof from individual interactions to collective realities, recognizing the context of violent inequality common to genocide.

MacKinnon, Catherine (2004). Genocide's sexuality, pp. 313-356. In Melissa Williams, and Stephen Macedo (Eds.), *Political Exclusion and Domination.* New York: New York University Press.

MacKinnon explores the genocidal functions of sexual forms of abuse, specifically examining how they relate to the Genocide Convention's definition of genocide. She asserts that it is not difficult to fit sexual forms of abuse within the Convention's sub-categories and that the International Criminal Tribunal for Rwanda has already recognized this. She distinguishes genocidal rape from rape in war in several ways, including by noting that rape in war is marked by an out-of-control quality, whereas rape in genocide is rape under control—rape done on purpose. MacKinnon's legal analysis centers on how the requirement of intent to destroy groups "as such" applies to women targeted for rape. "As such" means "the victim of the crime of genocide is the group itself and not the individual alone," and MacKinnon explains how rape occurring at the intersection of national, ethnic, racial or religious group affiliation and sex strikes at the heart of a group's definition of itself, replacing dignity, security and self-determination with fear, self-revulsion and a degraded identity. Using International Criminal Tribunal for the Former Yugoslavia case law as an example, MacKinnon observes that sexual atrocities thus give a distinctive content to the term "as such." MacKinnon concludes by arguing that, once the function of sexual abuse in genocide is more fully recognized, then the legal definition of genocide, as well as the advisability of a separate "gynocide" convention or protocol, can be revisited in a more realistic factual and theoretical construct.

Ni Aolain, Fionnuala (2000). Sex-based violence and the Holocaust – A re-evaluation of harms and rights in international law. *Yale Journal of Law and Feminism*, 12 (1), 43-84.

Harms caused by acts of violence in conflict, including genocidal conflict, can be bidirectional and multiple. For example, sex-based violence committed as part of genocide has a dual functionality: harming the victim and destroying her (or his) community. Ni Aolain argues that the international community's understanding of sex-based violation has been premised on notions of the female self that have little to do with how women actually experience and understand harms done to them. Using examples from the Holocaust, she identifies sex-based harms apart from rape and sexual violence, such as enforced nakedness, lewd verbal assaults and touching of intimate and other parts of the body, that clearly contribute to genocide and other human rights violations. She posits that the international community's understanding of sex-based harm must extend to include these related harms, as was done by the International Criminal Tribunal for Rwanda in the *Akayesu* judgments. In addition, she suggests that sex-based harm must be understood in international law as not only affecting the primary victim, but also the victim's family, friends and community. Sex-based harm is often chosen as a means of genocide or persecution because of its power to impose such extended damage. Thus, Ni Aolain urges that the international community not lose sight of nor diminish the individual harm experienced by the primary victim, but also accept that harm extends to secondary individuals and groups without lapsing into a patriarchal assumption that such communal harm is due to the loss of women's "honor."

Quénivet, Noëlle N. R. (2005). *Sexual Offences in Armed Conflict & International Law*. Ardsley, NY: Transnational Publishers Inc., 210 pp.

Quénivet explores feminist theorists' discussion of rape and genocide over the course of the past two decades. Pleading for a rigorous analysis of the international legal definition of genocide, she is critical of feminist writers who conflate sexual violence committed during ethnic cleansing operations and genocide, and who use the term "genocidal rape" without reference to the specific intent, physical and mental elements required in the definition of genocide. She views the term "gendercide" as an unhelpful addition to the analysis of genocide. Quénivet argues, in an analysis of sexual violence during genocide, that the most relevant category of analysis within the genocide definition is "causing serious bodily or mental harm to the group," as International Criminal Tribunal for the Former Yugoslavia and the International Criminal Tribunal for Rwanda jurisprudence and the International Criminal Court's Elements of Crime have recognized that serious sexual offenses can cause serious physical and psychological harm. Unlike de Brouwer, she does not support the use of the category of "killing members of the group" unless a great majority of rapes led to killing through sexually transmitted diseases or AIDS, and feels that sexual violence cannot qualify as "deliberately inflicting on the group conditions of life calculated to bring about its physical destruction." She contends that sexual violence can be linked to "imposing measures intended to prevent births within the group" but that forced impregnation should be considered under the category of "forcibly transferring children of the group to another group." In conclusion, she states that some feminists, by ignoring the legal definition of genocide and arguing instead on the basis of "genocidal rape" or "gendercide," have lost an opportunity to undertake an appropriate analysis of sexual offences as acts of genocide.

Russell-Brown, Sherrie L. (2003). Rape as an act of Genocide. *Berkeley Journal of International Law*, 21 (2), 350-374.

Russell-Brown explores the intersectionality of genocidal rape. She analyzes how the International Criminal Tribunal for Rwanda's *Akayesu* Trial Chamber judgment advanced international law's understanding of genocidal rape. Like Engle, she examines the contrasting approaches of Copelon and MacKinnon on the issue of whether to categorize the rapes committed against Bosnian Muslim women as "genocidal rape." She argues that the *Akayesu* judgement recognized: how rape was used to destroy a people; that "ethnicized" rape intersects with the gendered nature of the crime of genocidal rape; and that the rape victim is the subject (as opposed to the object) of the crime of genocidal rape. She concludes that the *Akayesu* judgement simultaneously recognizes the intersectionality of this rape (as per MacKinnon's approach) and that gender can be "surfaced" when considering genocide (as per Copelon's approach).

# 11

# The Post-Genocidal Period and Its Impact on Women

*Tazreena Sajjad*

*"Bombs and missiles kill men and women indis-criminately but other aspects of war affect women and girls disproportionately"—Ashford and Huet-Vaughn, 2000, p. 186.*

## Introduction

With its scale of atrocity and the systematic means in which it is carried out, the perpetration of genocide leaves behind not only material manifestations of its destruction, but also a psycho-social legacy that is borne by those who survive it. The study of psychological trauma induced by events such as genocide is to come face-to-face both with human vulnerability and with the capacity for evil in human nature. It demands one to be witness to a horrific set of events that do not fit in with a rational framework of reference. When the events are natural disasters or "acts of God," those who bear witness sympathize readily with the victim. But when the traumatic events are of human design, those who bear witness are caught in the conflict between victim and perpetrator and entangled in the battle of morality and ethics, of the need to remember and honor the dead, and for some survivors and emerging political structures, the urgency to forget and move forward. The tension between the will to deny horrible events and the will to proclaim them aloud is the central dialectic of psychological trauma (Herman, 1992, p. 1). In the post-conflict reconstruction period, the psychological needs of survivors, bystanders, and even the perpetrators of genocide can often be undermined in the effort to provide physical means of healing. The psychosocial recovery can only begin when the veil of secrecy is lifted, the survivors are given the space to speak about their experiences within the context of their cultures, and provided with the opportunities to establish themselves as productive members of their own communities. Only when the truth is finally recognized can survivors begin their road towards complete recovery. This chapter captures the phenomenon of post-genocidal trauma and examines the specific ways in which it impacts women, the context in which it plays out, the challenges involved in responding to such a horrifying reality and, ultimately, outlines some of the strategies that have been effective in responding to this sobering phenomenon.

## Understanding Trauma: The Personal Experience

It is estimated that more than one billion persons across the globe have been affected by mass violence (e.g., war, ethnic conflict, crimes against humanity, and genocide, among others) (Mollica and McDonald, 2003, p. 1). International relief and development organizations, public health experts and academics have increasingly acknowledged that such upheavals severely affect the mental health of survivors which manifest themselves as psychological distress, mental disorders, and trauma. "Psychological trauma" has been defined as an "experience that is emotionally painful, distressing, or shocking, which often results in lasting mental and physical effects" (MedicineNet, 2005). Judith Herman (1992), one of the leading theorists in trauma and trauma healing, provides a more complete definition of psychological trauma, explaining that "the ordinary human response to danger is a complex, integrated system of reactions, encompassing both body and mind" (p. 34). In instances of threat, the human body increases adrenaline production, heightened perception and awareness and typically causes actions of fight or flight. Herman (1992) defines trauma in comparison to the body's normal reaction to threat, noting that it occurs when normal reactions breakdown because they are overwhelmed by an event, leaving the victim feeling out of control and helpless. According to Eric Brahm (2004), emotional responses to trauma often include depression, anxiety, helplessness, flashbacks and a loss of connection. He goes on to provide several examples of physical responses to trauma, including headaches, stomach irritation, tightness of the chest, perspiration and psychosomatic complaints. Finally, Brahm (2004) lists several behavioral responses that can occur as a consequence of trauma: hyper-alertness, insomnia, and irritability.

The traumatic response studied most often in the individual is Post-Traumatic Stress Disorder (PTSD). PTSD symptoms include those mentioned above, but in PTSD the symptoms are chronic. PTSD is generally broken into three distinct categories: re-experiencing, hyper-arousal, and avoidant symptoms. The re-experiencing symptoms, such as flashbacks and nightmares, result in the inability to return to normal life in the post-trauma period. Traumatic events cause deep and abnormal memories which can be pervasive in the subconscious. Hyper-arousal symptoms include the inability to sleep and startled responses to loud noises and sudden movements. The avoidant symptoms, which include feelings of helplessness, depression, and indifference, arise from the feelings that occurred during the traumatic experience itself and results in the inability for the individual to make sense of their lives afterward. Feelings of disconnect with those around them and a sense that life is meaningless are typical (Barsalou, 2001; Herman, 1992). Furthermore, the shame and loss of self-confidence associated with such events may exacerbate the vulnerability of posttraumatic stress disorder and depression (Karunakara, Neuner, Schauer, Singh, Hill, Elbert, and Burnha, 2004). PTSD after war experiences has also been shown to be related to feelings of hatred and revenge (Cardozo, Kaiser, Gotway, and Agani, 2003).

In the context of this chapter and book, it is critical to highlight the trauma induced by rape and sexual violence. The immediate consequences of rape include: emotional symptoms (shock, intense fear, anger, shame, helplessness, nervousness, and numbness); psychological symptoms (confusion, disorientation, unwanted memories, decreased concentration); and physical symptoms (bodily injury; sexually transmitted diseases; muscular tension; fatigue; edginess; changes in sleep, appetite, and sex drive; gastrointestinal problems; racing heart; and bodily aches and pains) (National Center for PTSD, 2006).

Long-term consequences of rape-induced trauma can, of course, be complex and severe. The latter can include: injury; sexually transmitted diseases; marked interpersonal change such as distrust, the inability to establish and sustain intimate personal and family relationships, or fear of them; anger and isolation; depression (loss of hope, self-worth, motivation, or purpose in life, fatigue, decreased interest in previously enjoyed activities, changes in sleep in and/or appetite, and suicidal thoughts and actions); and alcohol and substance abuse (National Center for PTSD, 2006). Post-traumatic stress disaster symptoms, existential injuries, spiritual damage, depression, anxiety, somatic problems, fear, shame and humiliation are well-documented outcomes of rape in war (Agger 1989; Groenenberg 1993; Lunde and Ortman 1992; Sveass and Axelsen 1994; Sideris 1999; Van Willigen 1984).

## Postgenocidal Trauma and Collective (Un) Consciousness

The study of the effect of traumatic events on groups in the aftermath of World War II provided numerous and significant findings. As Volkan (2002) notes, "The survivors of Nazi concentrations camps generated a hitherto unprecedented need to study individual and mass reaction to overwhelming stress brought about by politically motivated cruelty" (p.1). Such research, though, was not conducted immediately after the war for the physical needs of the survivors were so extensive that the psychological needs took some time to be noticed by clinical workers (Volkan, 2002).

Volkan (2002) defines massive trauma as constituting an alarming experience that "takes precedence over the individual's past predispositions, which are obliterated" (p. 2). Massive trauma leaves the individual unable to function or recover on a very basic level; indeed, "chronically traumatized people no longer have a baseline state of physical calm or comfort" (Herman, 1992, p. 86).

Such experiences or catastrophes (e.g., natural disasters such as earthquakes and typhoons and man-made disasters such as war and genocide) can and do traumatize entire groups of people. When a major crisis or conflict affects all or most of a large group of people, there is a connection that forms, resulting in a shared memory of the event. These shared views and feelings by individual members of the group result in the group as a whole displaying these traumas collectively: "…new social processes and shared behaviors may appear throughout the affected community or communities, initiated by changes in the common psychological states of the affected individuals" (Volkan, 2002, p. 2).

One of the most critical contributions of Volkan's (2002) work is the differentiation between the trauma that a group experiences as a result of natural disasters, and that which arises when a person or group intentionally tries to destroy the other—even though both types of events create massive group trauma (pp. 9-10). The trauma that results as a consequence of genocide in particular, as opposed to other forms of mass killing, is more severe for both the individual and the society for a variety of reasons. "Traumas resulting from natural disasters may sometimes be distinguished from those caused by ethnic conflict (a form of human-generated trauma) by an important difference: the damaging effects of the latter can produce profound change in social and political processes that affect not only the generation that directly experienced the trauma but also subsequent generations. Volkan (2001) has referred to such changes as "'psychological degeneration'" (quoted in USIP, 2001, p. 2). Among the symptoms "of psychobiological degeneration in deeply traumatized societies are the loss of basic trust in the order of things, difficulty in mourning and difficulty in reversing a sense of helplessness and humiliation. Terrifying new social patterns, such as aggression, domestic violence, prostitution, rape, kidnapping, youth gangs and organized criminality tend to increase" (USIP, 2001, pp. 2-3). Under such a condition, there is total shock and disbelief both within and outside of the community that one's government would legitimize the extermination *of a people*. The existence of a systematic governmental or political plan to implement genocide can lead both the individual and the victimized group to mass trauma in terms of faith in the social structure. Part of the enormity of suffering endured by survivors include coping with the stigma that accompanies victimization, living with the generalized attitudes of suspicion and distrust and having a sense of psychological isolation (Patraka, 2001). The sense of estrangement from others often derives from traumatic experiences that cannot be shared with others. Talking about the "unspeakable" engenders a sense of discomfort for either the speaker or the listener or both (Nytagodien and Neal, 2004, p. 467). As collective traumas become embedded in the social heritage of any given group of people, a central and paradoxical dialectic consists of a desire to repress or deny what happened, as well as a perceived necessity to proclaim or speak loudly about the terrible events that occurred. The imperative of truth-telling involves a quest for justice and some degree of validation for beliefs about living in a just world. On the other hand, the emotional telling of stories by victims often results in credibility problems (Janoff-Bulman, 1992). Such stories are often dismissed as "emotional accounts" devoid of factual evidence.

The reality of post genocidal trauma is that all groups within a society from the victim to the perpetrator, and even the bystander, experience some form of trauma. Prior to and during the genocide, victims or the victims' loved ones experience violence, rape, torture, murder, destruction of homes, detention and institutional and structural harassment. While this type of trauma is undoubtedly graver for the individuals who directly experienced such events, the trauma can, and often is, experienced by members of the group who were not directly involved. In regard to the latter, the scale of the violence and human loss is inflicted upon the group identity and takes its toll on all of the members of the group experience—and these frequently include "....powerful, psychological, social, political and economic effects" (Volkan, 2002, p.23).

As previously noted, during the post-genocide period trauma manifests itself in several ways. Survivors of the victimized group may develop a sense of mistrust of other groups, especially the one that was dominant during the genocide and/or forms of authority such as the government that condoned the systematic killings and destruction. Like the individual, the victimized group may feel detached from the society as a whole, and both seek security and comfort from other members of the group. Under such circumstances, such feelings can result in a substantive social barrier to social reconciliation because of the traumatized group's inability to trust outsiders. For the victims, living among those who committed atrocities during the period of genocide can result in further trauma due to the constant reminder and the possible fear of future violence. The victimized group may also experience deep-seated anger and re- sentment, both towards their perpetrators and the international community who the group may feel should have done more. This, of course, has the potential for creating grounds for fomenting violence in the future.

A symptom of trauma that is particular to victims of large-scale catastro- phes and conflicts is *survivor guilt*. Survivor guilt is seen in natural disasters, survivors of war, mass killings, and genocide (Niederland, 1968). As Herman (1992) notes, survivor guilt is an extreme form of emotional helplessness where the survivor regrets not having had the power or ability to save the lives of those around him or her; and, having survived, while others did not, cannot understand why he or she survived.

Anger, as a consequence of trauma, can be passed from the group to the next generation, both consciously and subconsciously. When an individual or group passes their unresolved trauma onto their children, it is often referred to as transgenerational transmission (Volkan, 1992). Volkan (1997) notes that if healing does not take place and the trauma is passed on to the next generation, the large group remains bonded together through the memory of the traumatic event but "instead of raising a group's self-esteem, the mental image of the event links people through a continuing sense of powerlessness, as though members of the group existed under a large tent of victimhood" (p. 47).

Bystanders of genocide may also experience trauma due to having witnessed the event. They may be plagued by guilt for having done too little to prevent the event, to save lives and are often overwhelmed with a sense of helplessness and/or being out of control.

## Women and Mass Violence: The Things They Carry

During periods of mass violence, females (young girls, teenagers and women) not only experience various forms of torture, abandonment, displacement, and death, but are often also charged with the responsibility of protecting the youngest children, the elderly and the disabled as well as to nurse the injured in the midst of crossfire. And while women are crowned as protectors of the rest of the community, perpetrators of genocide often turn the bodies of the same women (and girls, for that matter) into a "battleground" (Ochieng, 2002). That is, females often become objects over which the perpetrators demonstrate their power and control. Hence, female victims' bodies are used as "envelopes" to send messages to the perceived "enemy." The female victims are subjected to rape, gang rape, forced pregnancy, abduction, and sexual slavery. Many are sexually tortured and mutilated. Concomitantly, they are often infected with HIV/AIDS and murdered by having their unborn babies ripped from their wombs. Ultimately, they also, frequently end up carrying indelible scars from the conflict through having their reproductive organs damaged beyond repair and/or being infected with HIV/AIDS. In Rwanda, for example, some survivors report that their persecutors told them they had been allowed to live so that they "might die of sadness" (Gordon and Crehan, 2002, p. 4). A survey of 304 Rwandan survivors reported that 35 percent of them had become pregnant following the rape and it is estimated that two in five "enfants de mauvais souvenir" (children of bad memories) resulted from rapes committed during the genocide" (Gordan and Crehan, 2002, p. 5). And, of course, on top of all this female victims are denied access to medical assistance and abortions, and forced to bear children conceived in rape.

## Beyond the Individual to the Larger Community

During periods of genocide, the mass rape of women can, and does, result in the social destruction of the communities of which they are an integral part, and which wartime rape strategically targets. Indeed, in this context, rape and its effects, more than any other act of violence perpetrated by one individual against another, highlights the political intention of interpersonal violence (Sideris, 2001, p. 146). Put another way, the calculated rationale of the act of wartime rape constitutes a political act and an attack on the collective political identity of the group of females under attack, not necessarily on their individual identities (Sideris, 2001, p. 149). Rape during some genocides, then, is not exclusively an attack on the body—it is an attack on the "body politic." Its primary goal is not to maim or kill a person (though that does, in fact, happen, in great numbers) but to control an entire socio-political process by crippling it. Rape and sexual violence not only reflect a patriarchal thinking of power and control over women's bodies as objects or property of men, but also the will to obliterate women's inner in-built reserve of strength, to perpetuate perverse myths about the "other," and, symbolically, destroy the ability and determination to hold the community together, since the woman is seen to be the nurturer, the care-giver and the carrier of culture.

Put another way, during certain genocides, rape has been used as a weapon of social control and cultural destruction, of devaluation and commodification. The discrete event of rape, then, is fundamentally linked to the process of social and cultural destruction (Sederis, 2001, p. 148). In places like Bangladesh, Rwanda, and Yugoslavia, rape was used (as it is now—2003 through today—in Darfur, Sudan) as a mechanism of genocide. Between 250,000 and 400,000 women were raped during the 1971 war for independence in Bangladesh, and an estimated 20,000 to 50,000 Muslim women were raped in Bosnia in "rape camps" in the 1990s where they were forced to conceive and bear Serbian children (Gordon and Crehan, 2002). Bosnian refugees describe how military forces publicly raped women to systematically force their families to leave their villages, contributing to the goal of "ethnic cleansing" (U.S. Department of Veteran Affairs, 2006; West, 2005).

It was not until late in the twentieth century that the phenomenon of sexual violence against whole communities of females was termed "genocidal rape." Genocidal rape is particular as well as part of the generic—and its particularity matters. Genocidal rape is ethnic rape as an official policy of war in a geno-cidal campaign for political control (Makinnon, 1994). That means, not only is the brutal desire of male power to control and inspire fear unleashed, which happens all the time in so-called peace; not only is it an instrument to defile, torture, humiliate, degrade, and demoralize the other side, which happens all the time in war; and not only is it a policy of men posturing to gain advantage and ground over other men. It is specifically rape under orders. This is not rape out of control. It is rape under control. It is also rape as massacre, rape to kill, rape unto death. It is rape to make the victims wish they were dead (MacKin-non, 1994).

In many cases, such rape is used "for the express purpose of impregnating the 'female other' in order to create a 'despised other' (a baby of mixed blood), knowing full well that the creation of a 'despised other' will constantly serve as a reminder of the humiliation, torture, and brutality that the bearer of the child and her people were subjected to" (Totten, 2009).

In the case of Bosnia-Herzegovina, mass rape became a tool, a tactic, and a policy—not to mention a practice. The "classic" case of such occurred when Serbs intentionally detained and raped Muslim women in camps to destroy them and their people by sexually "contaminating" the women.[1] The practice of raping on a mass-scale, that is genocidal rape, was repeated in Rwanda and is being currently witnessed in Darfur.

During the genocide in Rwanda, rape was widespread and tens upon tens of thousands of women were individually raped, gang-raped, raped with objects such as sharpened sticks or gun barrels, held in sexual slavery (either collectively or through forced "marriage") or sexually mutilated (Human Rights Watch, 1996). These crimes were frequently part of a pattern in which Tutsi women were raped after they had witnessed the torture and killings of their relatives and the destruction and looting of their homes (Gendercide Watch, 2002). Rwanda, therefore, also sadly stands as a paradigmatic example of "genocidal rape," owing to the fact that many of the Tutsi women who were gang-raped have subsequently tested positive for the HIV virus (Gendercide Watch, 2002). In the words of the *Guardian* (2001), "rape was a weapon of genocide as brutal as the machete" (p. 2).

Between early 2003 and December 2006, large-scale rapes in Darfur have continued relentlessly. According to Pamela Shifman (2004), a UN expert on violence and sexual exploitation, rape is being used "to terrorize individual women and girls...to terrorize their families and to terrorize entire communities. No woman or girl is safe" (p. 2).

## Coping with the Unspeakable: A Review of the Challenges for Women Survivors

Life after genocide has to be understood in the context of a wide array of social, cultural, and economic settings. While many suffer, as was discussed earlier, from PTSD, depression, anxiety disorder, agoraphobia, social phobia, reproductive complications, suicidal tendencies, they are also frequently forced to live in silence as social outcasts, with little or no economic, social or medical support. Indeed, vast numbers are forced to live in abject poverty.

The context of culture is critical in understanding how women in particular have to shoulder the burden of living with post genocidal trauma. Survivors of sexual violence are the evidence of the enemy's brutality and a symbol of the community's defeat. In many cases, female victims who attempt to return to their families are treated as pariahs as a result of the violence done to them (the women). Sadly, female survivors who have been sexually tortured and raped are regarded as "damaged property," shunned, divorced, or neglected because of the abuse they have undergone. In more conservative cultures, the belief that these women have brought dishonor and shame to their families and communities stigmatize them and brand them as "traitors." And the children born of rape remain as the permanent reminder of their "crime."

Not all societies, of course, react in the same manner to a survivor of genocidal rape. And some societies even act in contradictory ways. For example, in Bosnia-Herzegovina, a raped woman who was raped during the crisis years in the former Yugoslavia received a certain amount of sympathy but, at one and the same time, also evoked a negative reaction. A raped woman was and is considered defiled; she represents a disgrace to her family and her (national, religious, political) community. The shame of being raped in this case meant few identified themselves as being violated. They sought assistance only if they needed a psychiatric certificate in order to apply for a termination of pregnancy following, for example, a suicide attempt or if afflicted with one or another psychological disorder (Vera Folnegovic-Smalc, 1994).

Unsurprisingly, after being gang raped, held in a rape camp, or viciously raped during a genocide, females are left with a debilitating sense of self-esteem and left without little hope for a future. In the case that women are left without a male head of the household, the burden of shouldering family responsibility increases the stress and anxiety and often exacerbates the symptoms of the trauma of genocide. This, however, is *still* not the complete picture. It is painfully clear—despite increasing knowledge of science-based and culturally effective psychological interventions, and the value of such—that there exist vastly limited resources for assistance to post-genocidal communities. Indeed, such are only available to a minority of survivors. Thus, for a vast majority of females who are struggling to rebuild their lives from behind the veils of secrecy and shame, and whose immediate concerns involve physical survival of themselves and their children, the possibility of receiving specialized assistance for trauma recovery is a remote possibility.

Many post-genocidal societies lack a global and collaborative approach to the mental health and physical healing of traumatized groups. Far too many approaches in such settings fail to include important members of the healing system (doctors, counselors, religious leaders) within the society (Mollica and McDonald, 2003). Furthermore, individuals from post-genocidal communities have remained consistently absent from leadership positions in the international mental health movement, and therefore their expertise and views have been pushed to the background of debates in which major participants are more likely representatives from Western-based international and non-governmental organizations (NGOs) (Mollica and McDonald, 2003).

## Seeking a Way Forward

The core experiences of psychological trauma are disempowerment and disconnection from others (Herman, 1992, p.133). Recovery therefore must be based on the empowerment of the survivor and the creation of new connections. According to Herman (1992), recovery in most cases unfolds in three stages. The central task is the establishment of safety, the second is remembrance and mourning, and the third is reconnecting with ordinary life. Once safety has been established, the survivor is no longer under threat from physical or mental harm and can begin the process of seeking acknowledgement, truth-telling and defying the culture of denial and silence about the genocide. Vindication for the survivor can happen in the form of seeking procedural justice, through the legal system and/or through restorative justice mechanisms such as truth commissions which involve sharing personal accounts of the genocide: "Echoing the assumptions of psychotherapy, truth commissions presume that telling and hearing is healing" (Minow, 1998, p.8). Once the door to disclosing the horrors of the genocide is opened, the process of reconciliation can truly begin and pave the way for establishing new relationships. In renewing connections with other people, the survivor *begins* to *attempt* to recreate the psychological balance that was damaged or deformed by the traumatic experience.

It must be underscored that in the case of genocidal trauma, the multidimensional aspect of the experience calls for a complex and integrative method of treatment. Research has demonstrated the capacity of local primary health care systems, traditional healers, and national and international NGOs to play a major role in reducing the suffering and disability associated with mass violence (Mollica and McDonald, 2003). Experience has demonstrated that limiting the inclusion of experts from the conflict-affected countries themselves precludes valuable guidance while also limiting necessary buy-in, commitment and collaboration, each of which are cornerstones of effective and sustainable service design and delivery (Mollica and McDonald, 2003). Ultimately, sustainable funding, sound mental health policy and legislation, mental health capacity-building through multidisciplinary education and services, and integrated activities of international and local key stakeholders are absolutely key if the assistance provided to survivors is to be successful. Finally, it is highly recommended that any action plan be based on ensuring economic development and respect for human rights within the post-conflict context (Mollica and McDonald, 2003).

In developing a comprehensive and responsive program for female survivors of genocide, still other factors need to be consistently present in the design of trauma recovery strategies. Research in countries like Bosnia and Rwanda has indicated that the manifestations of trauma can often be culture- and gender-specific, and recovery mechanisms are most effective when cultural norms are incorporated in the healing process. As Gibbs (1997) notes, "How people embody and give meaning to their distress is significantly influenced by their particular cultural context, which indeed also affects how they identify and deal with it" (quoted in Weston, 2001, p. 5) Even if the core trauma symptoms that affect the body and mind are similar, they may be experienced differently. In this regard, Jenkins (1996) states that "in many cultures, people use somatic symptoms or talk of bodily illness as idioms of distress" (quoted in Weston, 2001, p. 5). For instance, women refugees from the political terror in El Salvador in the 1980s complained about "*nervios*," which encompassed such ills as anxiety, anger, and fear as well as body pains, shaking and trembling sensations, and "*calor*," a sense of heat related to the stress symptom (Kirkmayer, 1996 quoted in Weston, 2001, p. 5). Using somatic symptoms as a stress indicator also seems to be a pattern in

Bosnia-Herzegovina to some extent (Weston, 2001). Such manifestations call for culture-oriented intensive programs designed to acknowledge these reactions and to respond to the trauma in a way that helps reshape the lives of the survivors. Outside of individual treatment of post-traumatic stress, an appropriate strategy for responding to collective trauma is group therapy, a method that proved to be effective in the case of Bosnia. In a trauma support group, victims can meet other girls and women with similar experiences and have their own reactions validated. Judith Herman (1992) has summarized the many advantages of such a group:

> The solidarity of a group provides the strongest protection against terror and despair, and the strongest antidote to traumatic experience. Trauma isolates, the group creates a sense of belonging. Trauma shames and stigmatizes, the group bears witness and affirms. Trauma degrades the victim; the group exalts her. Trauma dehumanizes the victim; the group restores her humanity. (p. 241)

Herman (1992) also emphasizes the point that "trauma robs the victim of a sense of power and control," and thus the guiding principle of recovery must restore power and control to the individual and collective survivors. Such groups, then, not only provide the opportunity for mutually rewarding relationships, but also for collective empowerment (Weston, 2001). The importance of trust and space in re-establishing these social communities cannot be overemphasized. Agger and Mimica (1996) conclude that "the greatest need for war-traumatized people is to find a space in which trust in fellow human beings can be re-established and where normal human relationships can be formed. The activities offered in this space are less important than the general atmosphere of communal healing" (p. 4). Certainly the same seems to be true of those who survive genocide. In such spaces, after learning about trauma and stress symptoms, as well as various methods for coping with stress, female victims can finally begin the process of talking about their traumatic experiences.[2] In the end, the brutality of conflict and the horrific incidences of sexual violence strip female survivors of their multi-tiered identities and their capacity to believe in themselves. Healing for these survivors does not then fall only in the realm of physical and psychological recovery and the reconnecting of social relationships, but a reconstituting of their own political and public identities. Post-contexts must herald the opportunity of increased participation of women in public spheres and for institutionalizing social, cultural and legal reforms.

Such opportunities need to be created and expanded so that females can begin the process of rebuilding their lives, not only as mothers, caregivers and nurturers, but also as individuals, community leaders, and political figures who assert control and power over their own lives. Such measures, although not immediately within the folds of psychosocial healing, are critical in ensuring the establishment of safety and stability in the lives of such survivors and creating hope for a better future.

## Conclusion

Post-genocidal trauma is a disorder of identity, a horrifying distortion that destroys the thread of normalcy within which one weaves a sense of self, belonging and community. The reality of surviving trauma, and a trauma that involves mass and strategic extermination of one's own community and one that systematically dehumanizes the other, results in a life-long struggle to re-establish one's sense of individuality. It also presents one with a Herculean struggle to find a place in a complex, frightening world. The reality of post-genocidal conflict societies is the general neglect of the healing process of trauma because of the often absent mechanisms of coordinating facilities, limited funding for programs that can provide services such as cognitive behavior therapy that has proved to be effective for survivors, and ineffective pursuit of justice and reconciliation procedures that provide vindication for survivors of their experiences. All of these factors, together, make the task of responding effectively to post genocidal trauma daunting.

Girls and women who live through the horror of genocide experience, of course, different levels and kinds of trauma. Their levels of victimization can, and often do, occur at every level of existence: physical, emotional, political, sexual and communal. In the aftermath of genocide they, then, are not only likely to be affected by individual trauma and experience survivor guilt, but may also experience extreme levels of social ostracism and shame *for the crimes of sexual violence perpetrated against them.* The realities of bearing "enemy" children and being infected in many cases with HIV/AIDS constantly act as reminders of a past over which they had little, if any, control and one which mangled, if not destroyed, the very essence of their identity. The multifaceted complexities of facing post genocidal trauma by female genocide survivors serve as a sobering reminder of the need for humility about the extent of recovery that can truly happen.

Nevertheless, experiences from Bosnia and Rwanda have generated invaluable lessons about ways to move forward. What has become clear is that responding to the needs of female post genocidal survivors requires a comprehensive and sustained approach that harnesses the existing mechanisms of psychosocial processes with indigenous healing as the survivors struggle through stages of shock, anger, resentment, guilt, shame, humiliation, denial, rejection, mourning, and acknowledgement as they attempt the process of recovery.

## Notes

1.   In reality, women on all sides of the conflict were raped, a human rights violation that is endemic to war. Soldiers in World War I raped their own countrywomen in World War II and genocidal rape also took places in Bangladesh, Rwanda, and the U.S. war in Iraq.

2.    Be that as it may, it is important to keep in mind that talking publicly of traumatic events is not necessarily a cultural practice in many regions of the world. In such cases, ritual approaches are more relevant. For example, Michael Wessels (2000) describes the need for ritual cleansing models in Africa that takes into account the beliefs in the spirits of the dead.

## References

Agger, I. (1989). Sexual torture of political prisoners: An overview. *Journal of Traumatic Stress*, July, 2 (3), 305-318.

Agger, I. and Mimica, J. (1996). *Psychosocial Assistance to Victims of War in Bosnia-Herzegovina and Croatia: An Evaluation*. Brussels: European Community Humanitarian Office.

American Foundation for AIDS Research (AMFAR) (July 25, 2005). *Women, Sexual Violence and HIV*. Rio de Janeiro: Author, n.p.

Amiss, C. and Neal, A. (Summer 2006). Asylum from rape. *Critical Half* 4 (1), 29-32.

Ashford, M. W. and Huet-Vaugh, Y. (2000). The impact of war on women, pp. 186-196. In Barry S. Levy and Victor W. Siel (Eds.) *War and Public Health*. Washington, DC: American Public Health Association.

Barsalou, J. (2001). *Training to Help Traumatized Populations, Special Report 79*. Washington, DC: *United States Institute of Peace*. http://www.usip.org/pubs./specialreports/sr79.html.

Barsalou, J. (2005). *Training and Transitional Justice in Divided Societies, Special Report 135*. Washington, DC: United States Institute of Peace. http://www.usip.org/pubs/specialreports/sr135.html.

Brahm, E. (2004). Trauma healing. *Beyond Intractability*. January. http://www.beyondintractability.org/essay/trauma_healing.

Cardozo, B.L., Kaiser, R., Gotway, C.A., and Agani, F. (2003). Mental health, social functioning and feelings of hatred for Kosovar Albanians one year after the war in Kosovo. *Journal of Traumatic Stress*, August, 16(4), 351-260.

Crehan, K., and Gordon, P. (2002). Dying of sadness: Gender, sexual violence and the HIV Epidemic. Gender and the HIV Epidemic. *United Nations Development Programme (UNDP), Social Development and Poverty Elimination (SEPED) Conference Paper Series # 1*. New York: UNDP. http://www.undp.org/hiv/publications/gender/violencee.htm accessed October 25, 2006.

Dyregrove, A.; Gupta, L.; Gjestad, R.; & Mukanoheli, E. (2000). Trauma exposure and psychological reactions to genocide among Rwandan children. *Journal of Traumatic Stress*, 13(1), 3-21.

Eber, D. E., and Neal, A. G. (Eds) (2001). *Memory and Representation: Constructed Truths and Competing Realities*. Bowling, OH: Bowling Green State University Popular Press.

Elbert, T., and Schauer, M. (2002). Psychological trauma: Burnt in memory. *Nature*, 419 (6910), 419, 883.

Engle, K. (October 2005). Feminism and its (dis)contents: Criminalizing wartime rape in Bosnia and Herzegovina. *The American Journal of International Law,* 99 (4), 778-816.

Gendercide Watch (2002). *Case Study: Genocide in Rwanda, 1994*. http://www.gendercide.org/case_rwanda.html.

Gibbs, S. (1997). *Post-war Social Reconstruction in Mozambique: Reframing Children's Experiences in Trauma Healing*. In K. Krishna (Ed.) *Rebuilding Societies After War*. Boulder, CO: Lynne Rienner.

Groenenberg, M. (1992). Psychotherapeutic work with traumatized female refugees from different cultures, pp. 17-19. *Proceedings of an European Consultation initiated and organized by the UNHCR and Pharos Foundation for Refugee Health Care.* Utrecht: The Free Press.

Haynes, H. P. (2004). On the battlefield of women's bodies: An overview of the harm of war to women. *Women's Studies International Forum, 27,* 431-445.

Herman, J. (1992). *Trauma and Recovery: The Aftermath of Violence—From Domestic Abuse to Political Terror.* New York: Basic Books.

Human Rights Watch (1996). *Shattered Lives: Sexual Violence During the Rwandan Genocide and its Aftermath.* New York: Human Rights *Watch* (Africa Watch and Women's Rights Projects).

Janoff-Bulmann, R. (1992). *Shattered Assumptions: Towards a New Psychology of Trauma.* New York: The Free Press.

Jefferson, LaShawn R. (2004). In war as in peace: Sexual violence and women's status. *Human Rights Watch.* http://hrw.org/wr2k4/15.htm.

Jenkins, Janis H. (1996). *Culture, emotion and PTSD,* pp. 165-182. In A. J. Marsella (Ed.) *Ethnocultural Aspects of Posttraumatic Stress Disorder. Issues, Research and Clinical Applications.* Washington, DC: American Psychological Association.

Karunakara, U.; Neuner, F.; Schauer, M.; Singh, Hill, K.; Elbert, T.; and Burnha, G. (2004). Traumatic events and symptoms of post-traumatic stress disorder among Sudanese nationals refugees and Ugandan nationals in the West Nile. *African Health Sciences,* August, 4 (2), 83-93.

Keppel-Benson, J. M.; Ollendick, T.H.; & Benson, M.J. (2002) Post-traumatic disorders in children and adolescents, pp. 29-43. In C.F. Saylor (Ed.) *Children and Disaster.* New York: Plenum Press.

Kilpatrick, D. G.; Ruggiero, K. J.; Acierno, R.; Saunders, B. E.; Resnick; H. S.; and Best, C.L. (2003). Violence and risk of PTSD, major depression, substance/dependence and comorbidity. Results from the National Survey of Adolescents, *Journal of Consulting and Clinical Psychology.* August, 71(4), 692-700.

Kirmayer, L. J. (1996). *Confusion of the Senses: Implications of Ethnocultural Variations in Somatoform and Disassociative Disorders for PTSD, Ethnocultural Aspects of Post-traumatic Stress Disorder. Issues, Research and Applications.* Washington, DC: American Psychological Association.

Kritz J. N. (Autumn 1996). Coming to terms with atrocities: A review of accountability mechanisms for mass violations of human rights. *Law and Contemporary Problems*: *Accountability for International Crimes and Serious Violations of Fundamental Human Rights,* 59(4): 127-152.

*A Lingering Pain. Uganda* (40-minute Documentary. Produced by Isis Women's International Cross-Cultural Exchange, Kampala, Uganda, 2002).

Lunde, I. and Ortmann, J. (1992). Sexual torture and the treatment of its consequences, pp. 310-331. In M. Basoglu (Ed.) *Torture and its Consequences: Current Treatment and Approaches.* Cambridge: Cambridge University Press.

MacKinnon, Catherine A. (1994). Rape, genocide and women's human rights, pp. 183-196. In M. Stiglmayer and M. Faber (Eds.) *Mass Rape: The War Against Women in Bosnia-Herzegovina.* Lincoln: University of Nebraska Press.

McGreal, Chris (2001). A pearl in Rwanda's genocide horror. *Guardian,* December, pp. 1-3.

McKay, Susan. (1998). The effect of armed conflict on girls and women. *Peace and Conflict: Journal of Peace Psychology,* 4 (4):381-392.

MedicineNet (2005). "Definition of Trauma." *Online Medical Dictionary.* http://www.medterms.com/script/main/art.asp?articlekey=8171.

Miller, Patricia Omidian, and Kenneth E. (2006). Addressing the psychosocial needs of Afghan women. *Critical Half, Summer,* 4 (1):17-21.

Minow, M. (1998). *Between Vengeance and Forgiveness: Facing History After Genocide and Mass Violence.* Boston, MA: Beacon Press.

Mollica, F. R. (2001). The trauma story: A phenomenological approach to the traumatic life experiences of refugee survivors. *British Journal of Psychiatry,* Spring, 64 (1), 60-62.

Mollica, F. R., and McDonald, L. (2003). Project 1 billion: Health ministers of post-conflict nations act on mental health recovery. *UN Chronicle,* p. 56.

Mollica R. F.; McInnes K.; and Sarajlic N. (1998). *Trauma and Disability: Long-Term Recovery of Bosnian Refugees.* Cambridge, MA: Harvard Program in Refugee Trauma.

Mulhern de Jong K., and Ford M. (2000). The trauma of war in Sierra Leone. *Lancet, June,* 355 (9220):2067–2068.

Niarchos, N. C. (1995). Women, war and rape: Challenges facing the International Tribunal for the Former Yugoslavia. *Human Rights Quarterly,* November, 17(4), 640-690.

Niederland,W. (1968). Clinical observation on the survivor syndrome. *International Journal of Psycho-Analysis.* 49 (2), 313-315.

Nytagodien, L. R., Neal, G. A. (2004). Collective traumas, apologies and the politics of memory. *Journal of Human Rights,* December, 3 (4):465-475.

Ochieng, O. R. (July 1-5, 2002). The scars on their minds...and their bodies the battle-ground: Women's roles in post-conflict reconstruction. Paper read at 19th International Peace Research Conference, at Kyung Hee University, South Korea

Olujic, Maria B. (March 1998). Embodiment of terror: Gendered violence in peace time and wartime in Croatia and Bosnia-Herzegovina. *Medical Anthropology Quarterly,* March, 12 (1), 31-50.

Pynoos, R. S. (1994). Traumatic stress and psychopathology in children and adolescents. In R. S. Pynoos (Ed.) *Post-traumatic Stress Disorder. A Clinical Review.* Lutherville, MD: Sidran Press.

Reeves, Eric. (July 21, 2005). Genocidal rape and assault in Darfur. Testimony at Congressional Briefing, Washington D.C. At http://www.sudanreeves.org.

Saari, Salli. (2000). *A Bolt from the Blue: Coping with Disasters and Acute Traumas.* London and Philadelphia: Jessica Kingsley Publishers.

Saunders, R. and Aghaie, K. (2005). Mourning and memory. *Comparative Studies of South Asia, Africa and Middle East,* 25(1), 16-29.

Schaal, S., and Elbert, T. (2006). Ten years after the genocide: Trauma confrontation and posttraumatic stress in Rwandan adolescents. *Journal of Traumatic Stress.* February, 19(1), 95-105.

Sideris, T. (2001). Rape in war and peace: Social context, gender, power and identity, pp. 142-157. In S. Meintjes, A. Pillay, and M. Turshen (Eds.) *The Aftermath: Women in Post-Conflict Transformation.* New York: St. Martin's Press.

Silove, D. (2004). The challenges facing mental health programs for post-conflict and refugee communities. *Prehospital and Disaster Medicine* 19(1), 90-96.

Smalc, Vera Folnegovic. (1994). Psychiatric aspects of the rapes in the wars against the republics of Croatia and Bosnia-Herzegovina, pp. 174-182. In A. Stiglmayer and M. Faber (Eds.) *Mass Rape: The War Against Women in Bosnia-Herzegovina.* Lincoln: University of Nebraska Press.

Smith, P.; Perrin, S.; Yule, W.; Hacam, B.; and Stuvland, R. (2002). War exposure among children from Bosnia-Hercegovina: Psychological adjustment in a community sample. *Journal of Traumatic Stress,* April, 15 (2), 147-156.

Staub, E. (2005). Healing, reconciliation, forgiving and the prevention of violence after genocide or mass killing. *Journal of Clinical and Social Psychology*, 24(3):297-334.

Totten, Samuel (2009). The plight and fate of women prior to, during and following the 1994 Rwandan genocide." In Samuel Totten (Ed.) *Genocide: The Plight and Fate of Females. Genocide : A Critical Bibliographic Review.* New Brunswick, NJ: Transaction Publishers.

UNICEF (2004). Ten years after genocide, Rwandan children suffer lasting impact. *UNICEF Press Release*. April. http://www.unicef.org/media/media_20325.html.

United States Department of Veterans' Affairs (n.d.). *Rape of Women in a War Zone.* Washington, DC: Author.

United States Institute of Peace (2001). *Training to Help Traumatized Populations.* Washington, D.C.: Author.

Van Willigen, L. H. M. (1984). Women refugees and sexual violence. *Medisch Contact [Netherlands Medical Journal]* December, 50, 1613-14.

Volkan, V. (1998). *Bloodlines: From Ethnic Pride to Ethnic Terrorism.* Boulder, CO: Westview Press.

Volkan, V. (2002). *Third Reich in the Unconsciousness: Transgenerational Transmission and its Consequences.* New York: Brunner-Routledge.

Wessels, M., and Monteiro, C. (2000). Psychosocial interventions and post-war reconstruction in Angola: Interweaving western and traditional approaches. In Daniel Christie, Richard V. Wagner, and Deborah DuNann Winter (Eds.) *Peace, Conflict and Violence: Peace Psychology for the 21st Century.* New York: Prentice Hall.

West, Devorah. (2005). *Radical Racial Ideals and Sexual Violence: Rwanda, Bosnia, and Nazi Germany.* Providence, RI: Santa Fe Institute Research Experience for Undergraduate Program, Brown University.

Weston, Marta Cullberg (2001). *A Psychosocial Model of Healing From the Traumas of Ethnic Cleansing: The Case of Bosnia.* Johanneshov, Sweden: The Kvinna Till Kvinna Foundation.

## Annotated Bibliography

Askin, Kelly Dawn (2005). Gender crimes jurisprudence in the ICTR : Positive developments. *Journal of Criminal Justice*, August, 3(4), 1007-1018.

Askin, a lawyer and human rights activist, asserts that in light of the magnitude of rape and other sexual crimes perpetrated during the Rwandan genocide, gender crimes prosecutions at the International Criminal Tribunal for Rwanda (ICTR) have been inadequate thus far. Nonetheless, there is cause for ICTR case law to be commended for the impulse given, with and after Akayesu, to the criminalization and punishment of gender-related violence. This paper points to the achievements of the ICTR case law.

Barsalou, J. (2001). *Training to Help Traumatized Populations, Special Report 79.* Washington, DC: United States Institute of Peace. http://www.usip.org/pubs./specialreports/sr79.html.

This report provides a succinct understanding of the phenomenon of trauma, with a special focus on trauma and ethnic conflict. It recognizes that trauma caused by ethnic and other conflict—as distinguished from trauma stemming from natural disasters—can produce profound changes in social and political processes that affect not only the generation that directly experienced the trauma but subsequent generations. It also provides a short description of the activities involved in trauma training, the manifestations of trauma in communities that have experienced large-scale trauma and some of the most prominent individuals and institutes that are involved in designing trauma recovery approaches.

Barsalou, J. (2005). *Training and Transitional Justice in Divided Societies, Special Report 135*. Washington, DC: United States Institute of Peace. http://www.usip.org/pubs/specialreports/sr135.html.

In March 2004, the United States Institute of Peace (USIP), with assistance from the American Association for the Advancement of Science (AAAS), hosted a three-day conference entitled "Trauma and Transitional Justice in Divided Societies." The purpose of the conference was to explore, from different disciplinary perspectives, how divided societies emerging from violent conflict have sought justice and reconciliation through various transitional justice mechanisms and to assess what impact these mechanisms have had on trauma and reconciliation. The conference focused on societies that have (1) experienced political transitions following inter- or intrastate conflict, communal violence, and/or widespread human rights violations along ideological, ethnic, and/or historical lines; and (2) relied on different transitional justice mechanisms and public policy interventions. This report is a clear summary of the most salient issues relating to trauma as a consequence of large-scale violence and the processes of transitional justice that are critical for reconciliation and healing.

Brahm, Eric (January 2004). Trauma healing: Beyond intractability. http://www.beyondintractability.org/essay/trauma_healing.

Provides a short overview of the realities of trauma and the approaches to healing. Also outlines the special needs for women and children with trauma and engages in a short discussion of the approaches used to address trauma in post-genocidal former Yugoslavia and Rwanda.

Brunet, Ariane, and Helal, Isabelle Solon (1998). Monitoring the prosecution of gender-related crimes in Rwanda: A brief field report. *Peace and Conflict: Journal of Peace*, 4(4), 393-397.

This report describes the work of the International Centre for Human Rights and Democratic Development (ICHRDD) as it pertains to the prosecution of gender-related crimes in Rwanda. The ICHRDD organized a coalition of women's groups to advocate for prosecution, monitor prosecution proceedings, and support women involved in the process.

Cardozo, B. L.; Kaiser, R.; Gotway, C. A; and Agani, F. (2003). Mental health, social functioning and feelings of hatred for Kosovar Albanians one year after the war in Kosovo. *Journal of Traumatic Stress*, August, 16 (4), 351-260.

This article presents the results of a cross-sectional cluster sample survey that was conducted in June 2000 in Kosovo to assess the prevalence of mental health problems associated with traumatic experiences, feelings of hatred and revenge, and the level of social functioning among Kosovar Albanians approximately one year after the end of the war. Findings of the second cross-sectional survey were compared with those from 1999 mental health survey in Kosovo conducted by the same authors. Included in the survey were 1,399 Kosovar Albanians aged fifteen years or older living in 593 randomly selected households across Kosovo. Twenty-five percent of respondents reported PTSD symptoms, compared with 17.1 percent in 1999.

Drumbl, Mark A. (2005). The ICTR and justice for Rwandan women. *New Journal of International and Contemporary Law*, 12(1), 105-117.
    Drumbl raises three critical questions about the International Criminal Tribunal for Rwanda (ICTR) and its implications for Rwandan women: (1) What do both the gender jurisprudence and the jurisprudence at large of the ICTR mean to women, individually and collectively, in Rwanda?; (2) How do other modalities of accountability that operate in post genocide Rwanda respond to gender violence and promote gender equality?; and (3) What is the situation of Rwandan women today? He concludes that the ICTR plays a modest role within a much broader struggle for justice and equality for women. Although the ICTR's work carries significant expressive and didactic value, a need persists to connect that value more closely with other modalities of accountability, political reform, and daily life within Rwanda.

Dyregrove, A.; Gupta, L.; Gjestad, R.; and Mukanoheli, E. (2000). Trauma exposure and psychological reactions to genocide among Rwandan children. *Journal of Traumatic Stress*, January, 13(1), 3-21.
    This report summarizes the results of 3,030 interviews with children age eight through nineteen years old from Rwanda about their war experiences and reactions approximately thirteen months after the 1994 Rwandan genocide. Rwandan children had been exposed to extreme levels of violence in the form of witnessing the death of close family members and others in massacres, as well as other violent acts. The results indicated that a majority of these children (90 percent) believed that they would die, most had to hide to survive, and 15 percent had to hide under dead bodies to survive. Analyses showed that reactions were associated with loss, violence exposure, and, most importantly, feeling their life was in danger.

Eber, D. E., and Neal, A. G. (Eds) (2001). *Memory and Representation: Constructed Truths and Competing Realities*. Bowling, OH: Bowling Green State University Popular Press, 175 pp.
    The contributors to this volume address some of the theoretical issues connected with symbolic constructions of reality through human memory and its subsequent representation. It addresses the linkages between what we remember and how we represent it. Basically, humans construct reality from how they perceive the events in their lives and, from that reality, they create a symbol system to describe their world. It is through such symbolic

constructions that humans are provided with a usable backdrop for shaping their memories and organizing them into meaningful lines of action. With the use of case studies, the authors present a new and creative synthesis of the multiple meanings of memory and representation within the context of contemporary perceptions of truth.

Elbert, T., and Schauer, M. (2002). Psychological trauma: Burnt in memory. *Nature*, 419 (6910), 883.
> Provides a succinct understanding of trauma induced in the context of war and the relationship between trauma and memory.

Filice I.; Vincent, C.; Adams, A.; and Bajramovic, F. (1994).Women Refugees from Bosnia-Herzegovina: Developing a Culturally Sensitive Counselling Framework. *International Journal of Refugee Law* , 6(2), 207-226.
> This paper derives from work undertaken by the Research Resource Division for Refugees of Carleton University, Ottawa, in conjunction with the Ottawa Bosnian community, to assess the needs of Bosnian refugees in order to suggest guidelines and make recommendations for the development of a culturally and gender sensitive for a post-war counseling program. The general intervention framework is comprised of two phases. The first deals with general issues concerning orientation and information regarding Bosnian Muslims. The second offers more specific information relative to treatment techniques for survivors of sexual violence. Within this framework, suggestions are made for an overall specialized counseling approach.

Franz, Barbara (2005). *Uprooted And Unwanted: Bosnian Refugees in Austria and the United States*. College Station: Texas A&M University Press, 222 pp.
> The after-effects of war and genocide—the dislocation and relocation of civilians often loom large in the post-genocide period. The aftermath of the Bosnian conflicts left many refugees needing to establish new lives, often in radically different cultures. In *Uprooted and Unwanted,* Barbara Franz offers a cogent look at how these refugees have fared in two representative cities—Vienna and New York City. Between 1991 and 2001, some 30,000 Bosnian refugees settled in Austria, and 120,000 found their way to the United States. Franz focuses on the strategies, skills, and informal networks used by Bosnian refugees, particularly women, to adapt to official policies and administrative practices in their host societies. Her analysis concludes that historically inaccurate ideas on how to deal with displaced persons have led to policies in both Europe and North America that have adversely affected those whose lives have been devastated by violent conflict.

Greenberg, Marica E., and Zuckerman, Elaine (2006). *The Gender Dimensions of Post-Conflict Reconstruction: The Challenges in Development Aid. Research Paper No. 2006/62.* Helsinki, Finland: United Nations University, UNI-WIDER (World Institute for Development Economics Research), 26 pp.

Based on an analysis of World Bank and other donor post-conflict reconstruction (PCR) loans and grants from rights-based, macroeconomic and microeconomic perspectives, the authors conclude that few post conflict reconstruction (PCR) projects identify or address gender discrimination issues. Bank PCR investments hardly reflect bank research recognizing that gender inequality increases the likelihood of conflict and gender equality is central to development and peace. The paper's conceptual framework examining women's programs, gender mainstreaming, and gender roles in transforming violent into peaceful societies leads to recommendations that PCR projects systematically address gender issues and promote gender equality to make peace work.

Handrahan, Lori (2004). Conflict, gender, ethnicity and post-conflict reconstruction. *Security Dialogue*, December, 35(4), 429-445.

This article introduces the concept of ethnicity in relation to gendered security problems in conflict and post-conflict settings. Feminist research has established that men and women experience conflict and post-conflict situations differently owing to issues of identity and power. National and gendered identities and women's disadvantageous location within global and local power structures combine to put women at risk, while simultaneously providing little room for them to voice their security problems. Theories on women as female boundary-makers show how ethnicity appears in part to be created, maintained and socialized through male control of gender identities, and how women's fundamental human rights and dignity are often caught up in male power struggles. In post-conflict settings, gender construction appears to be further complicated by both national agendas of identity formation and re-formation.

Hart, Barry (2001). Refugee return in Bosnia and Herzegovina: Coexistence before reconciliation, pp. 291-310. In Mohammed Abu-Nimer (Ed.) *Reconciliation, Justice and Coexistence: Theory and Practice*. Lanham, MD: Lexington Books.

This essay looks at the multifaceted issues relating to the return of thousands of refugees and internally displaced people (IDPs) in the former Yugoslavia in the aftermath of the genocide. It recognizes the complex challenges posed by identity, the multi-levels of trauma caused by war, and the critical importance of healing in the post conflict environment. Hart is cognizant of the fact that there is "no simple panacea to trauma and reconciling people.... For critical change to take place it is important for the people themselves to finally want it" (p. 301). In particular, the author concentrates on a creative initiative involving trauma healing and conflict transformation undertaken in Zepce which involved two groups of Bosnian Muslim and Bosnian Croat women. The Bosnian Muslim group had suffered heavily in Zepce during the war, and despite their return, distrusted their Croat neighbors because of their role in expelling and killing many Bosnians during the conflict. Nevertheless, the effort to bring these two groups resulted in the creation of a network called The Women of Zepce, which focused on building relationships as well as creating effective economic initiatives for themselves and their families. The positive outcome of this encounter highlight "an example of boldness, of something greater than the measured and destructive power decisions made by manipulative political entities" (p. 303). The article does not gloss over the challenges relating to refugee reintegration, but focuses, instead, on the many and complex challenges vis-à-vis the numerous possibilities available of reconceptualizing identities and working past the conflict through creative means, political awareness and long-term commitment to changing ethnic relationships through taking ownership of the process of peace.

Herman, J. (1992). *Trauma and Recovery*. New York: Basic Books, 290 pp.
    Heralded as one of the most comprehensive and critical works on trauma, in this book Herman breaks new ground with an in-depth exploration of the aftermath of many kinds of violence—from domestic terrors like rape, incest, and child abuse to political traumas. *Trauma and Recovery* brings a new level of understanding to a set of problems usually considered individually. The book puts individual experience in a broader political frame, arguing that psychological trauma can be understood only in a social context.

Hunt, Swanee (2005). *This Was Not Our War: Bosnian Women Reclaiming the Peace*. Durham, NC: Duke University Press, 307 pp.
    Drawing on seven years of interviews, diplomatic and humanitarian work in the region, and personal visits to Bosnia throughout the 1990s, Hunt, a former U.S. ambassador to Austria and founder of Women Waging Peace, presents the testimony of twenty-six women who survived the region's horrific upheavals and in doing so delineates the challenges they face to rebuild their lives and society. Hunt juxtaposes private moments with public meetings and differences of opinion with common convictions. In presenting the interviews, the author provides a narrative framework that connects the women's stories, allowing them to "speak to one another."

Janoff-Bulmann, R. (1992). *Shattered Assumptions: Towards a New Psychology of Trauma*. New York: The Free Press, 256 pp.
    Janoff-Bulmann provides a cogent synthesis of cognitive, social and cultural psychology for a better understanding of human experience to traumatic events. It provides a comprehensive conceptual framework for evaluating and responding to the needs of traumatized people.

Karunakara, U.; Neuner, F.; Schauer, M.; Singh, K; Hill, K.; Elbert, T.; and Burhna, G. (2004). Traumatic events and symptoms of post-traumatic stress disorder among Sudanese nationals refugees and Ugandan nationals in the West Nile. *African Health Sciences*, August, 4 (2), 83-93.
    Using a single-round cross-sectional demographic survey, the authors compared the incidence of traumatic events and its association with symptoms of post-traumatic stress disorder in three population groups in northern

Uganda and southern Sudan. The report found that sex, age, education and occupation were significantly associated with the development of PTSD symptoms.

Keppel-Benson, J. M., Ollendick, T. H., and Benson, M. J. (2002) Post-traumatic disorders in children and adolescents, pp. 29-43. In C.F. Saylor (Ed.) *Children and Disaster*. New York: Plenum Press.

This paper provides a current review of the literature on PTSD pertaining to children and adolescents. Following a discussion of issues on diagnostic criteria and assessment of this affective disorder in this population, there is an overview of the existing literature on prevalence, comorbidity, risk factors, parental and family factors, and issues of gender and age of onset. The remainder of the paper focuses on the range of traumatic stressors in children and adolescents that can result in PTSD, including natural or human disasters, war and violence, chronic or life-threatening medical conditions, community violence and the witnessing of traumatic events, and physical and/or sexual abuse and other forms of interpersonal violence.

Krippner, Stanley and McIntyre, M. Teresa (Eds.) (2003). *The Psychological Impact of War Trauma on Civilians: An International Perspective*. Westport, CT: Praeger Publishers, 344 pp.

This book makes an invaluable contribution to the developing literature on the impact of war and the extreme stress on civilian populations. Not only are a great range of disrupted cultures and the survivors of such discussed, but the contributors take the necessary step of offering a conceptual and practical framework for effective treatment. The question as to how to provide appropriate clinical attention is addressed in great detail. The case studies and assessment section casts a wide net over the opportunities for healing at both individual and communal levels. The contributions not only examine the negative impacts of war on individuals, such as depression, anxiety, and post-traumatic stress, but they also investigate the legacy of warfare on a community level.

Lentin, Ronit, and Lentin, Ponit (Eds.) (1998). *Gender and Catastrophe*. New York: St. Martin's Press, 288 pp.

This book explores the gendered and gendering effects of violence against women in extreme situations such as major wars, genocides, famines, slavery, mass rape and ethnic cleansing. The female experience of methodical genocidal rape in the former Yugoslavia, women's coerced participation in the Rwandan massacre, the gendering of genocidal strategies during the Holocaust, and the reproduction "policy" in Tibet are all integrated into a wider framework—a framework which uncovers the consequences of identifying women as simultaneously sexual objects, transmitters of culture and symbols of the nation.

Mertus, Julie (2000). *War's Offensive on Women: The Humanitarian Challenge in Bosnia, Kosovo and Afghanistan*. Kumarian Press, pp. 157.

Mertus provides critical insights into the challenges that face both governmental and non-governmental organizations in providing specialized protection and assistance to women impacted by war. It not only captures the special needs capacities of vulnerable populations of women, but also points out failures in humanitarian responses, addresses the changes that have been brought about in the legal framework to recognize women as political entities affected by armed conflict in particular ways, and discusses the advances vis-à-vis women's human rights that have convinced humanitarian organizations to reject the dichotomous distinction between gender-based violence and abuse committed in the public and private spheres (p. 83). Most importantly, her argument is built on the platform of gender mainstreaming—the importance of integrating a gender analysis and perspective at every stage of humanitarian assistance and ensuring women in war-affected communities are allowed to exercise their agency and become key actors in implementing programs that are designed to help them recover.

Minow, M. (1998). *Between Vengeance and Forgiveness: Facing History After Genocide and Mass Violence*. Boston, MA: Beacon Press, 224 pp.

Minow explores the process of rebuilding lives and societies in the aftermath of atrocity. The central question of the book centers around the types of responses between vengeance and forgiveness that might result if legal and cultural institutions offered other venues for individuals and nations to deal with cases of collective violence. Minow makes clear from the outset that any response to societal-level violence will be inadequate, but that silence is not an acceptable alternative. The challenge, then, is to negotiate a path between securing justice for victims and attempting to rebuild a society. While clearly recognizing the three players in any conflict—the victims, the aggressors and the bystanders, all of whom, have wittingly or unwittingly play a role in collective violence. Minow pushes for the victims to occupy central stage in the post-conflict phase while making room for bystanders to also have a voice in expressing their contrition.

Mollica R.F., McInnes K, and Tor S. (1998). The dose-effect relationships of trauma to symptoms of depression and posttraumatic stress disorder among Cambodian survivors of mass violence. *British Journal of Psychiatry*, December, 173 , 482-489.

This study evaluates the dose-effect relationships of cumulative trauma to the psychiatric symptoms of major depression and post-traumatic stress disorder (PTSD) in a community study of Cambodian survivors of mass violence using a multi-stage random sampling design. Trauma history and psychiatric symptoms were assessed for two time periods. The study concludes that cumulative trauma continued to affect psychiatric symptom levels a decade after the original trauma events.

Mollica, F. R., and McDonald, L. (2003). Project 1 billion: Health ministers of post-conflict nations act on mental health recovery. *UN Chronicle*. http:// www.un.org/Pubs/chronicle/2003/issue4/0403p56.asp.

In part, the authors provide a synopsis of the UN project "1 Billion." In doing so, it spells out the key challenges to approaches to mental health and provides an illustrative framework of recovery that takes into account institutions, local capacity and the skills of local service providers and trained experts who have dealt with survivors of mass violence.

Mollica R.F., McInnes K., and Sarajlic N. (1998). *Trauma and Disability: Long-Term Recovery of Bosnian Refugees*. Cambridge, MA: Harvard Program in Refugee Trauma, n. p.

This report is a follow-up to previous research conducted by the same authors which found aspects of depression, posttraumatic stress disorder (PTSD), and disability in a Bosnian refugee cohort. This article investigates whether previously observed associations continue over time. The research concludes that former Bosnian refugees who remained living in the region continued to exhibit psychiatric disorder and disability three years after the initial assessment.

Nduwimana, Francoise (2004). Women and Rwanda's genocide: What goes unsaid. *Rights and Democracy*, 14(2), 1-6.

The victims of the Rwandan genocide did not all die during the 100 days in which most of the killings took place. Ten years after the massacre of an estimated 800,000 to one millions Tutsis and moderate Hutu, the genocide continues to take lives. Slowly, painfully and yet almost invisibly, thousands of Rwandan women are succumbing to HIV/AIDS as a result of having been raped during the genocide. Genocide, rape, and HIV infection have condemned these women to certain death.

Nelson, Brian S. (2003). Post-war trauma and reconciliation in Bosnia-Herzegovina: Observations, experiences, and implications for marriage and family therapy. *American Journal of Family Therapy*, July-August, 31(4), 305-316.

The 1992-1995 war in Bosnia-Herzegovina caused horrific devastation in that region of the world. This article describes the themes and issues that emerged from information gleaned from interviews with Bosnian professionals through a project entitled "Trauma and Reconciliation in Bosnia-Herzegovina," which was funded by the National Research Council. The findings of the report outline the ongoing issues facing Bosnia, including complex trauma-related and post-war issues, lack of coordination in professional services, limited outcome research and program evaluation, and the need for services for children and families. Recommendations and implications for marriage and family therapy are included in the report.

Niederland, W. (1968). Clinical observation on the survivor syndrome. *International Journal of Psycho-Analysis,* 49 (2), 313-315.

In this study of the impact of large-scale trauma on those who survive horrific events, Niederland coins the term "survivor syndrome." He states he used this term to sharpen the distinction (and to make clearer the understanding) of the multifold clinical manifestations encountered in survivors of persecution and to differentiate the clinical picture from other forms of psychopathology.

Palmary, Ingrid (2005). *Engendering War Time Conflict: Women and War Trauma.* Braamfontein, South Africa: Center for the Study of Violence and Reconciliation, 72 pp.

This report is a part of the Center for the Study of Violence and Reconciliation (CSVR's) Violence in Transition Project. It provides a detailed examination of conflict and violence as experienced by refugee women from the Great Lakes Region now living in Johannesburg, South Africa. The research is geared to influence existing trauma service delivery through offering a gender analysis of how war shapes gender relationships and gender-based violence that are not always incorporated into the services offered to refugees or asylum and peace-building processes. Ultimately, this report argues for broadening the scope of trauma interventions to provide integrated programs such as transitional justice initiatives, counseling, peace-building as well as projects for memorializing the past.

Pilch, Frances T. (2002). *Rape as Genocide: The Legal Response to Sexual Violence.* Center for Global Security and Democracy, Rutgers University, 25 pp. http://www.ciaonet.org/wps/pif01/pif01.pdf.

The last decade (1994-2007) has witnessed a profound transformation in the treatment of sexual violence in international law. The overwhelming evidence of the widespread use of rape as a policy tool in the former Yugoslavia, combined with the tragedy of the genocide in Rwanda, in which rape was also widely prevalent, has led to a legal reconceptualization of sexual violence in internal and international conflicts. The ad hoc tribunals for the former Yugoslavia (International Criminal Tribunal for the Former Yugoslavia [ICTY]) and Rwanda (International Criminal Tribunal for Rwanda [ICTR]), have genuinely broken new ground as they have confronted cases dealing with the issues of rape, torture, and genocide. They have struggled with determining the legal definition of rape. The revolutionary changes that have taken place in this area of the law in large part reflect the growing mobilization and influence of non-governmental organizations (NGOs) articulating the importance of the rights of women, and the increasing importance of the presence of women advocates, prosecutors, and judges.

Pilch addresses some of the most important changes in the legal interpretations of sexual violence and examines the importance of new actors in the international arena. In turn, in light of the experiences of the ad hoc tribunals (ICTR and ICTY), she analyses the proposed tribunal to deal with violations of international humanitarian and human rights law in Sierra Leone.

Powley, Elizabeth (2006). *Rwanda: The Impact of Women Legislators on Policy Outcomes Affecting Children and Families—State of the World's Children*. Geneva: UNICEF, 18 pp.

This paper provides a brief background on changing gender roles in Rwanda and in women's parliamentary representation, and highlights several of the factors that led to the election of women in such large numbers in 2003. Further, it examines the affect of gender on parliamentarians' attitudes, and investigates the impact of women parliamentarians on policies related to children and families, specifically with regard to the development of legislation, oversight of the executive, and influence on the national budget. The research is based on in-depth interviews with male and female parliamentarians, with practitioners working in the field of child welfare, and with representatives of the international community in Rwanda. It also draws on analysis of legislation and policies related to children, content analysis of local newspapers, and participant-observation research by the author, who directs a women's leadership project in Rwanda.

Saari, Salli. (2000). *A Bolt from the Blue: Coping with Disasters and Acute Traumas*. London and Philadelphia, PA: Jessica Kingsley Publishers, 280 pp.

Saari examines the psychological effects traumatic events can have on an individual. The book is a methodical step-by-step approach of the different stages of the process of understanding trauma and the process of recovery. Saari also examines the role and responsibility of social support, the media and the workplace in addressing trauma, and the methods that are effective in helping victims to cope after a traumatic event.

Schaal, S., and Elbert, T. (2006). Ten years after the genocide: Trauma confrontation and posttraumatic stress in Rwandan adolescents. *Journal of Traumatic Stress*, February 19(1), 95-105.

This article examines the war experiences and posttraumatic stress disorder (PTSD) symptoms of Rwandan orphans a decade after the genocide. All the youth interviewed had been exposed to extreme levels of violence. The study finds a significant relationship was found between the number of traumatic experiences and subsequent stress responses.

Sideris, T. (2001). Rape in War and Peace: Social Context, Gender, Power and Identity, pp. 142-157. In S. Meintjes, A. Pillay, and M. Turshen (Eds.).*The Aftermath: Women in Post-Conflict Transformation*. New York: St. Martin's Press.

Sideris examines the experience of sexual violence in particular contexts of war and peace, amongst Mozambican women refugees. The chapter draws on the work with marginalized groups of rural women who survived rape in times of war and peace. Sideris attempts to promote an understanding of how specific conditions impact women's interpretation of their violation and create the limits and possibilities to challenge the inequalities they experience. While the situation in Mozambique did not constitute genocide, the findings are still valuable.

Silove, D. (2004). The challenges facing mental health programs for post-conflict and refugee communities. *Prehospital and Disaster Medicine*, 19(1). http://pdm.medicine.wisc.edu.

This paper focuses on the experience of trauma experienced by refugee populations. It points out that the majority of refugees and communities exposed to warfare and oppression live in low-income countries with few resources or special skills, and that epidemiological studies have identified high levels of traumatic stress reactions in such populations. Such stress reactions can be intensified by harsh policies aimed at deterring survivors from seeking refuge in technologically advanced societies. The author proposes a model for low-income, post-conflict countries, based on a two-tiered formulation. At the eco-social level, he suggests that mental health professionals can play a supportive, but not a lead, role in facilitating recovery of core adaptive systems that hasten natural recovery from stress for the majority of the population. Where small-scale, community mental health services are established, he suggests that the emphasis should be on assisting persons and their families who are at greatest survival and adaptive risk.

Smith, P.; Perrin, S.; Yule, W.; Hacam, B.; and Stuvland, R. (2002). War exposure among children from Bosnia-Hercegovina: Psychological adjustment in a community sample. *Journal of Traumatic Stress*, April, 15 (2), 147-156.

The report is a summary of a study conducted by the United Nations Children's Fund (UNICEF)'s psychosocial program during the war in Bosnia-Herzegovina. The data was collected from a community sample of 2,976 children ages nine to fourteen years old. Children completed standardized self-report measures of posttraumatic stress symptoms, depression, anxiety, and grief, as well as a report of the amount of their own exposure to war-related violence. Results showed that children reported high levels of posttraumatic stress symptoms and grief reactions. Levels of distress were related to the amount and type of exposure. Girls reported more distress than boys, but there were few meaningful age effects within the age band studied.

Smith, Roger W. (1994). "Women and Genocide: Notes on an Unwritten History." *Holocaust and Genocide Studies* , 8(3), 315-334.

Narratives of the history of genocide have been based mainly on the experiences of men. Yet women's experiences with genocide have often differed from those of men in terms of participation, forms of victimization, and consequences. This essay explores these issues, focusing in particular on the relationship between women and the perpetration of genocide.

Staub, E. (2005). Healing, reconciliation, forgiving and the prevention of violence after genocide or mass killing. *The Journal of Clinical and Social Psychology*, 24(3):297-334

Staub describes a theory-based intervention in Rwanda to promote healing and reconciliation based on an experimental evaluation. The results of the research underscore the importance of understanding the origins of violence.

Volkan, V. (1998). *Bloodlines: From Ethnic Pride to Ethnic Terrorism*. Boulder, CO: Westview Press, 280 pp.

In *Bloodlines,* Volkan, a world-renowned psychiatrist specializing in international relations, explores ethnic violence by examining history and diplomacy through a psychoanalytic lens. The book lays the foundation for understanding the differences between ethnic groups as well as the common ground they share. It also provides fascinating insights into how personal identity intertwines with nationality, and why hatred of others becomes a part of a person's sense of self.

Volkan, V. (2002). *Third Reich in the Unconsciousness: Transgenerational Transmission and its Consequences*. New York: Brunner-Routledge, 224 pp.

*The Third Reich in the Unconscious* examines the third element of the psychological impact of massive human trauma: transgenerational transmission of psychological tasks. In order to study this topic and identify its pertinence to Third Reich-related case studies, the author both examines the effects of the Holocaust on second-generation survivors and outlines the mechanics of transgenerational transmission.

Describing in detail how transgenerational transmission occurs, Volkan focuses on the psychological processes of younger generations, outside of their identification with directly traumatized ancestors, and explains how historical images contaminate the expression of developmental conflicts at all levels.

Wagner, Carol (2002). *Soul Survivors: Stories of Women and Children in Cambodia*. Berkeley, CA: Creative Arts Book Company, 259 pp.

*Soul Survivors* give a voice to the women and children who stayed in Cambodia after the genocide (1975-1979), when nearly two million people perished due to execution, starvation, or disease. It includes the stories of two refugees who came to the U.S. as orphans, and then returned to Cambodia to help their country. The book effectively demonstrates the political, economic, and psychological links between the destruction of Cambodian society carried out in the 1970s and the suffering experienced by so many Cambodians today.

Weine, M. Stevan (1999). *When History is a Nightmare: Lives and Memories of Ethnic Cleansing in Bosnia-Herzegovina*. New Brunswick, NJ: Rutgers University Press, 259 pp.

In his attempt to develop a better understanding of ethnic cleansing in Bosnia, Stevan M. Weine focuses on the importance of developing a more complex and nuanced view of the dilemmas of memories of atrocity, both at the personal as well as the public level. He concludes, after decade-long work with Bosnian survivors, that the survivors' narratives of the genocide were capable of providing a more complex truth about the horrific events in Yugoslavia than that often found in analytic works, where much is "lost" in translation.

*When History is a Nightmare* explores how the many traumatic events affected not just individuals, but an entire society and its culture. Weine investigates the survivors' attempts to reconcile the contrasting, collective memories of having lived in a multiethnic society with the later memories of the ethnic atrocities. Weine concludes by describing how survivors of this terrible tragedy worked to confront the destructive nature of their memories while trying to bring about individual and collective healing.

Zawati, Hilmi M., and Mahmoud, Ibtisam M. (Eds.) (2004). *A Selected Socio-Legal Bibliography on Ethnic Cleansing, Wartime Rape, and Genocide in the Former Yugoslavia and Rwanda.* Lewiston, NY: Edwin Mellen Press, 587 pp.

The aim of this bibliography, comprising more than 6,000 entries, is to facilitate the research and writing of legal scholars, students and human rights activists in the fields of ethnic cleansing, genocide and sexual violence during national and international armed conflicts. It provides an overview of carefully selected socio-legal materials published in English and other European languages on ethnic cleansing, genocide and sexual violence during armed conflict in the Former Yugoslavia and Rwanda. This timely project, which commemorates the tenth anniversary of the ethnic cleansing and genocide in the Former Yugoslavia and Rwanda, has a great deal of interest for academics and those who are active in conflict/dispute settlement efforts in war-torn areas of the world.

Zinsstag, Estelle (2005). Sexual violence against women in armed conflicts: Standard responses and new ideas. *Social Policy & Society*, 5(1), 137–148.

Herein, the author assesses ways in which different justice schemes may operate together for an improved legal and political response to victims of sexual crimes in the aftermath of armed conflicts. In doing so, she addresses the problem of sexual violence against women in armed conflict and considers the evolution of criminal justice in regard to this crime. The latter focuses on the results of recent attempts to implement truth and reconciliation processes. The author also succinctly assesses reparation schemes. Finally, the author proposes a series of measures for coordinating the various schemes of justice in a way that guarantees women's rights in the aftermath of a conflict.

# Contributors

## Editor

*Samuel Totten* is a genocide scholar based at the University of Arkansas, Fayetteville.

In 2003, Israel W. Charny, the founding editor of *Genocide: A Critical Bibliographic Review*, named Totten managing editor of the bibliographical series. The first two volumes Totten edited for the series are: *Genocide at the Millennium* (New Brunswick, NJ: Transaction Publishers, 2005), *The Prevention and Intervention of Genocide* (New Brunswick, NJ: Transaction Publishers, 2007).

In 2005, Totten was named one of the inaugural co-chief editors of *Genocide Studies and Prevention: An International Journal*, which is the official journal of the International Association of Genocide Scholars (IAGS).

Among the essays/articles Totten has published on genocide are: "The Intervention and Prevention of Genocide: Sisyphean or Doable?" *Journal of Genocide Research*, June 2004, 6(2); "The U.S. Government Darfur Genocide Investigation." *Journal of Genocide Research*, June 2005, 7(2); "The U.S. Investigation into the Darfur Crisis and the U.S. Government's Determination of Genocide." *Genocide Studies and Prevention: An International Journal*, 1(1):57-78; and "Investigating Allegations of Genocide in Darfur: The U.S. Atrocities Documentation Team and the UN Commission of Inquiry" (with Eric Markusen) in Joyce Apsel (Ed.) *Darfur: Genocide Before Our Eyes*. New York: Institute for the Study of Genocide, 2005.

Among the books Totten's edited and co-edited are: *First-Person Accounts of Genocidal Acts Committed in the Twentieth Century* (Westport, CT: Greenwood Press, 1991); *Genocide in the Twentieth Century: Critical Essays and Eyewitness Accounts* (co-edited with William S. Parsons and Israel W. Charny) (New York: Garland Publishers, Inc., 1995); *Century of Genocide* (paperback version of *Genocide in the Twentieth Century* co-edited with William S. Parsons and Israel W. Charny (New York: Garland Publishers, Inc., 1997); *Teaching About Genocide: Issues, Approaches, Resources* (Greenwich, CT: Information Age Publishers, 2004); and *Genocide in Darfur: The Investigation and Findings of the Darfur Atrocities Documentation Team* (New York: Routledge, 2006). More recently, he co-authored, with Paul Bartrop, *Dictionary of Genocide* (Westport, CT: Greenwood Publishers, 2009).

In July and August of 2004, Totten served as one of twenty-four investigators on the U.S. State Department's Darfur Atrocities Documentation
Project whose express purpose was to conduct interviews with refugees from
Darfur, Sudan, in order to ascertain whether genocide had been perpetrated
or not in Darfur. Based upon the data collected by the team of investigators,
U.S. Secretary of State Colin Powell declared on September 9, 2004 that
genocide had been perpetrated in Darfur by Government of Sudan troops
and the *Janjaweed*.

Totten recently received a Fulbright Fellowship to Rwanda to conduct
research into the Rwandan genocide and to teach courses on genocide at the
National University of Rwanda during the 2008 spring academic semester.

## Authors

*Angela Debnath* holds a B.A. Honors in History from the University of
Toronto and a M.A. in Holocaust Studies from University College London
(UCL). She is currently pursuing a Ph.D. at University College of London on
genocide and systematic violence in South Asia during the Cold War. She is
also adjunct professor of international relations at the American University
of Rome, Italy.

*Nicole Hallett* is an instructor in human rights law at Yale University. A Tru-
man Scholar and Luce Scholar, she received her master's degree in Refugee
Studies from the University of Oxford and is currently pursuing her juris
doctor at Yale Law School. She has successfully represented asylum-seek-
ers, co-authored amicus briefs at every level of the federal court system
including the Supreme Court, and just recently helped bring one of the first
federal lawsuits under the Trafficking Victims Protection Act. She has also
participated in groundbreaking litigation under the Alien Tort Statute, which
allows non-citizens to sue in U.S. Courts for violations of international law,
including genocide. Ms. Hallett previously worked at the National Human
Rights Commission of Korea and the U.S. Department of State and has researched human rights in Chile, Denmark, the United Kingdom, Bangladesh,
Thailand, and South Africa.

*Judy L. Ledgerwood* is an associate professor in the Department of Anthropology and Center for Southeast Asian Studies at Northern Illinois University.
Her early work addresses changing Cambodian (Khmer) conceptions of
gender and includes research work with Cambodian refugees in the United
States as well as rural women in Cambodia. Her subsequent research has
focused on Khmer social organization, including gender, kinship, and ideas
of hierarchy and community. The latter involves comparative research across
the pre-revolutionary period, Democratic Kampuchea (the Khmer Rouge
era), and the postwar years (the People's Republic of Kampuchea, the State
of Cambodia, and the current Kingdom of Cambodia). She regularly teaches
about the Cambodian genocide and includes a focus on the use of first person
narratives to understand the Khmer Rouge era.

Among her publications are: "The Aftermath of Genocide: Cambodian Villagers" (with May Ebihara) in Alex Hinton (Ed.) *Annihilating Difference: The Anthropology of Genocide.* Berkeley: University of California Press, 2002; *Cambodia Emerges from the Past,* an edited volume. DeKalb, IL: Center for Southeast Asian Studies, Northern Illinois University, 2002; *Women in Development: Cambodia.* Manila: Asian Development Bank, 1996; *Cambodian Culture Since 1975: Homeland and Exile* edited with May Ebihara and Carol Mortland. Ithaca, NY: Cornell University Press, 1994; *The Situation of Women in Cambodia.* Bangkok: UNICEF, 1992; and *Changing Khmer Conceptions of Gender: Women, Stories and the Social Order.* PhD. Dissertation, Anthropology Department, Cornell University, 1990.

*Ivana Macek* is assistant professor in genocide studies at Uppsala University, Sweden, where she received her PhD in Cultural Anthropology. The title of her thesis was *A War Within: Everyday Life in Sarajevo under Siege* (2000).

She has had basic training in psychotherapy and works part-time as a counselor at the Red Cross Centre for Victims of War and Torture in Uppsala. Currently, her research concerns the consequences of work in war-zones on Swedish personnel.

*Valerie Oosterveld* is assistant professor in the Faculty of Law at the University of Western Ontario (Canada), where she teaches International Criminal Law, International Human Rights Law and Public International Law. She has degrees from Columbia University (J.S.D. and LL.M.), the University of Toronto (LL.B.) and the University of Ottawa (B.Soc.Sc.). Before joining the faculty in 2005, Valerie served in the Legal Affairs Bureau of Canada's Department of Foreign Affairs and International Trade. In this role, she provided legal advice on international criminal accountability for genocide, crimes against humanity and war crimes, and on international criminal justice institutions. She was a member of the Canadian delegation to the International Criminal Court negotiations and subsequent Assembly of States Parties. Her research and writing focus on gender issues within international criminal justice.

Her publications relating to genocide include: "Elements of Genocide," pp. 41-49 in Roy S. Lee (Ed.) *The International Criminal Court: Elements of Crimes and Rules of Procedure and Evidence* (Ardsley, NY: Transnational Publishers, 2001). Her publications relating to gender-sensitive prosecution of international crimes include: "Gender, Persecution and the International Criminal Court: Refugee Law's Relevance to the Crime Against Humanity of Gender-Based Persecution"(2006) in *Duke Journal of Comparative and International Law,* 17(1) 49-89; "Prosecution of Gender-Based Crimes in International Law"pp. 67-82 in Dyan Mazurana, Angela Raven-Roberts and Jane Parpart (Eds.) *Gender, Conflict and Peacekeeping* (Lanham, MD: Rowman & Littlefield Publishers, 2005); "The Definition of 'Gender' in the Rome Statute of the International Criminal Court: A Step Forward or Back for International Criminal Justice?" (2005) *Harvard Human Rights Journal*, 18, 55-84; "Gender-Sensitive Justice and the International Criminal Tribunal for Rwanda: Lessons Learned for the International Criminal Court" (2005) *New England Journal of International and Comparative Law*, 12(1): 119-133; and "Sexual Slavery and the International Criminal Court: Advancing International Law" (2004) *Michigan Journal of International Law*, 25(3): 605-651.

*Rubina Peroomian*, research associate in the Department of Near Eastern Languages and Culture at the University of California, Los Angeles (UCLA), received her PhD from the Near Eastern Languages and Cultures Department, Narekatsi Chair of Armenian Studies at UCLA. Her dissertation (1989) that was later published as a book, *Literary Responses to Catastrophe, A Comparison of the Armenian and the Jewish Experience* (Atlanta, GA: Scholars Press, 1993), marked her debut in the field of genocide studies.

She has published research papers in scholarly journals such as: *Journal of the Society for Armenian Studies*; *Pakin* (an Armenian literary journal); *Journal of Genocide Research*; and *Genocide Studies and Prevention: An International Journal*.

She has contributed chapters to scholarly collections such as *The Armenian Genocide* edited by Richard G. Hovannisian (New York: St. Martin's Press, 1992); *Remembrance and Denial, The Case of the Armenian Genocide* edited by Richard G. Hovannisian (Detroit, MI: Wayne State University Press, 1999); *Remembering for the Future – 2000, The Holocaust in an Age of Genocide* edited by John K. Roth (Palgrave Macmillan's Global Academic Publishing, 2001); *Looking Backward, Moving Forward, Confronting the Armenian Genocide* edited by Richard G. Hovannisian (New Brunswick, NJ: Transaction Publishers, 2003); and *Genocide Perspectives II, Essays on Holocaust and Genocide* edited by Colin Tatz, Peter Arnold, and Sandra Tatz (Sydney: Bradl & Schlesinger with The Australian Institute for Holocaust and Genocide Studies, 2003);

She has also authored *A Struggle to Comprehend the Catastrophe and Survive: A Comparative Study of the Armenian and the Jewish Literary Responses to Catastrophe*, a booklet published by the Republic of Armenia National Academy of Sciences, Museum-Institute of the Armenian Genocide (Yerevan, 2003).

*Frances T. Pilch* is professor of political science and Division Chair of International Relations and National Security Studies at the United States Air Force Academy. Among her many publications are: "The UN Response to the Unfolding Balkan Wars" (lead author with Major Joe Derdzinski) in *Reflections on the Balkan Wars: Ten Years After the Break-up of Yugoslavia*. New York: Palgrave Press/St. Martin's Publishers, 2004; "The Prosecution of the Crime of Genocide in the ICTY: The Case of Radislav Krstic." *USAFA Journal of Legal Studies*, March 2003; "Sexual Violence: The Role of NGO's in the Evolution of International Law" in special issue (Preventing Conflict, the Role of NGOs) of *International Peacekeeping*, Spring 2003, 10(1); "Rape as Genocide: The Legal Response to Sexual Violence" published on-line by the Center for Global Security and Democracy, Columbia University International Affairs On-Line (CIAO), fall 2002; "Sexual Violence During Armed Conflict: Institutional and Judicial Responses" published on-line by the Global Security Quarterly, Social Science Research Council, fall 2002; "The Crime of Rape in International Humanitarian Law." *USAFA Journal of Legal Studies*, Volume 9, 1999; and "Sexual Violence and the Crisis in Kosovo." August 1999, *Refuge: Canada's Periodical on Refugees*, 18(3).

*Tazreena Sajjad* is a third-year PhD student at the School of International Service at American University in Washington D.C. Her research interests include transitional justice, reconciliation in post-conflict countries, human rights and gender and conflict.

Her publications include: 'When Civil Society Fails Nation-Building" (co-authored with Julie Mertus) in Oliver P. Richmond and Henry F. Carey (Eds.) *Subcontracting Peace: The Challenges of NGO Peacebuilding*. Ashgate Publishers (2005); "Addressing the Gray Areas of International Law" in *Swords and Ploughshares: A Journal of International Affairs*, 2003; and "Human Rights and Human Insecurity" (co-authored with Julie Mertus, forthcoming) in *Journal of Human Rights* (forthcoming). She was a guest lecturer on women and post-conflict reconstruction at Dhaka University in 2006.

Sajjad also serves as Research Fellow for the women's program for Afghanistan for Global Rights in Washington D.C., where she provides research assistance and program development recommendations for women's rights violations documentation and training human rights investigators in the country. Previously, she served as the Program Associate for Afghanistan in Global Rights for the human rights legal program. She also has experience working at the Center for Victims of Torture (CVT) in Minnesota and at the Bangladesh National Women Lawyers Association in Bangladesh. She also conducts human rights investigation workshops for Human Rights and Gender courses at American University.

Sajjad holds a masters degree in International Peace and Conflict Resolution from American University and a Bachelor's degree from Macalester College, Minnesota. She was a Dean's Fellow for the Women and International Law Program at the Center for Human Rights and Humanitarian Law in the Washington College of Law in 2004. Ms. Sajjad is a recipient of the Graduate Leadership Award from American University and the Gandhi Memorial Scholarship for Peace from the Gandhi Center.

*Helene J. Sinnreich* is director of Judaic and Holocaust Studies at Youngstown State University and Editor in Chief of the *Journal of Jewish Identities*. Sinnreich, who received her Ph.D. from Brandeis University, has received numerous prestigious fellowships for her work, including a Charles H.

Revson Foundation Fellowship for Archival Research at the United States Holocaust Memorial Museum, a Kosciuszko Foundation Grant, a Dorot Travel Award, and a Civic Education Project Visiting Fellowship. She has also participated in two Center for Advanced Holocaust Studies' workshops: "The 'Final Solution' in the Ukraine" and "The Lodz Ghetto."

Her research focuses on the social history of the Holocaust. Her publications include "Baluty Market: A Study of a Food Space" in *Food, Culture and Society: An International Journal of Multidisciplinary Research* (March, 2007); "Polish and Jewish Historiography of Jewish-Polish Relations during World War II" in *Rethinking Poles and Jews: Troubled Past, Brighter Future* (Rowman & Littlefield, 2007); and "And We Eat Like on Yom Kippur: Women, Food, and the Struggle for Survival in the Lodz Ghetto," in *Lilith Magazine* (Fall, 2005). Her current book projects include one on history and memory of the Lodz Ghetto and another on rape and the Holocaust.

# Index